D0893358

# Interpersonal Sensitivity
## Theory and Measurement

୫ • ଔ

# The LEA Series in Personality and Clinical Psychology
## Irving B. Weiner, Editor

# Interpersonal Sensitivity
## Theory and Measurement

ॐ • ॐ

*Edited by*

**Judith A. Hall**
*Northeastern University*

**Frank J. Bernieri**
*University of Toledo*

2001
LAWRENCE ERLBAUM ASSOCIATES, PUBLISHERS
Mahwah, NJ                                    London

Lawrence Erlbaum Associates, Inc., Publishers
10 Industrial Avenue
Mahwah, New Jersey 07430-2262


Cover design by Kathryn Houghtaling Lacey

**Library of Congress Cataloging-in-Publication Data**

Interpersonal sensitivity : theory and measurement /
     Judith A. Hall & Frank J. Bernieri, eds.
          p. cm.
     Includes bibliographical references and index.
     ISBN 0-8058-3164-9 (hardcover : alk. Paper)
     1. Interpersonal relations—Research.     2. Sensitivity (Personality
     trait)—Research.     I. Hall, Judith A.     II. Bernieri, Frank J.
     HM1106.I59 2001
     302—dc21

                                                            00-044235


Books published by Lawrence Erlbaum Associates are printed on acid-free
paper, and their bindings are chosen for strength and durability.

Printed in the United States of America
10  9  8  7  6  5  4  3  2  1

*For Sally E. Snodgrass
a friend and colleague
whose life inspired many*

# CONTENTS

### III Toward the Creation of An Interpersonal Sensitivity Test

### IV Dyadic Interaction Approaches

# V   Where Can We Go From Here?

     Psychology: Theoretical and Methodological Applications
     *Ronald E. Riggio*

16   Three Trends in Current Research on Person Perception:    319
     Positivity, Realism, and Sophistication
     *David C. Funder*

17   Groping for the Elephant of Interpersonal Sensitivity    333
     *Leslie A. Zebrowitz*

18   Paradoxes of Nonverbal Detection, Expression,    351
     and Responding: Points to PONDER
     *Howard S. Friedman*

     Author Index    363

     Subject Index    375

# Series Editor's Foreword

This volume serves as a handbook of how to think about, measure, and study interpersonal sensitivity. It does so by using that most pedagogically proven procedure: showing how it has been done by the best and the brightest thinkers and researchers studying interpersonal sensitivity.

Readers of this book (and their students) will be rewarded with a greater appreciation of the strengths and weaknesses of the various methods used by the authors of these chapters. Readers will be rewarded, too, by the liberating effects of theoretical and methodological cross-fertilization. Exposure to the ideas and methods of other workers is liberating from habits of method that build up over time. When we know and really understand other approaches we can exercise more free choice in the methods we use. Our chosen method X is more likely to have been a wise choice when we thoughtfully preferred it over Y and Z than when we used it because it was the only method we knew how to use.

The editors and the authors evoke the spirit of earlier pioneers as they wrestle with some of the same fundamental issues. Among these pioneers are Don Campbell, Don Fiske, Lee Cronbach, Paul Meehl, and Gary Boring.

Campbell and Fiske's thinking about the multitrait, multimethod matrix may help to clarify when different measurement methods reflect truly distinguishable constructs, and when they merely reflect "problems of unique versus common method variance." Cronbach and Meehl's conceptions of construct validity allow us to describe more clearly the nomological nets created by (a) the superordinate construct of interpersonal sensitivity, (b) its nested major subtypes, (c) the more specific constructs within each of the subtypes, and (d) the measures used to assess the specific constructs and the higher-level constructs that subsume them. Until there was the more specific discussion of measures undertaken by this volume, we could hardly begin to describe the nomological net that defines interpersonal sensitivity theory.

Finally, there is the now-seen-as-radical but wisely cautionary message of Boring. Psychology's historian, Boring warned us of the problems we invite when we wander too far from a path of sensible operationism. Constructs should often be richer than any simple method used to measure them. But the prudent practice preached by Boring suggests that this richness, when excessive, can be theoretically troublesome.

Never has it been more clear that the domain of research on interpersonal sensitivity is a remarkable hybrid of personality and social psychology. It is a domain that seems intrinsically to call for the examination of individual differences in performance occurring in a context of a changing person existing in a changing environment, and an environment that is largely a social one at that.

This volume marks a new level of maturity of the research domain of interpersonal sensitivity. Never have we known as much about this fascinating topic as we do now, thanks to the editors and authors of this book.


*—Robert  Rosenthal*
*Riverside, California*

# Preface

People spend most of their waking hours perceiving and making judgments about others. The natural ecology within which people must survive is primarily social in nature. They necessarily must notice and make judgments about others' emotions, physical states, attitudes, personality, truthfulness, intentions (and much else, too), using many sources of information—verbal, nonverbal, and contextual. Our relative success as a species implies that these judgments must be sufficiently accurate, on average, over the long haul. In short, people possess some capacity to know each other. We call this ability *interpersonal sensitivity*.

But we also know that interpersonal judgments are not always accurate. There are many possible reasons for such inaccuracy. Messages and cues could be misunderstood because they are intrinsically hard to convey, or "encode," whereas others could be misjudged because they were conveyed in a flawed or confusing manner. These two examples illustrate the operation of "message" and "encoder" (i.e., expressor) factors in interpersonal judgment, respectively. But a message could also be misjudged because the person doing the judging (the "decoder") is not using the information in an optimal manner. Looking at the accuracy of interpersonal judgment from the perspective of the decoder is the main focus of this book. In other words, we discuss interpersonal sensitivity and its variability across individual decoders and across dyadic contexts.

The use of the terms "accuracy," "sensitivity," and "individual differences" naturally implies that the construct in question can be measured. We believe it can, as do the many investigators who have developed measurement techniques for doing so. The chapters of this book reveal the wide range of methods that have been developed as well as a wealth of validational findings for these methods.

You might ask, If interpersonal sensitivity is a single construct, why is there such a wide range of measurement approaches? Embedded within this question lies the fundamental motivation behind the present volume. The different methods that exist are certainly measuring something, but what are they measuring? A close look at different methods indeed reveals that different methods often imply different operational definitions of the interpersonal sensitivity construct. And if operational definitions differ, could not the underlying theoretical constructs also differ? And could there exist other definitions of interpersonal sensitivity that have not yet been captured in a measurement paradigm? Therefore, a main purpose of the present volume is to collect and systematize different theoretical definitions of interpersonal sensitivity, especially as these definitions are differently embodied in the tests and measurements available for empirical use.

Thus, our focus is on both theory and method. It is our hope that this volume will provide an integrated treatment of the interpersonal sensitivity construct, as well as detailed descriptions of measurement methodologies and instruments. Many of the authors will be well recognized as those most prominently associated with their respective approaches to measuring interpersonal sensitivity. We believe that these authors' insights, critiques, and proposals for new approaches will be a lasting resource for students and professionals working in almost any basic or applied area of study involving interpersonal judgments. The domain of relevance is relationships of all kinds, including personal, clinical, and functional, as well as the many settings in which the accuracy of interpersonal judgments may have significant consequences (including home, school, clinical, legal, and employment settings).

In suggesting that the present volume is a useful and thought-provoking resource, we are not claiming that it is the first in-depth treatment of interpersonal sensitivity. Over 20 years ago, Robert Rosenthal and his colleagues described the development and validation of the Profile of Nonverbal Sensitivity (PONS test) in a book that also discussed previous research on measuring interpersonal sensitivity (Rosenthal, R., Hall, J. A., DiMatteo, M. R., Rogers, P. L., & Archer, D., 1979. *Sensitivity to Nonverbal Communication: The PONS Test.* Baltimore, MD: The Johns Hopkins University Press). In the same year, Rosenthal edited a small but influential volume titled *Skill in Nonverbal Communication: Individual Differences* (Cambridge, MA: Oelgeschlager, Gunn & Hain, 1979). A number of the authors of the present volume are represented in both of these earlier works. Two decades have seen marvelous advances in the range of approaches that are available to measure interpersonal sensitivity. Nevertheless, the earlier volumes are still surprisingly timely; few chapters have been made obsolete with the accumulation of new methods and findings. We are proud to follow in the tradition established by this earlier work, and we believe that our emphasis on the description and evaluation of methodology serves to complement rather than supersede it.

This project has been helped along by two very important people. First is Susan Milmoe of Lawrence Erlbaum Associates, who suggested a book on interpersonal sensitivity and was willing to wait several years before we could commit to it. Everyone should hope for an editor as gentle and wise as Susan. Second is Steven Breckler, Program Director for Social Psychology at the National Science Foundation, who funded a chapter authors' workshop in June 1998. This 2-day opportunity for the contributors to discuss their work and their ideas, face to face, helped the authors to see commonalities and differences among their approaches and provided a sense of coherence and excitement for the project.

—*Judith A. Hall*
*Boston, MA*

—*Frank J. Bernieri*
*Toledo, OH*

# I

## Theoretical Issues

# 1

# Toward a Taxonomy of Interpersonal Sensitivity

Frank J. Bernieri
*University of Toledo*

Fundamentally, the contributors to this volume are interested in both the aptitude and achievement related to an individual knowing and understanding others. A person is considered sensitive if he or she can perceive or otherwise respond appropriately to the internal states (e.g., cognitive, affective, motivational) of another, understand the antecedents of those states, and predict the subsequent affective, cognitive, and behavioral events that will result. The presumption is that similar to other intellectual, physical, and emotional competencies, this ability should enable an individual to function more effectively in day-to-day life by facilitating interaction with others. *Interpersonal sensitivity*, then, can be defined most generally as the ability to sense, perceive accurately, and respond appropriately to one's personal, interpersonal, and social environment.

## FROM SENSATION TO BEHAVIOR

This definition clearly spans a number of distinct perceptual, cognitive, and motivational processes. An individual who is sensitive must first sense and perceptually *discriminate* various stimuli in his or her surroundings. If John's wife rolls her eyes in disgust at the breakfast table, but John doesn't notice it because he happened to be looking down at the newspaper when it occurred, his understanding of his immediate social environment will be compromised. Interpersonal sensitivity starts with sensation and perception. Thus, interpersonal sensitivity is a function of (a) one's opportunities to experience and interact with the environment, (b) attention, and (c) any constraints on the perceptual

3

system with respect to the range of stimuli one can detect and process. Any process that influences these three aspects of interpersonal sensation and perception will necessarily affect interpersonal sensitivity.

Information sensed and discriminated is also identified and interpreted (Gilbert & Malone, 1995; Trope, 1986). Here an individual labels a stimulus (e.g., a look of disgust, anger, contempt, or frustration) and perhaps the interpersonal context (e.g., the breakfast partner could have been surveying an attitude, failing a persuasion attempt, baiting a conflict, or getting a justifiable request rejected). The labeling of an event influences and is in turn influenced by any effortful or motivated analysis and interpretation. A correct perception of an interpersonal event is a function of not only the stimuli perceived but also any preexisting expectations regarding the stimulus person, the nature of the event itself, and the context within which the event occurred (Jones, 1990; Trope, 1986).

However, even if an eye-roll is correctly identified and understood by a perceiver as a manifestation of an exasperated state by one's breakfast companion, only an interpersonally sensitive individual will understand the implications of this event and how it will likely affect his or her immediate future and pursuit of subsequent interaction goals. In other words, after figuring out what it is that John has just witnessed he now must deal with the issues of what it means to him and how he should respond. People tend to view interpersonally sensitive individuals as those who know what an effective response would be and in what measure. Perhaps a small concession or acknowledgment of his partner's frustration is all that is needed to prevent a negative spiral of affective tone at this point in the conversation. Of course, simply knowing what the correct response should be does not ensure that it will be executed (e.g., Nowicki & Duke, chap. 10, this volume). Opportunity for interaction, encoding ability, and motivation all can influence the extent to which the effective response is ultimately executed.

In reviewing the various steps through which an interpersonally sensitive individual must successfully negotiate, Nowicki and Duke point out that "there are so many ways to fail interpersonally that it is surprising that children [and adults] succeed as often as they do socially" (chap. 10, this volume). And people do succeed, more or less.

The challenge for theoreticians and researchers is that the construct of interpersonal sensitivity can encompass the entire range of processes, from the detection of stimuli within a sensory field to the actual behaviors enacted toward another. The assessment of prosocial behavior in children (Losoya & Eisenberg, chap. 2, this volume), the study of deception detection (Malone & DePaulo, chap. 6, this volume), the judgment of interpersonal relations from videotaped interactions (Archer, Costanzo, & Akert, chap. 9, this volume), and the perception of nonverbal behaviors from very brief video clips (Ambady, LaPlante, & Johnson, chap. 5, this volume; Hall, chap. 8, this volume) are all very much related to an overlapping construct. However, it would be a mistake to consider these activities, tasks, and behaviors to be synonymous or generalizeable from one to another. This book makes clear that there is as much disparity between what interpersonal sensitivity researchers study as there is similarity.

The contributors to this volume are interested primarily in an individual's responsivity to, as well as the accurate perception and judgment of, the social environment. Whereas issues of encoding skill, expressive control, and interpersonal influence are relevant to the broad topics of emotional intelligence (Goleman, 1995; Salovey & Mayer, 1990) and social skill (e.g., Eisenberg, 1998; Gilbert & Connolly, 1991), their treatment is beyond the psychological construct on which we focus. Therefore, the interpersonal sensitivity construct that is dealt with in these pages relates more to receptive accuracy (i.e., detection, decoding, and comprehension) than to behavior expression, its control, and interpersonal manipulation.

## THE FUNDAMENTAL ISSUE

What is interesting to most psychologists and laypersons is not that individuals have interpersonal sensitivity (cf. Ambady, Bernieri, & Richeson, 2000; Funder, 1999, chap. 16, this volume), but that some individuals appear more interpersonally sensitive than others (Colvin & Bundick, chap. 3, this volume; Riggio & Riggio, chap. 7, this volume; Taft, 1955). Essentially, the quest in understanding how people come to know others has been driven all along by curiosity regarding how the "good ones" do it and why the "bad ones" fail.

One way to approach this general issue is to identify the good and not-so-good interpersonal perceivers and then study them to learn how they differ. This is precisely how psychologists went about their business until 1955, a year that is as notorious to contemporary interpersonal perception researchers as the year 1929 is to Wall Street stockbrokers. In 1955, Taft published his seminal review article on the ability to judge people, which adroitly summarized the preceding 40 years of research. In that same year, Cronbach and Gage published methodological papers that effectively undermined the validity of almost all of the relevant knowledge that had accumulated up to that point (Cronbach, 1955; Gage & Cronbach, 1955). It is beyond the scope of this chapter to detail those methodological points. However, the research described in nearly every chapter of this volume has, in some way, been inspired or influenced by those papers published over 45 years ago.

## PROBLEMS WITH INTERPERSONAL SENSITIVITY AND ACCURACY RESEARCH

Interpersonal sensitivity has been operationalized and measured in numerous ways, with the result being several distinct measurement paradigms, many of which are represented in the chapters of this volume. Typically, researchers have worked within one of these paradigms without fully appreciating the implicit assumptions, consequences, and implications of the existing methodological diversity. Unfortunately there has not been a great deal of communication among researchers as to the assumptions implicitly made with the adoption of each design. This has led to impoverished discussions detailing the precise constructs or competencies involved, which prevents a clear understanding of how one set of results relates or applies to those found elsewhere. Without a clear demarcation of interpersonal sensitivity subconstructs and a clear understanding of how specific data relate to each of these constructs, empirical results are subject to overgeneralization or inappropriate application, creating theoretical ambiguity. Unfortunately, this theoretical ambiguity grows with the introduction of each new paradigm no matter how insightfully or elegantly conceived.

The first step in removing the ambiguity is to make salient the alternatives that are possible. The following is a brief outline of the issues, alternatives, and assumptions that characterize research in interpersonal sensitivity and judgmental accuracy.

## Breadth of the Construct

As stated earlier, interpersonal sensitivity can pertain to everything from sensation thresholds (e.g., Hall, Carter, & Horgan, in press) to the execution of appropriate and effective behavior (e.g., Losoya & Eisenberg, chap. 2, this volume). Rarely, however, do researchers work with such a generalized construct. More often, as occurs in this volume, researchers constrain interpersonal sensitivity to the correct identification and comprehension of social stimuli. According to the work presented in this volume, the sensitive person can (a) perceive the emotion being experienced by another (Nowicki & Duke, chap. 10, this volume); (b) infer what a partner is thinking (Ickes, chap. 12, this volume); (c) decode what the partner is attempting to communicate (Noller, chap. 13, this volume), be it truth or deception (Malone & DePaulo, chap. 6, this volume); (d) ascertain the true relationship between interactants (Archer, Costanzo, & Akert, chap. 9, this volume) and how they are getting along (Bernieri & Gillis, chap. 4, this volume; Snodgrass, chap. 11, this volume); (e) assess the social context within which a person seems to be communicating (Hall, chap. 8, this volume); (f) know a target's stable dispositions, traits, and behavioral tendencies (Colvin & Bundick, chap. 3, this volume); and (g) do so with an exposure to an extremely thin slice of the target's ongoing behavioral stream (Ambady, LaPlante, & Johnson, chap. 5, this volume) when not afforded the opportunity of an entire series of interactions with multiple partners (Kenny & Winquist, chap. 14, this volume). Interpersonal sensitivity from the standpoint of this volume is mostly, if not exclusively, about knowing another or group of others.

One also can argue that a more global construct of interpersonal sensitivity should include knowing what to do (Nowicki & Duke, chap. 10, this volume). Constructs of social intelligence have emphasized the capacity of individuals to understand how social systems work and how people stereotypically behave within them (e.g., Riggio, 1986; Rosenthal, Hall, DiMatteo, Rogers, & Archer, 1979; Strang, 1930). For example, a young child sitting on a city bus may correctly ascertain and even feel empathically the physical fatigue of a pregnant woman standing and holding a heavy bag of groceries, but simply not realize that the thing to do is to offer up one's seat to this woman in need. One might view this child, then, as less interpersonally sensitive because of naiveté than the woman sitting nearby who immediately gives up her seat reflexively, though not empathically. Of course, even when someone is sensitive enough to perceive the fatigued woman and wise enough to know what the proper response should be, he or she must have the motivation to execute and deliver the appropriate response, in this case to offer up the seat. The interpersonal sensitivity discussed by Losoya and Eisenberg (chap. 2, this volume) illustrates how some researchers include behavior execution (i.e., prosocial behavior) in their construct of interpersonal sensitivity. Furthermore, execution is not always an all-or-nothing response but can sometimes vary in quality, such as when one delivers an obliged apology but does not express it with sufficient sincerity to be believed and accepted. In this case, sensitivity extends past the decoding of information into the realm of encoding: the expression and control of behavior (e.g., Friedman, chap. 18; Riggio & Riggio, chap. 7, both this volume).

In addition to knowing and doing, interpersonal sensitivity can refer to responsivity or reactivity to stimuli. For example, individual differences exist in the extent to which people attend to, notice, and remember nonverbal behaviors and physical appearance. Hall and colleagues have referred to this as *attentional accuracy* (Hall et al., 1998, in press). Interestingly, consciousness is not a prerequisite to responsivity. For example, individuals may differ in the extent to which their judgments are influenced by the presence or absence of certain nonverbal cues (Bernieri & Gillis, 1995b), and these differences may not be acknowledged by the perceiver (Gillis, Bernieri, & Wooten, 1995). Other, more visceral types of reactivity that some may wish to include as part of a general interpersonal sensitivity construct might include emotional contagion (Hatfield, Cacioppo, & Rapson, 1994) and interactional synchrony, which is the extent to which movements and behaviors become coordinated and matched during interaction (Bernieri, Davis, Rosenthal, & Knee, 1994; Bernieri & Rosenthal, 1991). Knowledge, comprehension, and execution are not issues here. Rather, this aspect of sensitivity refers to the difference in thresholds for response or reactivity that occurs either consciously or beyond awareness.

Thus, interpersonal sensitivity spans the domains of reactivity, knowledge, and behavior expression. The breadth of this construct becomes problematic when researchers working on different aspects that may involve different cognitive or psychological processes use language that might make others believe they are researching the same construct or process. Researchers need to locate their interpersonal sensitivity construct clearly within the domains of reactivity, knowledge, and behavior to avoid overgeneralization and misrepresentation.

## Content or Thing Perceived

Ickes (1993, chap. 12, this volume) has categorized interpersonal perception accuracy research on the basis of the constructs judged. For example, researchers have examined observer judgments of (a) personality traits; (b) attitudes, values, and self-conceptions; (c) emotional states; and (d) mental contents including thoughts and feelings (see also Kenny & Winquist, chap. 14, this volume). Bernieri et al. (1994) added a fifth category of constructs that included interpersonally defined constructs that exist at the dyad or group level, such as rapport, status, and kinship.

One of the recurrent themes the reader will notice throughout this volume is the acknowledgment by its contributing authors that there exists little evidence to show that the ability to judge one construct accurately generalizes to the perception and judgment of other constructs (Colvin & Bundick, chap. 3; Hall, chap. 8; Riggio & Riggio, chap. 7; Zebrowitz, chap. 17, all this volume). It is undeniably true that the abilities to (a) identify emotions in facial affect displays, (b) recognize a target's true extraversion, (c) infer what another is thinking, and (d) perceive which of two interacting targets holds the higher status, all contribute to one's overall skill in reading people and thus their interpersonal sensitivity. However, it does not necessarily follow—logically or empirically—that the ability for perceiving any one of these is necessarily predictive of the ability to perceive any other. The skill with which people judge various psychological constructs seems to be as much a function of the thing being judged as it is a function of the person doing the judging.

Researchers hope eventually to come to understand how the topic or content of interpersonal perceptions relates precisely to an individual's interpersonal sensitivity. At present, researchers are only now accepting the fact that it is an issue. Preliminary frameworks such as the one offered by Ickes (1993) and extended by Bernieri et al. (1994) are useful in that they begin to suggest systematic ways in which content may differ, which may in turn help elucidate corresponding perceptual, cognitive, and psychological processes associated with these differences.

To facilitate theorizing related to this issue, it might be useful at this stage to make finer discriminations within the content domains of interpersonal perception. By increasing the number of different domains possible, researchers will be compelled to look for, derive, and then test the similarities between constructs before generalizing across them. A working list of possible content domains appears in Table 1.1. The reader is advised to keep this list in mind while reading this volume because it may help clarify the interpretations and speculations made by the contributors to this volume given their reported results.

Despite this delineation of content and interpersonal judgment competencies, it still may be the case that interpersonal sensitivity is an enduring, global disposition. A major goal for researchers will be to determine whether there is, in fact, an interpersonal sensitivity trait. At the moment, empirical findings seem to be at odds with the notion of a "good judge." However, it will likely be the case that this trait is simply multifaceted and in many ways context-dependent. In other words, more is learned about various types of interpersonal judgment competencies and what moderates them, researchers may find systematic relations between the different content domains that will allow them ultimately to form a unifying theory of a global interpersonal sensitivity construct.

### TABLE 1.1
#### The Things Perceived and Judged Accurately
#### That Constitute Interpersonal Sensitivity

| Category of things judged | Example |
| --- | --- |
| Features | Does perceiver notice and remember the target's hair style? |
| Characteristics | Can the perceiver identify the target's gender, age, or educational level? |
| Behaviors | Does the perceiver notice and remember how much the target smiled? |
| Internal states | Can the perceiver detect a target's mood, attitude, or cognitions? |
| Interpersonal intentions | Can the perceiver recognize when a target wants to speak or terminate the interaction? |
| Deceptive intent and self-presentation | Can the perceiver detect a lie or tell when a target is self-presenting or persuading? |
| Traits and dispositions | Can the perceiver identify a target's personality, motivations, and competencies? |
| Social relations | Does the perceiver recognize who is the boss or who is related to whom? |
| Situation and cultural context | Does the perceiver recognize that the activity or task is cooperative and not competitive? |
| Role fulfillment | Can a perceiver tell when someone is conforming to a social role appropriately? |
| Future behaviors and outcomes | Can the perceiver predict how long a target will persist at a task? |

## Criterion Problem

When interpersonal sensitivity is understood in terms of accuracy of perception, a Pandora's box is opened regarding the very determination of an accurate judgment. How, exactly, are researchers to assess the accuracy with which people judge things in others, such as emotions, traits, attitudes, and motives? To determine accuracy of a judgment or reaction, one must know the reality. Kruglanski (1989) discussed the three distinct notions of judgmental accuracy that have been used throughout the interpersonal sensitivity literature. The most prevalent definition of accuracy involves a correspondence between a judgment and criterion. The challenge is up to the researcher to provide a compelling justification of the criterion as being representative of the reality (Hastie & Rasinsky, 1988).

Kenny (1994) categorized the criterion measures used implicitly or explicitly throughout the interpersonal sensitivity literature as follows: (a) self-report, (b) consensus, (c) expert judgments, (d) behavioral observations, and (d) operational criteria. *Self-reports* can be direct self-assessments of such things as preferences, internal states and cognitions, or behaviors. Results from personality inventories that are completed by a target are also considered self-reported criteria. Unfortunately, self-reports are problematic to the extent that a self-perception is intentionally distorted or incorrect for any other reason.

*Consensus* refers to the interpersonal agreement between judges (Funder, 1987, 1995; Kruglanski, 1989). Although accuracy does not necessarily follow from consensus (a million Frenchmen *can* be wrong), consensus is often thought of as a prerequisite for accuracy (see also Funder, chap. 16, this volume). *Expert judgments* are used as a criterion for judgmental accuracy when it can be argued that an individual, by definition, knows the true state or disposition of the target. Experts can range from a mother or teacher when the target is a child to a clinical psychologist who knows very well the target or psychological state or disposition. Of course, the accuracy of the experts themselves is an issue as unresolved as is the accuracy of the perceivers. Whereas there might not exist a true expert to yield the perfect criterion, it is reasonable to expect some experts to be more "expert" than others. For example, a track and field coach might be considered an appropriate expert to provide criterion data on targets with respect to their athletic motivation and competitiveness.

When used as a criterion measure, *behavioral observations* effectively reduce the perceiver's task from the judgment of psychological constructs (e.g., effort) to the prediction of more objectively operationalized behaviors (e.g., improvement in running times over a 6-week training period). The advantage of using behavioral observations as a criterion is increased conceptual clarity when the construct considered is nothing more than the behavior itself; however, the prediction of behaviors is a decidedly different task than is the identification of an internal state or psychological disposition. Because behaviors are multiply determined by any number of possible internal psychological states and dispositions, one might predict behaviors reasonably well but for all the wrong reasons. In other words, what is gained in objectivity and precision through the use of behavioral observations is lost in construct validity (i.e., the psychological meaning underlying these behaviors).

Also, although behavioral observations are operationalized more objectively than are psychological states and traits, they should not be thought of as perfectly objective realities that can be assessed with unbiased mechanical measurement devices. Even such clear-cut variables as interpersonal distance can involve a good deal of subjective interpretation. For example, in a 10-minute conversation between two targets sitting on chairs facing each other, what is the true physical distance separating them? Should the correct distance be measured nose-to-nose? Chest-to-chest? Waist-to-waist? Knee-to-knee? Foot-to-foot? Or between any two closest body parts? Because any measure will vary over time, which measure or mean of measures should be used? The distance at the beginning, middle, or end? Instead, perhaps, some mean should be used that samples several times over the course of the 10 minutes. But at what interval? Every second? 10 seconds? 60 seconds? It is important to acknowledge that even behavioral observations are inherently arbitrary and provide only possible improvements to the criterion problem. Behavioral observations do not solve the criterion problem.

Finally, *operational criteria* are sometimes used to determine the accuracy of perceivers. This is where the criterion is known directly through its definition (e.g., these two people are siblings) or is defined through experimental manipulation. Perhaps the most obvious example of this can be found in the deception detection literature (Malone & DePaulo, chap. 6, this volume). Researchers can ask individuals to report truthfully an attitude toward some object (e.g., a person or food item) and then ask them to lie about it. The accuracy with which a perceiver can detect such deception is straightforward. However, even with this criterion interesting nuances exist in exactly what constitutes an accurate perception of a lie. For example, asking people to make a dichotomous truth–lie judgment generates results that may not be directly comparable with scaled judgments of communication truthfulness (see Malone & DePaulo, chap. 6, this volume). Attempts at constructing standardized tests of interpersonal sensitivity are also notable in their use of operational criteria (Hall, chap. 8; Archer, Costanzo, & Akert, chap. 9; Nowicki & Duke, chap. 10, all this volume).

Each of the aforementioned treatments of the criterion issue can be found within the collection of research programs presented in this volume. The reason these criteria all appear is *not* because there is disagreement within the field as to which of the five categories of criteria constitutes the proper criterion. Rather, they all appear because each type of criterion is more or less appropriate given the precise nature and definition of the accuracy being assessed. In fact, an explicit goal of this volume is to make salient the nuances of the interpersonal sensitivity construct by having the empirical and theoretical work of the major contributors to the field side-by-side within a single reference volume.

As an illustration, consider the accuracy of perceiving friendliness. It might appear to be a straightforward task to have a perceiver judge how friendly a target is. In fact, a researcher can ask a perceiver this question but use many different criteria to assess the accuracy of the response. For example, simply using the five categories of criteria mentioned earlier, a researcher can compare a perceiver's judgment with (a) the target's self-description of friendliness, (b) reports of the target's friendliness from others, (c) the target's score on a state-of-the-art psychological inventory assessing sociability and friendliness, (d) how talkative and jovial the target is with people in general, or (e) in which of two observed interactions was the target interacting with a friend as opposed to an unliked colleague. Which is the judgment-to-criterion match that best captures the accuracy of perceiving friendliness? Add to this the fact that a researcher may ask the perceiver to assess friendliness or perhaps one of the five specific criteria listed earlier. The crossing of the categories of criteria with the corresponding categories of judgment creates an enormous potential for construct ambiguity and interpretive confusion. Alas, the problem facing interpersonal sensitivity researchers is that there may be as many types of accuracy as there are accuracy judgments and criteria. Only the use of precise language and the careful correspondence between theoretical discussion and research methodology can enable useful interpretations, extensions, and applications of the empirical data generated.

## Variance Components

Another difficulty that has impeded progress in this field involves the inherently componential nature of the judgment (and criterion). This issue becomes most noticeable when multiple perceivers make multiple judgments of many targets along several dimensions across different contexts at different times. For example, when a researcher requires perceivers to judge five different targets on 10 different traits to increase the robustness and generalizability of the accuracy construct, the meaning and interpretation of a single accuracy score for perceivers becomes multiply determined and problematic.

Essentially, in such designs an overall accuracy score can be driven by such different factors as: (a) rating bias (i.e., the way in which a perceiver understands and uses the assessment scale), (b) implicit personality theory accuracy (i.e., the existence of a reasonably accurate schema or person stereotypes for the constellation of traits or dispositions that exists within the typical person), (c) situation accuracy (i.e., the knowledge of how a typical person might behave within a given social context), and (d) unique target accuracy (i.e., the accuracy of perceiving unique targets after removing other accuracy components).

Kenny and Winquist (chap. 14, this volume) provide an overview of accuracy components and how they might be assessed empirically.

The reader should take note, however, that the delineation of variance components might turn out to be an ongoing issue in interpersonal sensitivity. Sources of variance due to target, perceiver, content (i.e., the variables judged, such as traits and emotions), situational context, and time are just the beginning. It will soon be advantageous to include other sources of variance to this list such as roles, relationships, social categories, and culture. With each source of variance systematically observed will come a new and precise aspect of interpersonal sensitivity never before assessed, perhaps each with its own set of moderators and diagnostic indicators. These developments will advance understanding of interpersonal sensitivity but only if researchers begin to appreciate the componential nature of accuracy and go beyond the use of a single, universal metric.

As was true in the discussion of accuracy criteria, it would be counterproductive to argue over how to define the single best accuracy metric. The reality is that for each research question there will be measures and statistically derived scores that are more or less relevant or appropriate. The challenge, and necessity, for theoreticians and researchers alike will be to identify the precise component of accuracy that is relevant to the theoretical discussion and match it accordingly to a proper research design.

It is ironic, perhaps, that the increasingly complex design features used to improve the external validity of an interpersonal sensitivity study tend to reduce the clarity of the interpretation of a single overall judgment-to-criterion agreement statistic (Cronbach, 1955; Gage & Cronbach, 1955; Kenny, 1994). In return, however, these design features hold great promise for delineating an entire taxonomy of interpersonal sensitivity constructs and competencies.

## METHODOLOGICAL CONSIDERATIONS

The number of different methodological approaches to the study of interpersonal sensitivity seems to be nearly equal to the number of investigators researching it. The reader will note several methodological issues that have been handled differently throughout this volume. Many times these issues are not explicitly addressed in published empirical reports because they are implicit within the theoretical framework being offered. In fact, a reader might easily overlook the issue entirely because of the intuitive appeal of the research methodology used given the presentation and formulation of the research problem. However, it should become quite clear after reading this volume that interpersonal sensitivity researchers have a frighteningly large number of alternative designs and methodologies at their disposal. Only by considering (and rejecting) other methodologies can researchers have more confidence in the correspondence between their data and their interpretations.

## Units of Analysis

What things or units are being judged? A target person? A group? A relationship? An interaction? A point in time within an interaction? A single thought?
A researcher interested in assessing the sensitivity with which a perceiver can
correctly identify an intended communication of a specific affect (e.g., Noller,
chap. 13, this volume) will need a different design than a researcher interested
in assessing the ability to identify kinship relations within dyadic interactions
(e.g., Archer, Costanzo, & Akert, chap. 9, this volume).

## Sampling of the Personal,
## Interpersonal, and Social Ecology

How much of the ecology constitutes a given trial? On one extreme, judgments
could be based on an entire life experience with the target, as is the case when
parents judge their children. On the other extreme are judgments based on extremely thin slices of the behavioral stream, lasting only seconds or less
(Ambady et al., 2000; Ambady, La Plante, & Johnson, chap. 5, this volume).
Clearly, the interpersonal sensitivity of first impressions or thin-slice perceptions cannot be equated with the interpersonal sensitivity regarding life-long
partners.

## Information Source

People typically form impressions and make judgments of others from a wide
array of information sources including face-to-face interactions, photographs, resumes and vitas, descriptions provided by others (e.g., gossip, stories, letters of recommendation), behavioral actions (e.g., job offers accepted
and refused, selection of friends and significant other), and personal produc-
tions (e.g., creative works of art, music, or literature; cluttered office; wedding
reception). Impression formation and interpersonal sensitivity researchers
have worked mainly with verbal information, audio and video recordings, and
face-to-face interactions. The important issue here is that the processes that
are uncovered by using one source of information may not generalize to others. For example, Gillis et al. (1995) presented half of their perceivers with
videotaped recordings of dyadic interactions. The rest of the perceivers were
presented with verbal descriptions that quantified the various behaviors encoded within the video segments that were viewed by the other perceivers
(e.g., interactants sat so many inches apart, smiled so many times, gestured
with their hands so many times). Results showed that judgments based on information presented verbally used available cues in a different way from judg-

ments based on information presented visually. Furthermore, the ability to modify one's judgment policy—as when instructed how to improve accuracy by attending to some behaviors and ignoring others—did not generalize across stimulus conditions even though the information communicated within the verbal presentations was yoked to that embedded within the videotaped displays. The lesson to be learned is that the medium or channel of information to which an observer has access may interact with his or her processing of that information. Closeness, for example, may be perceived and understood differently when observers see it compared with when they are informed about it (Gillis et al., 1995).

Social perceivers are exposed to all channels during face-to-face interactions. There has been much research looking at interpersonal sensitivity within isolated channels and channel communication, but it is not yet clear how these results should be incorporated into an overall construct (e.g., Hall, chap. 8, this volume).

One cause for the lack of integration is that comparisons of perceptions made on the various channels have revealed more independence than coherence (e.g., Berry, Pennebaker, Mueller, & Hiller, 1997; Ekman, Friesen, O'Sullivan, & Scherer, 1980; Grahe & Bernieri, 1999; Mehrabian & Ferris, 1967; Meiran, Netzer, Netzer, Itzhak, & Rechnitz, 1994; Rosenthal et al., 1979). In other words, issues such as what can be perceived, how accurate the perception is, and what moderates the accuracy of perception all need to be addressed by taking into account the channel of communication within which one is working. For example, one should not naïvely apply research findings based on the perception of audio clips to situations involving face-to-face interactions. This does not mean that isolated channel research is not ecologically valid or useful. On the contrary, social perceivers often have limited exposure to certain channels of communication. The fact is, we do form impressions and react to people even when all the information we have to process comes from only a photo of their face or perhaps a conversation with them over the phone.

## Spontaneous Versus Posed Behavior

Another critical issue in the design of interpersonal sensitivity research involves whether perceivers will be responding to unscripted spontaneous behavior, such as ongoing dyadic interaction (e.g., Ickes, chap. 12; Snodgrass, chap. 11, both this volume), or to behavior performed for the purpose of assessment, such as the communication of a specific affective message using standard content speech (e.g., Noller, chap. 13, this volume). On the basis of existing comparisons in the literature between spontaneous and posed encoding, it would be naïve to neglect this issue when designing research and interpreting empirical findings (e.g., Buck, 1984; Halberstadt, 1986). Clearly, the processes involved in spontaneous affective and interpersonal behavior are distinct from those involved in strategic, intentional, and controlled affective and communicative expression. However, neither form of interpersonal behavior and expression is more fundamental to the construct of interpersonal sensitivity. Human beings must identify and respond appropriately to expressions and behavior that are preplanned and intentionally acted out for their scrutiny, as well as to those encoded by their partners spontaneously.

## Online (Interactive) Versus
## Stimulus-Based (Passive) Judgments

The goals of construct clarity, comparability, reliability, and therefore utility have tended to compel researchers to use experimental designs that assess perceivers' ability to respond to or judge social stimuli passively by listening to or observing previously recorded targets. Such designs allow researchers to take their show on the road and compare different samples or populations with a single instrument (Bernieri & Gillis, 1995a; Hall, chap. 8, this volume; Rosenthal et al., 1979; Scherer & Wallbott, 1994).

Although enormously useful in this respect, stimulus-based paradigms have the burden of establishing their external validity or generalizability with respect to interpersonal sensitivity as it occurs in face-to-face interaction. An active perceiver in a face-to-face interaction is under high cognitive load (Gilbert, Pelham, & Krull, 1988; Patterson, 1995), is self-conscious (Carver & Scheier, 1981; Duval & Wicklund, 1972), and is subject to a host of motivational processes (e.g., DePaulo, 1992; Greenwald, 1980) that are typically minimized within perceivers. Each of these factors clearly influences how individuals perceive and think about others (Fiske & Taylor, 1991). The challenge for interpersonal sensitivity researchers will be to develop paradigms that can incorporate these interaction features into their assessments. Researchers have tapped interpersonal perceptions immediately following face-to-face interactions (e.g., Ickes, chap. 12, and Snodgrass, chap. 11, both this volume), but moment-to-moment face-to-face dyadic sensitivity is a largely unexplored phenomenon.

Obviously, perceptions and thoughts about others occur naturally: (a) on the fly while interacting with others; (b) spontaneously, while passively observing others (e.g., as one might do as a juror in a trial); and (c) later, after the fact, while ruminating about what one may have experienced. Therefore, each of these domains needs to be included within research. It is necessary therefore for researchers to distinguish between the perception and judgment of others as it occurs throughout ongoing social interaction and the perception and judgment of others as it occurs passively, or on reflection after the interaction has taken place (see also Kenny, 1994; McArthur & Baron, 1983).

## The Best Method

Throughout this volume, readers will be invited to take note of the ways each author has handled each of these issues. It should become obvious after only a few chapters that the research methodology used within any empirical investigation is highly customized to suit a precise and perhaps unique theoretical construct and research question. It should become obvious to all who survey the methodologies included in this volume that there exists no "canned research paradigm" for the investigation of interpersonal sensitivity.

## PURPOSE, GOALS, AND OBJECTIVES

The contributors to this volume are interested in the various ways to conceptualize and measure interpersonal sensitivity. It is our intention to discuss theoretical definitions, make explicit the resulting methodology that results, summarize representative findings, identify questions that need to be raised, and link those questions with the methods appropriate for their studies. Ultimately, we will need to map out a workable theory or taxonomy that will allow scholars and researchers unambiguously to understand the precise nature of the particular "sensitivity" measures we each are assessing. Only in this fashion will we be able to relate them meaningfully to other measures and to the more global construct of interpersonal sensitivity.

It is hoped that as readers make their way through the various chapters of this volume they will become aware of, but not intimidated by, the multifaceted nature and context-dependency of the construct referred to here as interpersonal sensitivity. The spirit of this volume then is of analysis rather than synthesis. Researchers are still in the nascent stages of theory and comprehension of this most complex and sophisticated of competencies. Methodologists and theorists are still developing methodology and terminology and are even still identifying the extent of content.

The metaphor of the blind men and the elephant used by Zebrowitz (chap. 17, this volume) to communicate the current state of our knowledge captures perfectly the reality that will be revealed throughout this book. Each of the contributors has grabbed firmly on a component of the beast we are each committed to understanding. We have always been aware that each of us has hold of the same beast but it has taken much longer to realize that the part with which we each are familiar may be entirely different in nature from the part understood by our colleagues. The publication of this volume represents a first step toward the big picture. Throughout these pages we are each explaining to one another not so much what we have learned in our labs, but more importantly, how we are making our observations and under what conditions. We are discussing as never before the implicit assumptions behind our preferred questions, methodology, and research style and are considering what impact these might have for the interpretation of our specific findings on the way to developing a unifying theory of interpersonal sensitivity.

## ACKNOWLEDGMENT

The contents of this chapter represent the products of a series of ongoing discussions with Judith A. Hall.

## REFERENCES

Ambady, N., Bernieri, F., & Richeson, J. (2000). Towards a histology of social behavior: Judgmental accuracy from thin slices of the behavioral stream. *Advances in Experimental Social Psychology, 32,* 201–271.

Bernieri, F., & Gillis, J. S. (1995b). Personality correlates of accuracy in a social perception task. *Perceptual and Motor Skills, 81,* 168–170.

Bernieri, F., Davis, J., Rosenthal, R., & Knee, C. (1994). Interactional synchrony and rapport: Measuring synchrony in displays devoid of sound and facial affect. *Personality and Social Psychology Bulletin, 20,* 303–311.

Bernieri, F., & Gillis, J. S. (1995a). The judgment of rapport: A cross-cultural comparison between Americans and Greeks. *Journal of Nonverbal Behavior, 19,* 115–130.

Bernieri, F., & Rosenthal, R. (1991). Coordinated movement in human interaction. In R. Feldman & B. Rimé (Eds.), *Fundamentals of nonverbal behavior* (pp. 401–432). New York: Cambridge University Press.

Berry, D. S., Pennebaker, J. W., Mueller, J. S., & Hiller, W. S. (1997). Linguistic bases of social perception. *Personality and Social Psychology Bulletin, 23,* 526–537.

Buck, R. (1984). *The communication of emotion.* New York: Guilford.

Carver, C. S., & Scheier, M. F. (1981). *Attention and self-regulation: A control theory approach to human behavior.* New York: Springer-Verlag.

Cronbach, L. J. (1955). Processes affecting scores on "understanding others" and "assumed similarity." *Psychological Bulletin, 52,* 177–193.

DePaulo, B. M. (1992). Nonverbal behavior and self-presentation. *Psychological Bulletin, 11,* 203–243.

Duval, S., & Wicklund, R. A. (1972). *A theory of objective self-awareness.* New York: Academic.

Eisenberg, N. (1998). The socialization of socioemotional competence. In D. Pushkar & W. M. Bukowski (Eds.), *Improving competence across the lifespan: Building interventions based on theory and research* (pp. 59–78). New York: Plenum.

Ekman, P., Friesen, W. V., O'Sullivan, M., & Scherer, K. (1980). The relative importance of face, body, and speech in judgments of personality and affect. *Journal of Personality and Social Psychology, 38,* 270–277.

Fiske, S. T., & Taylor, S. E. (1991). *Social cognition.* New York: McGraw-Hill.

Funder, D. C. (1987). Errors and mistakes: Evaluating the accuracy of social judgment. *Psychological Bulletin, 101,* 75–91.

Funder, D. C. (1995). On the accuracy of personality judgment: A realistic approach. *Psychological Review, 102,* 652–670.

Funder, D. C. (1999). *Personality judgment: A realistic approach to person perception.* San Diego, CA: Academic.

Gage, N. L., & Cronbach, L. J. (1955). Conceptual and methodological problems in interpersonal perception. *Psychological Review, 62*, 411–422.

Gilbert, D. G., & Connolly, J. J. (Eds.). (1991). *Personality, social skills, and psychopathology: An individual differences approach.* New York: Plenum.

Gilbert, D. T., & Malone, P. S. (1995). The correspondence bias. *Psychological Bulletin, 117*, 21–38.

Gilbert, D. T., Pelham, B. W., & Krull, D. S. (1988). On cognitive busyness: When person perceivers meet persons perceived. *Journal of Personality and Social Psychology, 54*, 733–740.

Gillis, J., Bernieri, F., & Wooten, E. (1995). The effects of stimulus medium and feedback on the judgment of rapport. *Organizational Behavior and Human Decision Processes, 63*, 33–45.

Goleman, D. (1995). *Emotional intelligence.* New York: Bantam.

Grahe, J. E., & Bernieri, F. J. (1999). The importance of nonverbal cues in judging rapport. *Journal of Nonverbal Behavior, 23*, 253–269.

Greenwald, A. G. (1980). The totalitarian ego: Fabrication and revision of personal history. *American Psychologist, 35*, 603–618.

Halberstadt, A. G. (1986). Family socialization of emotional expression and nonverbal communication styles and skills. *Journal of Personality and Social Psychology, 51*, 827–836.

Hall, J. A., Carter, J. D., & Horgan, T. E. (1998). *Assigned status and attention to nonverbal cues: Motivational effects of unequal status on accurate recall of a partner's behavior.* Unpublished manuscript.

Hall, J. A., Carter, J. D., & Horgan, T. E. (in press). *Status roles and recall of nonverbal cues. Journal of Nonverbal Behavior.*

Hastie, R., & Rasinsky, K. A. (1988). The concept of accuracy in social judgment. In D. Bar-Tal & A. W. Kruglanski (Eds.), *The social psychology of knowledge* (pp. 193–208). Cambridge, England: Cambridge University Press.

Hatfield, E., Cacioppo, J. T., & Rapson, R. L. (1994). *Emotional contagion.* Paris: Cambridge University Press.

Ickes, W. (1993). Empathic accuracy. *Journal of Personality, 61*, 587–609.

Jones, E. E. (1990). *Interpersonal perception.* New York: Freeman.

Kenny, D. A. (1994). *Interpersonal perception: A social relations analysis.* New York: Guilford.

Kruglanski, A. W. (1989). The psychology of being "right": The problem of accuracy in social perception and cognition. *Psychological Bulletin, 106*, 395–409.

McArthur, L. Z., & Baron, R. M. (1983). Toward an ecological theory of social perception. *Psychological Review, 90*, 215–238.

Mehrabian, A., & Ferris, S. (1967). Inference of attitudes from nonverbal communication in two channels. *Journal of Consulting Psychology, 31*, 248–252.

Meiran, N., Netzer, T., Netzer, S., Itzhak, D., & Rechnitz, O. (1994). Do tests of nonverbal decoding ability measure sensitivity to nonverbal cues? *Journal of Nonverbal Behavior, 18*, 223–244.

Patterson, M. L. (1995). A parallel process model of nonverbal communication. *Journal of Nonverbal Behavior, 19*, 3–29.

Riggio, R. E. (1986). Assessment of basic social skills. *Journal of Personality and Social Psychology, 51*, 649–660.

Rosenthal, R., Hall, J. A., DiMatteo, M. R., Rogers, P. L., & Archer, D. (1979). *Sensitivity to nonverbal communication: The PONS test.* Baltimore: Johns Hopkins University Press.

Salovey, P., & Mayer, J. D. (1990). Emotional intelligence. *Imagination, Cognition, & Personality, 9,* 185–211.

Scherer, K. R., & Wallbott, H. G. (1994). Evidence for universality and cultural variation of differential emotional response patterning. *Journal of Personality and Social Psychology, 66,* 310–328.

Strang, R. (1930). Measures of social intelligence. *American Journal of Sociology, 36,* 263–269.

Taft, R. (1955). The ability to judge people. *Psychological Bulletin, 52,* 1–23.

Trope, Y. (1986). Identification and inferential processes in dispositional attribution. *Psychological Review, 93,* 239–257.

# ❦ 2 ❧

# Affective Empathy

**Sandra H. Losoya**
**Nancy Eisenberg**
*Arizona State University*

Empathy has long been thought to contribute to individuals' abilities to understand, predict, experience, and relate to others' behaviors, feelings, attitudes, and intentions. Moreover, there are theoretical and empirical reasons to believe that empathy is a major contributor to moral development (Hoffman, 1990), altruistic and prosocial behavior (Batson, 1991, 1998; Eisenberg & Strayer, 1987; Eisenberg & Fabes, 1991, 1998; Roberts & Strayer, 1996), emotional intelligence (Davies, Stankov, & Roberts, 1998; Salovey & Mayer, 1990), social competence (Eisenberg & Fabes, 1992; Eisenberg, Fabes, Murphy, et al., 1996; Eisenberg & Miller, 1987; Saarni, 1990), interpersonal forgiving (McCullough, Worthington, & Rachal, 1997), and low levels of aggression toward others (Feshbach, 1978; Miller & Eisenberg, 1988). Thus, empathy, broadly defined, is a construct (and competency) that contributes to, or can be seen as an aspect of, interpersonal sensitivity and social competence.

The purpose of this chapter is to examine the conceptualization and operationalization of affective empathy-related responding as it is often used in contemporary research in developmental and social psychology. We begin with definitional and conceptual issues related to research on empathy. We then briefly review work on the relation of this multidimensional construct to prosocial behavior (i.e., voluntary action intended to aid or benefit another; Eisenberg & Miller, 1987), a body of research that provides support for the importance and validity of the construct of affective empathy. Finally, we review and evaluate past and present methods for assessing empathy-related reactions, including the use of various types of self-report measures, other-report measures, facial–gestural–behavioral responses, psychophysiological responding, and experimental manipulations.

21

## CONCEPTUAL ISSUES

Despite the fact that empathy has been an important area of research in a variety of disciplines including social, developmental, personality, and clinical psychology (e.g., Batson & Coke, 1981; Hoffman, 1984; Hogan, 1969; Ickes, 1993), there is little consensus regarding its meaning. One group of scholars takes a solely cognitive perspective and defines empathy as the ability to accurately understand or predict another person's thoughts, feelings, and actions (Deutsch & Madle, 1975; Dymond, 1949; Ford, 1979). In developmental work, cognitive empathy often has been labeled *perspective taking* or *role taking* (e.g., Eisenberg, 1986; Underwood & Moore, 1982) or has been framed as a lack of egocentrism (Ford, 1979). Perspective taking implies actively trying to take another's perspective, a process that researchers agree can involve a variety of cognitive processes such as accessing relevant information from memory or making relevant cognitive associations between another's emotional state or situation (perhaps from identifying relevant cues related to another's emotional state or situation) and one's own prior experience (e.g., Eisenberg, Shea, Carlo, & Knight, 1991; Higgins, 1981; Karniol, 1982, 1990).

Defined cognitively, the construct of empathy is similar to a traditional measure used in the study of person perception or interpersonal sensitivity. That is, an individual who is highly empathic by this definition is skilled at decoding cues related to another's feelings or behavior and therefore is accurate in predicting another's feelings or behavior. Accuracy in inferring another's thoughts and feelings, or *empathic accuracy* (Ickes, 1993; Ickes; Stinson, Bissonnette, & Garcia, 1990), and sensitivity to nonverbal cues (e.g., the PONS: Rosenthal, Hall, Archer, DiMatteo, & Rogers, 1979; Costanzo & Archer, 1991; Riggio, 1992) have been of considerable interest within the field of person perception and interpersonal sensitivity. The focus of researchers in this field, however, tends to be on the perceiver's ability to infer, from a variety of verbal and nonverbal cues, a target individual's thoughts, feelings, and personality characteristics, and on how this skill might be involved in processes of social influence such as in physician–patient or teacher–student relationships (Bernieri, 1991; Colvin & Funder, 1991; Marangoni, Garcia, Ickes, & Teng, 1995; Rosenthal, 1988; Rosenthal et al., 1979; Snodgrass, 1985).

Whereas cognitive definitions of empathy involve an observer's (or perceiver's) inferential skills, an equally useful and important definition of empathy emphasizes the vicarious emotional reactions that occur within the individual as a result of observing another's emotional state or situation (Eisenberg & Strayer, 1987; Feshbach, 1978; Hoffman, 1982; Mehrabian, Young, & Sato, 1988; Stotland, 1969). Building on the work of Feshbach (1978) and Hoffman (1982), we define empathy as a state of emotional arousal that stems from the apprehension or comprehension of another's affective state and which is similar to, or congruent with, what the other person is feeling (or would be expected to feel; Eisenberg & Strayer, 1987; Eisenberg, Shea, et al., 1991). For instance, if an individual observes another person who is sad, and then feels sad him- or herself, that individual is experiencing empathy. One also can be considered empathic if, in response to an individual's positive emotion, one feels similarly positive. One can empathize with a wide range of emotions, although empathy with emotions other than happiness, sadness, and upset or distress has seldom been studied.

Inherent in this conceptualization of empathy is the assumption that children and adults engage in spontaneous affect matching (or emotion contagion; Buck, 1984; Hatfield, Cacioppo, & Rapson, 1992), which may occur with or without conscious awareness or may require certain skills such as receiving and decoding cues related to the emotional state of another. Moreover, it is assumed that there are individual differences in the tendency to experience the same emotions as others (e.g., Bryant, 1982; Mehrabian & Epstein, 1972) and that some people, at least in some situations, tend to respond to others' negative emotions with little or no emotion or even positive emotion (e.g., Englis, Vaughan, & Lanzetta, 1982; Kestenbaum, Farber, & Sroufe, 1989; compare with McHugo, Lanzetta, Sullivan, Masters, & Englis, 1985). However, in order for the experience to be labeled empathy as it is defined here, the empathizer must recognize, at least on some level, that the emotion she or he is experiencing is a reflection of the other's emotional state. That is, there must be at least a minimal degree of self–other distinction. Otherwise, the response would be considered a primitive form or precursor of empathy (found in infancy and throughout the age-span, whereas empathy probably can occur only after the first year of life; Zahn-Waxler, Radke-Yarrow, Wagner, & Chapman, 1992).

Although the experience of empathy may result from "catching another's emotion" (which is then identified by the person as deriving from information about another person), it may also occur as a function of the empathizer's cognitive perspective taking, associating another's with one's own experiences (through conditioning or direct association), or retrieval of relevant information from memory that fosters an understanding of the other individual's feelings or situation (Eisenberg, Shea, et al., 1991; Eisenberg & Strayer, 1987; Hoffman, 1975, 1982; Karniol, 1990). For example, a person may observe a child falling from a swing and think about how the child must feel (i.e., take the perspective of the child) or remember what it felt like to fall from a swing or what the consequences of falling might be. As a result of these cognitive processes, the observer may experience an emotion similar to that of the child. To carry out such mental processes, however, the individual needs to be able to identify cues regarding another's emotion and its significance, a task that sometimes may be difficult for young children (Feshbach, 1978).

A second conceptual issue concerns distinguishing pure empathy from other empathy-related responses such as sympathy and personal distress (Batson, 1991, 1998; Eisenberg & Fabes, 1990). Sympathy is an other-oriented, emotional response that is based on the apprehension or comprehension of another's emotional state or condition and involves feelings of concern and a desire to have the other's distress alleviated. For instance, in the previous example of the child falling from the swing, a sympathetic observer would feel concern or sorrow for the child (in addition, perhaps, to empathic sadness). Sympathy may stem from the experience of empathy, or it may stem solely from cognitive processes such as perspective taking, mental associations, and accessing information about the other's situation from memory (Eisenberg, Shea, et al., 1991).

Personal distress, in contrast, involves a negative reaction such as anxiety or discomfort on perceiving cues related to another's distress (Batson, 1991). Like sympathy, personal distress may stem primarily from empathy or empathic overarousal, but it is also likely that personal distress could arise solely through cognitive processes (e.g., through negative associations between another's sadness and one's own past that lead to personal distress rather than experiencing empathic sadness). Hoffman (1982) referred to the experience of a negative emotional reaction to another's distress as empathic overarousal and hypothesized, as did Batson (1991), that it would lead to a focus on the self rather than to a focus on others. Consistent with this idea, researchers have found evidence that aversive emotional arousal induces self-focused attention (Wood, Saltzberg, & Goldsamt, 1990; Wood, Saltzberg, Neale, Stone, & Rachmiel, 1990). Thus, a person who is experiencing personal distress is believed to be more concerned with reducing his or her own vicarious emotional arousal than with reducing the distress of another (Batson, 1991).

There is a growing body of empirical evidence supporting the conceptual distinction between sympathy and personal distress. In a series of studies, Eisenberg, Fabes, and their colleagues have demonstrated that self-report, facial, and physiological markers of sympathy and personal distress differ across contexts chosen to elicit emotional reactions akin to personal distress versus sympathy (or these emotions vs. a baseline condition). Overall, they found that the experience of personal distress was associated with higher levels of physiological responding (i.e., heart rate and skin conductance) and, sometimes, more facial expressions of distress, anxiety, or fear than was the experience of sympathy (e.g., Eisenberg, Fabes, Schaller, Miller, et al., 1991; Eisenberg, Schaller, et al., 1988; also see Strayer, 1993). Verbal reports of sympathy tended to be consistent with expectations; that is, children and adults tended to report higher levels of sympathy and sadness (which is thought to foster sympathy) than personal distress in empathy-inducing contexts (Eisenberg, Fabes, et al., 1988; Eisenberg, Fabes, Schaller, Carlo, & Miller, 1991; Eisenberg, Fabes, Schaller, Miller, et al., 1991; Eisenberg, Schaller, et al., 1988). However, the pattern of findings sometimes varies in strength as a function of age and sex of the respondent (see Eisenberg & Fabes, 1990, for a review). For example, findings in regard to verbal reports have been stronger for older children and adults than for younger children (Eisenberg, Fabes, et al., 1988), and females sometimes report more distress than do males (although effects also have been found for men; Eisenberg, Fabes, et al., 1988; Eisenberg, Fabes, Schaller, Miller, et al., 1991).

In addition, there is considerable evidence that sympathy and personal distress differ in their association with interpersonal behavior. Much of the research on empathy-related responding and its link to social behavior is focused on other-oriented social behavior such as altruism and prosocial behavior (Batson, 1991, 1998; Eisenberg & Fabes, 1998; Eisenberg & Miller, 1987) and aggression (Miller & Eisenberg, 1988). Unfortunately, in much of the existing empirical literature, empathy, sympathy, and personal distress have been equated conceptually, making it difficult to obtain consistent relations between empathy-related responding and other variables. Nevertheless, in studies in which investigators have distinguished these constructs, they have found that individuals with high levels of sympathy (and sometimes global measures of empathy) are more likely than people low in sympathy or high in personal distress to offer assistance to distressed persons, even when they can easily escape from dealing with the distressed person (Batson, 1991; Eisenberg & Fabes, 1991, 1998; Eisenberg & Miller, 1987). Specifically, indicators of sympathy prior to and during exposure to a needy or distressed person have been associated with increased willingness to help, as well as social competence (Batson, 1991, 1998; Eisenberg & Fabes, 1990, 1991; Eisenberg & Miller, 1987; Eisenberg, Fabes, Murphy, et al., 1996). In contrast, markers of personal distress tend to be unrelated or negatively related to prosocial behavior when there is no easy escape for the potential helper (Batson, 1991; Eisenberg, Fabes, Miller, et al., 1989). Thus, there is evidence that sympathy and personal distress are different and result in different behavioral consequences.

However, whether one experiences sympathy or personal distress may vary with dispositional (relatively enduring) characteristics of the individual (i.e., temperament or personality of the individual; Davis, 1994; Eisenberg & Fabes, 1992). Recently, Eisenberg and Fabes (1992; Eisenberg, Fabes, Murphy, et al., 1994) argued that individual differences in tendencies to experience sympathy or personal distress are partly a result of individual differences in emotional reactivity and intensity as well as the capacity to cope with or regulate emotional reactions and emotionally arousing situations. Eisenberg and Fabes hypothesized that emotionally intense individuals are simply more likely to experience vicarious emotions (also see Mehrabian, Young, & Sato, 1988). Individuals who are able to maintain their emotional reactions within a tolerable range so that their vicarious emotion is not experienced as aversive may be more likely to feel sympathy than personal distress in response to another's distress. Because these individuals are able to experience the affect of the distressed other without becoming overly aroused, they are able to focus on the needs of the other rather than on their own emotional arousal. For these reasons, the experience of sympathy is thought to be fostered by the regulation of emotion. In contrast, individuals who are prone to intense emotional arousal in response to others' distress and who are unable to regulate their arousal are more likely to experience the vicarious emotion as aversive (i.e., to experience personal distress) and to focus on their own needs. Consequently, these individuals are likely to avoid the emotion-eliciting stimulus (Batson, 1991). Emotional overarousal may lead to a self-focus because aroused individuals' attentional capabilities are narrowed, and cognitions related to other people are consequently relatively unlikely to occur or be salient. Alternatively, empathic overarousal that is unmodulated may be interpreted as a signal of possible threat to the self.

In summary, empathy, as it is defined here, is a construct that centers on the affective experience that occurs within an observer in response to someone else's emotional state or situation. Related responses such as sympathy and personal distress are viewed as conceptually distinct from, but related to, the experience of empathy. Sympathy may stem from (or co-occur with) empathy (or perspective taking) but is characterized by other-oriented concern. Sympathy may be especially likely to occur if the individual is able to tolerate or modulate the experience of vicariously induced negative emotion. Personal distress may also stem from empathy (and, perhaps, solely from cognitive processes) but likely involves the experience of negative emotional overarousal and a self-focus (Hoffman, 1982). However, sympathy and personal distress differ in their relations to prosocial behavior.

## METHODOLOGICAL ISSUES

Like any emotional response, empathy and related vicarious emotions are multifaceted and occur in at least three levels: subjective, behavioral–expressive, and neurophysiological (see Dodge, 1989; Dodge & Garber, 1991). Consequently, we recommend a multimethod approach to the study of empathy, including the use of self-reports, facial–gestural measures, and measures of physiological responding. This approach, although not always possible or easy, is useful because different methods can be used to address different questions, and convergence among the different methodological findings increases one's confidence about their validity (Eisenberg & Fabes, 1998). Without a multimethod approach, the likelihood of differentiating among the various vicarious emotional responses is reduced, and the relations to socially valued behavior are likely to be underestimated.

For instance, in a meta-analytic review, Underwood and Moore (1982) reported no relation between empathy or sympathy and prosocial behavior. The studies in this review often operationalized empathy with children's self-reports of empathy or other measures of global empathy (e.g., babies' cries in response to the cries of other infants). However, Eisenberg and Miller (1987), in a subsequent meta-analysis, found that the strength and pattern of relations between empathy-related measures and prosocial behavior varied greatly as a function of the methodological approaches used to assess empathy. Thus, the measure of empathy seems to affect empirical findings regarding the associations between empathy and social behavior or social competence. Moreover, different measures may tap empathy-related responding better for different individuals, age groups, and situations.

## Self-Reports of Situational Empathy-Related Responding

Numerous measures of affective empathy consist of self-reports of emotional reactions experienced when individuals were exposed to stimuli expected to elicit empathy reactions. With such a procedure, one simply asks a research participant to report what she or he is feeling in a given empathy-inducing context. Such methods are easy and relatively quick to administer and have the potential to provide differentiated measures of vicarious emotional responding.

One of the early and most popular methods of assessing children's empathy was the picture-story index (see Feshbach & Roe, 1968). With this measure, children were presented with several story narratives in which characters were described and portrayed by drawings or photos in situations that are likely to evoke sadness, fear, anger, or happiness. For example, a child might be told a very short story about a child who lost his or her dog. Children were asked to report their emotional reactions to each story (and were often asked to label the character's emotion). If children reported feeling an emotion that was the same or quite similar to that of the story character, they were credited for experiencing empathy.

There are a number of problems with this type of self-report measure, particularly when used with children (Eisenberg & Lennon, 1983; Eisenberg-Berg & Lennon, 1980; Lennon, Eisenberg, & Carroll, 1983). First, verbal ability and comprehension may affect children's responding. Children may not be able to label accurately an emotion they observe, report accurately how they feel (Eisenberg & Miller, 1987; Strayer, 1987), or differentiate among emotion states with similar affective valences (Eisenberg, Fabes, & Miller, 1990; Eisenberg & Miller, 1987). Indeed, children's empathy scores have been associated with their verbal ability (Sawin, 1979) and reading comprehension (Feshbach, 1978). Children's self-reports to picture-story measures may also be affected by the demand characteristics of the experiment and self-presentational issues (Eisenberg & Lennon, 1983; Eisenberg-Berg & Hand, 1979). In addition, the report of empathy appears to be influenced by the interaction between gender of the child and gender of the experimenter. Girls' reports of empathy on picture-story measures have tended to be higher than those of boys, a finding that has not always been consistent with the results of nonverbal measures of empathy used with younger children (Eisenberg & Lennon, 1983; Lennon & Eisenberg, 1987). However, the degree of the gender difference varies as a function of the gender of the experimenter, such that children report more empathy if they are interviewed by same-gender experimenters. It may be that children are more comfortable reporting empathy to same-gender experimenters (Eisenberg & Lennon, 1983; Lennon et al., 1983), and most experimenters in early studies on empathy were women.

Another problem with picture-story measures is that the presentations of the emotion-depicting situation are generally brief (e.g., three or four sentences) and uninvolving and are unlikely to elicit genuine vicarious responding. One consequence of this is that children's reports of empathy likely have varied as a function of their attention to, and understanding of, the stories; what they thought the experimenter wanted to hear; and children's motivation to please the experimenter. Researchers have attempted to eliminate this problem by using more evocative empathy-inducing stimuli, both with children and adults (Batson et al., 1988; Eisenberg, Fabes, Schaller, & Miller, 1991; Eisenberg et al., 1994; Fultz, Schaller, & Cialdini, 1988). For example, adults have been presented with audio- or video-taped information about distressed or needy others (Batson, 1991; Carlo, Eisenberg, Troyer, Switzer, & Speer, 1991; Cialdini et al., 1987; Eisenberg, Fabes, Schaller, Miller, et al., 1991; Zahn-Waxler, Cole, Welsh, & Fox, 1995), and children or adults have been exposed to real people who they believe are needy or hurt (e.g., Zahn-Waxler, Friedman, & Cummings, 1983). Then study participants report their feelings of sympathy and personal distress, often using lists of adjectives (e.g., "sympathetic," "moved," "compassionate," "tender," "disturbed," "worried," "uneasy," and "upset" for adults, and "sorry for others," "concern for others," "anxious," and "upset" for children; Cialdini, Brown, Lewis, Luce, & Neuberg, 1997; Eisenberg, Fabes, Shepard, et al., 1998). Although these methods are likely much more valid than are the picture-story measures used with young children (e.g., they relate more strongly to prosocial behavior; Batson, 1991; Eisenberg & Miller, 1987; Eisenberg & Fabes, 1991), many of the same problems related to self-reports may hold for these measures of situational empathy-related responding.

## Questionnaire Measures of Dispositional Empathy-Related Responding

Another relatively straightforward self-report method of assessing empathy and related responses is the use of questionnaires. Questionnaires are generally used to assess dispositional, rather than situational, empathy-related responding. Although many researchers examining the relations of empathy to prosocial behavior and aggression have used this method with some success with adults and older children, some of these questionnaires assess empathy in a very global manner. For example, Mehrabian and Epstein (1972) developed a scale of global empathy for adults that likely taps emotional contagion, empathy, sympathy, personal distress, and other constructs. Sample items include the following:

(a) "I become nervous if others around me seem to be nervous," (b) "I tend to get emotionally involved with a friend's problems," (c) "Most foreigners I have met seemed cool and unemotional," (d) "Seeing people cry upsets me," and (e) "Little children sometimes cry for no apparent reason." Item (a) most clearly reflects empathy but could reflect personal distress; Item (b) could reflect empathy, sympathy, or personal distress; Item (c) may reflect stereotyping, lack of role taking, or lack of empathy; Item (d) most likely reflects empathy or personal distress, although sympathetic people would also tend to rate themselves highly on this item; and Item (e) seems to most clearly tap a lack of perspective taking. Similarly, Bryant's (1982) questionnaire measure of empathy for children, which was adapted from Mehrabian and Epstein's (1972) measure, consists of items that probably tap empathy, personal distress, and sympathy (e.g., "I get upset when I see an animal being hurt," "Kids who have no friends probably don't want any," "Seeing a girl who is crying makes me feel like crying," and "It makes me sad to see a boy who can't find anyone to play with").

In contrast, Davis (1983, 1994) developed a measure of empathy, the Interpersonal Reactivity Index (IRI), with four subscales: empathic concern (i.e., sympathy; e.g., "I often have tender, concerned feelings for people less fortunate than me" or "When I see someone being treated unfairly, I sometimes don't feel very much pity for them" [reversed]), personal distress (e.g., "Being in a tense emotional situation scares me" or "I tend to lose control during emergencies"), perspective taking (e.g. "I try to look at everyone's side of a disagreement before I make a decision" or "I sometimes try to understand my friends better by imagining how they look from their perspective"), and fantasy empathy (i.e., vicarious responding to characters in books or film; e.g., "When I am reading an interesting story or novel, I imagine how I would feel if the events in the story were happening to me" or "I am usually objective when I watch a movie or play, and I don't often get completely caught up in it" [reverse-scored]). These scales, or modifications thereof, have been used with considerable success with adults and adolescents (Davis, 1994; Eisenberg, Fabes, Schaller, Miller, et al., 1991; Eisenberg, Miller, Shell, McNalley, & Shea, 1991). In addition, Eisenberg and colleagues have developed a scale of dispositional sympathy for use with children (e.g., "I feel sorry for people who don't have the things that I have," "When I see someone being picked on, I feel kind of sorry for them;" Eisenberg, Fabes, Murphy, et al., 1996; Spinrad et al., 1999).

Questionnaire methods are vulnerable to many of the same kinds of methodological problems as are situational self-report measures of empathy. For instance, questionnaire items often are read to children who may have some difficulty reading. Under these circumstances, children may be especially influenced by demand characteristics of the experiment and may present themselves in socially desirable ways. In fact, social desirability has been related to children's reports of empathy and sympathy on questionnaires (e.g., Eisenberg, Miller, et al., 1991). However, in adulthood, the desire to present oneself in socially acceptable ways to others may be less of a problem than the desire to see oneself in ways consistent with one's own values, needs, and self-perceptions (including those stemming from one's same-gender role). In a study using a bogus pipeline procedure (a procedure in which participants are persuaded to think that their "true" attitudes and feelings can be accurately assessed with physiological measures; Jones & Sigall, 1971; Quigley-Fernandez & Tedeschi, 1978), Eisenberg, Miller, et al., (1989) found that adults' reports of sympathy and personal distress did not appear to change significantly as a function of their probable belief that others could tell if they were lying. Whether adults simply reported their sympathy and personal distress or did so in the bogus pipeline condition, women reported more of these characteristics than did men. Given that men and women generally do not differ as greatly on nonverbal measures of empathy-related responding as on self-reported reactions (Eisenberg & Lennon, 1983; Lennon & Eisenberg, 1987), it is likely that adults desire to see themselves in a manner consistent with gender roles (i.e., women are more invested in seeing themselves as caring and emotionally involved with others than are men, who may prefer to view themselves as rather detached and unemotional). In contrast, the significant gender difference in reports of fantasy empathy (empathy in response to books and the media) dropped to non-significance in the bogus pipeline condition. It is likely that men prefer to present themselves as unemotional to others whereas women are not concerned with being viewed by others as emotional in response to events depicted in movies, books, or TV. Thus, although social desirability likely influences reports of some types of empathic reactions (e.g., fantasy empathy), people's self-perceptions may play an equal or greater role in determining their reports of sympathy and personal distress reactions.

## Other-Reports of
## Empathy-Related Responding

Relatively few investigators have used reports by people other than study participants to assess empathy-related responding (e.g., Barnett, Howard, Melton, & Dino, 1982; Eisenberg, Fabes, Murphy, et al., 1996; Eisenberg, Fabes, Shepard, et al., 1998; Fabes, Eisenberg, & Eisenbud, 1993). Typically, items similar to those in the Mehrabian and Epstein (1972) empathy scale, Davis's empathy subscales, or Eisenberg and colleagues' self-report sympathy scale have been administered to parents or teachers (in studies of children) or friends (in studies of adolescents and adults) to obtain information about participants' empathy-related responding. One obvious benefit of the use of other-reports is that they can be used to obtain data on children too young to provide accurate self-reports. Moreover, other-reports are less likely to be biased than are self-report measures, especially if someone other than a family member is the respondent. Another possible benefit is that one could use multiple reporters to obtain information about individuals in a variety of settings (e.g., at school according to teacher and peer ratings and at home according to ratings of another family member). Information obtained from multiple reporters is generally more reliable than that obtained from one reporter (Epstein, 1979), and confidence in the validity of a measure of dispositional empathy-related responding is increased if it converges with other measures of a target individual's empathy-related responses. In fact, evidence of convergent validity has been found in the relatively few studies of the relations of dispositional to situational empathy-related responses (Eisenberg, Fabes, Murphy, et al., 1996; Eisenberg et al., 1998). For example, in elementary school children, teachers' and children's reports of sympathy were significantly related; also, in studies of older elementary school children and young adolescents, different teachers' reports tend to be significantly related over 4 years from age 6–8 to 10–12 (but not from age 8–10 to 10–12; Murphy et al., in press). Moreover, adults' reports of their own dispositional sympathy have been substantially positively related to friends' reports of their sympathy (Eisenberg et al., 1995). In addition, laboratory measures of children's situational sympathy sometimes have been positively related to teachers' reports of children's dispositional sympathy (e.g., Eisenberg, Fabes, Murphy, et al., 1996; Eisenberg et al., 1998).

## Facial and Gestural Measures of Empathy-related Responses

Markers of empathy-related reactions can also be obtained somewhat unobtrusively with facial or gestural reactions to empathy-inducing stimuli. Facial and gestural markers of empathy-related responses have been used with children as young as 15 months old (Zahn-Waxler, Radke-Yarrow et al. 1992; Zahn-Waxler, Robinson, & Emde, 1992). In studies of young children, facial–gestural reactions to observing others in need or distress have typically been obtained. For example, Zahn-Waxler, Radke-Yarrow, et al. (1992) asked mothers to describe in detail their young children's reactions to naturally occurring instances of another's distress that the children either caused or witnessed. Their reactions were coded for empathic concern, which was defined as emotional arousal that appeared to reflect sympathetic concern for the victim (e.g., sad looks, sympathetic statements such as "I'm sorry" said in a soothing or reassuring tone of voice, or gestures such as rushing to the victim while looking worried). Also coded was self-distress, which included emotions evoked by the other's distress that were more intense, negative, and reflective of personal distress (e.g., the target child sobs, cries, frets, or whimpers). In addition, positive affect expressed while viewing another's distress was coded. Methods such as these have been used not only with very young children but also with preschool and elementary school children (e.g., Miller, Eisenberg, Fabes, & Shell, 1996; Zahn-Waxler et al., 1983).

In studies of preschoolers, older children, and adults, researchers have sometimes coded individuals' facial and gestural reactions to viewing empathy-inducing films. Eisenberg and colleagues have tried to differentiate between facial expressions that likely reflect sympathy and those that more likely reflect personal distress. Facial expressions of concerned attention (e.g., eyebrows pulled down and inward over the nose, head forward, intense interest in evocative events in the film) are believed to indicate sympathy whereas fearful and anxious expressions and lip-biting are likely to indicate personal distress (Eisenberg & Fabes, 1990; Eisenberg, Schaller, et al., 1988). Signs of empathic sadness (sad facial expressions) in response to sad events likely tap empathy and may be more likely than other empathic emotions to engender sympathy. Although one can use microanalytic systems to code individuals' facial affect in situations of this type, researchers have found that more global ratings over periods of 10–30 seconds (or sometimes longer) appear to be reliable and valid measures of facial empathy-related reactions (e.g., Eisenberg et al., 1994; Lennon et al., 1983; Strayer & Roberts, 1997). Modest relations sometimes have been obtained between facial and other measures of empathy-related responding (e.g., Eisenberg, Fabes, et al., 1988; Eisenberg, Schaller, et al., 1988; Strayer & Roberts, 1997).

Facial expressions of emotion are somewhat less subject to some of the biases inherent in self-report methods, particularly when used in studies of younger children who have yet to learn socially appropriate facial display rules (Cole, 1986; Saarni, 1990). Moreover, children and adults are probably less likely to display socially expected reactions when they are videotaped unobtrusively through one-way mirrors than when they are directly reporting on their emotional reactions or observed by others who are visible.

However, although facial measures of vicarious emotional responses have clear benefits, they also have limitations. First, the nature of the empathy-inducing situation must be evocative enough to elicit an emotional facial response. If the stimulus or context is too mild, expressions of facial affect may not be sufficient to code, thus making it impossible to detect any emotion or to distinguish facial expressions of personal distress from empathic sadness or sympathy. A second limitation is that as children age, they increasingly become able to mask the expression of negative emotion (Cole, 1986; Shennum & Bugental, 1982; Strayer, 1983) and are able to do so in a variety of situations. Boys may be especially likely to mask emotion such as anxiety or fear (Cole, 1986; Eisenberg, Fabes, et al., 1988). Thus, as in the case of self-reports, self-presentational biases and demand characteristics may affect older children's and adults' willingness to display negative emotions. Consequently, facial indices alone may not always be accurate markers of older children's and adults' empathy-related responding.

## Physiological Measures of Empathy-Related Responses

In recent years, Zahn-Waxler and colleagues (Zahn-Waxler et al., 1995) and Eisenberg, Fabes, and their colleagues (see Eisenberg & Fabes, 1990, 1991, 1998) have explored the use of physiological indices as markers of empathy-related responses, particularly heart rate (HR) and skin conductance (SC) responses. Their work builds on the early research of Craig and Lowery (1969; Craig, 1968) and Lanzetta and colleagues (Englis et al., 1982; McHugo et al., 1985), among others. The value of this approach lies in the fact that physiological responses usually are not under systematic control of the research participant and thus, are not subject to the demand characteristics of the experiment or the self-presentational biases of the individual. The major disadvantage is that although there is a growing body of evidence that different emotional states reflect somewhat distinct patterns of physiological responding (Ekman, Levenson, & Friesen, 1983; Schwartz, Weinberger, & Singer, 1981), there is no one-to-one correspondence between a particular emotion and a single physiological response (Cacioppo & Tassinary, 1990; Schwartz, 1986). Physiological changes are influenced by a number of factors other than emotion, including the individual's attention and cognitive processing, physical activity, the temperature, or environmental nuisance (e.g., sudden noises). In addition, research participants may be reactive to the setting in which physiological reactions are assessed. For example, placement of electrodes on the body can be frightening as well as constraining, which could increase autonomic responding (Wilson & Cantor, 1985). These complications that are not necessarily associated with the stimulus itself make the interpretation of findings difficult. Nevertheless, there is reason to believe that physiological indices are associated with different empathic reactions.

*Heart Rate.*    There are conceptual and empirical reasons to expect differential relations of HR patterns to sympathy and personal distress. HR deceleration has been associated with the intake of information from the environment and an outward focus of attention in psychophysiological studies of arousal (Cacioppo & Sandman, 1978; Lacey, Kagan, Lacey, & Moss, 1963). Thus, HR deceleration is expected to be a marker of sympathy because sympathy involves an other-oriented focus of attention. HR acceleration, in contrast, has been associated with anxiety, distress, and active coping (Cacioppo & Sandman, 1978; Lazarus, 1974). Thus, HR acceleration would be expected to be a marker of personal distress in some contexts.

Recent studies of empathy-related responding have examined both mean HR while viewing an empathy stimulus, as well as change in HR (i.e., calculated as a slope representing linear change in an individual's HR during a specified period; see Eisenberg et al., 1992, for details) while individuals view a specific, especially evocative segment. When HR is measured as mean HR or as a slope, it tends to be higher (or to accelerate) in situations in which individuals are likely to experience vicariously induced distress than in situations more likely to elicit sympathy or in neutral conditions. Moreover, HR sometimes decelerates (or people exhibit lower mean HR) in sympathy-inducing contexts (Eisenberg, Fabes, et al., 1988; Eisenberg, Fabes, Schaller, Miller, et al., 1991; Eisenberg, Fabes, Schaller, Carlo, & Miller, 1991; Eisenberg, Schaller, et al., 1988). Thus, HR seems to be a crude marker of sympathetic versus personal distress reactions.

*Cardiac Vagal Tone.* Another physiological measure that is relevant to the discussion of empathy-related responding is cardiac vagal tone. Cardiac vagal tone, a measure derived from heart rate variability (HRV) and often respiratory sinus arrhythmia (Grossman, Karemaker, & Wieling, 1991), is viewed as a marker of dispositional emotional regulation (particularly individual differences in parasympathetic tone, a branch of the autonomic nervous system most related to soothing and restoration of calm in the body). Porges, Doussard-Roosevelt, and Maiti (1994) suggested that cardiac vagal tone might provide the physiological underpinning for an individual's ability to focus attentional processes and inhibit inappropriate behavior. High cardiac vagal tone and greater HRV, a measure that is highly related to cardiac vagal tone, have been associated with sustained attention (Suess, Porges, & Plude, 1994); uninhibited behavior; and the ability to cope with novel objects, new people, and new environments (Fox, 1989; Fox & Field, 1989; Izard et al., 1991). Although cardiac vagal tone (or HRV) is not expected to be a marker of empathy-related responding per se, it is predicted to be positively related to sympathy (which, as noted earlier, is believed to be fostered by emotion regulation) and negatively related to personal distress (which is fostered by low regulation). These measures were moderately predictive of sympathetic versus personal distress responding in a study of elementary school children's situational empathy-related responding (Fabes et al., 1993). However, in a study with preschoolers (some of whom were at risk in terms of behavior problems), cardiac vagal tone was negatively correlated with arousal during a film and empathic concern during simulations of distress (Zahn-Waxler et al., 1995). In studies of dispositional sympathy, the expected pattern of findings sometimes has been found only for boys (Eisenberg, Fabes, Murphy, et al., 1996), only for girls (Fabes et al., 1993), or no significant findings have been obtained (Eisenberg et al., 1997). Thus, it is not yet clear the degree to which cardiac vagal tone or HRV is linked to sympathy, especially when empathy-related responding is assessed with dispositional self-report or other-report measures.

*Skin Conductance.* SC (i.e., electrodermal activity) also has been used as a measure of emotional arousal (Eisenberg, Fabes, Schaller, Miller, et al.,

1991; Eisenberg, Fabes, Schaller, Carlo, & Miller, 1991; Fabes et al., 1993; Zahn-Waxler et al., 1995) and has a long history as a measure that has been used in studies of emotion, arousal, and attention (Dawson, Schell, & Filion, 1990). SC has been found to be sensitive to a wide range of stimuli including stimulus novelty (Raskin, 1973). Thus, the more an experimenter can control the empathy-inducing stimulus situation and eliminate other possible elicitors of SC, the more confident he or she can be that SC reflects a reaction to the empathy-related experimental stimulus.

In some studies, researchers have found that people tend to exhibit higher levels of SC reactivity when they report feeling anxious, fearful, or other unpleasant emotions, or are in stressful contexts (see e.g., MacDowell & Mandler, 1989; Wallbott & Scherer, 1991; Winton, Putnam, & Krauss, 1984). Thus, SC seems to be related to experiencing aversive negative emotions. Because feelings of distress or personal distress are believed to be more arousing than are feelings of sympathy, skin conductance is expected to be a better measure of personal distress than of sympathy (Eisenberg, Fabes, Schaller, Miller, et al., 1991; Shaver, Schwartz, Kirson, & O'Conner, 1987). In general, researchers have obtained findings consistent with this expectation (Eisenberg, Fabes, Schaller, Carlo, & Miller, 1991; Eisenberg, Fabes, Schaller, Miller, et al., 1991). However, there is some evidence in the literature that autonomic activity (particularly SC responses) is inversely related to facial emotional expressiveness (Buck, 1977; Cacioppo et al., 1992). That is, those who are considered "externalizers" with respect to facial expressions of emotion (i.e., high sending accuracy) will show lower levels of SC responses, whereas the "internalizing" response involves the opposite pattern. Thus, in studies that include SC as a marker of personal distress, it is important to include other measures that will help to illuminate the nature of the empathic experience.

## Experimental Manipulations

In studies with adults, sympathy has often been assessed with experimental manipulations. These include methods such as the following: (a) asking some study participants, but not others, to take the perspective of the person in need or distress (Batson et al., 1988, 1995, 1997; Fultz, Batson, Fortenbach, McCarthy, & Varney, 1986); (b) using a misattribution condition in which some individuals, but not others, have been led to believe that any arousal they experience during the study (including empathic arousal) is due to the effects of a pill (so they will not believe they are experiencing empathy or sympathy; e.g., Batson, Duncan, Ackerman, Buckley, & Birch, 1981, Manucia, Baumann, & Cialdini, 1984); and (c) inducing feelings of similarity between some participants and the person in need or distress (e.g., Batson et al., 1981; Stotland, 1969). On the basis of manipulation checks and relations of empathy-related responding to prosocial behavior, there is reason to believe that these manipulations have often been successful. However, the perspective-taking manipulation does not always work (e.g., Eisenberg, Fabes, Schaller, & Miller, 1991; Fultz, 1984), and these manipulations have not been used much with children.

## Summary

In summary, there are benefits and limitations associated with each of the aforementioned indices of empathy-related responses. We have suggested that the use of verbal self-reports with young children may be confounded by verbal and comprehension skills and that biases and demand characteristics associated with self-report measures and questionnaires may influence children's and adults' willingness to respond truthfully on these measures. Facial expressions of sadness, concern, and distress as well as behavioral reactions to empathy-inducing stimuli have typically been related in expected ways to sympathy and personal distress and thus are important markers of empathy-related responses. However, facial expressions may be masked as children get older and may not be as useful as other measures with adults (e.g., Eisenberg, Fabes, Schaller, Miller, et al., 1991). Finally, although sometimes difficult to interpret, physiological measures can be useful markers of sympathy and personal distress. Given the methodological issues associated with each individual method, we recommend a multimethod approach when assessing empathy-related responding (also see Strayer & Roberts, 1997).

## CONCLUSION

We have tried to demonstrate the usefulness of defining empathy in affective terms, especially when considering its relation to interpersonal behavior. We have shown that the empathy-related responses of sympathy and personal distress can be empirically distinguished and that these empathy-related reactions can be used to predict quality of social functioning. It is our view that each type of measure of empathy-related responding has its assets and problems and that researchers are best served by a multimethod approach to assessing affective empathy. No single marker of empathy-related responding is perfect, and all must be interpreted in a thoughtful manner. Moreover, empirical data suggest that age, sex, and personality (i.e., dispositional emotionality and reactivity) affect the way in which one experiences and expresses vicarious emotions. Thus, different measures of empathy-related responding may be most useful for different groups of individuals. The measure of empathy-related responding should be chosen in accordance with the characteristics (especially age) of the research participants and the context. Additional research is needed to determine the usefulness of some empathy-related measures and the situations in which they are most appropriate. Nonetheless, measures of affective empathy-related responding that are reasonably reliable and valid are available for current use.

## ACKNOWLEDGMENTS

This research was supported by grants from the National Institute of Mental Health (1 R01 HH55052) and a Research Scientist Award from the National Institute of Mental Health (K05 M801321) to Nancy Eisenberg.

## REFERENCES

Barnett, M. A., Howard, J. A., Melton, E. M., & Dino, G. A. (1982). Effect of inducing sadness about self or other on helping behavior in high and low empathic children. *Child Development, 53,* 920–923.

Batson, C. D. (1991). *The altruism question: Toward a social-psychological answer.* Hillsdale, NJ: Lawrence Erlbaum Associates.

Batson, C. D. (1998). Altruism and prosocial behavior. In D. T. Gilbert, S. T. Fiske & G. Lindzey (Eds.), *The handbook of social psychology* (Vol. 2, pp. 282–316). Boston: McGraw-Hill.

Batson, C. D., Batson, J. G., Todd, R. M., Brummett, B. H., Shaw, L. L., & Aldeguer, C. M. R. (1995). Empathy and the collective good: Caring for one of the others in a social dilemma. *Journal of Personality and Social Psychology, 68,* 619–631.

Batson, C. D., & Coke, J. S. (1981). Empathy: A source of altruistic motivation for helping? In J. P. Rushton & R. M. Sorrentino (Eds.), *Altruism and helping behavior: Social, personality, and developmental perspectives* (pp. 167–211). Hillsdale, NJ: Lawrence Erlbaum Associates.

Batson, C. D., Duncan, B., Ackerman, P., Buckley, T., & Birch, K. (1981). Is empathic emotion a source of altruistic emotion? *Journal of Personality and Social Psychology, 40,* 290–302.

Batson, C. D., Dyck, J. L., Brandt, J. R., Batson, J. G., Powell, A. L., McMaster, M. R., & Griffitt, C. (1988). Five studies testing two new egoistic alternatives to the empathy–altruism hypothesis. *Journal of Personality and Social Psychology, 55,* 52–77.

Batson, C. D., Sager, K., Garst, E., Kang, M., Rubchinsky, K., & Dawson, D. (1997). Is empathy-induced helping due to self–other merging? *Journal of Personality and Social Psychology, 75,* 495–509.

Bernieri, F. J. (1991). Interpersonal sensitivity in teaching interactions. *Personality and Social Psychology Bulletin 17,* 98–103.

Bryant, B. K. (1982). An index of empathy for children and adolescents. *Child Development, 53,* 413–425.

Buck, R. (1977). Nonverbal communication accuracy in preschool children: Relationships with personality and skin conductance. *Journal of Personality and Social Psychology, 33,* 225–236.

Buck, R. (1984). *The communication of emotion.* New York: Guilford.

Cacioppo, J. T., & Sandman, C. A. (1978). Physiological differentiation of sensory and cognitive tasks as a function of warning processing demands and reported unpleasantness. *Biological Psychology, 6,* 181–192.

Cacioppo, J. T., & Tassinary, L. G. (1990). Psychophysiology and psychophysiological inference. In J. T. Cacioppo & L. G. Tassinary (Eds.), *Principles of psychophysiology: Physical, social and inferential elements* (pp. 3–33). Cambridge, England: Cambridge University Press.

Cacioppo, J. T., Uchino, B. N., Crites, S. L., Snydersmith, M. A., Smith, G., & Berntson, G. G. (1992). Relationship between facial expressiveness and sympathetic activation in emotion: A critical review, with emphasis on modeling underlying mechanisms and individual differences. *Journal of Personality and Social Psychology, 62,* 110–128.

Carlo, G., Eisenberg, N., Troyer, D., Switzer, G., & Speer, A. L. (1991). The altruistic personality: In what contexts is it apparent? *Journal of Personality and Social Psychology, 61,* 450–458.

Cialdini, R. B., Brown, S. L., Lewis, B. P., Luce, C., & Neuberg, S. L. (1997). Reinterpreting the empathy–altruism relationship: When one into one equals oneness. *Journal of Personality and Social Psychology, 73,* 481–494.

Cialdini, R. B., Schaller, M., Houlihan, D., Arps, K., Fultz, J., & Beaman, A. L. (1987). Empathy-based helping: Is it selflessly or selfishly motivated? *Journal of Personality and Social Psychology, 52,* 749–758.

Cole, P. M. (1986). Children's spontaneous control of facial expression. *Child Development, 57,* 1309–1321.

Colvin, C. R., & Funder, D. C. (1991). Predicting personality and behavior: A boundary on the acquaintanceship effect. *Journal of Personality and Social Psychology, 60,* 884–894.

Costanzo, M. & Archer, D. (1991). A method for teaching about verbal and nonverbal communication. *Teaching of Psychology, 18,* 223–226.

Craig, K. D. (1968). Physiological arousal as a function of imagined, vicarious, and direct stress experiences. *Journal of Abnormal Psychology, 73,* 513–520.

Craig, K. D., & Lowery, H. J. (1969). Heart-rate components of conditioned vicarious autonomic responses. *Journal of Personality and Social Psychology, 11,* 381–387.

Davies, M., Stankov, L., & Roberts, R. D. (1998). Emotional intelligence: In search of an elusive construct. *Journal of Personality and Social Psychology, 75,* 989–1015.

Davis, M. H. (1983). Measuring individual differences in empathy: Evidence for a multidimensional approach. *Journal of Personality and Social Psychology, 44,* 113–126.

Davis, M. H. (1994). *Empathy: A social psychological approach.* Madison, WI: Brown & Benchmark.

Dawson, M. E., Schell, A. M., & Filion, D. L. (1990). The electrodermal system. In J. T. Cacioppo & L. G. Tassinary (Eds.), *Principles of psychophysiology: Physical, social and inferential elements* (pp. 295–325). Cambridge, England: Cambridge University Press.

Deutsch, F., & Madle, R. A. (1975). Empathy: Historic and current conceptualization, and a cognitive theoretical perspective. *Human Development, 18,* 267–287.

Dodge, K. A. (1989). Coordinating responses to aversive stimuli: Introduction to a special section on the development of emotion regulation. *Developmental Psychology, 25,* 339–342.

Dodge, K. A., & Garber, J. (1991). Domains of emotion regulation. In J. Garber & K. A. Dodge (Eds.), *The development of emotion regulation and dysregulation* (pp. 3–14). Cambridge, England: Cambridge University Press.

Dymond, R. (1949). A scale for the measurement of empathy ability. *Journal of Consulting Psychology, 13,* 127–133.

Eisenberg, N. (1986). *Altruistic emotion, cognition, and behavior.* Hillsdale, NJ: Lawrence Erlbaum Associates.

Eisenberg, N., Carlo, G., Murphy, B., & Van Court, P. (1995). Prosocial development in late adolescence: A longitudinal study. *Child Development, 66,* 911–936.

Eisenberg, N., & Fabes, R. A. (1990). Empathy: Conceptualization, assessment, and relation to prosocial behavior. *Motivation and Emotion, 14,* 131–149.

Eisenberg, N., & Fabes, R. A. (1991). Prosocial behavior and empathy: A multi-method, developmental perspective. In P. Clark (Ed.), *Review of personality and social psychology* (Vol. 12, pp. 34–61). Newbury Park, CA: Sage.

Eisenberg, N., & Fabes, R. A. (1992). Emotion, regulation, and the development of social competence. In M. S. Clark (Ed.), *Review of personality and social psychology, Vol. 14. Emotion and social behavior* (pp. 119–150). Newbury Park, CA: Sage.

Eisenberg, N., & Fabes, R. A. (1998). Prosocial development. In W. Damon (Series Ed.) & N. Eisenberg (Vol. Ed.), *Handbook of child psychology: Vol. 3. Social, emotional, and personality development* (5th Ed.; pp. 701–778). New York: Wiley.

Eisenberg, N., Fabes, R. A., Bustamante, D., Mathy, R. M., Miller, P., Lindholm, E. (1988). Differentiation of vicariously-induced emotional reactions in children. *Developmental Psychology, 24*, 237–246.

Eisenberg, N., Fabes, R. A., Carlo, G., Troyer, D., Speer, A. L., Karbon, M., & Switzer, G. (1992). The relations of maternal practices and characteristics to children's vicarious emotional responsiveness. *Child Development, 63*, 583–602.

Eisenberg, N., Fabes, R. A., & Miller, P. A. (1990). The evolutionary and neurological roots of prosocial behavior. In L. Ellis & H. Hoffman (Eds.), *Crime in biological, social, and moral contexts* (pp. 247–260). New York: Praeger.

Eisenberg, N., Fabes, R. A., Miller, P. A., Fultz, J., Mathy, R. M., Shell, R., & Reno, R. R. (1989). The relations of sympathy and personal distress to prosocial behavior: A multi-method study. *Journal of Personality and Social Psychology, 57*, 55–66.

Eisenberg, N., Fabes, R. A., Murphy, B., Karbon, M., Maszk, P., Smith, M., O'Boyle, C., & Suh, K. (1994). The relations of emotionality and regulation to dispositional and situational empathy-related responding. *Journal of Personality and Social Psychology, 66*, 776–797.

Eisenberg, N., Fabes, R. A., Murphy, B., Karbon, M., Smith, M., & Maszk, P. (1996). The relations of children's dispositional empathy-related responding to their emotionality, regulation, and social functioning. *Developmental Psychology, 32*, 195–209.

Eisenberg, N., Fabes, R. A., Schaller, M., Carlo, G., & Miller, P. A. (1991). The relations of parental characteristics and practices to children's vicarious emotional responding. *Child Development, 62*, 1393–1408.

Eisenberg, N., Fabes, R. A., Schaller, M., Miller, P. A., Carlo, G., Poulin, R., Shea, C., & Shell, R. (1991). Personality and socialization correlates of vicarious emotional responding. *Journal of Personality and Social Psychology, 61*, 459–471.

Eisenberg, N., Fabes, R. A., Shepard, S. A., Murphy, B. C., Guthrie, I. K., Jones, S., Friedman, J., Poulin, R., & Maszk, P. (1997). Contemporaneous and longitudinal prediction of children's social functioning from regulation and emotionality. *Child Development, 68*, 642–664.

Eisenberg, N., Fabes, R. A., Shepard, S. A., Murphy, B. C., Jones, J., & Guthrie, I. K. (1998). Contemporaneous and longitudinal prediction of children's sympathy from dispositional regulation and emotionality. *Developmental Psychology, 34*, 910–924.

Eisenberg, N., & Lennon, R. (1983). Sex differences in empathy and related capacities. *Psychological Bulletin, 101*, 91–119.

Eisenberg, N., & Miller, P. (1987). The relation of empathy to prosocial and related behaviors. *Psychological Bulletin, 101*, 91–119.

Eisenberg, N., Miller, P. A., Schaller, M., Fabes, R. A., Fultz, J., Shell, R., & Shea, C. (1989). The role of sympathy and altruistic personality traits in helping: A re-examination. *Journal of Personality, 57*, 41–67.

Eisenberg, N., Miller, P. A., Shell, R., McNalley, S. & Shea, C. (1991). Prosocial development in adolescence: A longitudinal study. *Developmental Psychology, 27*, 849–857.

Eisenberg, N., Schaller, M., Fabes, R. A., Bustamante, D., Mathy, R., Shell, R., & Rhodes, K. (1988). The differentiation of personal distress and sympathy in children and adults. *Developmental Psychology, 24*, 766–775.

Eisenberg, N., Shea, C. L., Carlo, G., & Knight, G. (1991). Empathy-related responding and cognition: A "chicken and the egg" dilemma. In W. Kurtines & J. Gewirtz (Ed.), *Handbook of moral behavior and development, Vol. 2. Research* (pp. 63–88). Hillsdale, NJ: Lawrence Erlbaum Associates.

Eisenberg, N., & Strayer, J. (1987). Critical issues in the study of empathy. In N. Eisenberg & J. Strayer (Eds.), *Empathy and its development* (pp. 3–16). Cambridge, England: Cambridge University Press.

Eisenberg-Berg, N., & Hand, M. (1979). The relationship of preschoolers' reasoning about prosocial moral conflicts to prosocial behavior. *Child Development, 50,* 356–363.

Eisenberg-Berg, N., & Lennon, R. (1980). Altruism and the assessment of empathy in the preschool years. *Child Development, 51,* 552–557.

Ekman, P., Levenson, R. W., & Friesen, W. V. (1983, September). Autonomic nervous system activity distinguishes among emotions. *Science, 221*(4616), 1208–1210.

Englis, B. G., Vaughan, K. B., & Lanzetta, J. T. (1982). Conditioning of counter-empathetic emotional responses. *Journal of Experimental Social Psychology, 18,* 375–391.

Epstein, S. (1979). The stability of behavior: 1. On predicting most of the people most of the time. *Journal of Personality and Social Psychology, 37,* 1097–1126.

Fabes, R. A., Eisenberg, N., & Eisenbud, L. (1993). Behavioral and physiological correlates of children's reactions to others' distress. *Developmental Psychology, 29,* 655–663.

Feshbach, N. D. (1978). Studies of empathic behavior in children. In B. A. Maher (Ed.), *Progress in experimental personality research* (Vol. 8, pp. 1–47). New York: Academic.

Feshbach, N. D., & Roe, K. (1968). Empathy in six- and seven-year-olds. *Child Development, 39,* 133–145.

Ford, M. E. (1979). The construct validity of egocentrism. *Psychological Bulletin, 86,* 1169–1188.

Fox, N. A. (1989). Psychophysiological correlates of emotional reactivity during the first year of life. *Developmental Psychology, 25,* 364–372.

Fox, N. A., & Field, T. M. (1989). Individual differences in young children's adjustment to preschool. *Journal of Applied Developmental Psychology, 10,* 527–540.

Fultz, J. (1984). Guilt-avoidance versus altruistic motivation as mediators of the empathy-helping relationship. *Dissertation Abstracts International, 46,* 1380B. (University Microfilms No. 8513744).

Fultz, J., Batson, C. D., Fortenbach, V. A., McCarthy, P. M., & Varney, L. L. (1986). Social evaluation and the empathy–altruism hypothesis. *Journal of Personality and Social Psychology, 50,* 761–769.

Fultz, J., Schaller, M., & Cialdini, R. B. (1988). Empathy, sadness, and distress: Three related but distinct vicarious affective responses to another's suffering. *Personality and Social Psychology Bulletin, 14,* 312–325.

Grossman, P., Karemaker, J., & Wieling, W. (1991). Prediction of tonic cardiac control using respiratory sinus arrhythmia: The need for respiratory control. *Psychophysiology, 28,* 202–218.

Hatfield, E., Cacioppo, J. T., & Rapson, R. L. (1992). Primitive emotional contagion. In M. S. Clark (Ed.), *Review of personality and social psychology. Vol. 14. Emotion and social behavior* (pp. 151–177). Newbury Park, CA: Sage.

Higgins, E. T. (1981). Role taking and social judgment: Alternative perspectives and processes. In J. H. Flavell & L. Ross (Eds.), *Social cognitive development* (pp. 119–153). Cambridge, England: Cambridge University Press.

Hoffman, M. L. (1975). Sex differences in moral internalization and values. *Journal of Personality and Social Psychology, 32,* 720–729.

Hoffman, M. L. (1982). Development of prosocial motivation: Empathy and guilt. In N. Eisenberg (Ed.), *The development of prosocial behavior* (pp. 281–313). New York: Academic.

Hoffman, M. L. (1984). Interaction of affect and cognition on empathy. In C. E. Izard, J. Kagan & R. B. Zajonc (Eds.), *Emotions, cognition, and behavior* (pp. 103–131). Cambridge, England: Cambridge University Press.

Hoffman, M. L. (1990). Empathy and justice motivation. *Motivation and Emotion, 14*, 151–172.

Hogan, R. (1969). Development of an empathy scale. *Journal of Consulting and Clinical Psychology, 33*, 307–316.

Ickes, W. (1993). Empathic accuracy. *Journal of Personality, 61*, 587–609.

Ickes, W., Stinson, L., Bissonnette, V., & Garcia, S. (1990). Naturalistic social cognition: Intersubjectivity in same-sex dyads. *Journal of Personality and Social Psychology, 59*, 730–742.

Izard, C. E., Porges, S. W., Simons, R. F., Haynes, O. M., Hyde, C., Parisi, M., & Cohen, B. (1991). Infant cardiac activity: Developmental changes and relations with attachment. *Developmental Psychology, 27*, 432–439.

Jones, E. E., & Sigall, H. (1971). The bogus pipeline: A new paradigm for measuring affect and attitude. *Psychological Bulletin, 76*, 349–364.

Karniol, R. (1982). Settings, scripts, and self-schemata: A cognitive analysis of the development of prosocial behavior. In N. Eisenberg (Ed.), *The development of prosocial behavior* (pp. 251–278). New York: Academic.

Karniol, R. (1990). Reading people's minds: A transformation rule model for predicting others' thoughts and feelings. *Advances in Experimental Social Psychology, 23*, 211-247.

Kestenbaum, R., Farber, E. A., & Sroufe, L. A. (1989). Individual differences in empathy among preschoolers: Relation to attachment history. In N. Eisenberg (Ed.), *New directions for child development: Vol. 44, Empathy and related emotional responses* (pp. 51–64). San Francisco: Jossey-Bass.

Lacey, J. I., Kagan, J., Lacey, B. C., & Moss, H. A. (1963). The visceral level: Situational determinants and behavioral correlates of autonomic response patterns. In P. H. Knapp (Ed.), *Expression of the emotions in man* (pp. 161–196). New York: International Universities Press.

Lazarus, R. S. (1974). A cognitively oriented psychologist looks at biofeedback. *American Psychologist, 30*, 553–561.

Lennon, R., & Eisenberg, N. (1987). Gender and age differences in empathy and sympathy. In N. Eisenberg & J. Strayer (Eds.), *Empathy and its development* (pp. 195–217). New York: Cambridge University Press.

Lennon, R., Eisenberg, N., and Carroll, J. (1983). The assessment of empathy in early childhood. *Journal of Applied Developmental Psychology, 4*, 295–302.

MacDowell, K. A., & Mandler, G. (1989). Constructions of emotion: Discrepancy, arousal, and mood. *Motivation and Emotion, 13*, 105–124.

Manucia, G. K., Baumann, D. J., & Cialdini, R. B. (1984). Mood influences on helping: Direct effects or side effects? *Journal of Personality and Social Psychology, 46*, 357–364.

Marangoni, C., Garcia, S., Ickes, W., & Teng, G. (1995). Empathic accuracy in a clinically relevant setting. *Journal of Personality and Social Psychology, 68*, 854–869.

McCullough, M. E., Worthington, E. L., Jr., & Rachal, K. C. (1997). Interpersonal forgiving in close relationships. *Journal of Personality and Social Psychology, 73*, 321–336

McHugo, G. J., Lanzetta, J. T., Sullivan, D. G., Masters, R. D., & Englis, B. G. (1985). Emotional reactions to a political leader's expressive displays. *Journal of Personality and Social Psychology, 49*, 1513–1529.

Mehrabian, A., & Epstein, N. A. (1972). A measure of emotional empathy. *Journal of Personality, 40*, 523–543.

Mehrabian, A., Young, A. L., & Sato, S. (1988). Emotional empathy and associated individual differences. *Current Psychology: Research & Reviews, 7*, 221–240.

Miller, P., & Eisenberg, N. (1988). The relation of empathy to aggression and externalizing/antisocial behavior. *Psychological Bulletin, 103*, 324–344.

Miller, P. A., Eisenberg, N., Fabes, R. A., & Shell, R. (1996). Relations of moral reasoning and vicarious emotion to young children's prosocial behavior toward peers and adults. *Developmental Psychology, 32*, 210–219.

Murphy, B. C., Shepard, S. A., Eisenberg, N., Fabes, R. A., & Guthrie, I. K. (1999). Contemporaneous and longitudinal relations of young adolescents' dispositional sympathy to their emotionality, regulation, and social functioning. *Journal of Early Adolescence, 19*, 66–97.

Porges, S. W., Doussard-Roosevelt, J. A., & Maiti, A. K. (1994). Vagal tone and the physiological regulation of emotion. *Monographs of the Society for Research in Child Development, 59*(Serial No. 240), 167–186.

Quigley-Fernandez, B., & Tedeschi, J. T. (1978). The bogus pipeline as lie detector: Two validity studies. *Journal of Personality and Social Psychology, 3*, 247–256.

Raskin, D. C. (1973). Attention and arousal. In W. F. Prokasy & D. C. Raskin (Eds.), *Electrodermal activity in psychological research* (pp. 125–155). New York: Academic.

Riggio, R. E. (1992). Social interaction skills and nonverbal behavior. In R. S. Feldman (Ed.), *Applications of nonverbal behavioral theories and research* (pp. 3–30). Hillsdale, NJ: Lawrence Erlbaum Associates.

Roberts, W., & Strayer, J. (1996). Empathy, emotional expressiveness, and prosocial behavior. *Child Development, 67*, 449–470.

Rosenthal, R. (1988, July). Interpersonal expectancies, nonverbal communication, and research on negotiation. *Negotiation Journal, 3*, 267–279.

Rosenthal, R., Hall, J. A., DiMatteo, M. R., Rogers, P. L., & Archer, D. (1979). *Sensitivity to nonverbal communication: The PONS test*. Baltimore: Johns Hopkins University Press.

Saarni, C. (1990). Emotional competence: How emotions and relationships become integrated. In R. A. Thompson (Ed.), *Socioemotional development* (pp. 115–182). Lincoln, NE: University of Nebraska Press.

Salovey, P., & Mayer, J. D. (1990). Emotional intelligence. *Imagination, Cognition and Personality, 9*, 185–211.

Sawin, D. B., (1979). *Assessing empathy in children: A search for an elusive construct*. Paper presented at the meeting of the Society for Research in Child Development, San Francisco.

Schwartz, G. E. (1986). Emotion and psychophysiological organization: A systems approach. In M. G. H. Coles, E. Donchin, & S. W. Porges (Eds.), *Psychophysiology: Systems, processes, and applications* (pp. 354–377). New York: Guilford.

Schwartz, G. E., Weinberger, D. A., & Singer, J. A. (1981). Cardiovascular differentiation of happiness, sadness, anger, and fear following imagery and exercise. *Psychosomatic Medicine, 43*, 343–364.

Shaver, G. E., Schwartz, J., Kirson, D., & O'Conner, C. (1987). Emotion knowledge: Further exploration of a prototype approach. *Journal of Personality and Social Psychology, 52*, 1061–1086.

Shennum, W. A., & Bugental, D. B. (1982). The development of control over affective expression in nonverbal behavior. In R. S. Feldman (Ed.), *Development of nonverbal behavior in children* (pp. 101–121). New York: Springer-Verlag.

Snodgrass, S. E. (1985). Women's intuition: The effect of subordinate role on interpersonal sensitivity. *Journal of Personality and Social Psychology, 49*, 146–155.

Spinrad, T. L., Losoya, S., Eisenberg, N., Fabes, R. A., Shepard, S. A., Cumberland, A., Guthrie, I. K., & Murphy, B. C. (1999). The relation of parental affect and encouragement to children's moral emotions and behavior. *Journal of Moral Education, 28*, 323–337.

Stotland, E. (1969). Exploratory studies in empathy. In L. Berkowitz (Ed.), *Advances in experimental social psychology* (Vol. 4, pp. 271–314). New York: Academic.

Strayer, J. (1983). Emotional and cognitive components of children's empathy. Paper presented at the biennial meeting of the Society for Research in Child Development, Detroit, MI.

Strayer, J. (1987). Picture-story indices of empathy. In N. Eisenberg & J. Strayer (Eds.), *Empathy and its development* (pp. 351–355). Cambridge, England: Cambridge University Press.

Strayer, J. (1993). Children's concordant emotions and cognitions in response to observed emotions. *Child Development, 64*, 188–201.

Strayer, J., & Roberts, W. (1997). Facial and verbal measures of children's emotions and empathy. *International Journal of Behavioral Development, 20*, 627–649.

Suess, P. E., Porges, S. W., & Plude, D. J. (1994). Cardiac vagal tone and sustained attention in school-age children. *Psychophysiology, 31*, 17–22.

Underwood, B., & Moore, B. (1982). Perspective-taking and altruism. *Psychological Bulletin, 91*, 143–173.

Wallbott, H. G., & Scherer, K. R. (1991). Stress specificities: Differential effects of coping style, gender, and type of stressor autonomic arousal, facial expression, and subjective feeling. *Journal of Personality and Social Psychology, 61*, 147–156.

Wilson, B. H., & Cantor, J. (1985). Developmental differences in empathy with a television protagonist's fear. *Journal of Experimental Child Psychology, 39*, 284–299.

Winton, W. M., Putnam, L. E., & Krauss, R. M. (1984). Facial and autonomic manifestations of the dimensional structure of emotion. *Journal of Experimental Social Psychology, 20*, 195–216.

Wood, J. V., Saltzberg, J. A., & Goldsamt, L. A. (1990). Does affect induce self-focused attention? *Journal of Personality and Social Psychology, 58*, 899–908.

Wood, J. V., Saltzberg, J. A., Neale, J. N., Stone, A. A., & Rachmiel, T. B. (1990). Self-focused attention, coping responses, and distressed mood in everyday life. *Journal of Personality and Social Psychology, 58*, 1027–1036.

Zahn-Waxler, C., Cole, P. M., Welsh, J. D., & Fox, N. A. (1995). Psychophysiological correlates of empathy and prosocial behaviors in preschool children with behavior problems. *Development and Psychopathology, 7*, 27–48.

Zahn-Waxler, C., Friedman, S. L., & Cummings, E. M. (1983). Children's emotions and behaviors in response to infants' cries. *Child Development, 54*, 1522–1528.

Zahn-Waxler, C., Radke-Yarrow, M., Wagner, E., & Chapman, M. (1992). Development of concern for others. *Developmental Psychology, 28*, 126–136.

Zahn-Waxler, C., Robinson, J., & Emde, R. N. (1992). The development of empathy in twins. *Developmental Psychology, 28*, 1038–1047.

# II

# Assessing the Performance of a Perceiver

# 3

# In Search of the Good Judge of Personality: Some Methodological and Theoretical Concerns

C. Randall Colvin
Matthew J. Bundick
*Northeastern University*

Jeff is looking for his friend and roommate, Mike, who is mingling with friends and acquaintances and no doubt enjoying the back-to-school dorm party. In contrast, Jeff, who is in no mood to mingle, sits and samples the party cuisine with vigor while keeping an eye out for his friend. His attention is drawn to an attractive young woman who, from hearing bits of her conversation, is telling a humorous story to three female friends about a male student who lives in their dorm. After another unsuccessful scan for Mike, Jeff's attention returns to the woman, whose demeanor has become more serious as she is talking to a man who Jeff guesses might be a current or former boyfriend. With the passing of minutes, the interaction between the woman and man lightens and a smile returns to the woman's face. Jeff, to his surprise, experiences a sense of relief on the woman's behalf, as though a critical impasse had been favorably resolved. Jeff finally spots Mike. To Jeff's surprise, Mike approaches the woman and man, shakes hands with the man and then embraces the woman. They talk in loud laughing voices for several minutes.

Later that evening when both roommates were back in their dorm room, Jeff asked Mike about the woman at the party. Mike indicated that he and Julie had known each other since high school and were pretty good friends. Jeff said he was attracted to Julie and wanted to get to know her. Jeff began telling Mike his impressions of Julie's personality, stating that he thought Julie is very outgoing and friendly, has a good sense of humor, is sensitive to other people's feelings, and is very self-confident. Mike told Jeff that his personality description of Julie was right on target. As the discussion continued, Jeff's judgments about Julie's personality traits were repeatedly confirmed by Mike with only minor exceptions.

This chapter explores the possibility that Jeff's ability to accurately judge Julie's personality traits is not typical of everyone, that people vary in their ability to accurately judge the personality traits of others. Whereas other chapters in this book focus on the ability of judges to accurately assess the current state of target individuals' thoughts or feelings, our focus is on the ability of judges to infer from limited behavioral information the target individual's personality traits or, in other words, the target individual's general behavioral tendencies across situations and over time. Moreover, we are particularly interested in the ability to be accurate over a wide range of personality traits as opposed to single traits such as extraversion or neuroticism. For example, we might ask Jeff to rate Julie's personality using 100 trait dimensions (e.g., "is critical, skeptical, not easily impressed," "is a dependable, responsible person," "has a wide range of interests") to determine whether Jeff is more accurate than other judges at rating Julie's global personality. The top half of Table 3.1 demonstrates how one might construct a judgmental accuracy score to determine Jeff's accuracy at rating Julie. Notice that for each judge a correlation coefficient is computed that indicates his or her agreement with the criterion rating. Although our example includes only one criterion, we recommend researchers use multiple criteria to overcome the inherent weaknesses of any single criterion. Finally, note that the correlation coefficient obtained in Step 1 becomes the judgmental accuracy score in Step 2 and is subsequently correlated with ratings of the judge's personality to develop a personality profile of the good and bad judge of personality.

We now define two terms that are frequently used in this chapter. First, to the extent that Jeff accurately judges Julie's personality traits and is relatively accurate in judging other people's personality traits, Jeff may be characterized as a good judge of personality. An important feature of this definition is that to be considered a good judge of personality, one must exhibit accuracy over a wide range of target persons. Second, the term *judgmental accuracy of personality traits* is used to denote a dimension marked by good judges of personality at one end of its continuum and poor judges of personality at the other end. For presentation purposes, we use the abbreviated term *judgmental accuracy* to refer to this individual difference dimension.

The chapter begins with a brief historical review of research on judgmental accuracy and then several methodological and theoretical issues are discussed. The historical review is necessarily brief as its intent is to set the stage for the remainder of the chapter. Our purpose is to indicate some of the trouble spots in

### TABLE 3.1
#### Example: Creation and Correlation of Judgmental Accuracy Scores

Step 1. Create Individual Judgmental Accuracy Score

| Personality Trait | Jeff's Rating | Julie's Criterion Rating |
|---|---|---|
| 1. Critical, skeptical | 4 | 3 |
| 2. Dependable, responsible | 7 | 8 |
| 3. Has a wide range of interests | 5 | 5 |
| 4. Is a talkative person | 8 | 7 |
| &#124; | | |
| &#124; | | |
| 97. Emotionally bland | 2 | 3 |
| 98. Is verbally fluent | 6 | 7 |
| 99. Is self-dramatizing | 5 | 5 |
| 100. Does not vary roles | 6 | 7 |

$r$ (Jeff & Julie) = .78

Step 2. Correlate Judgmental Accuracy Scores with Personality Ratings

| Judge | Judgmental Accuracy | Agreeableness |
|---|---|---|
| Jeff | .78 | 9 |
| Annie | .45 | 5 |
| &#124; | | |
| &#124; | | |
| Bill | .10 | 2 |
| Janet | .85 | 9 |

$r$ (Accuracy & Agreeableness) = .45

Note. The analysis in Step 1 is repeated for each judge. The correlation coefficient from Step 1 becomes the judgmental accuracy score for Step 2. Correlations computed in Step 2 are helpful in establishing a personality profile of good and bad judges of personality.

past research, offer some helpful suggestions for future research, describe our recently completed study, and ultimately to encourage readers to join the search for the good judge of personality. Finally, one question that may arise for newcomers to this topic as they discover all the problems that have been encountered is "Why bother?" The answer is that people make judgments about the personality traits of others every day, and inaccurate judgments may have negative consequences for the judge or the target person. When researchers gain a better understanding of the underlying processes and personality characteristics associated with good and bad judges of personality, training programs can be developed to improve people's judgmental accuracy.

## HISTORICAL BACKGROUND

From the 1920s through the 1940s, judgmental accuracy was a topic of interest to many researchers (for reviews, see Bronfenbrenner, Harding, & Gallwey, 1958; Cline, 1964; Cook, 1979; Taft, 1955). Dymond (1948, 1949, 1950) published a series of influential empirical papers on the good judge of personality that, ironically, marked the beginning of the end of the early era of judgmental accuracy research. In a typical study, college students rated themselves and rated each member of their 4–8 person group on six trait dimensions (i.e., self-confidence, superiority, selfishness, friendliness, leadership, humor) using a 5-point scale. In addition, participants predicted the other members' self-ratings and predicted the other members' ratings of them. Individual judgmental accuracy scores were derived by calculating the absolute difference between participants' "predictions" of other members' ratings with members' actual ratings. Judgmental accuracy was subsequently correlated with self-report measures, which revealed a positive relationship between judgmental accuracy and (a) concern and desire for positive interpersonal relationships and (b) close family relations (Dymond, 1950). Soon thereafter, several articles critical of judgmental accuracy research were published.

One of the first critiques argued that high judgmental accuracy scores could occur if judges projected their own personality characteristics onto target individuals whom they rated, and targets happened to possess personality characteristics that were similar to the judges' (Hastorf & Bender, 1952). Thus, people could be accurate but not because they were good judges of personality. Although several damaging critiques followed (Campbell, 1955; Cronbach & Gleser, 1953; Crow and Hammond, 1957; Gage and Cronbach, 1955; Hastorf, Bender, & Weintraub, 1955), Cronbach's (1955) was by far the most damaging.

He argued that judgmental accuracy scores, particularly summed difference scores such as those used by Dymond (1950), were comprised of several components, many of which were independent of a judge's ability to accurately describe a target's personality. One component, elevation, reflects the mean difference between a judge's trait ratings averaged over two or more targets and the targets' averaged criterion ratings. A related component, differential elevation, is simply the difference between a judge's trait ratings averaged for one target and the target's averaged criterion ratings. Both types of elevation may be influenced by response styles that are shared by judge and target (Bernieri, Zuckerman, Koestner, & Rosenthal, 1994). For example, if both people use a measurement scale in the same manner, judgmental accuracy scores could be high but artifactual. Stereotype accuracy is the comparison between a judge's mean rating of a single trait over all targets and the targets' average criterion rating on that same trait. More generally, stereotype accuracy occurs when a judge's ratings reflect the characteristics of the "average" person and, to the extent the target is similar to most people, obtains a high judgmental accuracy score even though the judge may possess little or no individuating information about the target. Consistent with Hastorf and Bender (1952), Cronbach argued that projection could result in high judgmental accuracy scores when a judge describes him- or herself as a proxy for describing the target's personality and the judge and target coincidentally possess similar personality characteristics. Differential accuracy is the one component, according to Cronbach, that resembles true judgmental accuracy and is essentially what is left over after controlling for the various artifactual components. Cronbach's critique effectively shut down research on judgmental accuracy. Researchers, unable to respond to Cronbach's critique and uncertain how to conduct methodologically sound research, moved on to other research topics.

In recent years, the accuracy of personality judgments has once again become an active research topic (Funder & Colvin, 1997), but a relatively small number of studies have focused specifically on the good judge of personality. A meta-analysis of post-Cronbach research on the good judge revealed that 78% of the analyzed effects pertained to judgments of emotion as opposed to personality traits (Davis & Kraus, 1997). Had it not been for Rosenthal and his colleagues, who contributed over 40% of all the analyzed effects (e.g., Rosenthal, Hall, DiMatteo, Rogers, & Archer, 1979), the number of studies may have been so small to render moot any conclusions about judgmental accuracy.

Davis and Kraus's (1997) review indicated that judgmental accuracy is positively related to intellectual functioning, cognitive style characterized by cognitive complexity and field independence, psychological adjustment, social sensitivity, and interpersonal orientation (i.e., value and seek out close relationships). These characteristics of the good judge are not inconsistent with research conducted prior to Cronbach's critique (e.g., Allport, 1937; Dymond, 1950; Taft, 1955), but because the David and Kraus review was based primarily on studies outside of the domain of personality trait judgments and the early pre-Cronbach research was methodologically limited, any conclusions drawn about the characteristics of the good judge of personality should be considered highly tentative.

A study by Ambady and her colleagues (Ambady, Hallahan, & Rosenthal, 1995) is particularly relevant although it was not included in the Davis and Kraus (1997) review. Participants were seated at a large table with 2–6 other individuals with whom they were unacquainted and told not to speak to. They rated themselves on several personality measures, completed two tests of nonverbal skill (the Profile of Nonverbal Sensitivity [PONS], Rosenthal et. al, 1979; Interpersonal Perception Task [IPT], Costanzo & Archer, 1989), and rated each group member on several personality traits that were subsequently reduced to four of the Big Five factors of personality (extraversion, agreeableness, emotional stability, and conscientiousness) and a fifth factor that was labeled positive affect. Judgmental accuracy scores were calculated for each of the five factors by correlating, for example, a judge's ratings on six extraversion-related adjectives for each target with each target's self-ratings on the same six adjectives and then averaging the correlations across targets. A complex set of results emerged, but in general women were more accurate than men and the most accurate women and men judges rated themselves as being relatively low in expressiveness, sociability, and self-esteem, which led the authors to speculate that psychologically vulnerable individuals may be better judges of others.

These results appear to be at odds with the results reviewed by Davis and Kraus (1997), who found good judges to be well-functioning individuals. However, as noted earlier, Davis and Kraus combined results from different kinds of judgmental accuracy studies. It is not clear to us, and probably should not be assumed, that investigations of trait accuracy, empathic accuracy, nonverbal decoding, lie detection, and so forth, all tap the same latent construct.

Empirical results support this claim. In the "good judge" project that are described later in this chapter, approximately half of our judges ($n = 60$) were tested on a variety of nonverbal decoding ability tests, including the PONS and the IPT, by our colleague Judith Hall (for details about these tests, see Hall, chap. 8, this volume). We correlated our measure of judgmental accuracy of personality traits with the nonverbal tests to determine whether the tests were related and assessed the same construct. The correlations between judgmental accuracy and the PONS ($r = .10$, ns, with audio PONS; $r = .15$, ns, with video PONS) and judgmental accuracy and the IPT ($r = .13$, ns) were not significant, nor were the intercorrelations among the nonverbal tests (rs range from -.02 to .05). These results suggest that the various tests assess different abilities (see also Hall, chap. 8, this volume).

Currently there are no theories that account for these results. However, it may be helpful to consider some of the characteristics of each test to better understand why these measures do not correlate. First, the PONS, IPT, and our test of judgmental accuracy differ in the amount of information presented to the observing judges. The PONS tests employed each had 40 2-s clips, the IPT thirty 28- to 124-s scenes, and the test of judgmental accuracy presents four 12-min videotaped dyadic interactions. Because the PONS presents audio and visual cues for such a short period of time, a high scorer on the PONS must necessarily be skilled at detecting different kinds of cues (e.g., hand movements, vocal intonation). In contrast, the IPT and test of judgmental accuracy provide considerably more information, thus placing a lesser burden on detecting all cues while placing a greater emphasis on the integration and interpretation of cues that are detected (Funder, 1999).

Second, the tests require different types of judgments. The PONS requires judges to evaluate what is being conveyed in the 2-s clip (e.g., is the person asking for a favor, talking about the death of a friend), the IPT requires judges to reach a conclusion about the people in the scenes (e.g., the actual relationship between a man and woman, the winner of a racquetball game), and the test of judgmental accuracy requires judges to infer the personality traits of a designated target person after observing his or her social behavior for 12 min. This suggests that the breadth of inference differs across the three tests, with the PONS requiring the narrowest and the test of judgmental accuracy the broadest inference, and the IPT falling in the middle. Although there are several other dimensions on which the tests differ, this brief analysis suggests that at least three variables—cue detection, cue integration/interpretation, and breadth of inference—may be factors that in part account for the divergent empirical results associated with the tests. Future research that uses the three tests, and other interpersonal sensitivity tests, may benefit from considering the influences due to these factors.

"Tentative" describes the current state of research on judgmental accuracy. Inconsistent results and Cronbach's continued influence on the field have led some researchers to call off the search for the good judge of personality (e.g., Kenny, 1994). Others are more optimistic, see the problem as inherently important, and continue to search for individual differences in judgmental accuracy with respect to personality (e.g., Ambady et al., 1995; Bernstein & Davis, 1982).

We fall into this latter group, and one of us has recently reported results from an extensive study on the good judge of personality (Vogt & Colvin, 1999). During the planning phase of the study, we consulted the literature on judgmental accuracy and attempted to develop a study that, although ultimately possessing its own flaws, was at least informed by the strengths and weaknesses of previous research. In the sections that follow, we discuss several methodological and theoretical issues that we confronted and the rationale for the choices we made. When finished, the reader will have a fairly good approximation of the study we conducted. Following that, we will review some of the results we obtained on the good judge of personality.

## METHODOLOGICAL ISSUES

### Selection of Targets

Researchers generally have not paid much attention to the number of target persons to be judged in their studies. Studies have been conducted that have used anywhere from 1 (Rosenthal et al., 1979) to 16 targets or more (Bernstein

& Davis, 1982; Borman, 1979) and many with some number in between (e.g., Ambady et al., 1995; Bronfenbrenner et al., 1958; Cline, 1964). There is rarely any rationale by researchers for the number of targets they use. This fact raises two issues. First, the number of targets used in a study will influence the reliability of the composite judgmental accuracy score (e.g., the mean score derived from multiple targets using the procedure described in the top half of Table 3.1), which raises the possibility that unpublished null findings might be due to inadequate sampling of targets and not necessarily due to the presumed lack of construct validity (e.g., Kenny, 1994). All things being equal, using more targets, like adding more good items to a test, produces a more reliable measure of judgmental accuracy resulting in stronger relationships with external variables (e.g., personality correlates of judgmental accuracy). All things are rarely equal, though, which raises the second issue.

The appropriate number of targets to be used is an important but difficult decision as it always represents a compromise between the goals set for the study and the resources available to conduct it. For example, Vogt and Colvin (1999) asked judges to rate four targets who had been videotaped for 12 min each. Each tape showed a target interacting with a person in three different situations. The purpose of each tape was to simulate the scenario we presented at the beginning of this chapter in which a judge observes an individual exhibiting a variety of behaviors across different situations. After watching each tape, judges used the California Adult Q-Set (CAQ; J. Block, 1978) to rate each target's personality characteristics. The CAQ is a measure of personality consisting of 100 personality traits each typed on separate cards that the judge sorts into nine piles ranging from 1 (extremely uncharacteristic of the target), to 9 (extremely characteristic of the target). In addition, judges rated themselves on more than 20 personality questionnaires and tests, and parents described judges' personality characteristics with the CAQ.

Relatively speaking, limited resources were not a serious issue for Vogt and Colvin's study, yet compromises still had to be made. Although they used only four targets, each videotape was 12 min long, and judges took approximately 45 min to complete the CAQ on each target. It would have been preferable to have judges observe a greater number of targets, but in the end, resources were finite. The participants, who had been tested, questioned, and observed for over 10 hours, could be expected to take only so much abuse in the name of science.

Ultimately, the optimal number of targets to be used in a study is a complex decision that requires the researcher to consider the phenomena being judged (e.g., extraversion vs. global personality), the attention span and motivation of the judges, the goal of the study (e.g., judgmental accuracy, correlates of judges' accuracy, or both), and the time and money available to conduct it. We have no rules of thumb to offer; we can only suggest that these factors be considered while planning a study.

## Criteria to Assess Accuracy

The use of imperfect criteria is, in part, responsible for the conceptual ambiguity in the personality judgmental accuracy literature. Many studies conducted in the 1940s and 1950s required judges to predict how target persons would describe themselves on a personality measure (e.g., Bender & Hastorf, 1950; Dymond, 1949, 1950). The criterion for determining judgmental accuracy was the match between judges' predictions and targets' self-ratings. Although this criterion was perfectly acceptable for the questions being asked, the questions we more often want answered are How does the judge actually perceive the target? and Are his or her judgments accurate? The former approach requires the judge to guess how the target will answer and whereas the latter approach results in a description of the target that the judge actually believes to be accurate.

A second problem is that a single criterion is likely to be unreliable and flawed and thus may produce biased assessments of judgmental accuracy. An assessment of judgmental accuracy is similar to conducting construct validation of a test in which multiple criteria are used to evaluate the underlying meaning of the test (Colvin & Funder, 1991; Cronbach & Meehl, 1955). Thus, when judgmental accuracy is assessed, it is useful to utilize multiple criteria to evaluate the accuracy of judges' personality descriptions. Vogt and Colvin (1999) used as criteria (a) targets' CAQ self-descriptions, (b) two friends' CAQ ratings, and (c) behavioral ratings of the targets' social behavior by a team of trained coders, which were used to evaluate the accuracy of judges' CAQ descriptions of each of four videotaped target persons. The multicriteria approach permits a more valid assessment of individual differences in judgmental accuracy by aggregating the strengths and canceling the weaknesses associated with different criteria (J. H. Block & Block, 1980; Funder, 1997).

## Cronbach's Components of Accuracy

Earlier in the chapter, we reviewed the components comprising judgmental accuracy as described by Cronbach (1955). He argued that at least four components—elevation, differential elevation, stereotype accuracy, and projection—could produce artificially high judgmental accuracy scores. The problems associated with these components at first appeared to researchers to be insurmountable, but there are now a number of techniques available to eliminate or control them (Funder & Colvin, 1997; Kenny, 1994). The elevation factors can be removed by using forced-choice rating techniques (e.g., Q-sort; J. Block, 1978) that constrain the ratings of all judges to have the same mean and variance across items, or they can be removed by standardization of judges' ratings (Bernieri et al., 1994). Stereotype accuracy and projection can be controlled by way of research design or statistical control (i.e., partial correlations).

Vogt and Colvin (1999), for example, developed indices of stereotype accuracy and projection and used partial correlation analyses to control for their effect on judgmental accuracy when judgmental accuracy was related to other substantive variables.

Recently, it has been argued that researchers' reflexive attempts to control for stereotype accuracy and projection may on occasion be misguided and that these two components may represent cognitive–perceptual processes that foster accuracy, not hinder it (Vogt & Colvin, 1999). It may be that stereotype accuracy and projection are processes that use relatively valid information about the self and about groups of people, respectively, and that judges use these processes to "fill in the blanks" when forming impressions about people behaving in informationally impoverished situations. A task for future research on judgmental accuracy is to determine the circumstances under which stereotype accuracy and projection produce substantive or artifactual gains in judgmental accuracy.

Another issue, pointed out long ago, arises when researchers control for stereotype accuracy and projection. The results, after controlling for a judge's use of a stereotype or for a judge's use of projection, are clearly and unambiguously interpretable only when the target is unlike the stereotype or when the judge and target are dissimilar (Cline, 1964). For example, when a judge and target possess similar personality traits, controlling for projection will sometimes result in an overcorrection whereby too much valid variance is removed from the judgmental accuracy score. The same principle applies if the judge's stereotype usage is controlled for when the target is very similar to the stereotype. As a demonstration of this point for projection, consider the simple case when a judge is a 7 on Extraversion and rates the assigned target 7 on Extraversion. Even if the target is a true 7, because the judge and target are similar on Extraversion, the judge will receive no credit for being accurate. The logic behind this statistical procedure is that the correct rating of the target is due solely to the fact that the judge and target possess the same amount of Extraversion. The true state of affairs for this single case cannot be determined, which leaves one to wonder whether projection is responsible for substantive or artifactual results.

One way to potentially circumvent this conundrum is to use multiple target persons whose personality characteristics differ from one another. In Vogt and Colvin's (1999) study, projection was highly related to judgmental accuracy for three of the targets but unrelated to judgmental accuracy for the fourth target. Further analysis revealed that the three targets were generally similar to the judges, whereas the fourth target was relatively dissimilar to the judges. Given that the best judges were relatively accurate at judging all four targets, it was suggested that the kind of projection used by the good judges was the "fill in the blanks" type, which was useful for the three targets but not useful and not used by the good judges to rate the fourth target. In other words, it appeared that the good judges were able to discriminate the personality characteristics of the targets, thereby indicating that "projection" was used only on those targets for whom it would increase judges' accuracy.

## Types of Data

Researchers often rely on quick and easy self-report measures to assess the characteristics of their participants. For some research purposes, self-report is a useful and necessary source of data. For other purposes, overreliance on self-report data can result in the dubious validity of an entire research area (e.g., Colvin, Block, & Funder, 1995). The inclusion of multiple types of data into a research design permits weaknesses associated with a particular type of data to be canceled out and individual strengths to be combined through data aggregation (J. H. Block & Block, 1980). In order to obtain a more valid and comprehensive portrait of the good judge of personality, it is important to move beyond self-report data and include other sources of data such as peer ratings, clinical interviews, and behavioral ratings.

Furthermore, it is necessary to cast a wide net of psychological measures to capture the personality characteristics associated with being a good and bad judge of personality. A comprehensive description of the good judge of personality traits is useful for generating hypotheses for future research and ultimately for developing and advancing theory. In Vogt and Colvin's (1999) study, judges completed over 20 self-report questionnaires and tests, and their parents rated their personality characteristics on the CAQ. The data were analyzed separately for men and women and by self and parent reports. The results were replicated in each analysis and indicated that judgmental accuracy, as defined in their study, was related to interpersonal orientation (i.e., value and desire close interpersonal relationships) and psychological communion.

## Types of Judgmental Accuracy

A recent review concluded that judgmental accuracy is a broad ability that generalizes across different categories of social objects and psychological dimensions (Davis & Kraus, 1997). Although this conclusion may ultimately prove correct, it seems useful, given the limited knowledge about judgmental accuracy, to identify and study different types of judgmental accuracy that may exist. At least four different types of judgmental accuracy for personality can be identified: the good judge of (a) strangers, (b) acquaintances, (c) close friends, and (d) self. Early research suggested that the psychological characteristics associated with one type of judgmental accuracy were independent of the other types (Allport, 1937; Vernon, 1933). Moreover, as future research investigates judgmental accuracy it may be found that each type emphasizes different aspects of the cognitive–perceptual system. The detection of behavioral cues, for example, might be more important for accurately judging strangers, whereas the integration of behavioral cues might be more important for accurately judging close friends (Funder, 1999).

At the beginning of this chapter, Jeff observed an unknown woman interacting with a variety of people. His accurate assessment of the woman marked him as a good judge of strangers. Of course, to correctly diagnose Jeff as a good judge of strangers, it would be necessary to assess his accuracy with a variety of unknown target persons. If he was consistently accurate, the good judge label would then be well deserved. Vogt and Colvin (1999) used this same logic when they assessed the ability of their judges to accurately describe the personality characteristics of unknown target persons. It is not known whether the good judge of strangers who is interpersonally oriented is also better than others at judging close friends, although Vernon (1933) suggested that they are not. Additional research is needed to provide an answer.

# THEORY

A review of research on judgmental accuracy reveals a notable absence of guiding theory. Empirical reviews, both old and new, report the personality characteristics associated with judgmental accuracy but have few theoretical assertions to offer to account for the observed results. As a result, the reported findings have a hodgepodge quality about them and lack a theoretical string to tie them together (e.g., Davis & Kraus, 1997; Taft, 1955).

Recently, two general theories of judgmental accuracy have been presented (Funder, 1995, 1999; Kenny, 1991, 1994). Kenny's Weighted-Average Model (WAM) focuses on the parameters that influence consensus (i.e., agreement between perceivers) and accuracy (i.e., validity of perceivers' judgments) and has been used, for example, to make interesting and provocative predictions about the influence of acquaintanceship on consensus. Probably because of Kenny's concern that accuracy research be "nomothetic, interpersonal, and componential," his initial model, although influential, does not address individual differences in judgmental accuracy (Kenny, 1994, p. 126). However, more recent writings revise this perspective (see Kenny & Winquist, chap. 14, this volume).

Funder's (1995) Realistic Accuracy Model (RAM; see also chap. 16, this volume), which at times compliments and competes with Kenny's model, is informative about individual differences in judgmental accuracy. According to RAM, for a personality judgment to be accurate, four steps must be successfully completed. First, the target must emit behavior that is relevant to his or her underlying personality characteristics (e.g., personality traits). Second, the behavioral information must be presented in a manner that makes it available to the judge's perceptual apparatus (e.g., visual, auditory). Third, the judge must detect the behavioral information (e.g., see it or hear it). Finally, the judge must correctly utilize the previously detected, available, and relevant behavioral information. If all four steps are completed without error, the judge will produce a judgment of personality that is accurate (see Fig. 3.1).

RAM indicates that differences between good and bad judges of personality are due to differences in either the detection or utilization of available and relevant behavioral information. Moreover, certain judgment tasks emphasize detection and utilization to different degrees. For example, differences in the judgmental accuracy in which husbands describe the personality traits of their wives probably reflect differences in how husbands use the vast amount of information available to them. In contrast, judgmental accuracy of strangers' personality traits emphasizes the detection of valid behavioral cues over the utilization of them. Because judgments about strangers are based on a relatively small set of behavioral cues, the detection of these cues represents the essential "input" for a subsequent judgment of personality. Of course, the cues must also be used correctly, but this last assertion simply recognizes that detection necessarily precedes utilization.

Funder (1999) suggested that at least three variables—motivation, ability, and knowledge—influence detection and utilization and, as a result, have an effect on judgmental accuracy.

The first variable, motivation, may play a role either in how much people care about making an accurate judgment or in how the judgments are made. For example, people may be more accurate when they believe their judgments will have important social outcomes (Flink & Park, 1991). To the extent that some people habitually seek out information about others and spend time analyzing it, they may exhibit higher judgmental accuracy than individuals who attend to different concerns. Motivational processes may at times hinder accuracy. Individuals who frequently use defensive processes (e.g., repression, denial) will, by definition, have less information available to them to make judgments about others.

FIG. 3.1   The realistic accuracy model of personality judgment.

Second, perceptual and cognitive ability are likely to have an effect on judgmental accuracy. Some people pay close attention to their partners and are sensitive to body movements, facial expressions, and voice qualities (Rosenthal et
al., 1979). Detection of these bits of information would seem to be necessary for
accurate personality judgments, despite our nonsignificant results reported earlier between judgmental accuracy and nonverbal decoding ability. Cognitive
ability or intelligence, long thought to be a correlate of judgmental accuracy
(e.g., Allport, 1937; Taft, 1955), is likely to play a role in how efficiently and successfully people use information they have gathered about another person. Recent advances in the cognitive sciences, social cognition, and object relations
point to additional cognitive variables that might influence judgmental accuracy, such as working memory (Baddeley, 1995), long-term memory, and complexity of mental representations (Leigh, Westen, Barends, & Mendel, 1992).

Third, individuals who possess considerable knowledge, particularly implicit
knowledge, about behavioral cues and their connections to personality traits
should be adept at detecting valid cues and using them to make accurate judgments. As Funder (1999) suggested, implicit knowledge of this sort is obtained
through experience, particularly as people make judgments of others and receive feedback about their accuracy. Interpersonally oriented persons are probably more likely than others to frequently engage in this process. This
knowledge not only allows interpersonally oriented individuals to accurately
judge others, it facilitates the more important goal of establishing close interpersonal relationships. By understanding the connection between cues and personality characteristics, these individuals can accurately assess others and make
adjustments to their own behavior in order to foster successful new relationships and maintain harmony in existing relationships (Davis & Kraus, 1997).

The concept of interpersonal orientation can be elaborated by relating it to
Bakan's (1966) writings on two broad and encompassing psychological constructs termed *agency* and *communion*. He viewed these constructs as the "two
fundamental modalities in the existence of living forms" (Bakan, 1966, p.15).
Agency is characterized by the individual, typically a man, who fulfills his needs
by controlling his environment and achieving individually based goals.
Self-satisfaction is the overreaching motivation of the agentic person. Communion, in contrast, is characterized by the individual, typically a woman, whose
needs are fulfilled by becoming one with a group of others. Personal feelings of
pleasure and pain often mirror the circumstances of those individuals for whom
she cares about. The communal individual is interpersonally oriented and will
frequently provide support to her friends and loved ones, perhaps while experiencing a cost to her own emotional well-being. Given that Bakan viewed agency
and communion as lenses through which people perceive and act on their
world, interpersonal orientation is best viewed as one facet of communion that
emphasizes the desire and need to have close interpersonal relationships.
Finally, although agency and communion are sometimes used to differentiate

men and women, Bakan believed that both characteristics are present to some degree in each gender (Spence & Helmreich, 1978).

RAM is useful for generating hypotheses for each type of judgmental accuracy. Because our focus is on judgmental accuracy for strangers, we will limit our discussion to this domain. One hypothesis derived from RAM asserts that judgmental accuracy for strangers and communion will be positively related. Communal individuals are more likely than less communal individuals to frequently seek out social contacts, evaluate the personality traits of their social partners, and obtain feedback about the correctness of their personality evaluations. This should lead communal individuals to have better knowledge of trait–behavior relations than less communal individuals, which in turn will facilitate their accuracy of strangers. A second hypothesis derived from RAM indicates that judgmental accuracy for strangers and intelligence will be unrelated. This hypothesis follows from the presumption that intelligence is related to the utilization of information and that judgmental accuracy of strangers places greater weight on valid detection than on utilization. These two hypotheses were evaluated in the study described next.

## VOGT AND COLVIN'S (1999) STUDY

In the preceding pages, several methodological and theoretical concerns were outlined that one might want to consider before conducting research on judgmental accuracy. The discussion of these concerns also served to acquaint the reader with some of the details of Vogt and Colvin's (1999) study, to which we now turn.

### Overview of Method

Judges, 55 women and 47 men, observed four videotaped 12 min dyadic interactions that featured a designated target person. Each of the four target persons served as participants in a previous study in which their personality characteristics were rated on the CAQ by themselves and by two close friends, and their videotaped social behavior was rated by a team of trained coders using the Behavioral Q-Sort (BQ; Funder & Colvin, 1991). After watching each videotape, judges described the personality of the designated target person using the CAQ and rated how confident they were of their descriptions. In addition, judges described their own personalities on numerous questionnaires and tests, and were rated by their parents on the CAQ.

### Construction of Judgmental Accuracy Score

Recall that for each of four target persons, CAQ self-descriptions, two CAQ friend ratings, and behavioral ratings (BQ) were obtained to serve as accuracy criteria. To construct the judgmental accuracy scores based on the self and friend criteria, the following was done: The judge's 100-item CAQ rating of the target was correlated with the target's 100-item self CAQ (or friends' aggregated CAQ; see Table 3.1). The resulting correlation coefficient was subsequently treated as a score; higher scores represented more agreement between the judge's personality description and the criterion rating for the target. The construction of the judgmental accuracy score based on the BQ required a slightly modified procedure. Forty items from the BQ have direct analogues in the CAQ (Funder, Furr, & Colvin, 1999). Therefore, the 40 matching items from the judge's CAQ rating of the target and the 40 items from the target's BQ criterion were correlated. Similar to the scores derived from self and friend criteria, the resulting correlation coefficient was treated as a score; higher scores represented better agreement with the behavioral criterion. These procedures were repeated for all judge and target–criterion pairings. As a result, each judge received three scores per target for a total of 12 judgmental accuracy scores. The scores were aggregated to create a composite score of judgmental accuracy of personality traits; Cronbach's alpha was .82. The results that are described next are based on this judgmental accuracy composite score.

## Personality Correlates of Judgmental Accuracy

Judgmental accuracy was correlated with self-descriptions and parents' ratings on the CAQ. The data were analyzed separately by gender as is customary in our lab. The personality characteristics descriptive of the good judge of personality were similar for men and women and across self- and parent ratings. The results indicated that men and women who were relatively accurate judges of personality are warm, outgoing, and sympathetic. Relative to poor judges, good judges of personality tend to be more empathic and egalitarian and are less manipulative, hostile, and autonomous. Good judges appear to be concerned with getting along with others and place a high value on their relationships with others. This constellation of personality descriptors is characteristic of individuals high in the construct of communion as elaborated by Bakan (1966). It refers to an interpersonal orientation marked by a motivation to develop and maintain positive relations with others. These results provide support for the hypothesis that judgmental accuracy for strangers and communion are positively related.

Judgmental accuracy was correlated with the Wonderlic, a 12-min test of intellectual ability, to evaluate the hypothesis that accuracy for strangers and intelligence are unrelated. Indeed, judgmental accuracy and intelligence were unrelated. Although the prediction and finding of a null result may not be reason for celebration, it is consistent with theory, and more importantly, future research will be able to evaluate whether intelligence is positively related to other forms of judgmental accuracy as RAM predicts.

Two additional findings are worth noting. First, women's judgmental accuracy scores were significantly higher than men's, suggesting that women on average are better judges of strangers' personality traits than men. This finding is consistent with a large body of conceptually related research that demonstrates women are better than men at decoding nonverbal behavior (Hall, 1978). Second, on two separate measures, judges' self-ratings of ability to accurately judge others were unrelated to their judgmental accuracy scores. These results mirror those found in the empathic accuracy literature and suggest that, in general, people do not possess valid self-knowledge about their ability to judge the personality traits of others (Ickes, 1993; Riggio & Riggio, chap. 7, this volume).

## SUMMARY

This chapter presented a number of issues that in our opinion need to be considered when conducting judgmental accuracy research. The methodological issues pertain to (a) selection of targets, (b) criteria to assess judgmental accuracy, (c) Cronbach's components, (d) need for wide range of data, and (e) the types of judgmental accuracy. We noted that, historically, judgmental accuracy research has been atheoretical and that recent theoretical frameworks should help to correct this limitation. Vogt and Colvin' (1999) study was discussed to indicate how these various issues might actually be dealt with in an empirical study. Finally, we mentioned only briefly the topic that lay people always want to know, "Can you teach me to be a better judge?" Training people to be better judges may be the ultimate goal of this research, but the first priorities are to search for and identify the characteristics of the good judge and to learn more about the cognitive–perceptual processes associated with judgmental accuracy.

## REFERENCES

Allport, G. W. (1937). Personality: A psychological interpretation. New York: Holt.

Ambady, N., Hallahan, M., & Rosenthal, R. (1995). On judging and being judged accurately in zero-acquaintance situations. Journal of Personality and Social Psychology, 69, 518–529.

Baddeley, A. (1995). Working memory. In M. Gazzaniga (Ed.), The cognitive neurosciences (pp. 755–764). Cambridge, MA: MIT Press.

Bakan, D. (1966). The duality of human existence. Chicago: Rand McNally.

Bender, I. E., & Hastorf, A. H. (1950). The perception of persons: Forecasting another person's responses on three personality scales. Journal of Abnormal and Social Psychology, 45, 556–561.

Bernieri, F. J., Zuckerman, M., Koestner, R., & Rosenthal, R. (1994). Measuring person perception accuracy: Another look at self–other agreement. Personality and Social Psychology Bulletin, 20, 367–378.

Bernstein, W. M., & Davis, M. H. (1982). Perspective-taking, self-consciousness, and accuracy in person perception. Basic and Applied Social Psychology, 3, 1–19.

Block, J. (1978). *The Q-sort method in personality assessment and psychiatric research*. Palo Alto, CA: Consulting Psychologists Press (Original work published 1961).

Block, J. H., & Block, J. (1980). The role of ego-control and ego-resiliency in the organization of behavior. In W.A. Collins (Ed.), *The Minnesota Symposia on Child Psychology* (Vol. 13, pp. 39–101). Hillsdale, NJ: Lawrence Erlbaum Associates.

Borman, W. C. (1979). Individual differences correlates of accuracy in evaluating others' performance effectiveness. *Applied Psychological Measurement, 3,* 103–115.

Bronfenbrenner, U., Harding, J., & Gallwey, M. (1958). The measurement of skill in social perception. In D. McClelland, A. L. Baldwin, U. Bronfenbrenner, & F. L. Strodtbeck (Eds.), *Talent and society: New perspectives in the identification of talent* (pp. 29–111). New York: Van Nostrand.

Campbell, D. T. (1955). An error in some demonstrations of the superior social perceptiveness of leaders. *Journal of Abnormal and Social Psychology, 51,* 694–695.

Cline, V. B. (1964). Interpersonal perception. In B. A. Maher (Ed.), *Progress in experimental personality research* (pp. 221–284). New York: Academic.

Colvin, C. R., Block, J., & Funder, D. C. (1995). Overly positive self-evaluations and personality: Negative implications for mental health. *Journal of Personality and Social Psychology, 68,* 1152–1162.

Colvin, C. R., & Funder, D. C. (1991). Predicting personality and behavior: A boundary on the acquaintanceship effect. *Journal of Personality and Social Psychology, 60,* 884–894.

Cook, M. (1979). *Perceiving others: The psychology of interpersonal perception*. London: Methuen.

Costanzo, M., & Archer, D. (1989). Interpreting the expressive behavior of others: The Interpersonal Perception Task. *Journal of Nonverbal Behavior, 13,* 225–245.

Cronbach, L. J. (1955). Processes affecting scores on "understanding of others" and "assumed similarity." *Psychological Bulletin, 52,* 177–193.

Cronbach, L. J., & Gleser, G. C. (1953). Assessing similarity between profiles. *Psychological Bulletin, 50,* 456–473.

Cronbach, L. J., & Meehl, P. E. (1955). Construct validity in psychological tests. *Psychological Bulletin, 52,* 281–302.

Crow, W. J., & Hammond, K. R. (1957). The generality of accuracy and response in interpersonal perception. *Journal of Abnormal and Social Psychology, 54,* 384–390.

Davis, M. H., & Kraus, L. A. (1997). Personality and empathic accuracy. In W. Ickes (Ed.), *Empathic accuracy* (pp. 144–168). New York: Guilford.

Dymond, R. F. (1948). A preliminary investigation of the relation of insight and empathy. *Journal of Consulting Psychology, 12,* 228–233.

Dymond, R. F. (1949). A scale for the measurement of empathic ability. *Journal of Consulting Psychology, 13,* 127–133.

Dymond, R. F. (1950). Personality and empathy. *Journal of Consulting Psychology, 14,* 343–350.

Flink, C., & Park, B. (1991). Increasing consensus in trait judgments through outcome dependency. *Journal of Experimental Social Psychology, 27,* 453–467

Funder, D. C. (1995). On the accuracy of personality judgment: A realistic approach. *Psychological Review, 102,* 652–670.

Funder, D. C. (1997). *The personality puzzle*. New York: Norton.

Funder, D. C. (1999). *Personality judgment: A realistic approach to person perception*. San Diego, CA: Academic.

Funder, D. C., & Colvin, C. R. (1991). Explorations in behavioral consistency: Properties of persons, situations, and behaviors. *Journal of Personality and Social Psychology, 60,* 773–794.

Funder, D. C., & Colvin, C. R. (1997). Congruence of self and others' judgments of personality. In R. Hogan, J. A. Johnson & S. R. Briggs (Eds.), Handbook of personality psychology (pp. 617–647). San Diego, CA: Academic.

Funder, D. C., Furr, M., & Colvin, C. R. (in press). The Riverside Behavioral Q-sort: A tool for the description of social behavior. Journal of Personality.

Gage, N. L., & Cronbach, L. J. (1955). Conceptual and methodological problems in interpersonal perception. Psychological Review, 62, 411–422.

Hall, J. A. (1978). Gender effects in decoding nonverbal cues. Psychological Bulletin, 85, 845–857.

Hastorf, A. H., & Bender, I. E. (1952). A caution respecting the measurement of empathic ability. Journal of Abnormal and Social Psychology, 47, 574–576.

Hastorf, A. H., Bender, I. E., & Weintraub, D. J. (1955). The influence of response patterns on the "refined empathy score." Journal of Abnormal and Social Psychology, 51, 341–343.

Ickes, W. (1993). Empathic accuracy. Journal of Personality, 61, 587–610.

Kenny, D. A. (1991). A general model of consensus and accuracy in interpersonal perception. Psychological Review, 92, 155–163.

Kenny, D. A. (1994). Interpersonal perception: A social relations analysis. New York: Guilford.

Leigh, J., Westen, D., Barends, A., & Mendel, M. (1992). Assessing complexity of representations of people from TAT and interview data. Journal of Personality, 60, 809–837.

Rosenthal, R., Hall, J. A., DiMatteo, M. R., Rogers, P. L., & Archer, D. (1979). Sensitivity to nonverbal communication: The PONS test. Baltimore: Johns Hopkins University Press.

Spence, J. T., & Helmreich, R. L. (1978). Masculinity and femininity. Austin, TX: University of Texas Press.

Taft, R. (1955). The ability to judge people. Psychological Bulletin, 52, 1–23.

Vernon, P. E. (1933). Some characteristics of the good judge of personality. Journal of Social Psychology, 4, 42–57.

Vogt, D. S., & Colvin, C. R. (1999). The good judge of personality: Gender differences, personality correlates, and Cronbachian "artifacts." Manuscript submitted for publication.

# ❧ 4 ❧

# Judging Rapport: Employing Brunswik's Lens Model to Study Interpersonal Sensitivity

Frank J. Bernieri
*University of Toledo*

John S. Gillis
*Oregon State University*

rapport *n.* 1. relationship or communication, esp. when useful and harmonious.

—*The Concise Oxford Dictionary, 1995*

Participants showing up for a psychological study on "Social Interaction" are greeted by an experimenter and told that in a few minutes they will be led in to a room where they will be seated next to another participant of the opposite sex whom they have never met. They are informed that they will be video-taped in a few different activities with their partner and at various points will be asked to report confidentially on how they are getting along. As they take their seats a few feet apart from each other—on armless typing chairs that roll easily—the experimenter tells them to introduce themselves and to get acquainted for a few minutes while she prepares for the study to begin. When the time comes, the participants are told they are to imagine that the Department of Psychology is going to provide them with $20,000 to travel around the world together as part of an investigation on relationship formation. They are asked to plan a trip around the world. Their only guidelines are that they must travel together (i.e., arrive and leave the same city at the same time taking the same

67

mode of transportation) and they must make it back home using no more than their allotted funds. They are given a large map of the world and $20,000 in play money and are asked to estimate the cost for each leg of the journey.

The map is picked up and unfolded. Someone grabs the pile of money. The inevitable question is asked, "Ok, where would you like to go?" Some dyads spend over 30 minutes squeezing in as many far-off locations as they can, demonstrating their prowess for shoestring budget travel. Their discussion becomes almost frenetic and slips into the absurd. "We can catch a fishing boat in Calcutta and hitch a ride to Bangladesh for free," the man declares. "I heard you can *do* that. It won't cost us anything. It will be great!" To an outside observer there is an apparent shared reluctance for these two to spend that last few hundred dollars that will get them home and end their fantasy journey.

Trips planned by other dyads are not so exotic. A woman in one pair grabs the remaining money after only 5 minutes, and as she plunks it down on Paris declares, "There! That'll do it. We go to Paris where we'll spend the rest. We're done," leaving her male partner gawking silently at the pile of play money strewn across Europe. Trip over. The participants in the first interaction reported being involved, interested, focused, attentive, friendly, cooperative, harmonious, and not awkward or frustrated. In short they achieved and enjoyed a good deal of *rapport* during their brief encounter. The participants in the latter interaction did not (Bernieri, Davis, Rosenthal, & Knee, 1994).

These interactions took place in a study investigating the behavioral manifestation of rapport (Bernieri et al., 1994; Bernieri, Gillis, Davis, & Grahe, 1996). Initially, the goal was to learn how rapport was manifest in expressive behavior. Over time, however, we became as interested in how outside observers judged rapport as we were in how rapport was expressed and revealed. We used Brunswik's Lens Model (Brunswik, 1956, 1966) as the organizing framework with which we examined simultaneously the expression of rapport and its accurate perception by others (see also Hammond & Stewart, in press). The lens model approach to the study of rapport has led to many insights regarding the expression of social constructs and their perception by others. In this chapter we summarize our research program, discuss the issues involved in the judgment of rapport, and relate them to the more general phenomenon of interpersonal sensitivity.

## THE CONSTRUCT OF RAPPORT

The very first issue in examining interpersonal sensitivity and social judgment accuracy involves knowing and defining the psychological construct that is being judged. In this regard, rapport is distinct from most constructs commonly considered because it applies to relationships, not people. Rapport exists between people, not within them. It is not an emotion or internal state. Rapport is a social construct that must be defined at the level of a dyad or larger group.

When rapport is felt within a group or with another person it is not in the same sense as anger or happiness is felt, for these are privately experienced internal states. Rather, rapport is a type of pleasant, engaging, and harmonious connection that exists between those interacting. The connection does not belong to only one individual but has as many points of contact as there are people contributing to it. In a sense, each individual has access only to their share of rapport. Each can only estimate the true and complete nature of the rapport (i.e., as it is experienced by all interactants) by extrapolating from their own direct experience. Although rapport is thought of as being shared by two people, it is a fact that although they each undoubtedly contribute to the total rapport between them, they are not likely to experience it and interpret it in exactly the same way. It is not a private internal state to which they both are privy but rather a condition characterizing the relation between them.

In terms of its content, rapport has been described as being composed of several subjectively and objectively defined components (Bernieri et al., 1994; Tickle-Degnen & Rosenthal, 1987, 1990). Most obviously, rapport feels good. Therefore, an important component involves the degree of positive affect being experienced. Another aspect of rapport involves a mutual focus of attention. It can be focused on the conversation at hand or on an external stimulus, such as a map. Finally, rapport is a harmonious relation that feels easy, smooth, and coordinated. People experiencing rapport demonstrate a degree of psychological and physiological coordination, symmetry, and closeness (Bernieri et al., 1994). Together, these three attributes of (a) positive affect, (b) mutual focus of attention, and (c) harmony constitute the construct of rapport, which this chapter discusses.

## BRUNSWIK'S LENS MODEL

Interpersonal sensitivity can be thought of as a specific case of a more general perception process where organisms need to perceive and respond effectively to the natural ecologies within which they live. Brunswik's (1956, 1966) description of the functioning and interrelationship of the ecology and the perceiving organism is represented most succinctly in his lens model (see Fig. 4.1). In essence, the model describes an organism that is not in direct contact with the distal stimuli it must respond to and react with. It has access only to a field of perceptual cues that emanate from the target stimulus. Unfortunately, these cues are imperfect indicators of the stimulus to be perceived and thus provide only probabilistic information regarding the identification or existence of the stimulus to be perceived. Furthermore, there may be much redundancy of the information conveyed by multiple cues. The perceiver's task is to assess a stimulus from mediated information about the target that is characterized by redundancy and uncertainty. According to Brunswik,

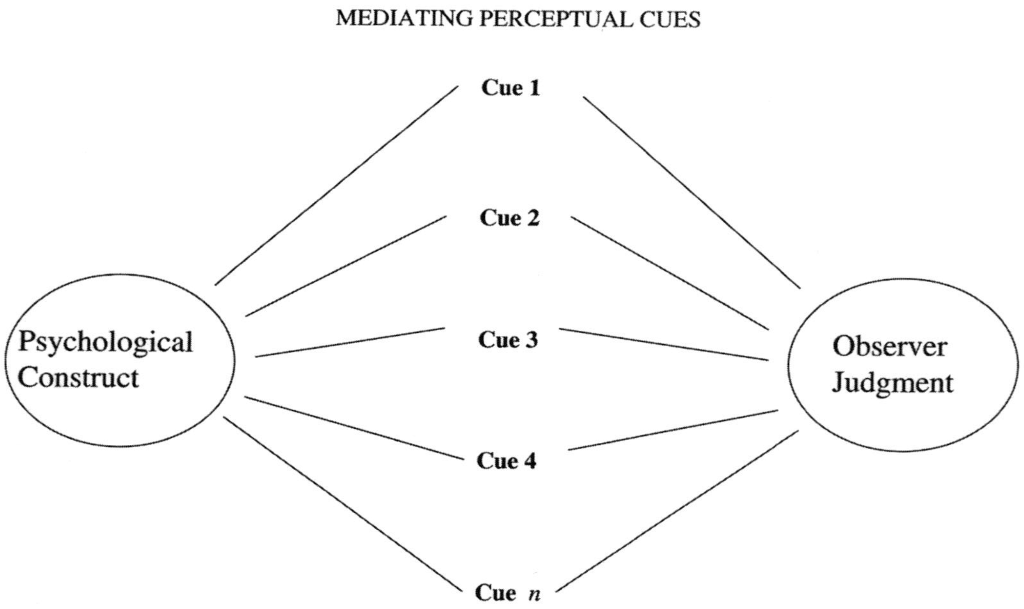

MEDIATING PERCEPTUAL CUES

FIG. 4.1   Generic lens diagram. The cues represent any feature that can be operationalized and measured within the behavioral stream. The empirical relationships observed between each cue and the observer's judgment and the relevant psychological construct are indicated by solid lines.

the general pattern of the mediational strategy of the organism is predicated upon the limited ecological validity or trustworthiness of cues.... This forces a probabilistic strategy upon the organism. To improve its bet it must accumulate and combine cues.... Hence the lens-like model ... which may be taken to represent the basic unit of psychological functioning. (1956, p. 20)

The lens model thus presents a schema in which the basic unit of perceiver and target can be studied with its probabilistic contingencies (see also Hammond & Stewart, in press).

Heider (1958) proposed Brunswik's scheme as the basic model for interpersonal perception in that it took account of the perceptual arc linking two end points: the object or person to be perceived and the percept itself, the way the object appeared to the perceiver. Furthermore, it allowed causal analyses to be made of both the ecological and perceiver's systems. That is, it guided the study of the relationships between mediators or behavioral manifestations of personality and both the "inner" personality processes themselves and the manner in which they are organized by the perceiver.

Scherer (1977) observed that the model was especially appropriate for the study of nonverbal behavior because it involved the expression, information transmission, and impression aspects of the communication process. Others have explored the utility of applying this framework directly in studying the perception of personality traits (Funder & Sneed, 1993; Gifford, 1994) and motivation (Gifford, Ng, & Wilkinson, 1985). Moreover, Brunswik's lens model has been an important inspiration in the development of more recent person perception models that acknowledge that in order to understand interpersonal perception one must understand, or at least be interested in, the things being perceived (Funder, 1995, chap. 16, this volume; Jones, 1990; Trope, 1986).

The remainder of this chapter summarizes some of the findings from a program of research that examined (a) how rapport was encoded within thin slices of the behavioral stream (see also, Ambady, Bernieri, & Richeson, 2000), (b) how observer judgments covaried with various cues embedded in the behavioral stream, (c) how the accuracy of rapport judgments were a function of various features of the stimuli observed, and (d) some potential moderator variables and individual differences of rapport judgment accuracy.

## RAPPORT AND ITS JUDGMENT

### Criterion

Although the establishment of a valid accuracy criterion may not be needed to examine the process of perception (Tagiuri, 1958), it is absolutely essential for evaluating the success or accuracy of perception (Funder, 1995; Kenny, 1994; Kruglanski, 1989; Swann, 1984).

We based our operationalization of rapport on the theoretical and empirical work by Tickle-Degnen and Rosenthal (1987, 1990). That is, we defined rapport as a composite construct made up of three distinct subconstructs that were free to vary independently but were likely to correlate naturally across the varying social ecology. Furthermore, we reasoned that the interactants themselves would be able to provide the most valid data regarding the assessment of these distinct subconstructs, even if they each could not provide the most comprehensive assessment of the complete construct.

Specifically, an 18-item rapport questionnaire was developed that asked each participant to assess his or her interaction on various items: (a) positive affect, (b) mutual focus, and (c) coordination and harmony. The 18 items can be found in Bernieri et al. (1994). Factor analyses failed to confirm the three-factor structure hypothesized, generating instead a single factor solution which we interpreted as rapport.[1] The reliability for this 18-item scale was correspondingly high (Cronbach's alpha = .94). The failure to confirm three independent factors was not completely unexpected in the present context. Although one can imagine situations in which interpersonal coordination and positive affect might differ markedly (e.g., among a medical team in a busy hospital emergency room), within the getting-acquainted social context examined, these features are likely to be more closely associated.

As stated earlier, the rapport experienced by two or more people interacting is not perfectly or completely assessed by any one member because the rapport itself does not reside within the members so much as it exists between or throughout them. Therefore, if self-reports are to be used as criteria for rapport they must be collected from every member within the interacting group. This raises the issue of interpartner reliability of rapport. In the study described in this chapter and reported in Bernieri et al. (1996), the self-reports of rapport correlated significantly but not impressively. The approximate correlation between reports of rapport within an interaction was .30, and this correlation varied across contexts. Reports of rapport correlated more strongly after the participants completed a subsequent debate with each other than they did after the initial trip-planning interaction. This increase in interpartner reliability of reporting rapport after the second interaction activity could have been the result of either an increase in acquaintance with their partner or because the adversarial context was more relevant to the rapport construct. In other words, psychological constructs relating to how well two people get along may be more relevant in the context of conflict than in any other mutual activity (Gottman, 1998; Gottman & Levenson, 1988). As Funder (1995, chap. 16, this volume) noted, some contexts will be more relevant to the expression of a given trait (or

---

[1]Although the initial published report (Bernieri et al., 1994) presented seven different sub-scores from the rapport questionnaire, their intercorrelations were still quite high. Furthermore, the redundancy in results from subsequent analyses provided compelling evidence to collapse the entire scale into a single composite item representing rapport.

social construct) than others. When relevance is high, so too should be the construct's expression. Of course, the observability of this expression to outside observers is another matter.

## The Encoding and Potential Mediation of Rapport

The next step in a lens model analysis is to identify the observable cues that have predictive covarying relationships to the criterion and thus are potentially available for a perceiver to use in assessment of the criterion. The procedures here are patterned after the general methodological procedures outlined in Beal, Gillis, and Stewart (1978). The cues considered in Bernieri et al. (1996) consisted of all nonverbal features of the recorded interactions that (a) could be coded reliably from relatively brief samples (i.e., less than 60 s) of behavior taken from the entire interaction and (b) had a theoretical, empirical, or intuitive relevance to rapport.

A meta-analysis by Ambady and Rosenthal (1992) revealed that the information contained within very brief samples (30 s or less) of the behavioral stream can be powerfully predictive of various behavioral outcomes including relationship status (see also Ambady, LaPlante, & Johnson, chap. 5, this volume; Ambady et al., 2000). Furthermore, increasing the length of the behavioral stream analyzed does not appear to increase its predictive validity (Ambady & Rosenthal, 1992; Ambady et al., 2000). For at least some subset of important behavioral and social outcomes, a thin slice of an entire interaction can contain as much predictive validity as a much larger slice.

From the stimulus tape containing video clips from 50 dyadic interactions, we coded a comprehensive set of potential behavioral cues to rapport (e.g., the number of times interactants smiled, the distance they chose to sit from their partners, the number of nervous behaviors they exhibited). Eventually, more than seventy distinct features were coded reliably. Because of the high intercorrelations among some of the coded features (duration and frequency of smiles for example), this list was reduced to a final set of 17 composite cues. The Appendix lists the cues along with their general descriptions. At this point it was possible to determine how interactant rapport was manifest or revealed via the nonverbal expressive behavior that characterized the behavioral stream. Simple zero-order correlation coefficients were computed to assess each cue-to-criterion relationship. In addition, multiple regression analyses determined the predictive strength of various subsets of cues.

Rapport during the trip-planning activity increased as interactants sat closer to one another and when their physical movements appeared more synchronous and coordinated (see Bernieri et al., 1994, and Bernieri & Rosenthal, 1991, for discussions of synchrony). Many more correlates of rapport were found in the second activity where the interactants were debating. Here, in addition to interpersonal proximity and movement synchrony, rapport was higher when interactants were talkative, exhibited head-nodding and responsive "hmms," increased their mutual eye contact, decreased their posture shifts, and sat back in their chairs. It is noteworthy to point out what nonverbal features did not encode rapport. Smiling, physical attractiveness, nervousness, orientation, and expressivity (general animation and activity level) showed no significant predictive relationship with reported rapport.

Multiple regression analyses performed on data from both interaction contexts showed that despite coding only 50-s slices taken from interactions ranging in length from 5 to 30 min, over half of the rapport criterion variance could be accounted for by subsets of three cues (i.e., Multiple $R > .70$).[2] Thus, rapport was encoded quite strongly within the targets' nonverbal behavior. Rapport is a social construct that generated a number of potential perceptual mediators, which is a necessary prerequisite for examining the right side of the lens model involving observer sensitivity or accuracy with respect to judgments.

## The Perception of Rapport

At this point the utility of the lens model becomes apparent. Knowing the empirical relationship between the observable attributes of a social stimulus and the psychological criterion under investigation allows a researcher to describe empirically the relationship between the judgment, criterion, and potential observable cues that mediate the accurate perception of that criterion. In this case, we know that observer judgments of rapport will be most accurate when they correlate with the targets' proximity to one another, their synchronizing, and positive responsivity to one another through head-nodding and "hmms" but not when their judgments correlate with smiling or target expressivity.

Bernieri et al. (1996) had 45 observers view the 50-s video clips of the targets debating and asked them to judge rapport. After a brief definition of rapport they were asked to rate how well the two targets were enjoying the interaction and how much they liked each other. In subsequent studies (Bernieri & Grahe, 1998; Gillis, Bernieri, & Wooten, 1995), where observers were asked to rate "rapport" explicitly, the data yielded virtually identical results. Observer judgments of rapport correlated significantly with targets' proximity, expressivity, smiling, and positive responsivity (head-nods and "hmms"). Thus, observer judgments covaried with two behavioral indicators of rapport (proximity and positive responsivity) and two nonpredictors.

Figure 4.2 displays the results in the form of a lens diagram. The solid lines on the left side of the figure represent significant relationships between the rapport criterion and the adjoining cue. The lines on the right side of the figure represent the significant relationships between the coded cues and observers' judg-

---

[2]More sophisticated nonlinear models are also possible (e.g., Cooksey, 1996).

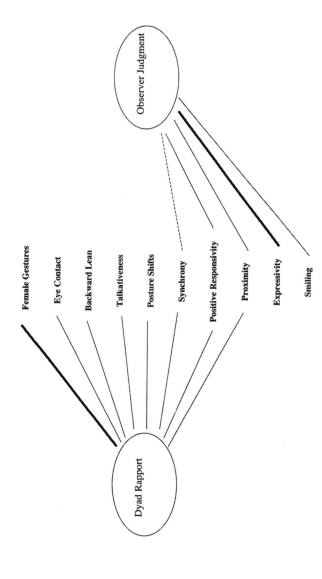

FIG. 4.2   Lens diagram of rapport in the debate context. Significant empirical relationships between coded cues, dyad rapport, and observer judgments are indicated by solid lines. A darkened line indicates the cue bearing the strongest relationship, whereas a dotted line indicates a near-significant empirical relationship.

ment. Cue-to-judgment correlations were computed separately for each observer. The lens diagram displays the mean effects for a cue-to-judgment relationship across a sample of judges. Mean effect sizes are computed by first transforming each effect size $r$ to its corresponding Fisher's $z$. The average Fisher's $z$ across a sample can then be converted back to a Pearson $r$ for interpretation (Rosenthal & Rosnow, 1991). Cues that do not correlate either with observer judgment or the rapport criterion are not included in the lens diagram. Visual inspection of the diagram reveals that rapport during the debates was encoded richly (i.e., redundantly) within thin slices of the behavioral stream but was perceived more simply by observers. In fact, multiple regression analyses indicated that no other coded cue predicted observer judgments significantly after taking into account the effect of expressivity.

When another sample of observers viewed the same targets in another context, planning a trip around the world, their judgments of rapport correlated significantly with expressivity and female gestures. Judgments covaried moderately with smiling and synchrony as well, but these correlations just failed to reach significance (see Fig. 4.3). The authors concluded from these results (and the dozen nonsignificant correlations that replicated across contexts) that observer judgments of rapport appear to be consistent across contexts. In other words, observer judgments of rapport seem to be a function of how expressive, how synchronous, and how happy two people appear to be. Such a judgment policy would reflect a corresponding and reasonable implicit theory of relationships and rapport. Two people who get along well with each other smile a lot (enjoy being together), are synchronous (do not look awkward), and are expressive (affectively and behaviorally uninhibited). Furthermore, this implicit judgment policy for estimating rapport seemed to be relatively unchanging across interaction contexts observers judged. The set of 17 cue-to-judgment correlations found within the debate context correlated well (.98) with the set of 17 cue-to-judgment correlations found within the trip planning context (Bernieri et al., 1996). Clearly the two samples of observers had judged rapport in a similar manner.

## Rapport Judgment Consensus

An important issue in interpersonal sensitivity involves the level of consensus between observers (Funder, 1995; Kruglanski, 1989; Swann, 1984). The higher the consensus, the easier it becomes for social perceivers to confirm and validate their perceptions by sharing them with others. Bernieri and Gillis (1995a) reported that the intraclass reliability of the rapport judgments reported in Bernieri et al. (1996) was .46. An intraclass correlation in this instance can be interpreted as estimating the expected correlation between the rapport judgments of any two observers selected at random (see also Rosenthal, 1987). This level of agreement is fairly high in thin-slice judgment research (Ambady et al.,

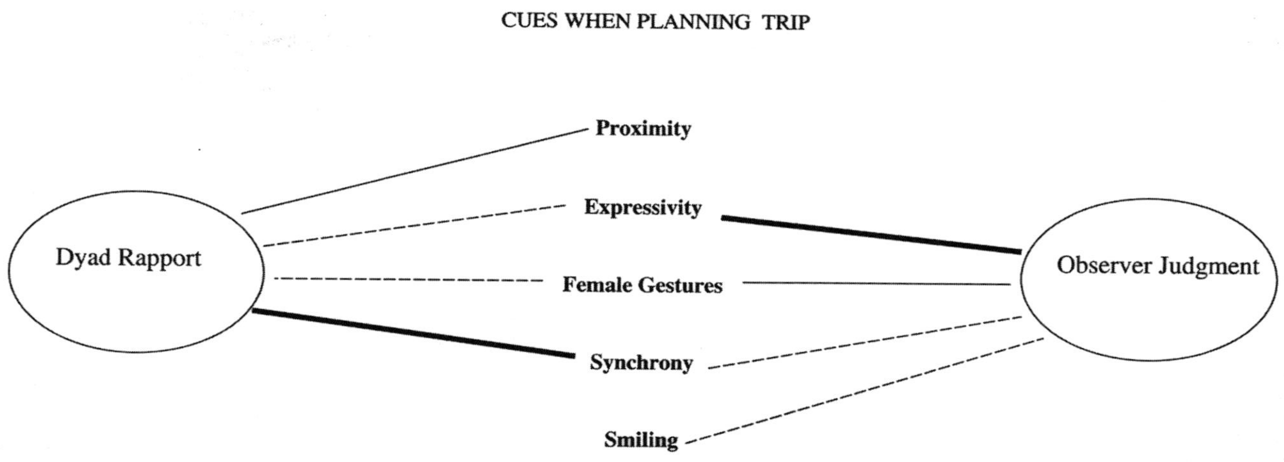

CUES WHEN PLANNING TRIP

FIG. 4.3   Lens diagram of rapport in the trip-planning context. Significant empirical relationships between coded cues, dyad rapport, and observer judgments are indicated by solid lines. A dark line indicates the cue bearing the strongest relationship, whereas a dotted line indicates a near-significant empirical relationship.

2000). It is also notably higher than the level of agreement found between the targets themselves. Similar levels of agreement have been found in subsequent samples (Bernieri & Grahe, 1998). Even cross-cultural samples of observers judging the rapport in the American targets described here have generated similar levels of consensus (Bernieri & Gillis, 1995a; Bernieri et al., 1999). Thus, it would seem that people agree in their perceptions of rapport at least when it is based on thin slices of the behavioral stream.

## Rapport Judgment Accuracy and Criterion Reliability

For each observer a correlation between rapport judgment and the target criterion across the 50 target dyads was computed. This correlation between judgment and criterion is a measure of perceptual achievement, the covariation of judgment with the rapport criterion being studied. For our purposes, it also represents a measure of rapport judgment accuracy (i.e., sensitivity). Accuracy ranged from a low of -.12 to a high of .54 across the 45 observers of the debates. The mean across all observers was .19. The $t$-test against zero for the sample of accuracy coefficients was significant. Across the 52 observers of the trip planning interactions, the mean accuracy achieved was .29, significantly higher than the accuracy achieved for observers of the debates.

These results should puzzle some psychometrically minded readers, especially those interested in accuracy issues. One would expect accuracy to increase as internal consistency of the rapport criterion increased. In other words, the higher the agreement between the two partners' self-reports of dyad rapport, the more reliable is their dyad mean self-report and thus the more valid a measure it is and the more strongly it should be predicted from observer judgments. Because targets showed higher agreement in their reports of rapport in the debate activity ($r = .37$) than when planning a trip ($r = .20$) one would expect the mean of these self-reports to be more stable and thus more predictable. In fact, accuracy in predicting the more internally consistent rapport criterion observed during the debating activity was lower than that found during the trip planning activity.

How can judgments be more predictive of a criterion when the apparent criterion reliability—and presumably its validity—decreases? The confusion lies in the fact that there often exists a multitude of ways in which the consistency (i.e., reliability) of a variable can be defined and assessed. Furthermore, these different measures of consistency may be unrelated to each other mathematically. For example, the tendency for a test to agree with itself over time is not necessarily determined by its internal consistency, and vice versa. One form of reliability does not substitute for another. The nature of the construct being assessed along with its network of theoretical relationships to other constructs determines which aspect of reliability is most relevant to its validity. For assessing affective states, for example, it is less relevant to establish temporal stability (e.g., day-to-day, week-to-week, or even hour-to-hour consistency) because the construct being assessed is expected to change over time. Temporal stability is more relevant for multifaceted dispositional constructs where the establishment of stable predictive relationships is paramount. In some cases (love and intelligence, for example) the intercorrelations between constituent subconstructs, although theoretically interesting, are not nearly as critical to the validity of the global construct as is its predictive utility.

For a construct like rapport that is defined at the dyad (or group) level, the information provided by both interactants is essential. Apparently, the level of agreement between the contributing sources is not a powerful determinant of its predictive utility (i.e., validity). For some reason yet to be determined, it was easier for our observers to correctly judge the mean self-reported rapport of people planning a trip than when they debated, although partner self-reports showed less agreement in this context.

The lens model becomes useful in this instance because it provides clues as to what may be happening. An inspection of Figures 4.2 and 4.3 shows that although there were fewer cues to rapport within the trip planning context, the concordance between the cues that drove observer judgments and the cues that were diagnostic of the criterion was higher in that context. In effect, the judgment policy of observers (i.e., their apparent implicit theory of rapport) more accurately reflected the true manifestation of the construct. Therefore, outside observers were more interpersonally sensitive to rapport in that context than in the debating context.

## Analyzing the Consensus Judgment Versus Individual Judgments

An additional methodological note is worth making. A true lens model analysis is performed on the judgment data generated by a single observer judging a single attribute over several stimulus trials (Beal et al., 1978; Bernieri et al., 1996). The outcome is a judgment policy of a single perceiver or judge. However, this framework can be used to model group mean consensus judgments on thin-slice stimuli as well (e.g., Gifford, 1994; Gifford & Hine, 1994). The distinction here is whether a researcher combines the judgments of all perceivers first and models the group mean judgment or chooses instead to model the judgments of each perceiver individually first, and then summarize the results across the observed sample.

The difference between these methodological procedures is noteworthy for interpersonal sensitivity researchers in both their interpretation and application (Bernieri & Gillis, 1995a; Bernieri et al., 1996; Hall & Carter, 1999). Group mean judgments will be more reliable and potentially more predictive of any given criterion than judgments from any single individual (Rosenthal, 1987). Thus, the accuracy or predictive utility of consensus (group mean) judgments will almost certainly overestimate the level that takes place for a typical individual.

In addition, it is not a mathematical necessity for the mean of a group of perceivers to represent or reflect the modal pattern of responses over a series of trials. Therefore, when the group mean consensus is modeled there might not be a single individual within that group for whom that consensus model applies. Therefore, the decision to analyze a pooled judgment over the individual observer judgments should be governed entirely on whether the goal of the research is to describe a group judgment or the judgment of a typical member within a given group.

## MODERATORS OF RAPPORT
## JUDGMENT ACCURACY

Across a number of studies run in our labs we have found that rapport judgment accuracy, defined as the correlation between an observer's judgments of rapport and the rapport criterion across a number of target dyads, typically ranges from .00 to .50 within any given sample with a central tendency around .20. There is plenty of variation to allow for moderator variables. Surprisingly, we have yet to uncover a robust moderator.

### Individual Differences

The initial sample of 45 observers (Bernieri et al., 1996) was assessed on a number of different individual-difference measures including, but not limited to, personality traits, paper-and-pencil measures of empathy and social sensitivity, performance measures of interpersonal sensitivity, and intelligence. The complete set of results is reported in Bernieri and Gillis (1995b). Rapport judgment accuracy did not correlate significantly with any of the hypothesized individual differences. In fact, only two significant predictors were found in the entire battery of moderator variables examined. However, the number of moderator variables tested increases Type I error in this instance so the reliability of these significant results is suspect. In an unpublished report, Gesn, Bernieri, Gada-Jain, and Grahe (1999) replicated the general failure to find hypothesized predictors of rapport judgment accuracy.

### Exposure Length

Some may think it remarkable that observers of a mere 50-s slice of an ongoing interaction can judge rapport at a level of accuracy above that which can be attributable to chance. Rapport may not be among the most sophisticated or complex of psychological constructs, but it is still impressive that it can be perceived almost immediately by an untrained outside observer. As a psychological construct detectable within thin slices, it joins the many others identified by

Ambady et al. (2000) in their review. But how thin is "thin?" And how much better could judgments be if they were based on the entire interaction sequence that extended from the initial greeting to the ultimate exit?

Bernieri and Grahe (1998) had a small group of observers watch the entire archive of videotapes from which the 50-s slices had been extracted. This meant that observers watched each dyad for as long as 60 minutes. They saw everything from the initial greeting, through the two interaction activities, right up to point when the experimenter sends the two targets home. Perhaps surprisingly, judgments of rapport were not significantly more accurate when based on the observation of the entire interaction than when based on a mere 50-s clip. In other words, there was no apparent gain to be had from watching the whole interaction sequence. Fifty seconds apparently contained all the information that observers could use. Bernieri and Grahe (1998) then shortened the length of the slices to 30 s, 20 s, 10 s, and 5 s. They found that reducing the exposure to 5–10 s had little effect on rapport judgment accuracy when observing targets plan a trip around the world and had only a small detrimental effect on rapport judgment accuracy when observing a debate. When judging rapport from thin slices of the behavioral stream, size doesn't seem to matter.

The relative insensitivity of accuracy to the length of thin slice observed, together with the fact that a small set of nonverbal features coded in a 50-s slice of behavior predicted over 50% of the target criterion variance (Bernieri & Grahe, 1998), suggests that rapport must be encoded chronically within an individual's expressive behavior (DePaulo, 1992). In other words, within the contexts examined, rapport is not a verbally based construct. As was implied by Tickle-Degnen and Rosenthal's (1990) review, rapport is very much a nonverbal phenomenon.

## Channel of Communication

Grahe and Bernieri (1999) looked at rapport judgment accuracy as a function of the channel of communication within which it was observed. Their results were quite conclusive; accuracy was a function of whether observers had access to the nonverbal visual channel. Access to the verbal channel, either in the form of transcripts or speech, did not increase judgment accuracy. Of course, these results were expected given the empirical results from the lens model analyses diagrammed in Figures 4.2 and 4.3.

## Training

Gillis et al. (1995) attempted to increase judgment accuracy by instructing observers on what to look for when making their judgments. Because the significant predictors of rapport were well documented it was a simple matter to tell observers that rapport correlated with proximity and talkativeness but not with smiling or expressivity. The instruction manipulation failed to increase accuracy. Although observers reported during the debriefing that they understood and followed the instructions as best they could, little evidence was found to show that the covariance between judgments and target talkativeness increased or that the covariance between judgments and target expressivity decreased after instruction.

Another training procedure simply gave observers explicit quantitative feedback after each judgment trial. The true rapport criterion value, transformed into a simple 10-point scale, was provided to observers immediately after they made each rapport judgment. Although we did not show them how to make their judgments, they could tell immediately how accurate their judgments were after each trial throughout the entire 50-dyad series. The rapport accuracy within this group of observers did increase. Outcome feedback provided immediately after each judgment helped to improve rapport perception accuracy.

The results reported by Gillis et al. (1995) confirm previous research that failed to demonstrate that interpersonal perception accuracy from thin-slice displays can be improved by providing prior instruction as to how it should be done (Costanzo, 1992; Hoffman, 1964; Rosenthal, Hall, DiMatteo, Rogers, & Archer, 1979). They also provide evidence to suggest that rapport judgments—and perhaps many other interpersonal judgments—involve automatic processes, especially when based on thin slices of the behavioral stream.

Although impression formation, in general, seems to be relatively automatic, it is not necessarily unconscious. At least one study has shown that social perceivers can be aware of how of nonverbal cues influence their perception of others (Smith, Archer, & Costanzo, 1991). However, at least when examined within the context of detecting deception, the relationship between confidence and accuracy is generally quite low (DePaulo, Charlton, Cooper, Lindsay, & Muhlenbruck, 1997). Furthermore, although people may be aware of using behavioral cues in their intuitive judgments, they are often unable to articulate or to control their processing and usage of cues (Smith, et al., 1991). After nearly 8 years of debriefing our participants who have judged rapport in our own lab, we strongly concur with this last point. Thus, we suggest that the rapport judgments, and perhaps many other interpersonal judgments, are largely reflexive, automatic, and perceptual rather than reflective, controlled, and analytical.

## CONCLUSION

Our investigation of rapport and how observers assess it in others has led us to several conclusions. First, the quality of a social interaction that we refer to as rapport is a visible construct. People who are getting along well together look different from those who are not. Therefore, it makes sense to investigate (a) whether social observers are sensitive to this and can perceive it accurately, (b) how this is accomplished (i.e., what cues are responsible for its accurate perception), (c) whether there are any individual differences in rapport perception sensitivity, (d) whether there are consequences of its accurate perception or misperception, and if so, (e) whether rapport perception accuracy can be increased through training or some other intervention. Second, it has become apparent through our experiments that the perception of rapport may be unrelated to conscious deliberative analytical processing. In other words, along the continuum from perception to cognition, rapport judgment seems to be more of an automatic perception process than a deliberative, cognitive judgment process. The cues that appeared to drive rapport judgments did not change when the cues that encoded rapport changed across contexts. We found little to suggest that interpersonal sensitivity can be enhanced simply by instructing people on what to look for. Social acuity was increased through practice and outcome feedback, not by simple instruction.

Third, we have been impressed by the fact that interpersonal sensitivity to rapport does not generalize to other related performance tasks. Performance tasks that seem to be conceptually and methodologically related, such as the Profile of Nonverbal Sensitivity (PONS; Rosenthal et al., 1979; Hall, chap. 8, this volume) and the Interpersonal Perception Task (IPT; Archer & Costanzo, 1988; Archer, Costanzo, & Akert, chap. 9, this volume), do not correlate with rapport judgment accuracy (Bernieri & Gillis, 1995b; Gesn et al., 1999). Nor is rapport judgment accuracy well predicted by current paper-and-pencil measures of social acuity (Bernieri & Gillis, 1995b; Gesn et al., 1999; see also Riggio & Riggio, chap. 7, this volume).

Finally, we have found that interpersonal sensitivity can be studied objectively, precisely, and informatively. The method described here has three requirements: A researcher must (a) define and operationalize interpersonal constructs reasonably, (b) objectively identify and describe all relevant or important potential perceptual mediators,[3] and (c) collect from each observer multiple interpersonal judgments of the same interpersonal construct (i.e., rapport, in this example) across targets and ideally within different social contexts. By doing so a researcher can investigate the relationships between mediators or behavioral manifestations of interpersonal constructs and both the latent interpersonal processes themselves and the manner in which they are understood by the perceiver.

Any single approach to the study of interpersonal sensitivity is imperfect, and the lens model is not without limitations. For example, the lens model approach depends on observing many perceptual events, but it is not clear how any given social event should be defined and sampled (Ambady et al., 2000). In other words, we do not yet know what precisely constitutes a bounded social stimulus. A photograph, thin slice, a complete interaction, or some other social

---

[3] Although the discussion within this chapter has emphasized nonverbal features of interpersonal behavior, the lens model has been applied successfully to verbal data as well (Gifford & Hine, 1994).

behavioral unit might be more or less appropriate depending on the given research objectives. Also, the model as it was presented here is linear, and in the multivariate case, difficulties in interpretation can surface as cues become more intercorrelated.

A more fundamental limitation is that the model does not solve problems of criterion definition or cue operationalization. It is well beyond the scope of this chapter and edited volume to declare exactly how our personality and interpersonal constructs should be defined. It will forever remain a goal for psychologists, philosophers, and poets to work out a final definition for such things as love, rapport, well-being, and openness to experience. The reader must keep in mind that Brunswik's lens model does not attempt to define these constructs but merely describes the perception and judgment process once these constructs have been given an objective definition by the researcher. Thus, the outcome, interpretations, and conclusions based on lens model analyses will always be subject to criticisms involving the definition and operationalization of the psychological construct being investigated.

In this chapter we hope to have demonstrated the utility of applying Brunswik's lens model to the study of interpersonal sensitivity. Although a relatively simplistic framework within which to work, the model provides enormous potential for uncovering the mediation process connecting psychological constructs to their social judgment. For all its shortcomings we feel much can be learned, and has already been learned, from a Brunswikian approach to interpersonal perception and the study of interpersonal sensitivity.

## ACKNOWLEDGMENT

The work described in this chapter was supported by a grant from the National Science Foundation to Frank J. Bernieri.

## REFERENCES

Ambady, N., Bernieri, F., & Richeson, J. (2000). Towards a histology of social behavior: Judgmental accuracy from thin slices of the behavioral stream. *Advances in Experimental Social Psychology, 32,* 201–271.

Ambady, N., & Rosenthal, R. (1992). Thin slices of expressive behavior as predictors of interpersonal consequences: A meta-analysis. *Psychological Bulletin, 111,* 256–274.

Archer, D., & Costanzo, M. (1988). *The Interpersonal Perception Task.* Berkeley, CA: University of California Media Center.

Beal, D., Gillis, J. S., & Stewart, T. (1978). The lens model: Computational procedures and applications. *Perceptual and Motor Skills, 46,* 3–28.

Bernieri, F., Davis, J., Rosenthal, R., & Knee, C. (1994). Interactional synchrony and rapport: Measuring synchrony in displays devoid of sound and facial affect. *Personality and Social Psychology Bulletin, 20,* 303–311.

Bernieri, F., & Gillis, J. S. (1995a). The judgment of rapport: A cross-cultural comparison between Americans and Greeks. *Journal of Nonverbal Behavior, 19,* 115–130.

Bernieri, F., & Gillis, J. S. (1995b). Personality correlates of accuracy in a social perception task. *Perceptual and Motor Skills, 81,* 168–170.

Bernieri, F., Gillis, J. S., Davis, J. M., & Grahe, J. E. (1996). Dyad rapport and the accuracy of its judgment across situations: A lens model analysis. *Journal of Personality and Social Psychology, 71,* 110–129.

Bernieri, F., & Grahe, J. (1998, May). *Thin-slice samples of the behavioral stream: Validating their use in social psychological research.* Paper presented at the Midwestern Psychological Association Convention, Chicago.

Bernieri, F., Grahe, J. E., Gillis, J. S., Gada-Jain, N., Ahadi, S. A., El Hajje, R., Vance, M., Williams, K. D., & Yuliandari, E. (1999). *Varying cultures, similar judgment policies: A cross-cultural study of rapport perception.* Unpublished manuscript.

Bernieri, F., & Rosenthal, R. (1991). Coordinated movement in human interaction. In R. S. Feldman & B. Rimé (Eds.), *Fundamentals of nonverbal behavior* (pp. 401–432). New York: Cambridge University Press.

Brunswik, E. (1956). *Perception and the representative design of psychological experiments.* Berkeley, CA: University of California Press.

Brunswik, E. (1966). Reasoning as a universal behavior model and a functional differentiation between "perception" and "thinking." In K. R. Hammond (Ed.), *The psychology of Egon Brunswik* (pp. 487–513). New York: Holt, Rinehart & Winston.

Cooksey, R. W. (1996). *Judgment analysis: Theory, methods, and applications.* San Diego, CA: Academic.

Costanzo, M. (1992). Training students to decode verbal and nonverbal cues effects on confidence and performance. *Journal of Education Psychology, 84,* 308–313.

DePaulo, B. M. (1992). Nonverbal behavior and self-presentation. *Psychological Bulletin, 111,* 203–243.

DePaulo, B. M., Charlton, K., Cooper, H., Lindsay, J. L., & Muhlenbruck, L. (1997). The accuracy–confidence correlation in the detection of deception. *Personality and Social Psychology Review, 4,* 346–357.

Funder, D. C. (1995). On the accuracy of personality judgment: A realistic approach. *Psychological Review, 102,* 652–670.

Funder, D. C., & Sneed, C. D. (1993). Behavioral manifestations of personality: An ecological approach to judgmental accuracy. *Journal of Personality and Social Psychology, 64,* 479–490.

Gesn, P. R., Bernieri, F. J., Gada-Jain, N., & Grahe, J. E. (1999, May). *Domains of interpersonal sensitivity: Performance accuracy and psychometric assessment of ability.* Paper presented at the Midwestern Psychological Association Convention, Chicago.

Gifford, R. (1994). A lens-mapping framework for understanding the encoding and decoding of interpersonal dispositions in nonverbal behavior. *Journal of Personality and Social Psychology, 66,* 398–412.

Gifford, R., & Hine, D. W. (1994). The role of verbal behavior in the encoding and decoding of interpersonal dispositions. *Journal of Research in Personality, 28,* 115–132.

Gifford, R., Ng, C. F., & Wilkinson, M. (1985). Nonverbal cues in the employment interview: Links between applicant qualities and interviewer judgments. *Journal of Applied Psychology, 70,* 729–736.

Gillis, J., Bernieri, F., & Wooten, E. (1995). The effects of stimulus medium and feedback on the judgment of rapport. *Organizational Behavior and Human Decision Processes, 63,* 33–45.

Gottman, J. M. (1998). Psychology and the study of marital processes. *Annual Review of Psychology, 49,* 169–197.

Gottman, J. M., & Levenson, R. W. (1998). The social psychophysiology of marriage. In P. Noller & M. A. Fitzpatrick (Eds.), *Perspectives on marital interaction*. Clevedon, England: *Multilingual Matters*, pp. 182–200.

Grahe, J. E., & Bernieri, F. J. (1999). The importance of nonverbal cues in judging rapport. *Journal of Nonverbal Behavior. 23*, 253–269.

Hall, J. A., & Carter, J. D. (1999). Gender-stereotype accuracy as an individual difference. *Journal of Personality and Social Psychology, 77*, 350–359.

Hammond, K. R., & Stewart, T. R. (Eds.). (in press). *The essential Brunswik: Beginnings, explications, applications*. Oxford, England: Oxford University Press.

Heider, F. (1958). *The psychology of interpersonal relations*. Hillsdale, NJ: Lawrence Erlbaum Associates.

Hoffman, M. (1964). *The effects of training on the judgment of nonverbal behavior: An experimental study*. Unpublished doctoral dissertation, Harvard University, Cambridge, MA.

Jones, E. E. (1990). *Interpersonal perception*. New York: Freeman.

Kenny, D. A. (1994). *Interpersonal perception: A social relations analysis*. New York: Guilford.

Kruglanski, A. W. (1989). The psychology of being "right": The problem of accuracy in social perception and cognition. *Psychological Bulletin, 106*, 395–409.

Rosenthal, R. (1987). *Judgment studies: Design, analysis, and meta-analysis*. Cambridge, England: Cambridge University Press.

Rosenthal, R., Hall, J. A., DiMatteo, M. R., Rogers, P. L. & Archer, D. (1979). *Sensitivity to nonverbal communication: The PONS test*. Baltimore: Johns Hopkins University Press.

Rosenthal, R., & Rosnow, R. L. (1991). *Essentials of behavioral research: Methods and data analysis* (2nd ed.). New York: McGraw-Hill.

Scherer, K. R. (1977). Methods of research on vocal communication: Paradigms and parameters. In K. R. Scherer & P. Ekman (Eds.), *Handbook of methods in nonverbal behavior research* (pp. 136–198). Cambridge, England: Cambridge University Press.

Smith, H. J., Archer, D., & Costanzo, M. (1991). "Just a hunch": Accuracy and awareness in person perception. *Journal of Nonverbal Behavior, 15*, 3–17.

Swann, W. B. (1984). Quest for accuracy in person perception: A matter of pragmatics. *Psychological Review, 91*, 457–477.

Tagiuri, R. (1958). Introduction. In R. Tagiuri & L. Petrullo (Eds.), *Person perception and interpersonal behavior* (pp. ix–xvii). Stanford, CA: Stanford University Press.

Tickle-Degnen, L., & Rosenthal, R. (1987). Group rapport and nonverbal behavior. *Review of Personality and Social Psychology, 9*, 113–136.

Tickle-Degnen, L., & Rosenthal, R. (1990). The nature of rapport and its nonverbal correlates. *Psychological Inquiry, 1*, 285–293.

Trope, Y. (1986). Identification and inferential processes in dispositional attribution. *Psychological Review, 93*, 239–257.

## APPENDIX

## Descriptions of the Perceptual Cues
## Coded in Bernieri et al. (1996)

1. *Adaptors* refer to manipulations of one's own body such as rubbing, scratching, preening, and, in the present study, rhythmically swiveling the chair back and forth.

2. *Expressivity* was a rated dimension that referred to the extent to which an individual's total behavior was active, animated, and exaggerated. Raters were told, for example, that people who are expressive show their emotions quite readily, whereas those who are not expressive tend to have "poker faces" and move very little.

3. *Mutual eye contact* refers to the amount of time the interactants were gazing into each other's eyes.

4. *Forward lean* refers to the total time spent by the interactants maintaining a postural configuration in which their head was forward of the upright, vertical position relative to their hips.

5. *Gestures* refer to nonverbal acts that have direct verbal translations (e.g., the "OK" sign) or are used to illustrate or punctuate speech (e.g., pointing and fist pounding).

6. *Mutual silence* refers to the total time spent in which interactant were simultaneously silent for periods longer than 1.5 s.

7. *Nervous behavior* was a rated variable. Raters were told that nervous behavior referred to any action or activity that suggested someone is scared, anxious, uncomfortable, or nervous (e.g., fidgeting, shaking, knees knocking, quivering voice, swallowing, and "freezing").

8. *Orientation* refers to the degree to which an individual's trunk was oriented directly toward his or her partner. This measure represents the average orientation of both interactants during the brief clip. Values for orientation increased as both interactants adopted a face-to-face orientation.

9. *Proximity* is a composite variable that represents the average distance separating the interactants' noses, chairs, and closest knees.

10. *Racial similarity* refers to the similarity of the racial composition of the interacting dyads. Although our sample contained African Americans, Asians, and Hispanics, racial match invariably meant that both interactants were Caucasian. Racial mismatch typically meant that one interactant was Caucasian and one was not. A dyad composed of one Hispanic and one Caucasian was coded as being more racially similar than a dyad that included a Caucasian and an African American or Asian.

11. *Back-channel responses* refer to head nods and "uh huhs."

12. *Smiling* refers to the total time spent by both interactants smiling and laughing.

13. *Synchrony* refers to the extent to which the behaviors and behavioral stream of each interactant were similar to and coordinated with each other (see Bernieri & Rosenthal, 1991). Manifestations of synchrony may take the form of posture mimicry, simultaneous movement, coordinated movement, or a combination of these.

14. *Attractiveness* refers to the dyad mean physical attractiveness of both interactants as rated by a group of naïve undergraduates.

15. *Attractiveness discrepancy* refers to the absolute difference between the rated physical attractiveness of each member of the dyad after standardizing within sex.

16. *Posture shifts* refers to the frequency with which the interactants changed their posture or appeared to shift their weight in the chair.

17. *Pointing* frequency refers to the number of times someone directed his or her partner's gaze to a specific location.

# ℬ 5 ℭ

# Thin-Slice Judgments as a Measure of Interpersonal Sensitivity

Nalini Ambady
Debi LaPlante
Elizabeth Johnson
*Harvard University*

Smooth, successful social interactions involve sensitivity to the feelings, affect, and behavior of others as well as to the ability to transmit and communicate cues in order to elicit desired responses from others. Thus, both the ability to judge and to be judged accurately serves an adaptive function in social interaction (Ambady, Hallahan, & Rosenthal, 1995). Consistent with our own experiences and intuitive judgments, research reveals that individuals exhibit high degrees of consensual accuracy in their judgments of others (Albright, Kenny, & Malloy, 1988; Funder, 1995; Kenny, Albright, Malloy, & Kashy, 1994; Passini & Norman, 1966; Paunonen, 1991; Watson, 1989). Such judgments have been found to be surprisingly accurate in predicting targets' self-reported characteristics on the basis of quite minimal information (Albright et al., 1988; Passini & Norman, 1966; Watson, 1989). This chapter discusses the implications of the interpretation of such minimal information, or "thin slices," of behavior for our understanding of interpersonal sensitivity. We define the characteristics of thin slices, discuss the methodology, describe two measures using thin slices to assess interpersonal sensitivity, review the moderators of interpersonal sensitivity as judged from thin slices, and suggest potential contributions of this methodology to the study of interpersonal sensitivity.

89

## DEFINING A THIN SLICE

Early research on expectancy effects has documented unambiguously that people can sense the subtle, unstated expectations that other people have of them and that people behave according to those expectations (Rosenthal, 1966, 1991; Rosenthal & Jacobson, 1992; Rosenthal & Rubin, 1978). These subtle expectations are communicated via cues from the expressive behavior of others. In their classic book *Studies in Expressive Movement*, Allport and Vernon (1933) defined expressive movement as "individual differences in the manner of performing adaptive acts, considered as dependent less upon external and temporary conditions than upon enduring qualities of personality" (p. 23). Expressive behavior captures the tone of what is expressed. We define a thin slice as a brief excerpt of behavior sampled from the behavioral stream, less than five minutes in length (Ambady, Bernieri, & Richeson, 2000). Thus, static, still frames (e.g., photographs) do not qualify as thin slices. Thin slices can be sampled from any available channel of communication, including the face, the body, audio clips, tone of voice clips, transcripts, or combinations of these.

Thin slices provide an efficient means of assessing personality, affect, and interpersonal relations from the lengthy behavioral stream. For example, results of a meta-analysis on the accuracy of predictions of various social and clinical outcomes based on thin slices of expressive behavior revealed moderately high rates of predictive accuracy (Ambady & Rosenthal, 1992). Further, this meta-analysis suggested that exposure length was not related to greater predictive accuracy: Predictions based on 30 seconds of information were as valid as those based on 4 or 5 minutes of information.

Thin-slice judgments represent a potentially useful tool in examining interpersonal sensitivity. First, thin-slice judgments have been found to be accurate and reliable predictors of a variety of different types of criterion variables, including those related to interpersonal sensitivity (Ambady & Rosenthal, 1992). Furthermore, such judgments are ecologically valid—they are precisely the type of judgments that people rely on in their everyday lives in intuitively judging other people on a host of different dimensions, such as in assessing others' intentions, affect, emotions, motivation, and personality. Intuition suggests that these rapid, often unarticulated judgments are the ones that underlie feelings of rapport and empathy—to put it colloquially, the sense of being "in" or "out of sync" with others. Moreover, thin-slice judgments provide a means to conduct fine-grained analyses of interpersonal sensitivity, such as identifying channels that are relied on to make different types of judgments and channels relied on to convey different types of messages.

## THIN-SLICE METHODOLOGY

Thin-slice methodology affords researchers a number of flexible alternatives that result in a methodology that is ecologically valid and informative. This approach can accommodate variations in the amount of exposure time presented to judges, communication channels presented to judges, and the types of variables judged from the slices.

## Length of Exposure

Typically, the slices usually fall in a fairly broad range, from 2 seconds to 5 minutes. Clips are drawn randomly from the first few minutes, the middle few minutes, and the last few minutes of an interaction. In addition to allowing for a wide representation of behavior, this technique conveniently allows for the assessment of behavior change over time. Although meta-analytic evidence indicates that length of exposure does not seem to affect accuracy (Ambady & Rosenthal, 1992), more research is needed to facilitate further understanding of potential moderators of sensitivity that may interact with exposure time, such as characteristics of the judge or characteristics of the target.

## Channels

Thin slices can be extracted from diverse channels of communication, including silent videotapes, audiotapes, content-filtered audiotapes (the removal of specific high band frequencies leaving only tone of voice cues), and standard videotapes. This flexibility in the type of channel allows researchers to assess the predictive value of various channels of communication. In addition, this flexibility also permits secondary analyses of existing datasets. Meta-analytic findings indicate that thin slices from both nonverbal and verbal channels of communication accurately predict criterion variables (Ambady & Rosenthal, 1992).

## Variables Judged

Variables judged from thin slices vary considerably as does the nature of such judgments. In general, judgments of impressionistic, fuzzy, molar variables related to affect and interpersonal functioning yield more accurate judgments than do counts of microlevel behaviors such as smiles and nods. This is because the same specific behavior might signal very different types of affect. Consider the example of a smile. A smile, depending on the context and accompanying behavior, may signal warmth, anxiety, or hostility (Ambady & Rosenthal, 1993). Molar judgments, by directly assessing warmth, anxiety, or hostility, capture the overall, gestalt impression conveyed in the slice. Thus, thin slices are typically rated by naïve (untrained) judges on a variety of molar variables theoretically related to the criterion variable. Such judgments can be used to form the basis of predictions regarding social and clinical outcomes or to measure acuity to individual characteristics (e.g., judging someone's personality or judging the level of rapport and empathy between members of a dyad).

## MEASURES OF INTERPERSONAL
## SENSITIVITY USING THIN SLICES

Thin slices have been used to assess individual differences in sensitivity to expressive cues. Two published measures of interpersonal sensitivity are composed of a series of thin slices. The Profile of Nonverbal Sensitivity (PONS; Rosenthal, Hall, DiMatteo, Rogers, & Archer, 1979) consists of 220 video clips, each lasting 2 seconds, from which observers are asked to make judgments about the expressor's affective state or the interpersonal situation he or she is in. Each slice is extracted from a brief scene where a woman portrays herself in a number of different social and interpersonal situations (e.g., admonishing a small child, asking for forgiveness, returning an item purchased at a store). Although the verbal content has been removed from each of these clips, judges' accuracy is above chance, demonstrating the richness of information contained within a mere 2 seconds of behavior (Rosenthal et al., 1979). Thus, the PONS is a useful tool for examining individual differences in sensitivity in general and also for examining sensitivity to different channels of communication.

Another measure, the Interpersonal Perception Task (IPT; Costanzo & Archer, 1989), is composed of longer clips ranging from 30 to 60 seconds, and unlike the PONS, the IPT preserves all of the channels of communication. The observer of the IPT views a series of brief clips and makes judgments regarding deception, intimacy, status, kinship, and competition. Given that all channels of communication are accessible to the observer, the IPT may tap into a different element of interpersonal sensitivity than the PONS (see Hall, chap. 8, this volume, and Archer, Costanzo, & Akert, chap. 9, this volume).

## ASSESSMENT OF INTERPERSONAL
## SENSITIVITY FROM THIN SLICES: MODERATORS

There is general consensus that individuals vary in their level of interpersonal sensitivity. A number of factors appear to moderate sensitivity to social and interpersonal characteristics of others. In this section we discuss the role of individual differences in personality, affect, and culture, as well as individuals' familiarity with the domain being judged on the assessment of sensitivity from thin slices.

## Personality and Individual Differences

What characteristics distinguish more from less interpersonally sensitive individuals on thin-slice judgment tasks? In a meta-analysis on the accuracy of person perception, Davis and Kraus (1997) found that people who are more accurate judges of others tend to be more intelligent, more cognitively complex, less dogmatic, better adjusted, and more interpersonally oriented. Although these findings are based on studies with a range of different methodologies, including self-reports and peer ratings, accurate judges of thin slices seem to possess similar attributes.

Characteristics of individuals who score higher on the PONS have been examined in some depth (Rosenthal et al., 1979). People who score higher tend to be less dogmatic and less Machiavellian and more democratic, extraverted, and socially adjusted than people who score lower. In addition, people who perform better on the PONS tend to be rated more interpersonally sensitive and more popular by people who know them well, such as their clients, teachers, supervisors, and spouses, than people who perform worse on the measure (Funder & Harris, 1986; Rosenthal et al., 1979). Furthermore, several studies have found that both adults and children who have more successful interpersonal relationships are more sensitive to the behavior of others (Baum & Nowicki, 1998; Boyatzis & Satyaprasad, 1994; Funder & Harris, 1986; Gottman & Porterfield, 1981; Noller, 1980; Noller & Feeney, 1994; Nowicki & Carton, 1997). In a similar vein, shyness and social anxiety have been associated with poorer sensitivity on the IPT (Schroeder, 1995a, 1995b). These results suggest that thin-slice judgment tasks are valid measures of interpersonal sensitivity—people who are rated by others as more interpersonally skilled and better adjusted perform better on these tasks than people rated as less skilled and less adjusted.

Are people who score better on tasks using thin slices to assess interpersonal sensitivity also more intelligent? The relationship between intelligence and sensitivity is less consistent. Whereas cognitive ability has been positively related to empathic accuracy (Davis & Kraus, 1997) and judgments of extraversion from thin-slice video clips (Lippa & Dietz, in press), other work suggests that intelligence is not related to performance on the PONS (Rosenthal et al., 1979) or the judgment of interactant rapport from thin slices (Bernieri & Gillis, 1995a). Thus, it might be useful to further explore under what conditions cognitive ability relates to interpersonal sensitivity judged from thin slices.

Recent work suggests that the role of individual differences in interpersonal sensitivity may depend on the type of judgment task. For instance, a recent study using the PONS (Rosenthal et al., 1979) and the IPT (Costanzo & Archer, 1989) in addition to two "in-house" thin-slice judgment tasks involving rapport assessment (Gesn, Bernieri, Gada-Jain, & Grahe, 1999) revealed fairly low intercorrelations between the four tasks with a median intercorrelation of

-.01. As previously suggested, this may be due to the type of channel information available for each task.

Another study found that occupational therapy students in a pediatric rehabilitation setting judged to be better performers by clinical fieldwork supervisors were more sensitive to body cues of emotions as assessed by the PONS, whereas those judged to be better performers in psychosocial rehabilitation were more sensitive to facial but not body cues on the PONS (Tickle-Degnen, 1997). Thus, people in different roles and contexts perform differently on different subscales (e.g., full body vs. face only), suggesting that different elements of sensitivity may be context relevant and dependent. This work also indicates that individuals' strengths in terms of sensitivity have real-world implications for their ability to work and interact efficiently. What remains ambiguous, however, is whether individuals bring their expertise to the context or whether exposure to particular contexts increases sensitivity to specific expressive cues.

## Affect

A considerable body of literature suggests that affect and mood influence many different domains of human performance (Forgas, 1992). There is some indication that induced mood influences the nature of impression formation judgments. For example, induced mood can increase the extremity of positive and negative judgments made by children (Forgas, Burnham, & Trimboli, 1988). There is also evidence for mood congruency in social judgments. For example, Forgas and Bower (1987) reported that happy participants formed more favorable impressions and made more positive judgments than did sad participants. Mood also appears to influence what information is attended to and how it is evaluated (Bower, 1991; Clore & Parrott, 1991; Fiedler, 1991; Forgas, 1992; Schwarz & Bless, 1991).

How might induced mood influence interpersonal sensitivity on the basis of thin slices? Some research suggests that positive moods should be associated with improved accuracy in interpersonal perception (Forgas, 1992; Sinclair, 1988). One study examined the differential effects of mood on thin-slice judgments of teacher effectiveness and dyadic relationships (Ambady, 2000). Positive and negative moods were induced by having subjects watch a 5-minute film clip. Interestingly, the positive mood condition was associated with improved accuracy in judging both teacher effectiveness and the type of dyadic relationships compared with a control group. Negative mood was associated with decreased accuracy compared with a control group with no mood induction. Thus, it seems that positive affective states facilitate and negative affective states impede the processing of thin slices. These findings complement work reviewed in the previous section suggesting that people who are more accurate judges tend to be better adjusted and more popular than those who are less accurate judges. Presumably, happier people are both better adjusted and more popular with others.

Whereas temporary positive moods facilitate the accuracy of thin-slice judgments, a mixed pattern of results emerges for stable, rather than laboratory induced, affective traits. Work on depressive realism would suggest that depressed people should be more accurate in their judgments of others (Alloy & Abramson, 1979, 1982). Chronic negative states, such as depression, have been associated with increased accuracy of judgment, particularly for negative stimuli (Bargh & Tota, 1988; Ruehlman, West, & Pasahow, 1985). On thin-slice judgments of rapport, Bernieri and Gillis (Bernieri & Gillis, 1993; Gillis & Bernieri, 1993) found that moderately depressed participants were slightly more accurate at judging rapport. Further, depressed observers were more likely to track the negative partner in the dyad, suggesting schematicity for negative information. Increased interpersonal sensitivity associated with depression has been documented in other research as well (Giannini, Folts, & Fiedler, 1989; Pietromonaco, Rook, & Lewis, 1992). However, other research has reported decreased interpersonal sensitivity associated with depression (Aube & Whiffen, 1996; Carton, Kessler, & Pape, 1999; Russell, Stokes, Jones, Czogalik, & Rholeder, 1993; Zuroff & Colussy, 1986), and still others have reported no differences between depressed and nondepressed individuals (Prkachin, Craig, Papageorgis, & Reith, 1977). Perhaps the severity of depression is relevant here. It is possible that severe depression might be associated with poor thin-slice judgments, whereas mild or moderate degrees of depression might be associated with more accurate judgment compared with nondepressed individuals.

In summary, both theory and research suggest that state- and trait-related affect seem to moderate interpersonal sensitivity assessed with thin slices. Because of the relative paucity of work in this area, however, the links between affect and interpersonal sensitivity need to be further examined.

## Culture

Culture is another important moderator of interpersonal sensitivity. For example, the PONS test was administered to over 2,000 individuals from 20 nations. Americans were the most accurate judges, suggesting that people are most accurate at judging targets from their own culture. Furthermore, people from cultures more similar to the United States were more accurate than people from less similar cultures. Thus, cultures whose languages most closely resembled English performed better than those whose language was not quite so similar (Rosenthal et al., 1979).

Bernieri and colleagues investigated thin-slice judgments of rapport in American student interactions in over a dozen countries including Greece, Colombia, Lebanon, and Indonesia (Bernieri, Gillis, & Grahe, 1999). (Bernieri & Gillis, 1995a) In contrast to the PONS work, similarity ratings were not made for each country. However, judgments still showed remarkable agreement with those made by their American counterparts although few participants could speak English or had ever traveled to the United States.

Additional evidence regarding the moderating role of culture on thin-slice judgments is provided by work on cultural differences in judgments of vocal cues from thin slices (Lee & Boster, 1992; Peng, Zebrowitz, & Lee, 1993). For example, whereas Korean speakers associated tension judged from thin-slice audio clips with power and competence, Americans exhibited the opposite reaction, associating vocal relaxation with power and competence (Peng et al., 1993). Thus, although some vocal cues seem to be interpreted consistently, other cues seem to be interpreted quite differently across cultures (Montepare & Zebrowitz-McArthur, 1987).

Cultural familiarity and accessibility of constructs also affect thin-slice judgments. Ambady and Hecht (2000) found that interpersonal sensitivity is affected by cultural norms, values, and practices. Thus, individuals from a more hierarchically structured culture, Korea, were more sensitive to the status of targets (whether the target being addressed was a subordinate, peer, or superior) than were Americans, who belong to a more egalitarian culture. Finally, it appears that certain characteristics are easier to judge cross-culturally than others. Thus, work on the accuracy of personality judgments in the zero-acquaintance paradigm suggests that extraversion can be judged most accurately across some cultures (Albright, Malloy, Dong, Kenny, & Fang, 1997). Thus, culture may affect interpersonal sensitivity judged from thin slices more on some dimensions than others, suggesting a culture–judgment relationship.

## Domain Familiarity and Sensitivity

The previous section regarding cultural effects on judgments suggests that familiarity with the domain and behaviors being judged influence sensitivity. Results from a study on the accuracy of judging sexual orientation from thin slices provides further evidence of familiarity effects (Ambady, Hallahan, & Connor, 1999). Whereas heterosexual and homosexual men and women were equally accurate at judging the 10s silent slices, gay men and lesbian judges were more accurate than heterosexuals as information became more sparse (1s clips). This result suggests that people who are more experienced or familiar with making judgments of a certain domain are more sensitive to cues in that domain.

Thus, interpersonal sensitivity as judged from thin slices is affected by a number of different moderators. Researchers using thin slices to assess interpersonal sensitivity should keep in mind potential moderators such as personality, culture, and familiarity with the domain being judged.

## THIN-SLICE JUDGMENTS AND INTERPERSONAL SENSITIVITY: SOME FUTURE DIRECTIONS

How can thin slices be used to assess individual differences in interpersonal sensitivity? This methodology promises to be useful in contributing to the knowledge of interpersonal sensitivity by addressing a number of interesting issues. We list a few of many potential avenues of inquiry. Is there a general ability to judge others regardless of the length of observation? Are some people better at judging thinner versus thicker slices? Similarly, does interpersonal sensitivity vary according to the channel of communication being judged? Thus, are certain people more accurate in judging slices from the audio channel and are others more accurate at judging video clips? Further, are there individual differences in sensitivity to different attributes or characteristics? Are individuals for whom certain attributes are chronically accessible or schematic more accurate at judging those attributes? Work on depressive realism reviewed earlier in this chapter suggests that this might be a possibility. Finally, what is the relationship between individual differences in personality and affect and the type of thin-slice judgment task? For example, are extraverts better at judging extraversion as opposed to judging conscientiousness and are such judgments affected by the channel being judged?

To increase understanding of interpersonal sensitivity, it seems important to develop more instruments to measure sensitivity along the lines of the PONS and IPT that tap different aspects of the construct. Although the correlation between the IPT and the PONS is generally low (Ambady et al., 1995; Bernieri & Gillis, 1995b; Hall, chap. 8, this volume), both measures seem to predict aspects of interpersonal functioning (Ambady et al., 1995), suggesting that interpersonal sensitivity is multifaceted and that other measures could be developed to evaluate other facets of the construct. For instance, measures could be developed to evaluate sensitivity to culturally appropriate and inappropriate behavior; to evaluate knowledge of social and cultural norms, standards, and patterns of behavior; and to evaluate the decoding of emotions beyond those evaluated by the PONS. Moreover, measures could be developed that assess sensitivity to brief slices as well as longer slices, that evaluate sensitivity to different channels of communication, and that evaluate sensitivity to people of different races, classes, and cultures.

## LIMITATIONS

Thin-slice methodology is still in need of development and refinement. First, the types of variables that can accurately be judged using this methodology need to be further established. The work reviewed earlier in this chapter suggests that judgments based on thin slices are probably most accurate for observable, interpersonal, or affective variables (Ambady & Rosenthal, 1992). This may be because affective, observable dimensions are the ones that need to be judged quickly for survival and adaptation to the environment (McArthur & Baron, 1983).

One's own experiences as a social being can attest to the fact that people do in fact make a broad range of judgments of other people in daily life. The consequences of such decisions often remind individuals of this. However, the question inevitably arises: Does the process of asking people to make these judgments substantially alter the process and accuracy of judgments? Although thin slices might be drawn from ecologically valid sources, is the making of such judgments as done in the laboratory also ecologically valid?

Thin-slice methodology, despite having a history within the nonverbal communication and interpersonal sensitivity literature, is still in its infancy. Knowledge of the predictive and diagnostic utility of this methodology is still developing. Thus, for instance, researchers still need to identify the domains in which certain variables and channels are maximally predictive of and maximally conducive to interpersonal sensitivity. Such attempts need however to parallel other emerging conceptualizations of sensitivity and take into account the multifaceted nature of sensitivity.

## CONCLUSION

With the advent of modern technology and inexpensive audio and video recorders, it is now fairly easy to capture thin slices of the behavioral stream. The availability of relatively inexpensive yet powerful computers suggests a number of intriguing avenues of exploration, such as the assessment of both accuracy and latency of judgments to provide further insights into interpersonal sensitivity. We are not suggesting that thin slices be used to the exclusion of other measures of interpersonal sensitivity, but we suggest that in tandem with other measures, judgments of thin slices can provide unique insights regarding the dynamics and processes underlying interpersonal sensitivity. The measurement of interpersonal sensitivity is still evolving. Thus, at this point, it is too early to assess the relative contributions of different types of measures to the assessment of interpersonal sensitivity. The use of multiple methodologies to examine interpersonal sensitivity will deepen our understanding of the construct and constituent processes.

In conclusion, intuitive judgments about others based on thin slices can be used to assess social acuity as well as to form the basis of predictions regarding social, clinical, and psychological outcomes. The use of thin slices can facilitate successful explorations of sensitivity and accuracy in several different domains, can contribute to the literature regarding interpersonal perception and communication, and has implications for health care, clinical psychology, and education (Ambady & Rosenthal, 1992; Ambady, Bernieri, & Richeson, 2000). Additionally, thin-slice methodology has considerable pragmatic utility. Briefly, this methodology has been found to yield rich insights while allowing researchers to save time and money, to predict several important outcome variables, and to assess social acuity. We are optimistic that the thin-slice methodology can be used to contribute to an understanding of interpersonal sensitivity.

## ACKNOWLEDGMENT

The authors gratefully acknowledge support from National Science Foundation (PECASE Award, BCS-9733706).

## REFERENCES

Albright, L., Kenny, D. A., & Malloy, T. E. (1988). Consensus in personality judgments at zero acquaintance. *Journal of Personality and Social Psychology, 55,* 387–395.

Albright, L., Malloy, T. E., Dong, Q., Kenny, D. A., & Fang, X. (1997). Cross-cultural consensus in personality judgments. *Journal of Personality and Social Psychology, 72,* 558–569.

Allport, G. W., & Vernon, P. E. (1933). *Studies in expressive movement.* New York: Haffner.

Alloy, L. B., & Abramson, L. Y. (1979). Judgment of contingency in depressed and non-depressed students: Sadder but wiser? *Journal of Experimental Psychology, 108,* 441–485.

Alloy, L. B., & Abramson, L. Y. (1982). Learned helplessness, depression, and the illusion of control. *Journal of Personality and Social Psychology, 42,* 1114–1126.

Ambady, N. (2000). *Feeling and judging: Mood and the automaticity of thin slice judgments.* Unpublished manuscript.

Ambady, N., Bernieri, F., & Richeson, J. A. (2000). Towards a histology of social behavior: Judgmental accuracy from thin slices of the behavioral stream. In M. P. Zanna (Ed.), *Advances in Experimental Social Psychology.*

Ambady, N., Hallahan, M., & Conner, B. (1999). Accuracy of judgments of sexual orientation from thin slices of behavior. *Journal of Personality and Social Psychology, 77*(3), 538–547.

Ambady, N., Hallahan, M., & Rosenthal, R. (1995). On judging and being judged accurately in zero acquaintance situations. *Journal of Personality and Social Psychology, 69,* 518–529.

Ambady, N., & Hecht, M. (2000). *Cultural frames: Domain accessibility and accuracy of judgments.* Manuscript in preparation.

Ambady, N., & Rosenthal, R. (1992). Thin slices of expressive behavior as predictors of interpersonal consequences: A meta-analysis. *Psychological Bulletin, 111,* 256–274.

Ambady, N., & Rosenthal, R. (1993). Half a minute: Predicting teacher evaluations from thin slices of nonverbal behavior and physical attractiveness. *Journal of Personality and Social Psychology, 64,* 431-441.

Aube, J., & Whiffen, V. E. (1996). Depressive styles and social acuity: Further evidence for distinct interpersonal correlates of dependency and self-criticism. *Communication Research, 23,* 407–424.

Bargh, J. A., & Tota, M. E. (1988). Context-dependent automatic processing in depression: Accessibility of negative constructs with regard to self but not others. *Journal of Personality and Social Psychology, 54,* 925–939.

Baum, K. M., & Nowicki, S., Jr. (1998). Perception of emotion: Measuring decoding accuracy of adult prosodic cues varying in intensity. *Journal of Nonverbal Behavior, 22,* 89–107.

Bernieri, F., & Gillis, J. (1993). Depressed mood and social perception: A cross-cultural replication. *Perceptual and Motor Skills, 77,* 154.

Bernieri, F., & Gillis, J. S. (1995a). The judgment of rapport: A cross-cultural comparison between Americans and Greeks. *Journal of Nonverbal Behavior, 19,* 115–130.

Bernieri, F., & Gillis, J. S. (1995b). Personality correlates of accuracy in a social perception task. *Perceptual and Motor Skills, 81,* 168–170.

Bernieri, F., J., Gillis, J. S., & Grohe, J. E. (1999). *Cross-cultural perceptions of rapport.* Unpublished data.

Bower, G. H. (1991). Mood congruity of social judgments. In J. P. Forgas (Ed.), *Emotion and social judgments* (pp. 31–53). Elmsford, NY: Pergamon.

Boyatzis, C. J., & Satyaprasad, C. (1994). Children's facial and gestural decoding and encoding: Relations between skills and with popularity. *Journal of Nonverbal Behavior, 18,* 37–55.

Carton, J. S., Kessler, E. A., & Pape, C. L. (1999). Nonverbal decoding skills and relationship well-being in adults. *Journal of Nonverbal Behavior, 23,* 91–100.

Clore, G. L., & Parrott, G. (1991). Moods and their vicissitudes: Thoughts and feelings as information. In J. P. Forgas (Ed.), *Emotion and social judgments* (pp. 107–123). Elmsford, NY: Pergamon.

Costanzo, M., & Archer, D. (1989). Interpreting the expressive behavior of others: The Interpersonal Perception Task. *Journal of Nonverbal Behavior, 13,* 223–245.

Davis, M. H., & Kraus, L. A. (1997). Personality and empathic accuracy. In W. J. Ickes (Ed.), *Empathic accuracy* (pp. 144-168). New York: Guilford.

Fiedler, K. (1991). On the task, measures and the mood in research on affect and social cognition. In J. P. Forgas (Ed.), *Emotion and social judgments* (pp. 83–104). Elmsford, NY: Pergamon.

Forgas, J. P. (1992). Affect in social judgments and decisions: A multi-process model. In M. P. Zanna (Ed.), *Advances in experimental social psychology* (Vol. 25, pp. 227–275). San Diego, CA: Academic.

Forgas, J. P., & Bower, G. H. (1987). Mood effects on person-perception judgements. *Journal of Personality and Social Psychology, 53,* 53–60.

Forgas, J. P., Burnham, D. K., & Trimboli, C. (1988). Mood, memory, and social judgments in children. *Journal of Personality and Social Psychology, 54,* 697–703.

Funder, D. C. (1995). On the accuracy of personality judgment: A realistic approach. *Psychological Review, 102,* 652–670.

Funder, D. C., & Harris, M. J. (1986). On the several facets of personality assessment: The case of social acuity. *Journal of Personality, 54,* 528–550.

Gesn, P. R., Bernieri, F. J., Gada-Jain, N., & Grahe, J. E. (May, 1999). *Domains of interpersonal sensitivity: Performance accuracy and psychometric assessment of ability.* Paper presented at the Midwestern Psychological Association Convention, Chicago.

Giannini, A. J., Folts, D. J., & Fiedler, R. C. (1989). Enhanced encoding of nonverbal cues in bipolar illness in males. *Journal of Psychology, 124,* 557–562.

Gillis, J., & Bernieri, F. (1993). Effects of depressed mood on social perception. *Perceptual and Motor Skills, 76,* 674.

Gottman, J., & Porterfield, A. L. (1981). Communicative competence in the nonverbal behavior of married couples. *Journal of Marriage and the Family, 43,* 817–824.

Kenny, D. A., Albright, L., Malloy, T. E., & Kashy, D. (1994). Consensus in interpersonal perception: Acquaintance and the Big Five. *Psychological Bulletin, 116,* 245–258.

Lee, H. O., & Boster F. J., (1992). Collectivism–individualism in perceptions of speech rate: A cross-cultural comparison. *Journal of Cross-Cultural Psychology, 23,* 377–388.

Lippa, R. A., & Dietz, J. K. (2000). The relation of gender, personality, and intelligence to judges' accuracy in judging strangers' personality from brief video segments. *Journal of Nonverbal Behavior,* 24(1), 25–43.

McArthur, L. Z., & Baron, R. M. (1983). Toward an ecological theory of social perception. *Psychological Review, 90,* 215–238.

Montepare J. M., & Zebrowitz-McArthur, L. (1987). Perceptions of adults with childlike voices in two cultures. *Journal of Experimental Social Psychology, 23,* 331–349.

Noller, P. (1980). Misunderstandings in marital communication: A study of couples' nonverbal communication. *Journal of Personality and Social Psychology, 39,* 1135–1148

Noller, P., & Feeney, J. A. (1994). Relationship satisfaction, attachment, and nonverbal accuracy in early marriage. *Journal of Nonverbal Behavior, 18*, 199–221.

Nowicki, S., Jr., & Carton, E. (1997). The relation of nonverbal processing ability of faces and voices and children's feelings of depression and competence. *Journal of Genetic Psychology, 158*, 357–363.

Passini, F. T., & Norman, W. T. (1966). A universal conception of personality structure? *Journal of Personality and Social Psychology, 4*, 44–49.

Paunonen, S. V. (1991). On the accuracy of ratings of personality by strangers. *Journal of Personality and Social Psychology, 61*, 471–477.

Peng, Y., Zebrowitz, L. A., & Lee, H. K., (1993). The impact of cultural background and cross-cultural experience on impressions of American and Korean male speakers. *Journal of Cross Cultural Psychology, 24*, 203–220.

Pietromonaco, P. R., Rook, K. S., & Lewis, M. A. (1992). Accuracy in interpersonal interactions: Effects of dysphoria, friendship, and similarity. *Journal of Personality and Social Psychology, 63*, 247–259.

Prkachin, K. M., Craig, K. D., Papageoris, D., & Reith, G. (1977). Nonverbal communication deficits and response to performance feedback in depression. *Journal of Abnormal Psychology, 86*, 224–234.

Rosenthal, R. (1966). *Experimenter effects in behavioral research.* Englewood Cliffs, NJ: Prentice-Hall.

Rosenthal, R. (1991). *Meta-analytic procedures for social research.* Newbury Park, CA: Sage.

Rosenthal, R., & Rubin, D. B. (1978). Interpersonal expectancy effects: The first 345 studies. *Behavioral and Brain Sciences, 3*, 377–415.

Rosenthal, R., Hall, J. A., DiMatteo, M. R., Rogers, P. L., & Archer, D. (1979). *Sensitivity to nonverbal communication: The PONS test.* Baltimore: Johns Hopkins University Press.

Rosenthal, R., & Jacobson, L. (1992). *Pygmalion in the classroom: Teacher expectation and pupils' intellectual development.* New York: Irvington.

Ruehlman, L. S., West, S. G., & Pasahow, R. J. (1985). Depression and evaluative schemata. *Journal of Personality, 53*, 46–92.

Russell, R. L., Stokes, J. M., Jones, M. E., Czogalik, D., & Rholeder, L. (1993). The role of nonverbal sensitivity in childhood psychopathology. *Journal of Nonverbal Behavior, 17*, 69–83.

Schroeder, J. E. (1995a). Interpersonal perception skills: Self-concept correlates. *Perceptual and Motor Skills, 80*, 51–56.

Schroeder, J. E. (1995b). Self-concept, social anxiety, and interpersonal perception skills. *Personality and Individual Differences, 19*, 955–958.

Schwarz, N., & Bless, H. (1991). Happy and mindless, but sad and smart? The impact of affective states on analytic reasoning. In J. P. Forgas (Ed.), *Emotion and social judgments* (pp. 55–71). Elmsdale, NY: Pergamon.

Sinclair, R. C. (1988). Mood, categorization breadth, and performance appraisal: The effects of order of information acquisition and affective state on halo, accuracy, information retrieval, and evaluations. *Organizational Behavior and Human Decision Processes, 42*, 22–46.

Tickle-Degnen, L. (1997). Working well with others: The prediction of students' clinical performance. *American Journal of Occupational Therapy, 52*, 133–142.

Watson, D. (1989). Strangers' ratings of five robust personality factors: Evidence of a surprising convergence with self-report. *Journal of Personality and Social Psychology, 57*, 120–128.

Zuroff, D. C., & Colussy, S. A. (1986). Emotional recognition in schizophrenia and depressed inpatients. *Journal of Clinical Psychology, 42*, 411–416.

# ☙ 6 ❧

# Measuring Sensitivity
# to Deception

### Brian E. Malone
### Bella M. DePaulo
*University of Virginia*

Since the 1980s, empirical study of deception has become quite popular. Many of the questions that have captured the attention of researchers pertain to people's skill at deception detection: How do people go about detecting deception? Are they good at it? Why or why not? Are some detectors better than others? Interest in these questions, as with many questions about nonverbal behavior, stretches beyond disciplinary boundaries. The work is relevant to topics in fields such as sociology, anthropology, communication, clinical psychology, law enforcement, and political science.

Sensitivity to deception differs in important ways from other kinds of interpersonal sensitivities and therefore warrants a separate treatment. Most significantly, detecting deception involves the perception of information that communicators are trying to hide. Because dishonest communicators are regulating their behaviors to create false impressions, sources of cues that ordinarily may be rich with useful information may instead be uninformative or even misleading. Facial expressions provide a compelling example. Just as people can regulate their facial expressions in nondeceptive interactions so as to make their feelings or sentiments especially clear, so too can they manipulate those expressions deliberately in order to mislead. The cumulative results of dozens of studies have shown that perceivers trying to detect deception typically are no more accurate when they have facial cues available than when they do not, and sometimes they are even a bit less accurate (B. M. DePaulo, Tornqvist, & Cooper, 2000).

Scholars discussing constructs such as skills, accuracies, and sensitivities often seem smitten with the assumption that more is better. With regard to deception detection, the assumption sometimes seems eminently reasonable. People do want to know who has stolen their computer and which candidate will raise taxes. On the other hand, there may be more than a few instances in which the truth hurts. Does one really want to know what politicians and their lovers do in the Oval Office, or how one's students mock him or her when not around? There are also situations in which knowing the truth would adversely affect one's relationships with other people. Perhaps individuals might be flattered to find out that someone has a crush on them; however, to that person, such knowledge may mean that he or she will have a hard time facing the object of the crush. So far, there is only suggestive evidence that too much insight into the truth behind certain lies may not be totally desirable (Rosenthal & DePaulo, 1979a, 1979b). We might suggest, then, that in certain situations, perceivers may be motivated not to find out the truth. Our prediction is not that motivated inaccuracy will be unique to the realm of deception detection, as we already know that it is not (e.g., Simpson, Ickes, & Blackstone, 1995). However, we do think that it may be an especially robust phenomenon in that arena.

In this chapter, we review the methods used most often to study deception detection. Over the course of this discussion, we describe the standard measurement approaches, flag the methodological deadends, and preview the approaches that we predict for future research. In addition, we also consider many of the theoretical issues that are implicit in discussions of methodology.

In addition to a descriptive component (i.e., which methods could be used?), our chapter contains a prescriptive component (i.e., what methods should be used?). We hope that the suggestions that we make in this chapter will improve the quality of deception research and, consequently, our understanding of the processes of deceptive communications.

## MEASURING ACCURACY IN DECEPTION DETECTION RESEARCH

### Standard Measures of Accuracy

*Percent Accuracy.*   In most studies of deception detection, perceivers make a binary judgment as to whether the message they just observed was a truth or a lie. Intuitively, it might seem that lie detection accuracy should be defined as the percentage of all of the lies that are accurately judged to be lies. Perceivers who guessed "lie" every time that the message they observed was indeed a lie would thereby earn a lie detection accuracy score of 100%. In fact, however, if scores are computed based only on judgments of lies, it is not possible to separate genuine accuracy from a bias to judge messages as deceptive. If the perceivers who guessed that all of the lies were lies had also guessed that all of the truths were truths, then they would have deserved accuracy scores of 100%. If, however, they guessed not only that all of the lies were lies but also that all of the truths were lies, then these perceivers would best be described not as accurate but as biased—biased to see others as lying.

When computing accuracy scores from binary truth versus lie judgments, then, it is essential to compute accuracy across both lies and truths. In the usual paradigm in which half of the messages that perceivers judge are lies and half are truths, perceivers who were just guessing would earn accuracy scores of 50%. This is exactly the score earned by perceivers who judge all of the messages to be lies (or who judge them all to be truths). Such perceivers show no ability whatsoever to distinguish lies from truths and thereby deserve their chance accuracy scores of 50%.

More than 100 studies have been reported in which percent accuracy scores (computed across truths and lies from dichotomous truth vs. lie judgments) were the dependent measure. In the studies in which the perceivers were adults with no special experience or training at detecting deception, who were judging adults from their own culture, the mean accuracy score was greater than chance in well over half of the studies. However, the mean accuracy score was only about 54%. This means that humans are only slightly better than chance at detecting deception. The mean accuracy score shows strikingly little variability. About two thirds of the group means were between 50 and 59%. Only a few studies have ever reported mean accuracy scores of greater than 70% for groups of untrained human lie detectors with no special deception detection experience, and none has reported accuracy scores greater than 80% (or less than 30%); (B. M. DePaulo, Tornqvist & Cooper, 2000).

One implication of the low overall accuracy and small variability in accuracy scores is that measurement issues are especially important. Researchers have reported dozens of manipulations of factors predicted to influence deception detection success; only occasionally do these manipulations succeed in pushing mean accuracy levels to 60% or higher. The value of measuring accuracy as precisely as possible may therefore be even greater in the field of deception than in other areas of nonverbal sensitivity in which the range of accuracy scores is typically greater.

*Rating Scale Measures of Accuracy.*    Perceivers are sometimes asked to indicate their perceptions of the deceptiveness of messages on rating scales (typically 7- or 9-point scales, but others have been used as well). The endpoints are variously labeled *deceptive, (dis)honest, (in)sincere, truthful,* and so forth. Although scholars may see shades of different meanings in these labels, research participants apparently do not, as there is no indication that the precise synonym selected is of any consequence.

On the theory that accurate perceivers are those who rate the lies as more deceptive than the truths, accuracy scores are computed by subtracting deceptiveness ratings of the truths from deceptiveness ratings of the lies. Scores of zero indicate that perceivers were completely unsuccessful at distinguishing the truths from the lies. Positive scores indicate successful detection, and negative scores indicate that perceivers were fooled into seeing the lies as even more honest than the truths.

This rating scale method should not be confused with another rating method that has appeared in the literature (Burgoon, Buller, Ebesu, & Rockwell, 1994). Recently, some researchers have computed accuracy as a difference score between the sender's rating of his or her own truthfulness and the judge's rating of the sender's truthfulness. Such a method is statistically problematic, as Cronbach and Gage pointed out nearly half a century ago (Cronbach, 1955; Gage & Cronbach, 1955).

In the influential conceptualization of accuracy offered by Cronbach (1955), a difference score representing the difference between the target's and judge's ratings of a certain trait actually contains four components of accuracy. (For a detailed explanation of this component model, see Kenny, 1994; see also Kenny & Winquist, chap. 14, this volume.) Only two of these four components have any relevance to accuracy: the target component, which captures how a judge rates a target as compared with the other targets; and the uniqueness component, which captures how a judge rates a specific target on a specific trait. To the extent that the target judgment and the uniqueness judgment correspond with the criteria, the judgments are considered accurate. Accuracy of the target judgment is called *differential elevation* and accuracy of the uniqueness judgment is called *differential accuracy*.

The other two components of the difference score do not contain accuracy information; in fact, they are measures of bias. The constant term tells us about the general response tendency of the judge to rate high or low all targets in all judgments. Some judges may, as a general rule, center their judgments around a mean of 5; others may tend toward a mean of 3. This difference between means, however, does not provide meaningful information about the accuracy of the judgments. A second bias term, the trait component, represents how judges, when rating numerous traits, tend to view the incidence of such traits in the population at large. For example, if a judge believes that honesty is more common than selfishness, he or she will rate people as more honest than selfish. Such a difference in ratings, again, does not provide information about the accuracy of that judgment.

Such a component model is somewhat simpler for studies in which only one trait, such as honesty, is of interest. However, the logic remains the same: Calculating difference scores between judge and target ratings produces a score that is a mixture of both accuracy and bias. In the case of deception judgments, a correspondence between the judge's rating of honesty and the target's rating of honesty could result from several factors. On the one hand, the correspondence could reflect meaningful accuracy: The judge may have accurately perceived the honesty of the communication. On the other hand, the correspondence could reflect bias: the judge may believe that almost every communication is probably true (a biased response set). The correspondence could also indicate that the judge and target just happen to share the same use of ratings scales; for example, perhaps both tend to make ratings on the low end of the scale.

The problem of confounding bias and accuracy is not encountered in the rating scale approach that we described at this beginning this section. When judges' ratings of deceptiveness are compared for both truths and lies, biases due to response set are removed. For example, if a judge has a response tendency to rate all messages as deceptive, he or she will rate lies as very deceptive; however, this same bias will lead him or her to rate truths as deceptive also. Comparing the means for truths and lies will show that the judge is not accurate. The key difference is that the accuracy score we endorse involves a within-judge comparison (the judge's perceptions of the lies are compared with the same judge's perceptions of the truths), whereas the difference score that Cronbach has attacked involves the subtraction of a rating made by one person from a rating made by another.

Proposed methods of untangling the confounds that are intrinsic to discrepancy scores are elegant but also complex (e.g., Kenny, 1994). There is, however, a simple but workable solution available when each judge and each target have made a series of deceptiveness ratings of the target's messages: The judges' ratings can be correlated with the targets', and the resulting coefficient is a measure of accuracy (Snodgrass, chap. 11, this volume; see also Bernieri & Gillis, p. 4, this volume and Kenny & Winquist, chap. 14, this volume, for variations on the same approach). Because correlations compare patterns of ratings (rather than mean differences in the use of the rating scales), important artifactual interpretations are eliminated. However, this correlational measure, and other similar ones, appear infrequently in the deception literature (e.g., Kraut & Poe, 1980).

*Comparing the Percent Accuracy Measure With the Rating Scale Measure of Accuracy.* Potentially, rating scale measures of accuracy are more sensitive and precise than binary choices, for judges can indicate not only whether they think the message was deceptive, but also the degree to which they perceive it as such. For the kinds of messages that really do vary in degrees of deceit (e.g., "How do you feel about whales?" as opposed to "Is your name Ishmael?"), it may be especially appropriate to allow respondents to indicate the extent to which they noticed the shades of deceit.

The most fundamental question about lie detection skill—Can people detect lies?—is answered similarly by studies that use a rating scale measure and those that use percent accuracy. In both sets, the majority of studies show that accuracy is better than chance (B. M. DePaulo, Tornqvist & Cooper, 2000). Because of the greater precision of the rating scale measures, we expect that experimental manipulations will show more powerful effects on those measures than on percent accuracy measures, but the relevant work remains to be done.

There is a subtle way in which percent accuracy and rating scale measures of accuracy differ. By the percent measure, perceivers who judge all messages (both the truths and the lies) as truths, in the usual paradigm in which half of the messages are truths and half are lies, will be assigned accuracy scores of 50%, indicating chance accuracy (none at all). By the rating scale measure, in contrast, perceivers could assign all messages a rating on the truthful end of the scale, but still earn positive accuracy scores if they rated the truths as even more truthful than the lies. This is not inappropriate if accuracy is construed as the ability to distinguish between truths and lies. The tendency to see most messages as truthful (see discussion later) is a separate issue, both theoretically and statistically. If, for example, suspicious and trusting perceivers observe truths and lies and rate them on a 9-point scale of deceptiveness, and those raw ratings of deceptiveness are used as the dependent measures in an analysis of variance (ANOVA), a main effect of suspiciousness might indicate that the suspicious perceivers saw the messages as more deceptive than did the trusting perceivers; a main effect of truths versus lies might indicate that perceivers were significantly more accurate than chance; and an interaction between suspiciousness and message type would indicate that the suspicious perceivers were more (or less) accurate than the trusting ones.

Although the potentially greater precision of the rating scale measure in an area in which precision is of the essence might seem to argue for the preferential use of that measure, in fact the reverse has been true. Percent accuracy scores are far more widely used (B. M. DePaulo, Tornqvist & Cooper, 2000). We think they are favored because of the ease with which both professionals and laypersons can interpret them. Percent accuracy is a familiar metric; and the chance score of 50% is easily understood as the common description of odds as "50–50." In contrast, the interpretation of a mean difference between truths and lies (e.g., .14 on a 7-point scale) is far less intuitive. It is possible to compute the degree to which the lies were rated as more deceptive than the truths in effect size units (e.g., $d$s or $r$s), thereby setting aside the ambiguities of interpreting difference scores generated from different rating scales (e.g., 5-point scales vs. 100-point scales). Even so, most effect size measures are far less familiar and understandable to laypersons than are percent accuracy measures. The field of deception detection has been of especially great interest to practitioners and to the audiences of the popular press. The interpretability of the measures selected for research is therefore of special importance.

Truth Bias.    Previously, we argued that percent accuracy measures must be defined in terms of accuracy at recognizing both truths and lies. However, it can also be of interest to examine separately the percentage of lies that are identified as lies and the percentage of truths that are identified as truths. Levine and his colleagues (Levine, Park, & McCornack, 1999) have done just that in a series of studies, and their results are consistent with the cumulative results of dozens of other studies (B. M. DePaulo, Tornqvist, & Cooper, 2000 ) in showing that the percentage of truths accurately recognized as such is typically higher than the percentage of accurately identified lies. This pattern of results, which Levine et al. (1999) dubbed the "veracity effect," is conceptually similar to the equally well-documented "truth bias," which is the bias to see most communications as truths (typically defined as the percentage of all messages perceived as truthful). In fact, when there are equal numbers of truths and lies to be judged (as is the case in the vast majority of studies), the veracity effect and the truth bias are perfectly correlated.

Most of the early work on the communication of deception focused on accuracy. Only rarely was truth bias the predicted outcome variable in experimental studies or the correlate of interest in nonexperimental work. Increasingly, however, the theoretical and practical significance of perceivers' tendency to see most communications as truths has been recognized and analyzed. The truth bias, it has now been shown, is interestingly responsive to norms, expectations, and the qualities of the person being judged (e.g., see Levine & McCornack, 1991). For example, a study of experienced salespersons (P. J. DePaulo & DePaulo, 1989) provided a rare example of a context in which perceivers were biased to judge communications as lies instead of truths. In contrast, when perceivers are judging their close relationship partners, compared with when they are judging strangers, they are typically even more biased to believe that what they are hearing is the truth (Anderson, 1999; Anderson, Ansfield, & DePaulo, 1999). Classic social psychological phenomena, such as the anchoring heuristic and sensitivity to self-serving biases, provide other examples of perceivers' theoretically predictable inclination to believe or disbelieve other people's communications (e.g., Jones, 1990). The study of accuracy and bias in contexts that vary in theoretically meaningful ways is a useful direction for future research.

*Signal Detection Measures.* In areas of psychology such as cognition and psychophysics, measures of accuracy and bias are often based on signal detection theory (SDT; Green & Swets, 1974). This is well-developed measurement perspective with important variants (e.g., Luce's 1959 choice theory) and many refinements and nuances (e.g., see Macmillan & Creelman, 1991). We present only some very basic concepts.

The components of accuracy and bias in SDT are the familiar ones we have described, with different labels. Correct judgments of truths as truths are called *hits*; when this number is computed as a percentage of all messages that actually were truths, the index is called the *hit rate*. Mistaken judgments of lies as truths are called *false alarms*; when this number is computed as a percentage of all messages that actually were truths, the index is called the *false-alarm rate*. Correct judgments of lies as lies are called *correct rejections*, and mistaken judgments of truths as lies are called *misses*. The logic of accuracy (called *sensitivity* in SDT) is also the same as we have described: Accurate judges more often label communications as truths when they really are truths than when they are lies; that is, the hit rate is greater than the false-alarm rate. The index of accuracy (sensitivity) in signal detection theory is d' (d-prime), which is the hit rate minus the false alarm rate, after each has been transformed into a Z-score. The units of hits and false alarms that are used in the sensitivity equation are therefore standard deviation units.

What we have been calling the truth bias is called *response bias* in signal-detection theory. It is computed analogously to the truth bias as the hit rate (percentage of truths that are judged to be truths) plus the false-alarm rate (mistaken judgments of lies as truths as a percentage of all truthful messages). Both components are first transformed into Z-scores before they are combined.

One point underscored by signal detection theorists that is less often discussed by deception researchers is that the same accuracy or sensitivity score can be produced by many different combinations of hit rates and false-alarm rates. For example, a hit and false-alarm pair of .80 and .40 results in the same sensitivity (accuracy) as the pair .60 and .20. The difference is that the perceiver who produced the first pair was more biased to see messages as truths than was the perceiver who produced the second pair. The various pairings that result in the same sensitivity score are often plotted as a curve, called an isosensitivity or receiver operating characteristic (ROC) curve.

Although signal detection measures could be used effectively in studies of deception detection, reports of such measures in the literature are extremely rare. Again, we suspect this is because the SDT measures are less widely understood than simple percent measures, both within and of course outside of academic psychology.

*Actual Affect (Leakage) Accuracy.*     As Ekman and Friesen (1969) pointed out several decades ago, perceivers who see another person as deceptive have noticed only that the person seems to be hiding or falsifying the truth. They may or may not appreciate the nature of the truth that is being concealed. For example, perceivers may feel suspicious of a person who is claiming great fondness for a new acquaintance, but if the person's true sentiment is not liking, then what is it? Strong disliking? Ambivalence? Indifference? The ability to identify another person's true attitudes or feelings has been called *actual affect accuracy* or *leakage accuracy*.

The popular person–description paradigm provides examples of ways in which leakage scores are sometimes computed. Senders describe people they like and dislike truthfully. They also pretend to like the people they really dislike, and pretend to dislike the people they really like. Judges who are accurate at knowing how the senders really do feel about the people they are describing would rate the senders as feeling more liking for the people they are only pretending to dislike (whom they really do like) than for the people they are only pretending to like (but really do dislike). Therefore, leakage accuracy (sometimes called absolute leakage accuracy) can be computed as liking ratings on the pretend-to-dislike descriptions minus liking ratings on the pretend-to-like descriptions. Higher scores indicate greater accuracy. Because perceivers often take what they hear at face value, it is not unusual for leakage scores to be negative: Perceivers often believe that senders feel more liking for the people they are deceptively claiming to like than for the people they are deceptively claiming to dislike.

However, even perceivers who earn negative absolute leakage accuracy scores are not always totally fooled. Although they may think that the false claims of liking indicate more genuine liking than the false claims of disliking, they may still realize that the liking expressed in the false claims is not quite as extreme as the liking expressed in the genuine claims. That is, judges may appreciate that senders truthfully describing people they really do like feel more liking than senders falsely claiming to like people they really dislike. Similarly, they may realize that senders truthfully describing people they really do dislike feel more disliking than senders falsely claiming to dislike people they really like (e.g., B. M. DePaulo, Jordan, Irvine, & Laser, 1982). Relative leakage scores capture these understandings. For example, liking ratings of the pretend-to-like messages can be subtracted from liking ratings of the truthful liking messages; more positive numbers indicate greater accuracy.

## Standard Paradigms

To interpret the levels of accuracy reported in the hundreds of studies that have already been conducted, one must consider not only the statistical properties of the accuracy scores that are used, but also the experimental paradigms used to generate the truthful and deceptive communications.

In the most common paradigms used to study the communication of deception (reviewed by B. M. DePaulo, Tornqvist & Cooper, 2000), people describe honestly or dishonestly their opinions on current controversial issues; or they describe their feelings toward other people; or they answer questions about films, slides, or pictures they have seen. In more than half of the studies, there is another person present asking the sender questions. Typically, though, that interviewer asks questions from a prepared script and does not challenge or probe. Most often, these interviews are videotaped and later viewed by judges who then try to determine the deceptiveness of the senders.

A series of objections to this paradigm occurs readily to many undergraduates hearing about it for the first time, and even to some seasoned investigators. There are no rewards for telling a successful lie, nor any punishments for telling an obvious one, they say; there are no incentives for the judges to detect the lies skillfully either. Importantly, they think, the paradigms are not truly interactive.

Judges have no opportunity actively to try to uncover the deceit: They cannot ask follow up questions or set traps. Moreover, the critics continue, the lies are about matters of little consequence, such as feelings of fondness for other people. These are not what the lies of real life are like, they say.

In fact, however, the standard paradigms may well capture with amazing accuracy what most of the lies of everyday life are really like. It is amazing because at the time most of the studies were designed, little was known about the nature of everyday lies. A pair of diary studies of lying among students as well as people in the community (B. M. DePaulo, Kashy, Kirkendol, Wyer, & Epstein, 1996) has since shown that most lies are indeed about feelings, such as feigning greater liking than one really does feel. Importantly, according to people's diaries, most lies of everyday life are little lies of little consequence. People report that they do not plan their lies very much, they do not regard their lies as very serious, they experience little concern about whether they will get caught in their lies, and they rarely do get caught in those lies (or rarely learn about it if they do). They also experience little discomfort while telling their lies.

The participants in the diary studies rarely reported conversations in which they were challenged or interrogated by the target of the lie or in which the target tried to trick them into "fessing up." In general, only the most trivial interactivity seemed to be present in that the liar was talking to another person.

There is another perhaps even more important problem with the claim that the standard paradigms are ecologically invalid. It seems to be leveled in ignorance of the most basic distinction between internal and external validity. The lie telling and lie detecting modeled in the lab in order to study the process of communication do not need to resemble the superficial features of the deceptive interactions of everyday life in order to be internally valid. It may have been fortunate that the standard paradigms resembled everyday lies in many ways, but scientifically it was not necessary (Mook, 1983).

The critics of the most commonly used paradigms have a favorite alternative paradigm, one in which some of the participants are induced to cheat and then lie about it (e.g., see Exline, Thibaut, Hickey, & Gumpert, 1970). Those participants are then questioned in a challenging way. This paradigm is often heralded for its external validity, but as we have argued, most of the lies of everyday life are not like this. Those who would like to study adversarial lie detection because of a special interest in that particular process should of course do so, but not because they want to capture the characteristics of most everyday lies.

More importantly, the cheating paradigm often suffers from internal invalidity. Participants who are induced to cheat sometimes refuse to do so in nontrivial numbers and are therefore eliminated from the study; those who are not induced to cheat almost never drop out. This differential response rate undermines random assignment and makes it impossible to know whether differences between the liars and the truth tellers reveal anything about deception or whether they instead reveal something about the kinds of people who readily agree to cheat and then lie about it. The reluctant liars (who dropped out of the study), when they do lie, may do so in different ways.

## Where Do Perceptions of Deceptiveness Come From?

Our focus on the deception detection skills of perceivers may seem to suggest an assumption that success at detecting deceit follows most directly from the insightfulness of the perceiver. We believe that there are important differences among perceivers that account for the impressions of deceptiveness that they form (Tornqvist et al., 2000). However, we also believe that a particular speaker, or a particular message, can be so compelling that many different perceivers will form the same impression of that person or message.

*Nature of the Stimulus.* Because perceivers can distinguish lies from truths at an accuracy that is better than chance, it must follow that there are discernible differences between truthful and deceptive communications. In fact, there are many such veridical cues to deceit (B. M. DePaulo, Lindsay, Malone, Muhlenbruck, Charlton, & Cooper, 2000). But the degree to which most of these behaviors differentiate truths from lies is small, and there is no one cue that is totally valid (e.g., always occurs when people are lying and never occurs when they are telling the truth). Cues to deception differ for different kinds of lies and different kinds of liars. For instance, verbal cues to deception are different when people are faking liking than when they are faking disliking (B. M. DePaulo, Rosenthal, Rosenkrantz, & Green, 1982). In addition, the ways in which women fake disliking are different from the ways men do so (B. M. DePaulo, Rosenthal, et al., 1982). There may also be personal styles of lying, as suggested by the results of attempts to train perceivers to detect the lies of particular communicators; the training was effective for the communicators included in the training program but did not generalize to other communicators (Zuckerman, Koestner, & Alton, 1984).

Moreover, for any particular communicator, small behavioral differences between their truthful and deceptive communications may occur in the context of more striking consistencies in overall demeanor. Some people look and sound honest both when lying and when telling the truth, and others appear consistently dishonest (Bond, Kahler, & Paolicelli, 1985; Zuckerman, DeFrank, Hall, Larrance, & Rosenthal, 1979). This research on demeanor bias suggests the possibility that deception judgments are primarily stimulus-driven. It is possible that most of the variance in these judgments is due to differences in the judgeability of targets as opposed to the sensitivity of the perceivers.

*In the Eyes of the Perceiver?* Perceivers use some valid cues to deceit when deciding whether someone is lying, but they also use some cues that are not valid (Malone, DePaulo, Adams, & Cooper, 2000). In a meta-analytic review of more than 1000 estimates of actual cues to deception (B. M. DePaulo, Lindsay, et al., 1999), the average absolute value of the difference between truths and lies was about a quarter of a standard deviation. The comparable value from a meta-analytic review of the degree to which perceivers infer deceptiveness from behavioral cues was about a half of a standard deviation (Malone et al., 2000).

Perceivers may also be insufficiently discriminating in the ways that they use cues to infer deceit. For example, in the same study in which cues to faked liking were shown to be different from cues to faked disliking (B. M. DePaulo, Rosenthal, et al., 1982), it was also reported that perceivers used mostly the same cues to judge both kinds of lies. In fact, there are striking consistencies in the cues used by very different kinds of people to infer deceit. For example, laypersons and professional customs inspectors generally agree with each other on who seems to be trying to smuggle contraband; so do more and less successful inspectors and perceivers with low or high levels of self-monitoring (Kraut & Poe, 1980). In other studies, striking similarities between men and women (B. M. DePaulo, Rosenthal, et al., 1982) and among people from different cultures (Bond et al., 1992; Bond & Atoum, 2000) have been reported.

Consensus in judgments of deceptiveness has also been assessed by calculating the number of perceivers in a given sample who, by chance alone, would arrive at the same decision about the deceptiveness of a communicator, and the number who actually do agree with each other. By that measure, too, there are noteworthy levels of agreement (Bond et al., 1985; Kraut & Poe, 1980).

The high level of agreement among different kinds of perceivers in the inferences they draw about deceptiveness suggests that deceptiveness judgments may be largely stimulus driven. That is, a particular communication will strike most people as either truthful or deceptive; individual differences among perceivers seem less consequential. Yet there are significant individual differences in skill at detecting deceit and also in judgmental biases, such as the tendency to see most communications as truthful. For example, anxious and neurotic perceivers are especially unsuccessful at detecting deceit (Tornqvist et al., 2000), and dispositionally suspicious people are especially unlikely to believe other people (McCornack & Levine, 1990). There is also evidence that, at least for lies that are similar in important ways (e.g., all are told under high-stakes conditions and to the same interviewer), people who are successful at detecting one kind of lie (about personal opinions) are also skilled at detecting another (about a theft; Frank & Ekman, 1997).

It is possible to assess precisely the degree to which judgments of deceptiveness are attributable to (a) the impressions conveyed by the communicators (i.e., stimulus driven), (b) the impressions formed by the perceivers (i.e., the eye of the beholder), or (c) the special ways in which particular perceivers form impressions of particular communicators (relationship effects). Kenny's social relations model, for example, was designed to address precisely these kinds of questions (Kenny, 1994; Kenny & Albright, 1987; Kenny & Winquist, chap. 14, this volume). However, the model has not yet been applied to judgments of deceptiveness.

## A Note on the Generalizability of Lie-Detection Skill

The realm of human lying and lie detecting, when considered exhaustively, is remarkably varied. The little lies of everyday life that pass with little notice or consequence ("I had a great time") differ in countless ways from the lies told by philanderers to suspicious spouses or by murderers to hostile cross-examining prosecutors. It is of great relevance to the construct validity of "general lie-detection skill" to know whether there is anything general about it. As theoretically motivated scientists, we want to know whether there are many lie-detection skills or just one or a few. For practitioners, however, the answer to this question may be of little consequence. The Secret Service, for instance, may want to hire agents who are talented at discerning the credibility of threats on the life of the President. If they then go home and believe their teens' tall tales of spending Friday night at the library, the President's safety may be no more imperiled because of it.

## Nonverbal Sensitivity and Skill at Detecting Deception

The ideas that nonverbal cues betray deceit and that sensitivity to such cues should therefore facilitate lie-detection success have long been part of the lore of the deception–detection literature. But are they true?

First, does sensitivity to particular kinds of cues predict success at detecting deception? It should, but only if the cues are valid indicators of deceit. If, for example, some perceivers were especially attentive to postural shifts, and accurately recognized when they did and did not occur, this sensitivity may be of no use whatsoever to deception detection success if postural shifts do not occur any more or less often when people are lying than when they are telling the truth. In that case, attending to such an irrelevant cue could even undermine lie-detection success if it takes attention away from other more promising sources of information.

In contrast, Ekman and his colleagues suggested that when people tell lies under high-stakes conditions, very brief displays of the emotions that they are trying to hide may be evident to perceivers who are sensitive to such displays and who will then uncover the deceit. Consistent with their predictions, they reported positive correlations between accuracy at recognizing micromomentary facial expressions of emotions and accuracy at detecting several different high-stakes lies (Ekman & O'Sullivan, 1991; Frank & Ekman, 1997).

In two studies of accuracy at detecting low-stakes lies, Littlepage reported small positive (nonsignificant) correlations with nonverbal sensitivity, measured by the Profile of Nonverbal Sensitivity (PONS; Rosenthal, Hall, DiMatteo, Rogers, & Archer, 1979; Littlepage, McKinnie, & Pineault, 1983), and accuracy at recognizing discrepancies between vocal and visual nonverbal cues, measured by the Nonverbal Discrepancy Test (B. M. DePaulo, Rosenthal, Eisenstat, Rogers, & Finkelstein, 1978; Littlepage, Maddox, & Pineault, 1985). If nonverbal cues more clearly separate the lies from the truths under high-stakes conditions than low (B. M. DePaulo, Lindsay, et al., 1999), then it should also follow that nonverbal sensitivity is a more powerful predictor of success at detecting high- than low-stakes lies, as the data seem to suggest.

From the correlational data on nonverbal sensitivity and lie-detection success, it is, of course, impossible to know whether nonverbal sensitivity played a causal role in perceivers' lie-detection success, nor even whether nonverbally sensitive perceivers were tuning in to the nonverbal cues when trying to detect the deceit. In other studies, perceivers make a decision as to whether a message was truthful or deceptive, then explain the basis for their decision (often in an open-ended fashion). These studies, too, have provided some evidence for a link between attunement to (certain) nonverbal cues and success at detecting deception. For example, Ekman and O'Sullivan (1991) found that perceivers who reported using nonverbal cues, alone or in combination with verbal cues, were more accurate at detecting deception than perceivers who reported using only verbal cues. Anderson, DePaulo, Ansfield, Tickle, and Green (1999) also found that the reported use of verbal cues did not predict lie-detection success, but neither did the use of visual cues; only paralinguistic cues predicted success. Anderson, DePaulo, Ansfield, et al. (1999) conceptually replicated experimental work in which perceivers who were instructed to attend to tone-of-voice cues were more successful at detecting deceit than perceivers who were given no special instructions, but perceivers who were instructed to attend to words or to visual cues did no better than control participants (B. M. DePaulo, Lassiter, & Stone, 1982).

Just as deception detection success may be improved by the accurate reading of, or attunement to, nonverbal cues, it may also be undermined by interpretive biases in the reading of those cues. When nonverbal cues conflict, for example, such that some cues suggest that the communicator feels positively, and others suggest negative feelings, some perceivers reliably trust one emotional tone more than the other. Similarly, when visual nonverbal cues conflict with tone-of-voice cues, women, more so than men, may favor the visual cues, especially facial cues (Rosenthal & DePaulo, 1979a,1979b). The lies of everyday life are far more likely to be ones in which people falsely claim positive feelings than ones in which they feign negative feelings (B. M. DePaulo et al., 1996). There is also evidence suggesting that tone-of-voice cues, relative to visual cues (and especially facial cues) may be more likely to leak information that liars are trying to hide (B. M. DePaulo, Stone, & Lassiter, 1985; Ekman & Friesen, 1969). It is likely, then, that perceivers who are biased to trust positive affects and those who are biased to weigh visual cues more than tone-of-voice cues may be especially unlikely to succeed at telling truths from lies.

However, although perceivers might enjoy certain lie detection successes if they do not trust positive affect and ignore facial cues, such an approach to interpersonal perception in everyday social interactions could be hazardous. Imagine how unpleasant it would be to completely disregard the positive affect of your communication partners or to avoid looking at their faces. Such behaviors may provide a boost to the detection of the occasional deceptive communication, but will probably not get you invited back to many parties. For this reason, strategies that could in theory improve your chances of deception detection success may involve a sobering tradeoff—you may have to be willing to spoil your interactions in order to avoid being suckered by a lie.

## FUTURE DIRECTIONS

### Indirect Deception Detection

In the earlier sections, we reviewed the ways in which researchers can measure perceivers' explicit judgments about the veracity of communication. We consider making a binary choice or rating the deceptiveness of a message to be a conscious process regardless of the level of awareness with which the decision actually was reached. We also suggested that, in general, perceiver decisions about veracity are not very accurate. However, is it possible that, at some level, perceivers are accurately judging the truthfulness of messages? If so, is there some way in which this nonexplicit knowledge can be measured?

Such knowledge of the differences between truths and lies has been dubbed indirect or implicit deception detection (Anderson, DePaulo, Ansfield, et al., 1999; B. M. DePaulo, 1994). One way to tap into this implicit knowledge is to examine aspects of the perceivers' feelings and attitudes while they are observing truths and lies. If the attitudes and feelings differ when the perceivers are judging lies compared with when they are judging truths, it can be said that the perceivers are, in some way, detecting the deception.

There is growing empirical support for the construct of implicit deception detection. In one of the first studies to show (or to be recognized as showing) an indirect detection effect, judges ranging in age from sixth graders to college students rated the deceptiveness and ambivalence of speakers who were honestly or dishonestly describing people they liked and disliked (B. M. DePaulo, Jordan, et al., 1982). The 12th graders and college students accurately rated the lies as more deceptive than the truths, thereby showing explicit deception detection accuracy. By their explicit ratings of deceptiveness, the 10th graders seemed not to be able to distinguish the lies from the truths. However, they did see the lies as significantly more ambivalent than the truths (as did the older judges), thereby showing that in some way they could tell the messages apart.

In a subsequent study in which judges observed truthful and deceptive messages and then talked out loud as they tried to decide whether the message they just heard was deceptive, the judges more often mentioned the possibility that the message might be a lie when it was in fact a lie than when it was a truth (Hurd & Noller, 1988). These hunches, however, were uncorrelated with the perceivers' final judgments of the deceptiveness of the messages. Similarly, in a study in which participants guessed whether messages were lies or truths and then were asked to describe the cues that they relied on to make their decision, perceivers mentioned more verbal cues when the story was truthful than when it was a lie, and mentioned more visual nonverbal cues when the story was a lie than when it was a truth (Anderson, DePaulo, Ansfield, et al., 1999). These results were especially noteworthy because the participants did no better than chance at detecting deception when asked explicitly to classify the stories as lies or truths.

By now, a number of different kinds of indirect measures have been shown to distinguish truths from lies. A meta-analytic review showed that in studies in which judges reported their impressions of the senders, they described the senders as appearing more nervous, more indifferent, less verbally and vocally involved in the telling of their tales, and less spontaneous when they were lying than when they were telling the truth. They also formed a less positive impression of the senders who were lying than of those who were telling the truth (B. M. DePaulo, Lindsay, et al., 2000). An important issue for future research is to predict and understand the kinds of indirect measures that do and do not distinguish truths from lies. In the B. M. DePaulo, Lindsay et al.'s (2000) report, only judges' impressions of the senders were reviewed. Another promising direction is to look at the judges' own feelings and reactions. Already several studies have shown that judges feel more confident when judging truths than when judging lies, although their feelings of confidence bear no relationship whatsoever to the accuracy of their explicit judgments of deceptiveness (B. M. DePaulo, Charlton, Cooper, Lindsay, & Muhlenbruck, 1997).

Anderson, DePaulo, and Ansfield (2000) reported other promising leads. They found, for example, in a study in which senders and judges interacted face to face and the judges were no better than chance at detecting deception explicitly, that the judges distinguished the lies from the truths in many indirect ways. For example, the judges were more likely to report that they did not get enough information after their partner had just lied to them than after their partner had just spoken truthfully. They thought the senders seemed more comfortable when telling the truth, and they felt more comfortable themselves after hearing the truth than after hearing a lie. They also reported feeling more suspicious after the lies than after the truths. The researchers then showed videotapes of the interactions to new raters. These raters also failed to distinguish the lies from the truths by their explicit categorizations of the stories as truths or lies. But in making some of the same indirect ratings as the original judges, they too could distinguish the truths from the lies on almost every one. In addition, these raters observed the original judges on the tape, and their perceptions of the suspiciousness of those judges also significantly separated the truths from the lies.

Another important issue for future research is whether perceivers' indirect knowledge can ever be tapped in such a way as to improve explicit deception detection. Is there a way to teach judges to notice and use the differences in their feelings and beliefs? The obvious way to approach this question would be to explain to judges that there is a link between their feelings of confidence, or their impression that the speaker is for example ambivalent or distant, and the truthfulness of the message that they have just heard. Although such studies should be attempted, it is not clear that they will succeed. If perceivers attempt deliberately to form the same impressions that they had previously formed unself-consciously, it is possible that they will not arrive at the same conclusions.

## Behavioral Measures

Although conceptually it is just a short step from looking at perceivers' cognitive and affective reactions to looking at their overt behavioral responses, it is a step that to our knowledge has never been taken. The possibilities range from the micro to the macro. If reaction times to truths and lies were measured, would results show that perceivers react more quickly to the truths than to the lies? If it could be determined with certainty that particular citizens were or were not being lied to by their leaders, would an assessment of the feelings of the citizens show that those listening to the dishonest leaders felt more anxious or insecure than those listening to the honest leaders, even if the unlucky victims had not yet explicitly formed the hypothesis that their leader might be lying?

## Detection Over Time

For the most part, deception detection studies have examined the judgments that perceivers made almost immediately after an exposure to a communication. However, outside of the lab, people frequently make decisions about the truthfulness of a communication after hours, days, or even weeks have passed. For example, it might not even occur to you that a student's excuse must have been a lie until you are driving home from work. Future detection research should examine the ways in which detection ability may change over time.

One possibility is that accuracy might actually improve over time. In the context of an ongoing interaction, it may be difficult to set aside our inclination to accept whatever "face" the other person is presenting (Goffman, 1959). However, once perceivers have temporal (or spatial) distance from the communicator and the message, they may be less likely to accept the message at face value. Differences in cognitive resources during an interaction versus afterwards may also be important. Gilbert, Tafarodi, and Malone (1993) argued that initially, perceivers effortlessly believe what they hear; the process of unbelieving, however, takes additional mental work. Perceivers may have more available mental capacity when they are not involved in an ongoing interaction in which they need to attend to the other person in addition to planning and executing their own self-presentations. More simply, after the interaction is over and they are by themselves, they have time to think (and the mental resources to do so effectively).

Accuracy may also change over time as a result of changes in the information that perceivers use to make deception judgments. When perceivers are in the immediate context of an interaction, they have access to a great deal of information: the verbal content of the message, microlevel nonverbal cues, macrolevel impressions. In contrast, when perceivers think back on a past interaction, they are limited by what they remember (explicitly or implicitly). The documented biases and shortcomings of memory based judgments might seem to point to the prediction that such judgments will be less accurate than the ones made during or directly after the processing of a particular message (Hastie & Park, 1986). However, we think that the opposite prediction is at least equally plausible. The global impressions that stay with perceivers may contain a bigger grain of truth than the first impressions formed at the time of the initial deceptive or truthful encounter. The relevant research needs to be done.

## Noticing Deception in Everyday Interaction

In all research on the detection of deception, perceivers are asked to indicate their perceptions of the deceptiveness of the messages they observe. It is from those reports that their accuracy and bias are assessed. However, would they have noticed the deceits if they had not been explicitly asked about them? The question we are asking is, we think, one of the most fundamental ones in the field: What is the rate of naturalistic lie detection in everyday life? It is also one of the most difficult to address. Without asking people what they noticed about deception, how will researchers know? But once they are asked, their naturalistic social cognition has been intruded on, which may elicit an observation or an inference that they would not have made without being nudged.

Researchers can make changes in paradigms so as to be a bit less directive in their questioning. For example, in laboratory experiments, perceivers could be asked to make open-ended judgments of messages instead of deception judgments. For example, the participants could be asked to list the words that best describe each communicator or message. Mentions of words such as "deceptive" or "honest" could then be compared for the truths and lies. This method, however, is still not totally unobtrusive in that perceivers are making their judgments self-consciously and recording them for researchers. What they notice in such circumstances could differ from what they notice when left completely to their own devices. A second problem is that perceivers' feelings about the veracity of the communications might be too weak to make it onto their list. In this way, it is possible that judges may be getting the right sense but not reporting it.

A hint about the possible rates of lie detection in everyday life came from the diary studies mentioned earlier in which participants kept diaries, every day for a week, of all of their social interactions and all of the lies that they told during those interactions (B. M. DePaulo et al., 1996). About a week after the recording period was over, participants were asked to indicate, for each of the lies they recorded, whether—to their knowledge—the lie had ever been discovered. The answer was a clear "yes" for only 19% of the lies, and for another 19%, the participants reported that they did not know. Of course, the feedback liars receive from the targets of their lies is incomplete and open to misinterpretation. The data from that research, then, can only be regarded as suggestive about the rates of naturalistic lie detection.

However, it may be possible to modify the diary paradigm in order to attain a better estimate of lie detection in everyday life. For example, participants who are close relationship partners could be asked to keep a diary, for just 1 day, of all of their interactions with each other. At the end of the day, the participants could be asked to indicate, for each of the interactions they recorded, whether they had told any lies during that interaction and whether they think their partner lied to them. Participants' reports of the lies they told to their partners in particular interactions can be compared with their partners' reports of believing that they had been told lies during the same interactions. Even this methodology, however, is not totally naturalistic. It is possible that the process of recording social interactions will change the nature and rate of lying and lie detecting.

Our best guess about the outcome of future research on detection accuracy is that it will demonstrate both lesser and greater accuracy than the rates documented by the first several hundred studies. The rates of explicit naturalistic lie detection, we suspect, will be lower than the current best guess of 54%. On the other hand, when researchers allow for the indirect ways in which perceivers might accurately sense when a lie has or has not been told (including cognitive, affective, and behavioral ways), and when researchers also begin to look at perceivers' second and third thoughts about the veracity of stories they were told, after they are removed from the demands of the immediate interaction in which the lies may have been told, we surmise that greater insights will be found than have heretofore been documented. We look forward to the replacement of our hunches with data.

122                                                                              MALONE AND DEPAULO

# REFERENCES

Anderson, D. E. (1999). Cognitive and motivational processes underlying the truth bias. Unpublished doctoral dissertation, University of Virginia, Charlottesville.

Anderson, D. E., Ansfield, M. E., & DePaulo, B. M. (2000). Love's best habit: Deception in the context of relationships. In P. Philippot, R. S. Feldman, & E. J. Coats (Eds.), *The social context of nonverbal behavior* (pp. 372–409). Cambridge, England: Cambridge University Press.

Anderson, D. E., DePaulo, B. M., & Ansfield, M. E. (2000). *The development of deception detection skill: A longitudinal study of same sex friends.* Manuscript submitted for review.

Anderson, D. E., DePaulo, B. M., Ansfield, M. E., Tickle, J. J., & Green, E. (1999). Beliefs about cues to deception: Mindless stereotypes or untapped wisdom? *Journal of Nonverbal Behavior, 23,* 67–88.

Bond, C. F., & Atoum, A. O. (2000). International deception. *Personality and Social Psychology Bulletin, 26,* 385–395.

Bond, C. F., Jr., Kahler, K. N., & Paolicelli, L. M. (1985). The miscommunication of deception: An adaptive perspective. *Journal of Experimental Social Psychology, 21,* 331–345.

Bond, C. F., Jr., Omar, A., Pitre, U., Lashley, B. R., Skaggs, L. M., & Kirk, C. T. (1992). Fishy-looking liars: Deception judgment from expectancy violation. *Journal of Personality and Social Psychology, 63,* 969–977.

Burgoon, J. K., Buller, D. B., Ebesu, A. S., & Rockwell, P. (1994). Interpersonal deception V: Accuracy in deception detection. *Communication Monographs, 61,* 303–325.

Cronbach, L. J. (1955). Processes affecting scores on understanding of others and "assumed similarity." *Psychological Bulletin, 52,* 177–193.

DePaulo, B. M. (1994). Spotting lies: Can humans learn to do better? *Current Directions in Psychological Science, 3,* 83–86.

DePaulo, B. M., Charlton, K., Cooper, H., Lindsay, J. J., & Muhlenbruck, L. (1997). The accuracy–confidence correlation in the detection of deception. *Personality and Social Psychology Review, 1,* 346–357.

DePaulo, B. M., Jordan, A., Irvine, A., & Laser, P. S. (1982). Age changes in the detection of deception. *Child Development, 53,* 701–709.

DePaulo, B. M., Kashy, D. A., Kirkendol, S. E., Wyer, M. M., & Epstein, J. A. (1996). Lying in everyday life. *Journal of Personality and Social Psychology, 70,* 979–995.

DePaulo, B. M., Lassiter, G. D., & Stone, J. I. (1982). Attentional determinants of success at detecting deception and truth. *Personality and Social Psychology Bulletin, 8,* 273–279.

DePaulo, B. M., Lindsay, J. J., Malone, B. E., Muhlenbruck, L., Charlton, K., & Cooper, H. (2000). *Cues to deception.* Manuscript submitted for publication.

DePaulo, B. M., Rosenthal, R., Eisenstat, R. A., Rogers, P. C., & Finkelstein, S. (1978). Decoding discrepant nonverbal cues. *Journal of Personality and Social Psychology, 36,* 313–323.

DePaulo, B. M., Rosenthal, R., Rosenkrantz, J., & Green, C. R. (1982). Actual and perceived cues to deception: A closer look at speech. *Basic and Applied Social Psychology, 3,* 291–312.

DePaulo, B. M., Stone, J. I., & Lassiter, G. D. (1985). Deceiving and detecting deceit. In B. R. Schlenker (Ed.), *The self and social life* (pp. 323–370). New York: McGraw-Hill.

DePaulo, B. M., Tornqvist, J. S., & Cooper, H. (2000). *Accuracy at detecting deception: A meta-analysis of modality effects.* Manuscript in preparation.

DePaulo, P. J., & DePaulo, B. M. (1989). Can attempted deception by salespersons and customers be detected through nonverbal behavioral cues? *Journal of Applied Social Psychology, 19,* 1552–1577.

Ekman, P., & Friesen, W. V. (1969). Nonverbal leakage and clues to deception. *Psychiatry, 32,* 88–106.

Ekman, P., & O'Sullivan, M. (1991). Who can catch a liar? *American Psychologist, 46,* 913–920.

Exline, R. V., Thibaut, J., Hickey, C. B., & Gumpert, P. (1970). Visual interaction in relation to Machiavellianism and an unethical act. In R. Christie & F. Geis (Eds.), *Studies in Machiavellianism* (pp. 53–75). New York: Academic.

Frank, M. G., & Ekman, P. (1997). The ability to detect deceit generalizes across different types of high-stake lies. *Journal of Personality and Social Psychology, 72,* 1429–1439.

Gage, N. L., & Cronbach, L. J. (1955). Conceptual and methodological problems in interpersonal perception. *Psychological Review, 62,* 411–422.

Gilbert, D. T., Tafarodi, R. W., & Malone, P. S. (1993). You can't not believe everything you read. *Journal of Personality and Social Psychology, 65,* 2221–2233.

Goffman, E. (1959). *The presentation of self in everyday life.* Garden City, NY: Doubleday/Anchor.

Green, D. M., & Swets, J. A. (1974). *Signal detection theory and psychophysics.* Huntington, NY: Robert E. Krieger.

Hastie, R., & Park, B. (1986). The relationship between memory and judgment depends upon whether the judgment task is memory-based or on-line. *Psychological Review, 93,* 258–268.

Hurd, K., & Noller, P. (1988). Decoding deception: A look at the process. *Journal of Nonverbal Behavior, 12,* 217–233.

Jones, E. E. (1990). *Interpersonal perception.* New York: Freeman.

Kenny, D. A. (1994). *Interpersonal perception: A social relations analysis.* New York: Guilford.

Kenny, D. A., & Albright, L. (1987). Accuracy in interpersonal perception: A social relations analysis. *Journal of Personality and Social Psychology, 102,* 390–402.

Kraut, R. E., & Poe, D. B. (1980). Behavioral roots of person perception: The deception judgments of customs inspectors and laymen. *Journal of Personality and Social Psychology, 39,* 784–798.

Levine, T. R., & McCornack, S. A. (1991). The dark side of trust: Conceptualizing and measuring types of communicative suspicion. *Communication Quarterly, 39,* 325–340.

Levine, T. R., Park, H. S., & McCornack, S. A. (1999). Accuracy in detecting truths and lies: Documenting the veracity effect. *Communication Monographs, 66,* 125–144.

Littlepage, G. E., Maddox, J., & Pineault, M. A. (1985). Recognition of discrepant nonverbal messages and detection of deception. *Perceptual and Motor Skills, 60,* 119–124.

Littlepage, G. E., McKinnie, R., & Pineault, M. A. (1983). Relationship between nonverbal sensitivities and detection of deception. *Perceptual and Motor Skills, 57,* 651–657.

Luce, R. D. (1959). *Individual choice behavior.* New York: Wiley.

Macmillan, N. A., & Creelman, C. D. (1991). *Detection theory: A user's guide.* Cambridge: Cambridge University Press.

Malone, B. E., DePaulo, B. M., Adams, R. B., & Cooper, H. (2000). *Perceived and believed cues to deception.* Manuscript in preparation.

McCornack, S. A., & Levine, T. R. (1990). When lovers become leery: The relationship between suspicion and accuracy in detecting deception. *Communication Monographs, 57,* 219–230.

Mook, D. G. (1983). In defense of external invalidity. *American Psychologist, 38,* 379–387.

Rosenthal, R., & DePaulo, B. M. (1979a). Sex differences in eavesdropping on nonverbal cues. *Journal of Personality and Social Psychology, 37,* 273–285.

Rosenthal, R., & DePaulo, B. M. (1979b). Sex differences in accommodation in nonverbal communication. In R. Rosenthal (Ed.), *Skill in nonverbal communication: Individual differences* (pp. 68–103). Cambridge, MA: Oelgeschlager, Gunn & Hain.

Rosenthal, R., Hall, J. A., DiMatteo, M. R., Rogers, P. L., & Archer, D. (1979). *Sensitivity to nonverbal communication: The PONS test.* Baltimore: Johns Hopkins University Press.

Simpson, J. A., Ickes, W., & Blackstone, T. (1995). When the head protects the heart: Empathic accuracy in dating relationships. *Journal of Personality and Social Psychology, 69,* 629–641.

Tornqvist, J. S., DePaulo, B. M., Mahaffey, A., Muhlenbruck, L., Kernahan, C., & Cooper, H. (2000). *Sex differences and personality differences in detecting deception: A meta-analytic review.* Manuscript in preparation.

Zuckerman, M., DeFrank, R. S., Hall, J. A., Larrance, D. T., & Rosenthal, R. (1979). Facial and vocal cues to deception and truth. *Journal of Experimental Social Psychology, 15,* 378–396.

Zuckerman, M., Koestner, R., & Alton, A. O. (1984). Learning to detect deception. *Journal of Personality and Social Psychology, 46,* 519–528.

# III

## Toward the Creation of an Interpersonal Sensitivy Test

# ❦ 7 ❧

# Self-Report Measurement
# of Interpersonal Sensitivity

**Ronald E. Riggio**
*Claremont McKenna College*

**Heidi R. Riggio**
*California State University, Fullerton*

This chapter reports on the use of self-report techniques for measuring interpersonal sensitivity and related constructs. There are two main advantages to using self-report measures to assess interpersonal sensitivity. First and foremost, self-report methods are relatively easy to administer. This is particularly important when researchers have limited access to research participants, as is the case in much applied research (see Riggio, chap. 15, this volume). Second, self-report methods allow assessment of a broad range of sensitivity-related constructs. Although most of this book focuses on interpersonal sensitivity from an "accuracy" perspective (e.g., accuracy of decoding emotions, accuracy of personality judgments), it may be fruitful to broaden the definition of interpersonal sensitivity to include individual differences in sensitivity to emotional messages, such as empathically (vicariously) responding to others' emotional states. Some of these broader sensitivity constructs may be more amenable to self-report methodology.

Although self-report assessment of interpersonal sensitivity has a great deal of potential, research to date has shown only weak relationships between direct self-report assessments of accuracy of decoding emotions (i.e., nonverbal sensitivity) and performance-based measures of decoding accuracy. We review this research, explore the broader range of sensitivity-related constructs that are typically assessed through self-reports, discuss measurement issues regarding the use of self-report methods, and suggest guidelines for developing and using self-reports in interpersonal sensitivity research.

## SELF-REPORT VERSUS
## PERFORMANCE-BASED MEASUREMENT

Self-report methods are used extensively for measuring attitudes, emotional states, and personality traits. Attitudes and emotional states are subjective experiences that are not easily assessed via observation, so self-report assessments are deemed appropriate. Similarly, self-report methods are a generally accepted means for assessing personality constructs. Although self-report assessments of attitudes are indeed the norm, observational methods of assessing attitudes have been developed. For example, Wrightsman (1969) used bumper stickers to measure voting preferences, whereas Milgram and others have used the forwarding of "lost letters" to measure attitudes toward political candidates or causes (Milgram, Mann, & Harter, 1965; Simmons & Zumpf, 1983). However, these types of measures are usually difficult to develop and use, tend to be imprecise, and are viewed as indirect measures of the constructs (Oskamp, 1991).

Behavioral assessments of emotional states are more common than behavioral assessments of attitudes, but self-reports are also most typically used to measure emotional states. For example, there has been considerable success in using observations of facial expressions and other nonverbal displays of emotional cues as a more "direct" method of measuring basic emotional states (most notably, the six or so basic emotions of happiness, anger, disgust, fear, surprise, and sadness outlined by Ekman and Friesen, 1975). However, individual control over the expression of felt emotional states and the influence of social "display rules" on emotional expression (e.g., Ekman, 1972) decrease the accuracy of these observational assessments of emotional states. Because of these and other limitations, it is more common, and thought to be more accurate, to assess emotional states via self-report (Robinson, Shaver, & Wrightsman, 1991). In a similar vein, personality traits are most typically assessed using self-report inventories, although trained clinicians often attempt to assess personality through direct observations of behavior. For research purposes, however, self-report measures are most typically used (Robinson et al., 1991). In short, self-report measures are typically the preferred assessment mode when measuring attitudes, emotions, or personality. The exact opposite is the case for measuring interpersonal skills, such as interpersonal sensitivity.

Skills or abilities are more typically measured through behaviorally based, or performance-based, methods of assessment. For example, cognitive skills are usually assessed via performance tests requiring the solving of problems that measure facility in using the particular skill. Similarly, measurement of interpersonal skills is most commonly accomplished through direct observation and/or designing a test, such as the performance-based measures of interpersonal sensitivity discussed elsewhere in this volume. Self-reports of skills are viewed as less precise and strongly affected by response biases (Cronbach, 1990; Oskamp, 1991) and are thus used less frequently in research. We argue that despite limitations, validated self-report assessments of interpersonal skills and of interpersonal sensitivity in particular are viable alternatives to behaviorally based measures for investigating particular research questions.

The primary advantage of self-report measures of interpersonal skills is their ease of use and relative low cost in terms of time, technology, and resources. The development of standardized, performance-based measures of interpersonal skills is laborious, and usually such measures are time-consuming to administer. Self-report measures of skill are relatively easy to develop, and once validated, are easy and inexpensive to administer. This is particularly important for research in applied settings, such as in work organizations (see Riggio, chap. 15, this volume), where time limitations usually prohibit the use of more time-consuming, performance-based measures.

A second advantage of self-report measures of interpersonal skills is that they can reflect skill levels across a variety of domains and situations. For instance, items can assess skill in both intimate and nonintimate dyadic interactions as well as interpersonal skills in formal and informal group settings. If constructed correctly, individuals can use self-report measures to recount both the history of their success with particular skills and how successfully they use certain skills in a variety of typical situations. This is a particular advantage in considering the relative usefulness of self-report measures in comparison with behavioral assessments of interpersonal skills. Generally, behaviorally based assessments of interpersonal sensitivity involve observing a participant in a specific structured or unstructured laboratory situation, often requiring the participant to report on his or her perceptions of the feelings experienced by an unknown target person involved in a particular interaction (e.g., Ickes, 1997, chap. 12, this volume; Snodgrass, Hecht, & Ploutz-Snyder, 1998; Snodgrass, chap. 11, this volume). Although such methods may yield precise results concerning individuals' interpersonal sensitivity in response to the particular social situation used, these methods may not be indicative of interpersonal sensitivity as it occurs in the variety of social situations the typical individual encounters on a daily basis.

Finally, self-report measures of interpersonal skills can focus on both individual perceptions of abilities (i.e., individual metaknowledge of communication skill and success), experiential responses to communication events, and estimates of the frequency with which an individual engages in particular behaviors in everyday social interaction. In other words, some self-report measures may assess self-perceptions of communication success or skill level (e.g., "I am very good at figuring out what other people are feeling"), other items may inquire as to feelings about communication experiences (e.g., "I dislike hearing about other people's troubles"), and others may ask respondents to rate the frequency with which they engage in prototypical communication behaviors (e.g., "I must admit I rarely notice irritation in other peoples' voices"). This important feature of self-report instruments is a clear advantage over behavioral assessments or direct observation because respondents may provide information concerning processes that are not observable but that the respondent has become aware of through feedback from others (e.g., "Other people have told me that I am a sensitive person"), rather than reflecting just self-perceptions. Self-report instruments are thus highly flexible, are useful for examining self-reported behavior as well as psychological judgments, and may be tailored specifically for particular research questions.

## CONSTRUCT VALIDITY OF SELF-REPORT MEASURES OF INTERPERSONAL SENSITIVITY

Major criticisms of self-report measures of interpersonal sensitivity generally focus on the construct validity of such measures. Researchers evaluating the usefulness of self-report measures of interpersonal skill must decide whether respondents are truly aware of the degree of their communication ability or the frequency with which they engage in particular communication behaviors and whether they are reporting accurately on these factors (Oskamp, 1991). An obvious way to evaluate the construct validity of self-report assessments of interpersonal sensitivity is to determine whether self-reports of a decoding skill are significantly correlated with behavioral assessments of such skill—convergent validity evidence that supports the construct validity of certain self-report measures (Campbell & Fiske, 1959).

The earliest attempt to use self-report methods to measure nonverbal decoding skill was Zuckerman and Larrance's (1979) Perceived Decoding Ability (PDA), and Perceived Encoding Ability (PEA), scales. The PDA consists of 32 self-report items written to assess decoding skill in both facial–visual and vocal–auditory channels. Items are also designed to assess decoding skill across the four quadrants created by the intersection of the positive–negative and dominant–submissive dimensions. For example, an item such as "I can usually tell when someone is angry from his or her tone of voice" measures vocal sensitivity to negative–dominant affect (anger). The item, "When someone tries to please me, I can usually tell from his or her facial expression" assesses facial sensitivity to positive–submissive affect.

The results of initial validity studies of the PDA were mixed. For example, scores on the PDA did not correlate significantly with the full version of the Profile of Nonverbal Sensitivity (PONS; $r = .13, n = 88$), which is a standardized test of accuracy in decoding nonverbal cues (Rosenthal, Hall, DiMatteo, Rogers, & Archer, 1979; see Hall, chap. 8, this volume), although the correlations between the PDA and the "Brief Exposure" version of the PONS were higher ($rs = .26$ and $.28$, $n = 45$ and $158$, respectively). Although the PDA did not correlate with success at decoding posed facial cues of affect ($r = -.03$), the correlation between the PDA and decoding of spontaneous facial affect was higher ($r = .22$; both $n = 46$).

There are several possible reasons why these results for the PDA were not more encouraging. First, the PDA items directly ask about abilities to decode cues from tone of voice and facial expressions. Critics of the use of self-reports of interpersonal skill have argued that it is virtually impossible for individuals to accurately and directly report their level of skill, including skill in interpersonal sensitivity. For example, Ickes (1993) suggested that individuals rarely seek explicit feedback concerning their communication skill and that any feedback they do receive may be inaccurate. Respondents may be largely unaware of their ability to decode facial expressions, vocal and paralinguistic cues, their accuracy in judging personality, and the like. Moreover, they may be unable to differentiate among these various skills.

Another potential problem with self-report measures of interpersonal sensitivity in general, and the PDA in particular, concerns socially desirable responding. The great majority of PDA items use the item stem, "I can usually tell … " (e.g., "I can usually tell when someone feels guilty from the person's facial expression"—an item designed to assess skill at decoding deception clues). It seems that an affirmative response to such positively worded items would imply interpersonal communication accuracy and high skill, whereas affirmative responses to negatively worded items (e.g., "I usually cannot tell when someone is impressed from the person's tone of voice") would imply deficiency in communication ability. Thus, responses to such items seem highly susceptible to the influence of social desirability. Other PDA items also appear to be highly suggestive of responses that are socially desirable or indicative of high communication skill, a socially desirable trait. For instance, it seems unlikely that many participants would agree with items such as "I am usually unaware of other people's feelings," or disagree with items such as "I think I have a lot of insight into people," regardless of their actual ability to decode the vocal and nonverbal displays of others. The susceptibility of responses to PDA items to social desirability is indicated by a significant positive correlation ($r = .20$, $n = 253$) between the Marlowe–Crowne Social Desirability Scale (Crowne & Marlowe, 1964) and the PDA total score (Zuckerman & Larrance, 1979).

The researchers who developed the PONS (Rosenthal et al., 1979) also explored the relationship between the performance-based PONS and self-reports of nonverbal decoding skill. Specifically, the PONS researchers used three 9-point rating scales of how much respondents believed they understood voice tone, body movements, and facial expressions. Each rating scale was correlated with its corresponding PONS subscale (tone, body, face). The most encouraging result was a .30 median correlation (for the three correlations) for 53 U.S. college students. However, the median correlation of 28 different samples of participants was only .08[1] It seems obvious that these self-report items suffer from the same problems as the PDA—the fact that respondents may not be able to directly report on their understanding of specific channels of nonverbal communication and the possibility that such self-reports are distorted by social desirability. Although correlations of approximately .20 between self-reports of decoding skill and scores on performance tests are small and disappointing, it is interesting to note that both single- and multiple-item self-reports of intelligence and correlations with IQ test scores are essentially the same ($rs$ = .20–.26; Paulhus, Lysy, & Yik, 1998).

In addition to research on emotional decoding, there have been some attempts to correlate scores on the more complex measure of interpersonal sensitivity, the Interpersonal Perception Task (IPT; Archer & Costanzo, 1988; Costanzo & Archer, 1989; see also Archer, Costanzo, & Akert, chap. 9, this volume), with self-reported success on the IPT. Smith, Archer, and Costanzo (1991) found a slight positive relationship between IPT accuracy and self-reported accuracy ($r$ = .08, $n$ = 476). Patterson and Stockbridge (1998) found a nonsignificant correlation of -.08 between self-reported accuracy and actual performance on the IPT, but they also noted a tendency for participants to greatly overestimate their accuracy—a bias that might affect ability to accurately self-report one's accuracy and skill on performance-based measures. Interestingly, this same overestimation bias occurs in self-reports of intelligence (Paulhus et al., 1998).

Riggio's Social Skills Inventory (SSI; 1986, 1989) represents an attempt to formally use self-report methods to assess interpersonal sensitivity and other social/communication skills. However, rather than using direct reports of interpersonal skill, as was the case in Zuckerman and Larrance's PDA, the SSI uses a more indirect, traitlike self-report method.

The SSI is a 90-item instrument designed to assess basic social/communication skills. The SSI consists of six scales that measure social and emotional (essentially nonverbal) expressivity, sensitivity, and control. Expressivity refers to the skill with which individuals send messages; sensitivity refers to the skill with which individuals receive and interpret the messages of others; control refers to the skill with which individuals are able to regulate the communication process in a social situation.

Two of the SSI's six scales are, in effect, self-report measures of interpersonal sensitivity. The 15-item Emotional Sensitivity scale measures skill in receiving and interpreting (decoding) the nonverbal affective messages of others. Yet the definition of emotional sensitivity is broader. In addition to emotional decoding

---

[1]Although it is clear that people are not very good at assessing their own nonverbal decoding accuracy, others (peers, supervisors, acquaintances) are only slightly more successful at judging a person's nonverbal sensitivity. For instance, the median correlation between other-ratings and scores on the PONS is .22 (as opposed to the .08 median correlation obtained between self-reports and PONS across all samples).

skill, emotionally sensitive persons are simply more attentive to emotional cues—perhaps related to what Hall (chap. 8, this volume) refers to as "attentional accuracy"—and they are more susceptible to becoming emotionally aroused by others, empathically experiencing their emotional states.

The second SSI scale that measures interpersonal sensitivity is the Social Sensitivity (SS) scale. The 15-item SS scale assesses ability to interpret and decode social situations and the subtle verbal communication of others. It also assesses an individual's sensitivity to and understanding of the norms governing appropriate social behavior. As with other scales of the SSI, most items on the SS scale reflect reports based on social behaviors for which respondents have received direct feedback and involve descriptions of the frequency of typical social communication behaviors (e.g., "While growing up, my parents were always stressing the importance of good manners" and "I would much rather take part in a political discussion than to observe and analyze what the participants are saying" [reverse-scored]). This self-report scale is more aligned with the decoding skill captured in the performance-based IPT. In addition, individuals who are socially sensitive are conscious and aware of the appropriateness of their own actions. Extremely high scores on this scale, particularly in conjunction with persons who are low on expressiveness (i.e., low scores on the Emotional Expressivity and Social Expressivity scales of the SSI), may suggest a social self-consciousness that inhibits participation in social interaction. This may explain why there are positive correlations between the SS scale and measures of public self-consciousness, social anxiety, and the Other-Directedness subscale of Snyder's Self-Monitoring Scale (1974; also see Briggs, Cheek, & Buss, 1980; Riggio & Friedman, 1982). It is assumed that some level of social awareness and social anxiety may be a prerequisite for being interpersonally sensitive—acting somewhat like a social conscience (Riggio, 1986; Riggio, Throckmorton, & DePaola, 1990).

The SSI scales were constructed in an attempt to indirectly assess interpersonal skills. Broad and detailed definitions were created for each of the scales, and items were based on social behaviors that were presumably indicative of socially skilled interactants. Whenever possible, items were worded to reflect reports on skills about which the respondent had presumably received some performance feedback (e.g., "People have told me that I am a sensitive and understanding person" rather than "I am a sensitive and understanding person"), or items were written to assess the frequency and typicality of particular sensitivity-related behaviors (e.g., "I am easily able to give someone a comforting hug or touch someone who is distressed"). It is important to note that the domain of social behaviors related to interpersonal sensitivity is quite broad. An attempt was made in constructing the SSI sensitivity scales to sample from this broad domain of behaviors (i.e., the issue of content validity of the scales). Yet, there are undoubtedly limitations to the breadth of measurement in the existing SSI sensitivity scales.

For the most part, correlations between the SSI sensitivity scales and performance-based assessments of interpersonal sensitivity follow the same pattern as the earlier attempts to measure sensitivity via self-report methods.[2] For example, the Emotional Sensitivity (ES) scale of the SSI was significantly positively correlated with total score on the PONS, but the magnitude of the correlation was small ($r = .18, n = 119$; Riggio, 1986). The SSI ES scale was also slightly positively correlated ($r = .17, n = 31$) with the total score on the IPT (Riggio & Carney, in press). The SS scale of the SSI was not correlated with these performance measures. In another study, the ES scale of the SSI was combined with the Emotional Expressivity scale of the SSI to create a scale of emotional empathy—ability to read others' emotions and express them back. This composite scale was found to be significantly positively correlated with performance on a behaviorally based emotion recognition task and an ability to empathize with authors of emotionally laden written essays (Riggio, Tucker, & Coffaro, 1989). Validation studies for the SS scale found significant positive correlations between Social Sensitivity and several other self-report measures of empathy and perspective-taking (Riggio et al., 1989). In addition, scores on the SS scale predicted performance on a perspective-taking task, but only for male participants ($r = .25$). These results provide some limited support for the use of the SS scale in assessing individual differences in sensitivity to others in social situations.

Although self-reports of general levels of interpersonal sensitivity or general ability to decode facial expressions of emotion may be somewhat inaccurate, individuals are likely to be more accurate in reporting the frequency and typicality with which they engage in particular social behaviors, such as initiating or taking part in a conversation at a party or social event or the degree to which the social behavior of others affects their felt emotional states. Further, items may be worded such that they tap reports on skills about which the respondent has presumably received some performance feedback (e.g., "People have told me that I am a sensitive and understanding person"). Therefore, although an individual's assessment of his or her own level of communication skill may be somewhat deficient, individual ratings of the frequency of communication behaviors and events as well as reports of feedback received from others are likely to be more accurate. As might be expected, scores on the ES scale of the SSI are indeed sig

---

[2]Whereas self-reports of decoding skill are weakly correlated with decoding performance, self-reports of nonverbal encoding, or emotional expressiveness, have been found to have stronger positive correlations with behavioral assessments of encoding (e.g., Riggio, Widaman, & Friedman, 1985; Tucker & Riggio, 1988). In addition, self-report measures of emotional control, or the ability to control the outward expression of felt emotional states, have been found to be significantly negatively correlated with behavioral measures of the spontaneous expression of emotion and yet have been found to be uncorrelated with behavioral assessments involving the posed expression of emotion (Tucker & Riggio, 1988). In other words, individual emotional control, as reflected by self-report assessment, is strongly negatively associated with spontaneous expressive behavior, yet it is unrelated to expressive behavior in response to a prompt to pose emotions. This pattern of results is intuitively sensible and supports the construct validity of such self-report assessments.

nificantly correlated with self-reported social behaviors, such as numbers of close friends ($r = .37$), the size of social networks (rs = .28–.37; Riggio, 1986; Riggio, Watring, & Throckmorton, 1993), and desire to go into jobs in teaching and the "helping professions" ($r = .22$; Riggio & Ritter, 1986). This has important implications for how self-report measures of interpersonal sensitivity and other interpersonal skills and abilities are constructed. Of course, a critical need is to map out the domain of social behaviors that may be indicative of possession of interpersonal sensitivity. To date, this work has not been done, so self-report measures of interpersonal sensitivity rely primarily on the authors' implicit assumptions of what constitutes interpersonally sensitive behavior.

As mentioned earlier, self-report measures of interpersonal skill are also likely to be easily affected by response biases, particularly social desirability (Oskamp, 1991). Individuals may respond to questions concerning their social or interpersonal skills in ways that reflect positively on them. However, there are scale development procedures that may serve to prevent the strong influence of social desirability on self-reports. Items may be pretested on social desirability and dropped from the scale accordingly (Robinson et al., 1991). Further, the forced-choice format in which the alternatives have been equated on the basis of social desirability ratings may be used to further reduce the influence of this response set (Oskamp, 1991; Robinson et al., 1991). In addition, items asking for reports of the frequency of certain behaviors may be less influenced by social desirability than items asking for reports of success or ability. Although clearly a disadvantage that is highly particular to the use of self-report assessments, the influence of response biases may be strongly reduced when rigorous scale development and validation procedures are followed (Robinson et al., 1991).

As mentioned earlier, social desirability may play a significant role in explaining why direct self-report measures of interpersonal sensitivity, and measures such as the PDA, do not correlate well with actual decoding and sensitivity abilities. Instruments such as the PDA may not be as useful as other self-report assessments of interpersonal sensitivity in that many items are apparently based on self-perceptions of communication ability rather than on the frequency of particular social behaviors or events or actual feedback that the respondent has received from others concerning typical communication behaviors. As discussed earlier, items reflecting typical interaction behaviors appear less likely to be influenced by social desirability, particularly if they are worded in such a way that communication accuracy, success, or deficiency are not associated with any particular response (e.g., "I sometimes cry at sad movies"). It seems that rather than reflecting actual vocal and facial decoding ability, the PDA assesses individual beliefs and desires about decoding skill and endorsement of socially desirable communication abilities. It is interesting to note that the ES scale was found to be non-significantly correlated with the Marlowe–Crowne Social Desirability Scale (SDS; Crowne & Marlowe, 1964; $r = .12, n = 149$; see Riggio, 1986) and with the Lie scale of the Eysenck Personality Inventory (EPI; Eysenck

& Eysenck, 1968; $r = .05, n = 95$), suggesting that the ES scale of the SSI is not particularly prone to distortion or response bias. Interestingly, the SS scale of the SSI is significantly *negatively* correlated with the SDS ($r = -.31$) but uncorrelated with the EPI Lie scale ($r = .05$).

## SELF-REPORT MEASURES OF CONSTRUCTS RELATED TO INTERPERSONAL SENSITIVITY

As can be seen throughout this book, interpersonal sensitivity is a broad construct, encompassing accuracy in decoding others' emotions, cognitions, personalities, and social relationships. We have already explored self-report assessment of one subset of interpersonal sensitivity—emotional sensitivity, or emotional decoding skill—as well as a second construct related to social perception and social sensitivity. There have also been a few attempts to assess other interpersonal sensitivity-related constructs via self-reports. However, the definitions of these constructs vary with each measure. We review several here.

As part of the development of a self-report Interpersonal Competence Questionnaire, Buhrmester and his colleagues (Buhrmester, Furman, Wittenberg, & Reis, 1988), constructed a scale of Emotional Support that included elements of emotional sensitivity. This emotional support scale correlated strongly with the ES scale of the SSI and with friends' ratings of the respondents' levels of emotional support. The Emotional Support scale also predicted respondents' self-reported popularity and dating frequency. However, it does not appear that this Emotional Support scale has been correlated with performance-based measures of emotional decoding skill or interpersonal sensitivity, and it does not appear that this measure has been widely used.

The Interpersonal Sensitivity Measure (IPSM; Boyce & Parker, 1989) is not what the title suggests. According to the authors, the IPSM is designed to measure depression-prone personality style. Yet it illustrates one of the dilemmas associated with both the construct and the measurement of interpersonal sensitivity. Being interpersonally sensitive requires attention to and an awareness of others' social behavior, an ability to "read" social situations, as well as the ability to judge others' feelings, cognitions, and personalities. Taken to the extreme, interpersonal sensitivity may overlap with constructs such as public self-consciousness and social anxiety (see Buss, 1980; Fenigstein, Scheier, & Buss, 1975; Leary, 1983). The IPSM deals with this extreme end of the interpersonal sensitivity continuum. This measure identifies individuals with an undue or excessive awareness of and sensitivity to the behavior and feelings of others. The authors suggest that the IPSM assesses aspects of interpersonal relationships, generally close relationships, rather than aspects of general social behavior. The use of the IPSM is limited and it has generally been used in research examining aspects of melancholic and nonmelancholic depression. It is unclear how this instrument is related to other self-report measures of interpersonal sensitivity, to self-report and behavioral measures of nonverbal decoding, and to overall communication skill.

Additionally, there are a number of personality constructs that are closely related to interpersonal sensitivity, and all of these are measured through self-report methods. Most closely aligned with notions of interpersonal sensitivity is empathy—a topic discussed in depth by Losoya and Eisenberg (chap. 2, this volume). The primary distinction in the definition and measurement of empathy concerns the difference between emotional empathy and cognitive empathy, or perspective-taking (Eisenberg, Murphy, & Shepard, 1997; Hogan, 1969; Riggio et al., 1989). For example, Mehrabian and Epstein's Questionnaire Measure of Emotional Empathy (Mehrabian & Epstein, 1972), is the most commonly used measure of emotional empathy, although Davis (1983) developed a measure that assesses empathy from the cognitive, perspective-taking standpoint. This distinction parallels attempts to measure interpersonal sensitivity as emotional and nonverbal decoding skill, as well as a more global social sensitivity. Davis (1983; 1994) further divided empathy, differentiating empathic concern ("other-oriented feelings of sympathy") and personal distress ("feelings of personal anxiety and unease in tense interpersonal settings"—similar to a tendency toward emotional contagion that we discuss shortly), from perspective-taking. Because all of these measures treat empathy as a personality dimension, the use of self-report methods is rarely challenged. It may very well be the case that empathy, in its broadest sense, represents the "personality" manifestation of the skill or ability of interpersonal sensitivity (for further discussions of the relationship between personality traits and abilities, see Friedman, 1979; Paulhus & Martin, 1987; Wallace, 1966).

As mentioned earlier, personality dimensions such as public self-consciousness, social anxiety, and other-directedness (and perhaps other personality dimensions; see Davis & Kraus, 1997) have also been linked to interpersonal sensitivity, and these personality characteristics are typically assessed via self-report methods. There is some evidence that empathy measures as well as measures of other sensitivity-related personality constructs predict performance, such as nonverbal decoding and perspective-taking tasks (e.g., Riggio et al., 1989). Yet, these correlations are weak. An obvious goal is to develop sound self-report measures of interpersonal sensitivity—measures that view sensitivity as a skill rather than a trait. These measures should show stronger associations with decoding skill, empathic accuracy, and accurate social perception.

Quite recently, there has been renewed interest in the construct of emotional contagion. Emotional contagion is described as a process involving a tendency to automatically mimic and synchronize expressions, postures, vocalizations, and movements with those of another person, and thus converge emotionally with that person (Hatfield, Cacioppo, & Rapson, 1994). Emotional contagion occurs as individuals attend to others and unconsciously mimic their emotional and nonverbal expressions in a continuous manner. This social mimicry leads to and occurs simultaneously with a congruent emotional experience. Emotional contagion is clearly linked to the experience of empathy, and has been distinguished from empathy by being described as the primitive, affective, more basic component of empathy (Hatfield, Cacioppo, & Rapson, 1992; Hatfield et al., 1994; Thompson, 1987). It also represents a primitive form of interpersonal sensitivity.

Research has indicated that there are individual differences in susceptibility to emotional contagion. For instance, Eisenberg et al. (1991) found that people who are more affected by high-intensity emotional reactions in others may be especially prone to vicarious emotional responding. Doherty (1997) developed and has done preliminary validation work with the Emotional Contagion Scale (ECS). The scale's 15 items were designed to assess the consistency of congruent responses to five basic emotions (happiness, love, anger, sadness, and fear), as well as attention to the emotions of others. Each item presents an event in which another's emotional expression is present, and a congruent emotionally expressive response to the event follows (e.g., "Being with a happy person picks me up when I'm feeling down"; "It irritates me to be around angry people"). The construct validity of the ECS is supported by a lack of correlation with the Marlowe–Crowne SDS, a significant negative correlation with emotional stability, and significant positive correlations with self-consciousness and empathy measures. Scores on the ECS correlate significantly with the ES scale of the SSI ($r = .33, n = 30$; Carney, unpublished data, 1999). The ECS may be a potentially useful measure in research investigations of emotional contagion and the related, more inclusive constructs of empathy and interpersonal sensitivity.

## SUMMARY AND RECOMMENDATIONS

Although attempting to measure interpersonal sensitivity via self-report methods has received only limited attention, this chapter argues that there is merit in continuing this line of research. The advantages of self-report instruments include their ease of use, relative low cost, and breadth of assessment. However, due to the limited and potentially biased perspective of respondents, accurate self-report measures of interpersonal skills are not easy to construct. It is believed that the key to developing such measures is first to map out the domain of sensitivity-related social behaviors and then to construct items that solicit reports of the frequency or typicality with which respondents engage in particular social behaviors indicative of persons with interpersonal sensitivity or sensitivity-related patterns of behavior from which the respondent has received some performance feedback.

Although correlations between self-reports of interpersonal sensitivity and performance-based assessments of decoding accuracy have been largely positive, they are small in magnitude (approximately .20). On the surface, this is discouraging. However, research on self-reported intelligence correlates at about the same level with performance-based IQ tests—despite the fact that people should be much more aware (i.e., they have received more concrete feedback) of their intellectual skills than their nonverbal decoding skills. Moreover, correlations between different performance-based measures of interpersonal sensitivity are rarely larger than .20—despite the fact that they usually share method variance and that these are purportedly measures of the same or similar constructs (see Hall, chap. 8, this volume).

There have only been a few attempts to develop standardized self-report measures of interpersonal sensitivity. Although there is clearly room for improvement in the existing measures, the initial results are somewhat encouraging. However, more research is needed with existing measures, and there is a need for additional self-report measures of interpersonal sensitivity, particularly given the broad definitions and approaches to the construct.

As demonstrated in this book, most research on interpersonal sensitivity has been conducted in the laboratory with performance-based measures of interpersonal sensitivity. These methods are typically elaborate and accurate (although quite specific and narrow in scope) and have led to a greater understanding of the construct of interpersonal sensitivity. Yet the use of these methods typically requires strict experimental control and a large investment of time and resources. However, if research on interpersonal sensitivity is going to move to the next level—and that means moving beyond the laboratory into real-world settings—self-report measures of interpersonal sensitivity will certainly be useful.

A review of research using the existing self-report measures of interpersonal sensitivity and related constructs, and the literature on self-report methods in general,[3] suggest certain guidelines for developing self-report measures of interpersonal sensitivity.[4]

The first guideline is that the items should be understood and interpreted in the manner in which they were intended by the author or researcher. To this end, the items should be simple, clear, unambiguous, and free of jargon. Care should be taken to anticipate how respondents might interpret and frame the question or item and their responses (see Schwarz, 1999).

As a second guideline, the content of the items must adequately sample the domain to which the scale generalizes. As we have discussed, interpersonal sensitivity is a broad and multifaceted construct. To date, there is no comprehensive theory of interpersonal sensitivity to chart out the various definitions and domains that might be included in the broad construct (see Bernieri, chap. 1, this volume).

The third guideline is that care must be taken to prevent or minimize systematic biases and distortion of responses. This includes avoiding response set, particularly the related problems of acquiescence and social desirability.

---

[3]Robinson et al. (1991) offered a concise overview of considerations in constructing self-report personality and attitude scales.

[4]We thank Frank Bernieri for suggesting this outline and framework.

As was mentioned, it is likely that respondents will acquiesce to self-report skill items that ask directly about skill or ability ("I am easily able to read others' emotions"; "I can usually tell what others are feeling"). In addition, interpersonal competence is, by its very nature, socially desirable. Therefore, it is imperative that self-report measures of interpersonal sensitivity be constructed carefully to minimize distortion due to social desirability. This might require finessing items through careful wording and encouraging respondents to admit shortcomings ("I have to admit it, I often completely misread the feelings of a close friend"; "Although I disagree, people close to me have sometimes called me "aloof" and "insensitive" [both reverse-scored for interpersonal sensitivity]).

As a fourth guideline, if items require respondents to report on the frequency of social behaviors, then (a) these behaviors must be theoretically relevant to interpersonal sensitivity; (b) the respondents must be aware of these behaviors when they occur; and (c) the respondents must be able to accurately recall and properly quantify or scale their frequency of occurrence.

As a fifth guideline, if items require respondents to report on feedback that they have received from others, then (a) the opportunity to receive such feedback needs to be typical (i.e., feedback about an aspect of interpersonal sensitivity must typically occur; e.g., "People have told me that I am a good listener"), and (b) respondents must be able to accurately recall and properly quantify or scale this feedback.

The final guideline suggests that items that require respondents to report on the behavioral consequences or outcomes of interpersonal sensitivity, as opposed to its manifestations, should be theoretically derived. For example, the item "I am easily able to calm a person who is agitated or distressed" might be appropriate if this outcome (i.e., calming others down) is theoretically linked to being empathically sensitive to others' distressed states.

Interpersonal sensitivity is a broad and important construct—one that is relevant to all facets of social life. Clearly, there are many ways to assess interpersonal sensitivity. One method that has received surprisingly little attention is the use of self-reports. It is anticipated that as research on interpersonal sensitivity moves away from the laboratory and into applied settings, the demand for sound self-report measures of interpersonal sensitivity will increase. Careful attention to the construction and validation of self-report measures of interpersonal sensitivity will not only lead to better measurement of this interesting phenomenon, but encourage the breadth and scope of interpersonal sensitivity research.

## REFERENCES

Archer, D., & Costanzo, M. (1988). *The Interpersonal Perception Task (IPT)*, Berkeley, CA: University of California Extension Media Center.
Boyce, P. M., & Parker, G. (1989). Development of a scale to measure interpersonal sensitivity. *Australian and New Zealand Journal of Psychiatry, 23*, 341–351.

Briggs, S. R., Cheek, J. M., & Buss, A. H. (1980). An analysis of the Self-Monitoring Scale. *Journal of Personality and Social Psychology, 38*, 679–685.

Buhrmester, D., Furman, W., Wittenberg, M. T., & Reis, H. T. (1988). Five domains of interpersonal competence in peer relationships. *Journal of Personality and Social Psychology, 55*, 991–1008.

Buss, A. H. (1980). *Self-consciousness and social anxiety*. San Francisco: Freeman.

Campbell, D. T., & Fiske, D. W. (1959). Convergent and discriminant validation by the multitrait-multimethod matrix. *Psychological Bulletin, 56*, 81–105.

Costanzo, M., & Archer, D. (1989). Interpreting the expressive behavior of others: The interpersonal perception task. *Journal of Nonverbal Behavior, 13*, 225–235.

Cronbach, L. J. (1990). *Essentials of psychological testing* (5th ed.). New York: HarperCollins.

Crowne, D. P., & Marlowe, D. (1964). *The approval motive*. New York: Wiley.

Davis, M. H. (1983). Measuring individual differences in empathy: Evidence for a multidimensional approach. *Journal of Personality and Social Psychology, 44*, 113–126.

Davis, M. H. (1994). *Empathy: A social psychological approach*. Madison, WI: Brown & Benchmark.

Davis, M. H., & Kraus, L. A. (1997). Personality and empathic accuracy. In W. Ickes (Ed.), *Empathic accuracy* (pp. 144–168). New York: Guilford.

Doherty, R. W. (1997). The Emotional Contagion Scale: A measure of individual differences. *Journal of Nonverbal Behavior, 21*, 131–154.

Eisenberg, N., Fabes, R. A., Schaller, M., Miller, P., Carlo, G., Poulin, R., Shea, C., & Shell, R. (1991). Personality and socialization correlates of vicarious emotional responding. *Journal of Personality and Social Psychology, 61*, 459–470.

Eisenberg, N., Murphy, B. C., & Shepard, S. (1997). The development of empathic accuracy. In W. Ickes (Ed.). *Empathic accuracy* (pp. 73–116). New York: Guilford.

Ekman, P. (1972). Universals and cultural differences in facial expressions of emotion. In J. Cole (Ed.), *Nebraska Symposium on Motivation* (Vol. 9, pp. 207–283). Lincoln, NE: University of Nebraska Press.

Ekman, P., & Friesen, W. V. (1975). *Unmasking the face*. Englewood Cliffs, NJ: Prentice-Hall.

Eysenck, H. J., & Eysenck, S. B. G. (1968). *Manual for the Eysenck Personality Inventory*. San Diego, CA: Educational and Industrial Testing Service.

Fenigstein, A., Scheier, M. F., & Buss, A. H. (1975). Public and private self-consciousness: Assessment and theory. *Journal of Counseling and Clinical Psychology, 43*, 522–527.

Friedman, H. S. (1979). The concept of skill in nonverbal communication: Implications for understanding social interaction. In R. Rosenthal (Ed.), *Skill in nonverbal communication* (pp. 2–27). Cambridge, MA: Oelgeschlager, Gunn & Hain.

Hatfield, E., Cacioppo, J., & Rapson, R. (1992). Primitive emotional contagion. In M.S. Clark (Ed.), *Review of personality and social psychology* (pp. 151–177). Newbury Park, CA: Sage.

Hatfield, E., Cacioppo, J., & Rapson, R. (1994). *Emotional contagion*. New York: Cambridge University Press.

Hogan, R. (1969). Development of an empathy scale. *Journal of Consulting and Clinical Psychology, 33*, 307–316.

Ickes, W. (1993). Empathic accuracy. *Journal of Personality, 61*, 587–610.

Ickes, W. (Ed.). (1997). *Empathic accuracy*. New York: Guilford.

Leary, M. R. (1983). *Understanding social anxiety*. Beverly Hills, CA: Sage.

Mehrabian, A., & Epstein, N. A. (1972). A measure of emotional empathy. *Journal of Personality, 40*, 525–543.

Milgram, S., Mann, L., & Harter, S. (1965). The lost-letter technique of social research. *Public Opinion Quarterly, 29*, 437–438.

Oskamp, S. (1991). *Attitudes and opinions* (2nd ed.). Englewood Cliffs, NJ: Prentice-Hall.

Patterson, M. L., & Stockbridge, E. (1998). Effects of cognitive demand and judgment strategy on person perception accuracy. *Journal of Nonverbal Behavior, 253–263*.

Paulhus, D. L., Lysy, D. C., & Yik, M. S. M. (1998). Self-report measures of intelligence: Are they useful as proxy IQ tests? *Journal of Personality, 66*, 525–554.

Paulhus, D. L., & Martin, C. L. (1987). The structure of personality capabilities. *Journal of Personality and Social Psychology, 52*, 354–365.

Riggio, R. E. (1986). Assessment of basic social skills. *Journal of Personality and Social Psychology, 51*, 649–660.

Riggio, R. E., & Carney, D. (in press). *Manual for the Social Skills Inventory.* Palo Alto, CA: Consulting Psychologists Press.

Riggio, R. E., & Friedman, H. S. (1982). The interrelationships of self-monitoring factors, personality traits, and nonverbal social skills. *Journal of Nonverbal Behavior, 7*, 33–45.

Riggio, R. E., & Ritter, L. (1986, April). *Communication skills in various occupational groups.* Paper presented at the meeting of the Western Psychological Association, Seattle, WA.

Riggio, R. E., Throckmorton, B., & DePaola, S. (1990). Social skills and self-esteem. *Personality and Individual Differences, 11*, 799–804.

Riggio, R. E., Tucker, J., & Coffaro, D. (1989). Social skills and empathy. *Personality and Individual Differences, 10*, 93–99.

Riggio, R. E., Watring, K., & Throckmorton, B. (1993). Social skills, social support, and psychosocial adjustment. *Personality and Individual Differences, 15*, 275–280.

Riggio, R. E., Widaman, K. F., & Friedman, H. S. (1985). Actual and perceived emotional sending and personality correlates. *Journal of Nonverbal Behavior, 9*, 69–83.

Robinson, J. P., Shaver, P. R., & Wrightsman, L. S. (Eds.), (1991). *Measures of personality and social psychological attitudes.* New York: Academic.

Rosenthal, R., Hall, J. A., DiMatteo, M. R., Rogers, P. L., & Archer, D. (1979). *Sensitivity to nonverbal communication: The PONS test.* Baltimore: Johns Hopkins University Press.

Schwarz, N. (1999). Self-reports: How the questions shape the answers. *American Psychologist, 54*, 93–105.

Simmons, C. H., & Zumpf, C. (1983). The lost letter technique revisited. *Journal of Applied Social Psychology, 13*, 510–514.

Smith, H. J., Archer, D., & Costanzo, M. (1991). "Just a hunch": Accuracy and awareness in person perception. *Journal of Nonverbal Behavior, 15*, 3–18.

Snodgrass, S. E., Hecht, M.A., & Ploutz-Snyder, R. (1998). Interpersonal sensitivity: Expressivity or perceptivity? *Journal of Personality and Social Psychology, 74*, 238–249.

Snyder, M. (1974). The self-monitoring of expressive behavior. *Journal of Personality and Social Psychology, 30*, 526–537.

Thompson, R. A. (1987). Empathy and emotional understanding: The early development of empathy. In N. E. Strayer & J. Strayer (Eds.), *Empathy and its development* (pp. 119–143). Cambridge, England: Cambridge University Press.

Tucker, J. S., & Riggio, R. E. (1988). The role of social skills in encoding posed and spontaneous facial expression. *Journal of Nonverbal Behavior, 12*, 87–97.

Wallace, J. (1966). An abilities conception of personality: Some implications for personality measurement. *American Psychologist, 21*, 132–138.

Wrightsman, L. S. (1969). Wallace supporters and adherence to "law and order." *Journal of Personality and Social Psychology, 13*, 17–22.

Zuckerman, M., & Larrance, D. (1979). Individual differences in perceived encoding and decoding abilities. In R. Rosenthal (Ed.), *Skill in nonverbal communication* (pp. 171–203). Cambridge, MA: Oelgeschlager, Gunn & Hain.

# 8

# The PONS Test and the Psychometric Approach to Measuring Interpersonal Sensitivity

Judith A. Hall

*Northeastern University*

The question of whether people can judge others' emotions and communicative intentions from behavioral cues has a long history. Darwin (1872/1965) posed it while mustering evidence for his concept that emotion displays are universal and therefore universally recognizable, an idea that had an important place in his arguments for natural selection. Throughout the 20th century, psychologists have investigated the decoding of expressions, asking questions such as whether the sexes differ in their accuracy of judgment, which emotions are easier and harder to judge, and whether the meanings of spontaneous (as opposed to posed) cues can be identified; some of this research dates to the earliest decades of social psychological experimentation (e.g., Feleky, 1914).

Early on, investigators began using fixed sets of expressive stimuli in the form of film clips, photos, drawings, and later, video and audio tape clips. The advantages of using reusable stimulus sets instead of live interaction as a source of cues are many, including the relative ease of establishing criteria for scoring of accuracy. With a standard set the "right answers" need be established only once, instead of again each time a study is undertaken with a new set of expressors or stimuli. One common way of determining what cues have

143

been expressed, and how successfully, is to show expressive stimuli to an independent group of judges whose collective responses then become the operational criterion for the scoring of accuracy.

Another great advantage of using standard stimuli is that, for purposes of comparing accuracy scores among decoders, the method unconfounds the intrinsic clarity or judgeability of the cues from the skill of the judge; in a live interaction, whether one person judges the other correctly is a function both of the sender's clarity of expression and the judge's ability (or motivation) to notice the cues and successfully apply a judgment algorithm. The round-robin design does offer one solution to this confounding of sender and receiver effects (Kenny & Winquist, chap. 14, this volume); in a typical round-robin study, a group of people engages in live interaction in all possible pairs, and in each pair judgments are made by participants of their partners. However, the statistical analysis of this design was far in the future for early investigators. Other difficulties also limit the widespread use of round-robin methodology: Such studies are dauntingly laborious to conduct and generalization of results from one study to another remains a problem because the stimuli (cues to be judged) are not the same from study to study.

Thus, if the question concerns individual differences in judgment accuracy, many issues are simplified by holding the expressive cues constant either within or across studies. Once the decision is made to hold the cues constant, one has entered the world of psychometric test development, for the standard cue set becomes, as with any test, a set of items that can be appraised for its reliability and validity. In other words, the items are intended to measure an ability possessed by the test-taker.

This chapter is concerned with the method of assessing individual differences in interpersonal sensitivity using standard cue sets, which I call the *psychometric* approach. A number of investigative teams have developed such instruments. In this chapter I discuss one of them at length, the Profile of Nonverbal Sensitivity, commonly called the PONS test (Rosenthal, Hall, DiMatteo, Rogers, & Archer, 1979). I also describe several other tests briefly, and for two of them I am especially brief because whole chapters in this volume are devoted to them (the Interpersonal Perception Test, or IPT, Archer, Costanzo, & Akert, chap. 9, this volume; and the Diagnostic Analysis of Nonverbal Accuracy, or DANVA, Nowicki & Duke, chap. 10, this volume).

## OTHER TESTS OF NONVERBAL DECODING ACCURACY

Many investigators have measured people's accuracy in decoding cues that reveal other people's traits and states. Here, the focus is on instruments that have been deliberately developed for the assessment of individual differences in cue judgment accuracy—that is, instruments that have undergone some amount of psychometric analysis, construct validation, and repeated usage.[1]

## Brief Affect Recognition Test
## (BART; Ekman & Friesen, 1974)

This test consists of photographs of faces showing "basic" emotions identified in the research program of Paul Ekman (happiness, sadness, disgust, fear, surprise, and anger), presented tachistoscopically (e.g., less than 1/25 s; Ekman & Friesen, 1974). Test-takers choose which emotion was shown from a multiple choice. More recently Matsumoto and colleagues engaged in comprehensive development of an improved test on this format, called the JACBART, which includes equally Japanese and Caucasian, male and female encoders, and seven emotions (Matsumoto et al., 2000). On the JACBART, a facial expression is embedded in a 1-s presentation of that poser's neutral expression. Reliability is high (internal consistency > .80, retest $r = .78$), and scores correlate with an array of personality measures.

## CARAT (Buck, 1976)

The "slide-viewing technique" (Buck, 1979) measures spontaneous expression of emotional cues, that is, cues that are revealed on the expressor's face without awareness or intention. Although variations on this technique exist, the basic paradigm consists of showing affectively arousing color slides to individuals whose faces are surreptitiously recorded on videotape as they watch the slides. The videotape is then shown to naive judges, who are typically asked which slide was being viewed. If the slide can be accurately identified, one can infer that the expressor (encoder) unintentionally revealed his or her emotional response to the slide.

Most research using the slide-viewing technique is concerned with accuracy of encoding, not accuracy of decoding. However, Buck (1976) incorporated one set of these facial expressions into a decoding accuracy test. Test-takers view a series of faces and can response either categorically, as described earlier (i.e., which slide was being viewed), or dimensionally by rating how pleasant the encoder rated his or her own experience; accuracy for the dimensional measure (which Buck called the pleasantness measure) consists of correlating these ratings with the original encoders' ratings across the different encoders' expressions. Thus, there are two different criteria for accuracy: the category of the slide (sexual, unusual, scenic, and unpleasant) and the encoders' self-ratings of

---

[1] Some researchers who have conducted large programs of research on expressive cue judgment have been primarily interested in studying group, rather than individual, differences (e.g., Ekman et al., 1987; Izard, 1971). These researchers have not been as concerned with establishing the psychometric properties of their tests as those coming from the individual-differences direction.

pleasant affect. The CARAT has not been extensively used in individual-differences research, though validational findings have been reported (Buck, 1976; Hall, Halberstadt, & O'Brien, 1997).

## IPT (Costanzo & Archer, 1989; Archer et al., chap. 9, this volume)

The IPT presents both nonverbal and verbal cues. The criteria for accuracy on this 30-item multiple-choice test (there is also a 15-item version) are objective facts about the encoders or the circumstances under which their cues were expressed. An example would be a videotape clip of a woman talking to someone on the telephone; is she talking to her mother or her boyfriend?

## DANVA (Baum & Nowicki, 1998; Nowicki & Duke, 1994; Nowicki & Duke, chap.10, this volume)

This team of investigators has developed several tests based on posed expressions of fear, sadness, happiness, and anger, conveyed via face, gesture, posture, and paralanguage. The tests use a multiple choice among the four emotion labels.

## Child and Adolescent Social Perception Measure (CASP; Magill-Evans, Koning, Cameron-Sadava, & Manyk, 1995)

The CASP consists of 10 naturalistic scenes acted out by children and adolescents, presented on videotape with electronic filtering of the soundtrack to prevent verbal comprehension. Test-takers do not mark a preprinted answer sheet but rather respond in an open-ended fashion to probes about which emotions they perceive. A standardized scoring system is used. This test shows age and gender differences in a normative sample of children, but little other validity data has been gathered thus far. The test's authors developed the test with clinical populations in mind, but the test may be useful in normal populations as well.

Perusal of this line-up of tests reveals interesting similarities and differences. Most are multiple-choice instruments. The BART, JACBART, DANVA, and CASP inquire directly about emotional state, whereas the others ask for a variety of different judgments, which may involve emotional judgments to varying degrees. For example, when the IPT asks which of two people is the other person's boss, the test-taker might look for emotion cues (maybe the boss looks happier), but other cues could be informative as well—for example, maybe the boss initiates the conversation or talks louder, cues that have no obvious relation to emotion. Similarly, an IPT item showing deceptive communication might contain emotion cues (e.g., negative affect) but also might contain cues indicating cognitive uncertainty. On the CARAT's categorical measure of accuracy, the test-taker translates affective cues on the face into a judgment about which slide was being watched, a process that involves various inferences. For example, does a person look disgusted or fascinated by an unpleasant slide; does a person look happy or embarrassed by a sexual slide, and so forth?

Thus, at a broad level these tests are all measuring accuracy in judging communicative cues, but they may be tapping a variety of specific domains of judgment, a point taken up again later. This applies equally to the PONS test, which I describe now.

## THE PONS TEST: WHY IT CAME TO BE

As is explained in more detail later, the PONS is a multi-item test of accuracy in identifying the meanings of nonverbal cues expressed by a woman through face, body, voice tone, and combinations of these cue channels. The test assesses sensitivity in the sense that one can successfully interpret cues by applying previously acquired knowledge about how a person is likely to behave in various situations and emotional states.

The history of the PONS test is not rooted in the study of emotion judgment, nor even in an individual differences tradition, but in the study of interpersonal expectations. Starting in the 1960s, Robert Rosenthal began publishing experimental demonstrations that experimenters in psychological experiments can bias their human participants (and animal subjects) by simply believing that certain kinds of behavior could be expected from them (reviewed in Rosenthal, 1976). In the classic photograph-rating paradigm, experimenters were led to expect that some participants would see affective positivity in bland faces, whereas others would see negativity in them. These expectancies were experimentally implanted on a random-assignment basis by the investigator, unknown to the laboratory experimenters. As every psychologist now knows, the mere belief that some participants would see more positivity, and some less, caused these very differences to occur. The self-fulfilling prophecy effect is now well established in many settings, including teaching, work, and everyday relationships (e.g., Rosenthal & Rubin, 1978; Snyder, Tanke, & Berscheid, 1977).

What has this to do with measuring interpersonal sensitivity? Two missing pieces must be added before the answer is clear. First, from the beginning researchers understood that the transmission or mediation of interpersonal expectancies involved interpersonal, often nonverbal, cues. Investigations of what kinds of subtle behaviors could account for the fulfillment of expected outcomes in another person eventually led to the identification of four categories of mediating cues (Harris & Rosenthal, 1985), specifically input, output, feedback, and affective climate. Affective climate is especially relevant to non-verbal behavior. The self-fulfillingness of the expectancy comes about, in part, because the expectancy-holder inadvertently sends subtle nonverbal cues that are congruent with the expectancy—for example, lots of eye contact and looks of approval for the student who is expected to be smart or a deadpan face and a limp handshake for the new roommate who is expected to be a bore. If the student or the roommate responds reciprocally to the expecter's nonverbal cues, then the out-of-awareness cycle of expectancy, response, and confirmed expectancy (followed by further cues and responses) is set into motion.

So, after pinpointing a crucial role for nonverbal cues in the fulfillment of expectancies, the final step leading to the development of the PONS test was the recurrent observation that in experiments not all expectancy-holders (experimenters, teachers, and so forth) produced biasing cues, and not all targets of expectancies (research subjects, students) were vulnerable to the effects of biasing cues. The question then was: Why are some people more vulnerable than others? Rosenthal speculated that nonverbal communication skills were important to understanding this puzzle in that they served as a moderator of the expectancy transmission phenomenon. So was born the idea for a standardized test that would identify which people were more and less sensitive to nonverbal cues—the reasoning being that a person who is not sensitive to such cues would simply miss, or misjudge, the biasing cues and therefore not be influenced by them.

Thus, the PONS test was born out of the desire to understand better the operation of interpersonal expectancy effects. The test was made in 1971, and the monograph describing its development and validation was published in 1979 (Rosenthal et al., 1979). During the intervening years, the PONS was subjected to an extensive program of validational research.

## DESCRIPTION OF THE PONS TEST

The full-length PONS test consists of 220 two-second audio clips, video clips, or both, and a printed answer sheet on which 220 pairs of brief verbal descriptions are presented, which are responded to in multiple-choice style. The person expressing the cues in the clips is the present author at the age of 24. There are also shorter forms of the test, which are discussed later.

The nonverbal cues contained in the test were originally recorded on different video cameras which captured, for each scene, cues in the following "channels" of communication: the full figure (head and body down to knees of the standing expressor), the face only (filling the screen), and the body only (neck to knees). The vocal channel was also recorded simultaneously. During the editing process, the voice clips were content-masked in two ways, electronic filtering and randomized splicing. Electronic filtering removes the highest frequencies, making the voice sound muffled. Randomized splicing physically rearranges short segments of the unfiltered audiotrack in a random order. The 11 channels shown in the test consisted of all possible combinations of the visual and audio cues, as follows: the three visual channels alone, with no voice; the two vocal channels alone, with no visual cues; and the six combinations of the three visual and two vocal channels.

The PONS test has an a priori structure consisting of these 11 channels crossed by 20 affective scenes, for example "returning faulty item to a store" or "expressing jealous rage," which themselves fall into a 2 x 2 configuration (with 5 scenes in each) representing the dimensions of positivity and dominance. Thus, the four affective quadrants are positive-submissive, positive-dominant, negative-submissive, and negative-dominant. Examples of positive-submissive scenes are asking for a favor, helping a customer, and ordering food in a restaurant; examples of positive-dominant are admiring the weather, talking about one's wedding, and expressing motherly love; examples of negative-submissive are asking forgiveness, talking about the death of a friend, and returning a faulty item to a store; and examples of negative-dominant are threatening someone, criticizing someone for being late, and nagging a child. Assignment of scenes to quadrants was based on ratings of the encoder's actual portrayals (see discussion later).

The portrayals were made largely without a prepared script to maximize spontaneity. As taped, the videotaped scenes were roughly 5 s in length, but they were shortened to 2 s in order to make a test of optimal difficulty; optimal difficulty for a two-item choice is 75% correct. This goal was approximately achieved in that the overall accuracy of the largest normative sample was 78%.

During videotaping, a number of different portrayals were taped for each scene, following which a small panel of judges, including the investigators, rated the portrayals for adequacy in conveying the desired communication, positivity, and dominance. The panel's ratings were used to make the final selection of the best portrayal of each scene and also to assign the scenes to affective quadrants. Thus, for example, the panel's ratings determined which portrayal of "talking to a lost child" was the best and also that "talking to a lost child" fell into the positive-dominant quadrant. On the test, "talking to a lost child" became the correct answer for that scene. When a different scene was presented, "talking to a lost child" or one of the 18 remaining scene descriptions were used as distractors.

It is a feature of the PONS that items were selected according to a predetermined factorial structure that required five scenes in each of four quadrants, crossed by 11 channels which themselves represent the crossing of two vocal channels with three video channels plus each channel in isolation. This is in contrast to the item-analysis approach common to psychometric test development. In the latter tradition, a large number of items is weeded down to a smaller number based on inter-item (alternatively, item-total) correlations, which are desired to be high. How many items are retained is joint function of a desired overall reliability (e.g., Cronbach's alpha) and the actual interitem correlations (Rosenthal & Rosnow, 1991). In contrast, the items included on the PONS were not selected on the basis of their intercorrelations with other items. Reliability of the PONS is an issue to which I return later.

Short forms of the PONS test consist of sets of selected items. The two most frequently used are a 40-item test containing the voice-only items and a 40-item test containing the 20 face-only and the 20 body-only items.

Norm groups were established for elementary school, junior high school, and high school. Numerous large college samples were also tested, as well as a smaller number of older samples. Additionally, 58 groups from 20 non-U.S. locations were tested, mostly in university settings. In many samples, external variables were also measured such as personality and other background characteristics.

## RELIABILITY AND INTERNAL ANALYSES OF THE PONS TEST

Although most analyses of the PONS involved external correlates, a number of analyses were made internally (for a much fuller description of psychometric analyses, see Rosenthal et al., 1979). Reliability was assessed in terms of internal consistency and stability over time. Internal consistency (KR-20) for the full-length test was .86. This is high enough reliability by conventional standards, yet it conceals the interesting fact that the average interitem correlation is only about .03, quite a low correlation by any standard. The adequate overall reliability figure was achieved only because the test has so many items. As one might expect from the low interitem correlation, short forms of the PONS have very poor reliability; the channels that include video information have an internal consistency reliability of less than .40, and the audio-only channels have reliability well below that figure (e.g., alphas of .30, .21, and .17; Hall & Halberstadt, 1994; unpublished data from Hall et al., 1997).[2]

Retest reliability for the full PONS test over periods of 10 days to 10 weeks is .69 (median over 6 samples), indicating adequate consistency of measurement over time.

---

[2]In Rosenthal et al. (1979), internal consistency reliability for the individual channels of the test were presented as coefficients equated for length with the full-length test, using the Spearman–Brown formula (Rosenthal & Rosnow, 1991). This was done for purposes of direct comparability of subscales with unequal numbers of items in them. However, in hindsight these figures may give a misleading impression of how high the reliability for individual channels (and short forms of the test) actually are. Working the Spearman–Brown formula backwards from these "corrected" coefficients yields internal consistency coefficients similar to those reported in this chapter.

## VALIDATIONAL FINDINGS
## FOR THE PONS TEST

I give only a brief summary of validational findings. Convergent validity correlations were often in the range of .20 or so, meaning that in isolation the correlations of the PONS with external criteria would comprise rather weak evidence of validity. However, many convergent validity correlations were collected for the PONS, which together indicated that the test measures something that deserves to be called "sensitivity to nonverbal cues." In other words, the test has meaningful and predicted relations to many other variables.

The most frequently examined correlate of the PONS test is gender: women scored better than men in 80% of the 133 samples that had been tested at the time the monograph was published (Rosenthal et al., 1979). The size of this difference was about 3 percentage points on the test, or stated differently, a point-biserial correlation between gender and performance of about .20. Among children, the gender difference was the same size as among adults. In order to compare this result with gender differences found for other nonverbal decoding tests, I conducted several nonoverlapping meta-analyses of gender differences in accuracy of judging nonverbal cues (Hall, 1978, 1984; Hall, Carter, & Horgan, 2000). In these reviews, deliberately few results based on the PONS were included in order not to overrepresent that test in the data set. Remarkably, these meta-analyses, involving dozens of other studies, showed almost identical results to those based on the PONS test alone.

Many other validational results were reported in Rosenthal et al.'s (1979) monograph. Among those results were the findings that high scorers had healthier, more well adjusted personalities; were rated as more interpersonally sensitive by peers or supervisors; were more democratic as teachers; and were rated as better in their job performance as clinicians and teachers. The accuracy of different national and cultural groups varied with how similar to the United States they were on indices of modernization. Performance improved from middle childhood to college, women performed better than men, psychiatrically impaired groups performed more poorly than nonimpaired samples, and married women with toddler-age children scored higher than a matched sample of married women without children.

Interestingly, the original goal of elucidating interpersonal expectancy effects was only partially achieved, mainly because of the difficulty of mounting full-fledged expectancy studies in which the PONS test was given to the participants. By and large, the results that were obtained did not give much support to the idea that people who scored higher on the PONS would be more susceptible to the biasing effects of others' expectancies (Rosenthal et al., 1979). Subsequent studies that tested this moderation hypothesis also were not successful (Cooper & Hazelrigg, 1988; Hazelrigg, Cooper, & Strathman, 1991). However, a study that looked simultaneously at perceivers' nonverbal encoding skill and targets' nonverbal decoding skill did indicate that the strongest expectancy effects occurred when both skills were high (Zuckerman, DeFrank, Hall, & Rosenthal, 1978).

In the years since the original monograph was published, many other validational results have been published. As examples, physicians scoring higher on the PONS had more satisfied patients (DiMatteo, Friedman, & Taranta, 1979); also, people scoring higher on the PONS learned more in an interpersonal teaching situation (Bernieri, 1991), possessed more accurate knowledge of differences in men's and women's behavior (Hall & Carter, 1999), were liked more and seen as more honest and open (Funder & Harris, 1986), and were more accurate in judging the extraversion and positive affect of people with whom they interacted (Ambady, Hallahan, & Rosenthal, 1995).

## CRITIQUE OF THE PONS TEST

Although the collective evidence in favor of validity is compelling, the test has a number of potential limitations and weaknesses.

### Reliability and the Associated Problem of Test Length

The trade-off between reliability and the number of items on a test confronts an investigator wishing to use the PONS with a difficult decision. The full-length test has good reliability but takes about an hour to administer. It is also tiring for participants, as the format becomes quite repetitive even though, in the literal sense, the same item is never shown twice. The time required to administer the test and the fatigue it causes are serious obstacles in many research settings. On the other hand, the shorter tests are less problematic in terms of time and fatigue, but they have extremely poor internal consistency.

Weak internal consistency seems to be a hallmark of some other nonverbal decoding tests and is thus not a characteristic only of the PONS. Normative reliability data for the 30-item IPT indicate internal consistency (KR-20) of only .52 (Costanzo & Archer, 1989), and other investigators have found even lower figures (Cronbach's alpha of .31, Patterson & Stockbridge, 1998; alpha of .27, unpublished results from Hall et al., 1997). In our laboratory the 15-item IPT had Cronbach's alphas of .26, .31, and .06 in three studies (unpublished data). The 32-item CARAT test had a normative Cronbach's alpha of .56 (Buck, 1976), and Hall et al. (1997) found an alpha of .46 (unpublished data). Sternberg and Smith (1985) developed two tests of sensitivity to the nature of interpersonal relationships and also found weak internal consistency, .34 and .47 respectively (Barnes & Sternberg, 1989). Although this list is not exhaustive, it makes the point that internal consistency for several decoding tests (including the short forms of the PONS) is not strong.

Because the PONS and other tests have accumulated a good track record of validity coefficients, it does not appear to be the case that random error completely swamps true variance. In particular, the audio items of the PONS, which have essentially no internal consistency by conventional standards, have repeatedly been shown to have predictive validity (e.g., Buller & Aune, 1988; Buller & Burgoon, 1986; Hall, 1980). How is this possible?

It is possible if weak internal consistency is not necessarily an indicator of random error, as classic test theory would assume. Other models of construct structure are possible. In particular, one can conceptualize quasi-independent discrete variables as collectively defining a concept, much as income, education, and occupational prestige collectively define socioeconomic status (Bollen & Lennox, 1991). Socioeconomic status is the empirical consequence of one's standing on these indices rather than being a latent construct of which each of the indices is simply an indicator. Thus, the fact that income, education, and occupational prestige are not strongly correlated with one another would not lead one to conclude that these variables are merely flawed indicators of the latent construct or that one had created a psychometrically bad scale of socioeconomic status. Applying the same logic to the case of nonverbal decoding tests, one could argue that such tests may actually gain validity by including items that represent a number of different skills, in contrast to the more typical psychometric situation in which items are seen as imperfect replications of each other. In other words, the weak intercorrelations among items may not be exclusively a reflection of random error.

Against this landscape of weak internal consistency, the DANVA, JACBART, and CASP stand out in having impressive internal consistencies (.77–.88 for the DANVA, Nowicki & Duke, 1994; better than .80 for the JACBART, Matsumoto et al., 2000; .88 for the CASP, Magill-Evans et al., 1995). It is interesting that all of these tests are concerned with only one domain of judgment—emotions—in contrast to the PONS and IPT, which, as mentioned earlier, tap a wide variety of domains (emotions but also social scripts and contexts, status roles, deception, relationship cues, etc.) as well as different nonverbal channels within the same test. Ability to identify discrete emotions from expressive cues may indeed be a consistent skill: If you can judge one emotion, you can judge others too. But being a good judge of deception, for example, does not necessarily predict one's ability to discern the kind of relationship two people have; being a good judge of facial emotions does not necessarily predict one's ability to judge vocal emotions; and so forth.

The fact that retest reliability is respectable even for measures with weak internal consistency (.70 for IPT, Costanzo & Archer, 1989; .79 and .80 for the CARAT, Buck, 1976; .69 for the PONS, Rosenthal et al., 1979) clearly indicates that these tests are measuring something. Considering their internal consistency, however, it may be more appropriate to conclude that these tests each measure some thing, a diverse collection of skills rather than only one skill.

Buck (1976) showed considerable foresight when he said that "nonverbal receiving ability is inherently complex and multidimensional" (pp. 168–169).

## The "One-Sender" Problem

The fact that the PONS test has but one expressor sometimes has been raised as a possible threat to its validity, the concern being that accuracy may not generalize to other expressors. Although it is legitimate to ask about limitations on generalizability, in the case of the PONS the amassed quantity of validity data makes it virtually inconceivable that test scores are tied to idiosyncratic characteristics of its expressor. Moreover, as reported earlier in this chapter, the gender difference has been replicated so many times with other tests, not only in direction but also in magnitude and with male expressors, that the one-sender criticism loses force. The number of different expressors to be represented among test stimuli does have interesting implications for test development and interpretation, however; for example, one might argue that a test with fewer expressors would have improved internal consistency but reduced content validity (see Colvin & Bundick, chap. 3, this volume). Nevertheless, the widespread evidence for the predictive validity of the PONS test seems to suggest that the decision to use only one expressor was not a significant compromise.

## What is Being Measured?

As mentioned earlier, the concept of sensitivity to nonverbal communication is rather vague in meaning. The term "sensitivity" could apply at different stages in the processing of cues (Barnes & Sternberg, 1989). For example, sensitivity could refer to alertness to or awareness of nonverbal cues—Does a person pay attention to and notice such cues?—versus the accuracy with which cues are interpreted once they are noticed (see Meiran, Netzer, Netzer, Itzhak, & Rechnitz, 1994 for an empirical examination of different meanings of sensitivity). The first kind of sensitivity received almost no research until recently (Hall, Carter, & Horgan, in press). On the PONS, both of these kinds of sensitivity may contribute to accuracy. Although intuition suggests that the most likely process is an inferential one, DiMatteo and Hall (1979) developed a test for measuring individual preferences for attending to different nonverbal channels, and then used these preferences to predict accuracy at judging the corresponding channels on the PONS. Preference for attending to both the face and body predicted accuracy on those channels, suggesting that attentional processes do contribute to accuracy in addition to the ability to draw accurate inferences.

Another construct validity question concerns what kinds of inferences are being drawn on the PONS. As pointed out by Nowicki and Duke (chap. 10, this volume), the PONS requires a multistep judgment process. Although some PONS items ask the test-taker to judge emotion directly, as in "expressing jealous rage," most of them ask the test-taker to make a judgment about whether the expressor is in a particular social context, such as "ordering food in a restaurant," "talking about one's wedding," "helping a customer," or "talking about one's divorce." Some scenes may reflect a complex blend of emotions (e.g., talking about one's divorce could entail sadness, anger, and relief), whereas others may be rather neutral with respect to emotion (ordering food in a restaurant). The PONS's situational as opposed to emotional focus means that complex knowledge about norms for social behavior must be brought to bear on the test-taker's judgments.

The point here is not that the PONS is flawed because it requires a complex judgment process (in this respect it is similar to the IPT), but only that it draws on a skill that is rather hard to name. If pressed, I would say the PONS measures "accuracy at identifying interpersonal scenarios from nonverbal cues." This kind of skill may have as much relevance to the judgments we make in daily life as do tests of ability to judge pure emotions. In real life, opportunities to judge pure emotions are probably rare, but there are many opportunities to judge what kind of interpersonal scenario is ongoing and whether the cues being displayed are appropriate to it.

## THE BIGGER PICTURE: RELATIONS AMONG TESTS

As noted earlier, items in nonverbal decoding tests tend to be weakly correlated with one another, raising the possibility that many distinct skills are being measured (Buck, 1984). With this logic in mind, and recalling also that different tests seem to be tapping different kinds of judgments, we might not be surprised to discover that different tests correlate very imperfectly with one another. Indeed, this is the case. Ambady et al. (1995) found a correlation of only .03 between a 110-item version of the PONS and the 30-item IPT. Hall et al. (1997) administered the 30-item IPT, the 32-item CARAT, and 80 audio-only items from the PONS (40 new male items added; Rosenthal et al., 1979), and found the following intercorrelations: PONS with IPT, .20; PONS with CARAT, .16; and IPT with CARAT, .10. Also, in our laboratory we have found a correlation of only -.02 between the 15-item IPT and the 40-item video form of the PONS (unpublished data). Gesn, Bernieri, Grahe, & Gada-Jain (1999) reported a correlation of .22 between the 30-item IPT and the full-length PONS test. Buck (1979) reported a correlation of .02 between the CARAT and the full-length PONS test. Sternberg and Smith (1985) developed two tests, one that measured ability to discriminate photographed couples in relationships from pairs of strangers posing as couples and one that measured ability to identify which member of a photographed dyad was the supervisor and which was the supervisee. The correlation between these two tests was -.09 in one study (Sternberg & Smith, 1985) and .14 in another (Barnes & Sternberg, 1989). Furthermore, these two tests were correlated only

.16 and .14 with the 40-item still-photo form of the PONS test (Sternberg & Smith, 1985). Davies, Stankov, and Roberts (1998) found a correlation of -.09 between the 15-item IPT and a 24-item test they made to measure accuracy at judging emotions from facial expressions. In light of these findings, it should come as no surprise that different tests can have very different correlations with external criteria (e.g., Hall & Carter, 1999).

Thus, psychometric tests of decoding interpersonal cues are not interchangeable. Unfortunately, at the current stage of knowledge there is little theoretical or empirical grounding for a researcher's choice of instruments. Choices appear to be made according to personal preference or convenience. It is important eventually to discover whether different tests have differential validity for different categories of external variables, and, if so, why.

## RECOMMENDATIONS FOR INVESTIGATORS

In light of the foregoing, it is premature to recommend particular tests to investigators except along very broad criteria. For example, if an investigator is interested only in vocal sensitivity, he or she would choose either the DANVA or PONS audio tests. If an investigator is clearly interested in emotion judgment, then the DANVA or JACBART would be chosen over the PONS or IPT. At present it is not possible to argue that one test is generally more valid than another.

It is possible, however, to offer a strong recommendation regarding sample sizes. The correlations between these tests and external variables tend to be modest at best. To give an example, the ubiquitous gender difference in decoding, which is based on hundreds of studies, is equivalent to a point-biserial correlation of .20. Many other validity coefficients fall into this range. Considering that for $r = .20$, a sample size of 96 is required to achieve $p = .05$, two-tail, it is clear that investigators hoping to achieve statistical significance need a full recognition of the statistical power issues inherent in detecting effects of this size (Cohen, 1988).

## WHAT IS THE FUTURE
## OF THE PSYCHOMETRIC APPROACH?

Although many questions have been investigated using psychometric tests of decoding accuracy, the state of knowledge is still very incomplete. At present, theoretical knowledge of nonverbal sensitivity consists of little more than catalogues of correlates of nonverbal decoding accuracy (e.g., Hall, 1998). A theory of nonverbal sensitivity would speak to the origins and development of individual differences, a topic about which almost nothing is known. Similarly, gender differences in decoding accuracy have been well documented but not explained.

We also know almost nothing about the relative contributions of motivation and knowledge to scores on nonverbal sensitivity tests.

Thus, there is much need for good psychometric instruments. It may be possible to build a better mousetrap in nonverbal decoding assessment, but test development is both time-consuming and expensive. It is also not clear what an improvement would consist of. Reliability may be improved by limiting the test to a rather narrow domain of judgment, but this compromises content validity. Perhaps what is needed is a large battery of tests, each of which measures a distinctive ability with high reliability. However, this could amount to a great many tests. As yet there is no comprehensive list of discrete interpersonal sensitivities (see Bernieri, chap. 1, this volume), but any such list would be very long.

Thus far, the available tests are all intended to measure inferential accuracy. As mentioned earlier, sensitivity in the sense of paying attention to, or noticing, interpersonal cues is also a legitimate kind of sensitivity, but one that has not yet been captured with a standard test.

In two laboratory experiments, Hall, Carter, & Horgan (1998; see also Hall et al., in press) measured this attentional accuracy by measuring how much dyad members could remember about each other's physical appearance and nonverbal behavior following their interaction. Accuracy was based on comparison of these reports with coding made by independent observers. Attentional accuracy was related to dyad members' reports of how they felt during the interaction (e.g., how much they had felt a desire to please the other person), to assigned roles in the interaction, and to participants' gender. These promising results suggest that it may be fruitful to develop a standardized measure of attentional accuracy.

Another skill for which standardized measurement might be valuable is the ecological sensitivity construct recently discussed by Hall and Carter (1999). By ecological sensitivity is meant the ability to detect covariations that exist in the social environment, for example between group membership and group members' behavior, which would translate into accurate knowledge of group differences. A recently developed test of this construct, the Observational Test of Ecological Sensitivity, shows promising correlations with several personality constructs and tests and nonverbal cue decoding accuracy (Carter, 2000).

A final issue with psychometric decoding tests, no matter what specific version of the construct is being measured, is that they assess accuracy as a trait, that is, as a characteristic of the person. The very concept of retest reliability embodies the assumption that people maintain their skill level relative to other people after a passage of time. The individual-differences model implies that even if skill levels can be improved through intervention, the newly attained skill level would replace the old one as one's trait accuracy. Thus, tests of this sort are not useful for research questions on transient or role-related factors in accuracy. An example would be the relation between marital satisfaction and accuracy in decoding one's own spouse (Noller, chap. 13, this volume). Obviously for such a question, a test specific to the relevant target (in this case the spouse) is called for. Another example is the relation between relative status or dominance between two people and their sensitivity to each other's cues (Hall et al., in press; Snodgrass, chap. 11, this volume). Methodological difficulties with measuring dyadic sensitivity are well known and have not been completely solved.

## ACKNOWLEDGMENT

Preparation of this chapter was supported by a grant from the National Science Foundation to the author.

## REFERENCES

Ambady, N., Hallahan, M., & Rosenthal, R. (1995). On judging and being judged accurately in zero-acquaintance situations. *Journal of Personality and Social Psychology, 69,* 518–529.

Barnes, M. L., & Sternberg, R. J. (1989). Social intelligence and decoding of nonverbal cues. *Intelligence, 13,* 263–287.

Baum, K. M., & Nowicki, S., Jr. (1998). Perception of emotion: Measuring decoding accuracy of adult prosodic cues varying in intensity. *Journal of Nonverbal Behavior, 22,* 89–107.

Bernieri, F. J. (1991). Interpersonal sensitivity in teaching interactions. *Personality and Social Psychology Bulletin, 17,* 98–103.

Bollen, K., & Lennox, R. (1991). Conventional wisdom on measurement: A structural equation perspective. *Psychological Bulletin, 110,* 305–314.

Buck, R. (1976). A test of nonverbal receiving ability: Preliminary studies. *Human Communication Research, 2,* 162–171.

Buck, R. (1979). Measuring individual differences in the nonverbal communication of affect: The slide-viewing paradigm. *Human Communication Research, 6,* 47–57.

Buck, R. (1984). *The communication of emotion.* New York: Guilford.

Buller, D. B., & Aune, R. K. (1988). The effects of vocalics and nonverbal sensitivity on compliance: A speech accommodation theory explanation. *Human Communication Research, 14,* 301–322.

Buller, D. B., & Burgoon, J. K. (1986). The effects of vocalics and nonverbal sensitivity on compliance: A replication and extension. *Human Communication Research, 13,* 126–144.

Carter, J. D. (2000). *Ecological sensitivity: Individual differences in accuracy of covariation judgments in social interaction.* Unpublished doctoral dissertation, Northeastern University.

Cohen, J. (1988). *Statistical power for the behavioral sciences* (2nd ed.). Hillsdale, NJ: Lawrence Erlbaum Associates.

Cooper, H. M., & Hazelrigg, P. (1988). Personality moderators of interpersonal expectancy effects: An integrative research review. *Journal of Personality and Social Psychology, 55,* 937–949.

Costanzo, M., & Archer, D. (1989). Interpreting the expressive behavior of others: The Interpersonal Perception Task. *Journal of Nonverbal Behavior, 13,* 225–245.

Davies, M., Stankov, L., & Roberts, R. D. (1998). Emotional intelligence: In search of an elusive construct. *Journal of Personality and Social Psychology, 75,* 989–1015.

Darwin, C. (1965). *The expression of the emotions in man and animals.* Chicago: University of Chicago Press. (Original work published 1872)

DiMatteo, M. R., Friedman, H. S. & Taranta, A. (1979). Sensitivity to bodily nonverbal communication as a factor in practitioner–patient rapport. *Journal of Nonverbal Behavior, 4,* 18–26.

DiMatteo, M. R., & Hall, J. A. (1979). Nonverbal decoding skill and attention to nonverbal cues: A research note. *Environmental Psychology and Nonverbal Behavior, 3,* 188–192.

Ekman, P., & Friesen, W. V. (1974). Nonverbal behavior and psychopathology. In R. J. Friedman & M. M. Katz (Eds.), *The psychology of depression: Contemporary theory and research.* Washington, DC: Winston.

Ekman, P., Friesen, W. V., O'Sullivan, M., Chan, A., Diacoyanni-Tarlatzis, I., Heider, K., Krause, R., Le Compte, . A., Pitcairn, T., Ricci-Bitti, P. E., Scherer, K., Tomita, M., & Tzavaras, A. (1987). Universals and cultural differences in the judgments of facial expressions of emotion. *Journal of Personality and Social Psychology, 53,* 712–717.

Feleky, A. (1914). The expression of the emotions. *Psychological Review, 21,* 33–41.

Funder, D. C., & Harris, M. J. (1986). On the several facets of personality assessment: The case of social acuity. *Journal of Personality, 54,* 528–550.

Gesn, P. R., Bernieri, F. J., Grahe, J. E., & Gada-Jain, N. (1999, April). *Domains of interpersonal sensitivity: Performance accuracy and self-reports of ability.* Presented at Midwestern Psychological Association convention, Chicago.

Hall, J. A. (1978). Gender effects in decoding nonverbal cues. *Psychological Bulletin, 85,* 845–857.

Hall, J. A. (1980). Voice tone and persuasion. *Journal of Personality and Social Psychology, 38,* 924–934.

Hall, J. A. (1984). *Nonverbal sex differences: Communication accuracy and expressive style.* Baltimore: The Johns Hopkins University Press.

Hall, J. A. (1988). How big are nonverbal sex differences? The case of smiling and sensitivity to nonverbal cues. In D. J. Canary & K. Dindia (Eds.), *Sex differences and similarities in communication: Critical essays and empirical investigations of sex and gender in interaction* (pp. 155–177). Mahwah, NJ: Lawrence Erlbaum Associates.

Hall, J. A., & Carter, J. D. (1999). Gender-stereotype accuracy as an individual difference. *Journal of Personality and Social Psychology, 77,* 350–359.

Hall, J. A., Carter, J. D., & Horgan, T. E. (1998). *Assigned status and attention to nonverbal cues: Motivational effects of unequal status on accurate recall of a partner's behavior.* Unpublished manuscript.

Hall, J. A., Carter, J. D., & Horgan, T. E. (2000). Gender differences in nonverbal communication of emotion. In A. Fischer (Ed.), *Gender and emotion* (97–117). Cambridge, England: Cambridge University Press.

Hall, J. A., Carter, J. D., & Horgan, T. E. (in press). Status roles and recall of nonverbal cues. *Journal of Nonverbal Behavior.*

Hall, J. A., & Halberstadt, A. G. (1994). "Subordination" and sensitivity to nonverbal cues: A study of married working women. *Sex Roles, 31,* 149–165.

Hall, J. A., Halberstadt, A. G., & O'Brien, C. E. (1997). "Subordination" and nonverbal sensitivity: A study and synthesis of findings based on trait measures. *Sex Roles, 37,* 295–317.

Harris, M. J., & Rosenthal, R. (1985). Mediation of interpersonal expectancy effects: 31 meta-analyses. *Psychological Bulletin, 97,* 363–386.

Hazelrigg, P. J., Cooper, H., & Strathman, A. J. (1991). Personality moderators of the experimenter expectancy effect: A reexamination of five hypotheses. *Personality and Social Psychology Bulletin, 17,* 569–579.

Izard, C. E. (1971). *The face of emotion.* New York: Appleton-Century-Crofts.

Magill-Evans, J., Koning, C., Cameron-Sadava, A., & Manyk, K. (1995). The Child and Adolescent Social Perception Measure. *Journal of Nonverbal Behavior, 19*, 151–169.

Matsumoto, D., LeRoux, J., Wilson-Cohn, C., Raroque, J., Kooken, K., Ekman, P., Yrizarry, N., Loewinger, S., Uchida, H., Yee, A., Amo, L., & Goh, A. (2000). A new test to measure emotion recognition ability: Matsumoto and Ekman's Japanese and Caucasian Brief Affect Recognition Test (JACBART). *Journal of Nonverbal Behavior, 24, 179–209.*

Meiran, N., Netzer, T., Netzer, S., Itzhak, D., & Rechnitz, O. (1994). Do tests of nonverbal decoding ability measure sensitivity to nonverbal cues? *Journal of Nonverbal Behavior, 18,* 223–244.

Nowicki, S., Jr., & Duke, M. P. (1994). Individual differences in the nonverbal communication of affect: The Diagnostic Analysis of Nonverbal Accuracy Scale. *Journal of Nonverbal Behavior, 18,* 9–35.

Patterson, M. L., & Stockbridge, E. (1998). Effects of cognitive demand and judgment strategy on person perception accuracy. *Journal of Nonverbal Behavior, 22,* 253–263.

Rosenthal, R. (1976). *Experimenter effects in behavioral research* (enlarged ed.). New York: Irvington.

Rosenthal, R., Hall, J. A., DiMatteo, M. R., Rogers, P. L., & Archer, D. (1979). *Sensitivity to nonverbal communication: The PONS test.* Baltimore: The Johns Hopkins University Press.

Rosenthal, R., & Rosnow, R. (1991). *Essentials of behavioral research* (2nd ed.). New York: McGraw-Hill.

Rosenthal, R., & Rubin, D. B. (1978). Interpersonal expectancy effects: The first 345 studies. *Behavioral and Brain Sciences, 3,* 377–386.

Snyder, M., Tanke, E. D., & Berscheid, E. (1977). Social perception and interpersonal behavior: On the self-fulfilling nature of social stereotypes. *Journal of Personality and Social Psychology, 35,* 656–666.

Sternberg, R. J., & Smith, C. (1985). Social intelligence and decoding skills in nonverbal communication. *Social Cognition, 3,* 168–192.

Zuckerman, M., DeFrank, R. S., Hall, J. A., & Rosenthal, R. (1978). Accuracy of nonverbal communication as determinant of interpersonal expectancy effects. *Environmental Psychology and Nonverbal Behavior, 2,* 206–214.

## APPENDIX

## Acquiring and Administering the PONS Test

The PONS test is available from Judith Hall, Department of Psychology, Northeastern University, Boston, MA 02115 (send email to hall1@neu.edu). Available are alternate forms of the test, a test manual, and answer forms. Scoring is done by the individual investigator using the keys provided. The PONS can be administered in group sessions using standard audiovisual equipment and dim lighting. All answer forms are multiple-choice. The most complete source of information on test development and validation is Rosenthal et al. (1979).

# The Interpersonal Perception Task (IPT): Alternative Approaches to Problems of Theory and Design

**Dane Archer**
*University of California, Santa Cruz*

**Mark Costanzo**
*Claremont McKenna College*

**Robin Akert**
*Wellesley College*

This chapter describes the theoretical issues and concrete design features that inspired the Interpersonal Perception Task (IPT). The IPT is a broadcast quality videotape that has 30 scenes, and each scene contains a sequence of naturalistic interaction. The IPT scenes reflect the spectrum of simultaneous communication channels found in everyday interaction, and the IPT viewer is presented with naturally co-occurring cues that are verbal, coverbal, and nonverbal.

For each IPT scene there is an interpretive question, and for every question there is an objectively correct answer. The IPT items include a range of qualitatively different interpretive areas. In one IPT scene, a man and a woman interact with two children, and the viewer is asked to infer which of the two children is theirs. In a second IPT scene, a woman tells two different accounts of her childhood, and the viewer is asked to judge which of the two accounts is true. In a third IPT scene, two men discuss a game of basketball they have just played, and the viewer is asked to identify which man won the game. In a fourth IPT scene, two co-workers talk to one another, and the viewer is asked to determine which of the two workers is the boss. In a fifth IPT scene, a woman talks on the telephone, and the viewer is asked to infer whether she is talking to her mother, a female friend, or her boyfriend.

Each of the 30 IPT scenes taps one of five interpretive areas: kinship, lies, competition, status, and intimacy. For each IPT scene, the chance (or mere guessing) level of accuracy reflects the number of multiple-choice alternatives for that question—that is, chance is 33.3% if there are three alternatives, and 50.0% if there are two alternatives. Figure 9.1 graphs the mean scores on the 30 IPT scenes for a sample of 438 college and university students, and also indicates the chance level of accuracy for each scene. For the very first IPT scene ("Who is the child of the two adults—only the little boy, only the little girl, or neither child?"), Figure 9.1 shows that 64.5% of the sample answered this question correctly, which greatly exceeds the corresponding chance level of 33.3%. Figure 9.1 provides similar information for the other IPT scenes as well.

In Figure 9.2, the 30 IPT scenes are grouped in the five interpretive areas. This graph compares three different accuracy levels: the actual performances of women and men (which are graphed separately), and the corresponding chance accuracy levels for each interpretive area. As shown in Figure 9.2, women were slightly more accurate than men in all five interpretive areas, and both genders were substantially more accurate than chance in all five areas.

Despite the important differences reflected in the data summaries in Figure 9.1 and Figure 9.2, the consistencies in these graphs demonstrate that the IPT meets two of the most fundamental requirements for a task of this sort. Above-chance scores such as those shown in these graphs are impossible unless: (a) important cues are present somewhere (text, coverbal, nonverbal) in the IPT scenes and (b) judges are able to decode these cues to arrive at accurate interpretations. Accuracy scores that rise substantially above chance levels are impossible unless both of these qualities are present in an interpretive task such as the IPT.

Naturally, it is not easy for the print page to demonstrate the nature of a videotape task such as the IPT. Although the video is in color, the black-and-white photographs in Figure 9.3 reflect some of the visual content and variation of the IPT scenes. These images were taken directly from the screen and therefore include scan lines. Each of the photographs shown in Figure 9.3 is paired with the corresponding IPT question and multiple-choice answers.

Another indication of the variety of interactions in the IPT scenes can be obtained from the text channel—that is, transcripts of the spoken words. Naturally, transcripts are only text, and they lack all the subtlety contained in vocal paralanguage. A transcript is therefore a minimal source of cues compared with seeing and hearing the actual IPT videotape, but it can indicate some of the manifest content of the interactions. The Appendix contains transcripts made from several of the IPT scenes. It is of course possible to try to answer the IPT interpretive questions using only the photographs in or only the verbal

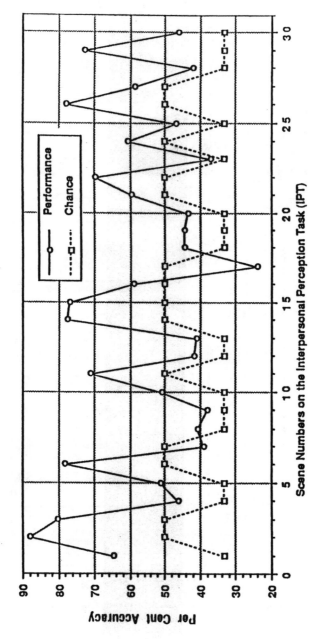

FIG. 9.1. Performance on the Interpersonal Perception Task (IPT): Norm group ($n = 438$) versus chance levels of accuracy.

163

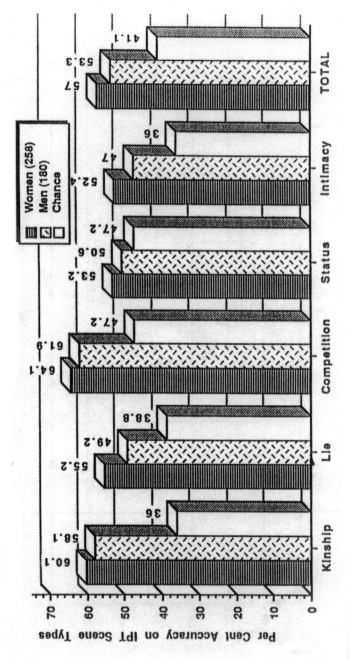

FIG. 9.2. Gender differences in performance on the Interpersonal Perception Taks (IPT).

IPT: Scene 1

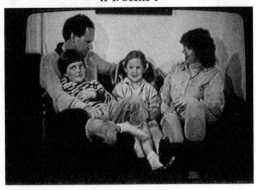

1. Who is the child of the two adults?

a) only the little boy.

b) only the little girl.

c) Neither the boy or the girl is the child of the adults.

| *Left* | | *Right* | |
|---|---|---|---|
| *Person 1* | *Person 2* | *Person 3* | *Person 4* |
| *(man)* | *(boy in man's lap)* | *(girl)* | *(woman)* |

1: Complain a lot . . .

4: You complain, yeah

1: Who do you talk to your pillow, or, or, just yell out the window, or what do you do, slam the door?

3: No, just

1: None of that, huh?

2: When Brendan has a tantrum he throws his math book.

4: Huh?

1: Does Brendan . . . ?

2: That's what he did yesterday!

4: He threw his math book?

1: Uh huh.

2: On his desk!

4: You're kidding Nate!

1: You mean he looks through all his books and picks out the math book?

3: I know

1: And then throws that? Is that what he does?

3: Yeah, he's . . .

4: Oh my goodness.

3: He's all mad just because . . . um

2: Lauren's going to move in where Cory is.

1: Oh . . .

4: Oh . . .

3: Yeah, so . . .

FIG. 9.3 Sample items from the IPT.

2. What is the relationship between the man and the woman?

a) they are lovers who have been together for about 10 months.

b) They are lovers who have been together for about 3 years.

IPT: Scene 2

*Left*                              *Right*

*Person 1 (woman)*              *Person 2 (man)*

1: I think maybe one child's nicer to have from the parent's point of view . . . Less work. Um. But as 1 of 3, I felt a lot different. I grew up sharing a room with my sister, as you know.

2: Right.

1: And that way, sharing a room in college with a roommate was a lot easier. And didn't fight over things . . . And then there were a lot of times where I think I would have been really lonely, if I didn't have her, and also a little brother. I grew up where there weren't very many kids my age, and we had each other. We wouldn't have had each other.

2: Uh huh.

1: If they weren't there. I mean I can see your point, about

2: I don't know, I just . . .

1: I guess all the advantages, but I think there's other advantages too, not just advantages of all the attention

2: Uh huh.

1: But advantages of having playmates, um, peers.

2: Yeah, I just remember how I felt when I had a step—I have a step-brother and a step-sister, and when they'd come for the summer, and I always felt, when I was a little kid, I always felt like . . . My turf was being invaded on just a little bit.

(FIG. 9.3., continued)

transcripts in Fig. 9.3 but readers are cautioned that both are cue-impoverished compared with the full-channel repertoire of the scenes in the IPT videotape.

Because the original IPT was about 45 min long, it seemed desirable to have a briefer version of the IPT available as well. As a result, the IPT-15 videotape contains only 15 of the 30 scenes in the original IPT. More detailed data on the reliability and validity of both the IPT and the IPT-15 are given elsewhere, along with careful descriptions of the actual verbal and nonverbal behaviors in the IPT scenes (Archer & Costanzo, 1987; Costanzo & Archer, 1989, 1991, 1993).

IPT: Scene 8

*Person 1 (woman)*

8. Who is the woman talking to on the telephone?

a) her mother.

b) a female friend she has known for many years.

c) a male friend she has known for many years.

1: Well Chris freaks out, she says that to me all the time, she goes "Oh my God, you're so spacey" you know, she . . . Don't worry about that (laugh) yeah . . . I had a blast, I'm psyched to come up for your birthday . . . . Oh, I know, there's supposed to be like three more coming, but I mean, it's ah, we can figure something out . . . . Yeah, . . . All right.

26. Who won the game of one-on-one basketball?

a) the man on the left.

b) the man on the right.

IPT: Scene 26

*Left Person 1 (man)*                    *Right Person 2 (man)*

2: So he got me practicing pretty often. I've been playing ball since I was 8 years old, and he's been playing less than that, a lot less than that. And I got my shot down pretty pat, even . . . Even if I'm cold, I know I'm still gonna eventually hit, and I don't know about, about himself.

1: Um. My shot isn't down pat. I just have to feel the ball. I'm, I'm like a weather player. I f the weather's all right, then I'm all right. Lately, so like the past three weeks I've been getting confident, 'cept I make a mistake that he knows that if I, when I shoot, I'm not gonna tell everyone, but when I shoot I happen to, do it on only on one move, either side, but, I don't know, I hate doing that, 'specially when I play him, cause he knows, he knows I'm gonna do it, but then I try not to do it and mess up my whole game.

(FIG. 9.3., continued)

## RESEARCH DESIGN:
## INFLUENCES, REFLECTIONS, AND FIRST EFFORTS

It is quite clear that there would never have been an IPT if not for the ground broken by the Profile of Nonverbal Sensitivity (PONS), a film developed at Harvard University in 1971 and described in a book published by the end of that decade (Rosenthal, Hall, DiMatteo, Rogers, & Archer, 1979). The PONS research project was led by Robert Rosenthal, and he generously (and characteristically) invited several of his graduate students to participate in all phases of the PONS project.

The PONS film was a pioneering effort and one that led to many discoveries, including the first evidence that (a) sensitivity to nonverbal communication is not the same as conventional intelligence; (b) this new ability seemed reliable, and also linked to a number of important and favorable outcomes; and (c) women were more accurate readers of nonverbal cues than men. There were also less global (but no less intriguing) findings. For example, the researchers found evidence that mothers of prelanguage toddlers were unusually accurate on the PONS—presumably because the women had been taught to read nonverbal behavior by decoding messages from their wordless toddlers.

The PONS project has several links to the present volume. Dane Archer was the "decoder" who stood just off camera while the PONS scenes were filmed. This provided someone for the "encoder" to address, and the encoder on the PONS project was one of the editors of this volume, Judith Hall. With three separate video cameras trained separately on (a) her face, (b) her body from the neck down, and (c) her combined face and body, Hall enacted emotional situations (jealous anger, leaving on a trip, admiring nature, trying to seduce someone, etc.). The PONS was an ambitious conception and a trail-blazing research program. It offered a systematic approach to nonverbal behavior, and it also offered members of the research team insights into the strengths and also the limits of the PONS paradigm.

In 1971, the PONS film was completed, and 16mm "kinescope" (film) versions were created from the original videotapes. That summer, Dane Archer took the PONS film to Great Britain, testing samples in England and Northern Ireland. Along the way, Dane Archer stumbled—inadvertently and with no laudable scientific forethought at all—on evidence of the powerful impact that cultural differences stamp on nearly all human communication, including the nonverbal channels.

The unanticipated insight occurred in Belfast, Northern Ireland, during a resurgence of "The Troubles." In the midst of bomb craters and surreal discussions of how to avoid buildings likely to be targets for either Protestant or Catholic extremists, the PONS film was shown to clinical faculty and staff at a psychiatric hospital. After the PONS test had been screened, the participants were thanked warmly for patiently sitting through the long task.

Then members of the audience were asked if they had any questions. A middle-aged woman raised her hand and said, "Well, one of the alternative answers on the PONS test is 'discussing a divorce,' and I really couldn't answer this because I had no idea whether this woman would be mildly disappointed or else suicidal—you see, I have never known anyone who had a divorce."

It was at that moment that Dane Archer realized that the PONS research group had been operating under unstated presumptions about how people would try to answer the PONS questions. Basically, it was assumed that there would be two routes to a correct answer: direct personal experience or informed imagination. We assumed that people watching the PONS would try to "map" the images in the PONS film on to the viewer's own experiences and observations. For example, a loud celebratory interaction might be recognized because everyone has experienced loud celebrations. Even if viewers lacked direct personal experience with celebration, they might try to imagine what this would look like—having observed friends and family members, media images, and so forth.

In Northern Ireland at the time of the visit, however, there was no direct experience with an emotional event like divorce and also little or no vicarious observation of the experience. What the woman in Belfast was saying, in other words, is that in her culture people lacked both experiential data and observational data on what talking about divorce might look like. Naturally, cultural differences are not limited to interactions about divorce. If this is true, one might begin to wonder about what other interpretive situations might be remote, irrelevant, or even alien to perceivers in different ethnic, cultural, and national groups. This experience increased Dane Archer's interest in how understanding another person's communicative behavior may depend on culture, society, gender, and other social factors.

Indirectly, therefore, the PONS project catalyzed a very different research program, one using video to explore how interpretation, perception, attributions, and the accurate decoding of nonverbal behavior often hinge on systematic patterns of cultural, social, and gender differences. Years later, this led to the creation of a University of California documentary video series dedicated to capturing and exploring the nature, nuances, and power of nonverbal communication. The University of California video series examines cultural differences, gestures, vocal paralanguage, facial expressions, the human body, proxemics, and cross-cultural communication (Archer 1991, 1992, 1993, 1995, 1997a, 1997b, 1998, 1999; Archer & Costanzo, 1987; Costanzo & Archer, 1993).

## Interpersonal Sensitivity: Problems of Theory and Method

The PONS research project was a watershed, making its mark as the first systematic, large-scale effort to evaluate individual differences in the ability to decode nonverbal behavior. The legacy of this effort is evident and, no doubt, lasting.

The approach and design of the PONS project also had other effects. For Dane Archer, participation in the PONS project catalyzed ideas about alternative theoretical approaches and design decisions. In this section, we describe ways in which the design of the IPT departs from previous approaches. We wish to emphasize that this in no way diminishes the historic role and multiple accomplishments of the PONS project. All research designs (including our own) have both strengths and constraints.

The issues discussed in this section are theoretical, methodological and, at the intersection of these two domains, epistemological. These issues lie at the heart of what we intend our research to illuminate:

- What types of interpersonal sensitivity are we addressing?
- What "level" of behavior are judges being asked to observe—manifest acts, implicit emotions, probable motives, verbal assertions, or some combination?
- How and where do we sample behavior for a judgment task—what is the relative acceptability of acted behavior, spontaneous behavior, or "hidden camera" behavior?
- Is there a "right answer" (one that is objectively correct) to the questions we ask the judges and, if there is, how do we know it is right?
- Are the interpretive questions concerned with emotions alone, or do they also address biography, truthfulness, and relationships such as those involved in love, family, work, and friendship?
- When we use terms such as interpersonal sensitivity, perception, inference, and interpretation, are these near-synonyms, or do we use them to mean qualitatively different tasks?
- What channels of verbal and nonverbal communication do we regard as essential, and how do we decide which ones (and how many) to include in our research design?

In our view, these questions are neither frivolous or discretionary. Researchers do not always make explicit their design choices on these fundamental dimensions, and in some cases these choices are made by default. The point is that these design choices are being made. Consciously or not, all researchers in this field must adopt an epistemological stance on these issues. It is our hope that by articulating these critical design issues, we can assist other researchers in recognizing the range of possible choices so they can optimize their own design decisions. Understanding the constraints inherent in previous approaches can be enormously fruitful—just as the hiker who observes the difficulties of the traditional route may discover alternative, as yet untraveled paths.

Many of the design issues and choices described in this article were first used in a black-and-white videotape task known as the Social Interpretations Task (SIT) developed during the 1970s by Dane Archer and Robin Akert. Using the

SIT, Archer and Akert found evidence that the accuracy of interpretations was relatively poor when judges saw only printed transcripts of interactions, and far more accurate when shown the full-channel (verbal and nonverbal) videotape of the same interactions. Archer and Akert called this result "Words and Everything Else" (Archer & Akert, 1977).

The black-and-white SIT was also used in a test of three different theoretical models that sought to explain the relationship between information and interpretation. The researchers compared accuracy obtained with a whole video sequence with accuracy obtained from only parts disaggregated from the whole sequence. A part could be one channel alone (e.g., only the audio channel, or only the silent video channel) rather than the multichannel whole. A part could also be temporal—for example, a whole 20-s video sequence could be broken into four 5-s parts.

The vital theoretical question compares the accuracy obtained with the whole with the accuracy obtained with just a part. This theoretical issue addresses the fundamental nature of interpretation: How does interpretation use information, and what cues are needed for an interpretation to achieve accuracy? We presented three strikingly different theories, each leading to different predictions:

### Significant Cue Theory

This assumes that accuracy results from one key part of an interaction (e.g., the first 5 s), or from one key channel (e.g., one person's facial expressions). Significant cue theory predicts that only those judges who happen to have this key part will get the right answer. Judges shown other parts that do not contain the significant cue will do poorly.

### Additive Theory

This assumes that no part of an interaction will suffice, and that the right answer is possible only when the parts accumulate into the whole. Additive theory is deeply contextual, and it assumes that accurate understanding accumulates incrementally. As a judge sees more and more parts, the judge becomes more accurate. This theory predicts that judges shown only a part—any part—will do poorly.

### Diffusion-Redundancy Theory

This assumes that virtually all parts of an interaction possess cues that enable judges to reach an accurate interpretation. According to this theory, the important qualities of an interaction are diffused or redundant. This theory holds that vital cues are encoded redundantly in two ways: (a) across many channels at any given instant, and (b) across the time segments of an interaction. As a result, this theory predicts that judges shown different channels, or different time intervals—indeed, almost any part—will all be exposed to important cues, and they should do as well as judges who saw the whole.

In a series of experiments, we found evidence that strongly and consistently supported Diffusion-Redundancy Theory (Archer & Akert, 1980). When different groups of judges were given only one part of an interaction (e.g., only the audio channel, or only the first 5 s of the video), the groups performed equally well, above chance, and—perhaps most curiously—roughly as well as judges who saw the whole interaction. This finding contradicts both significant cue theory (which predicts that only some parts of the interaction can lead to accurate interpretation) and Additive Theory (which predicts that individual parts will not lead to accuracy, whereas wholes will).

Alas, a major drawback of the SIT was not scientific but cinematic. The black-and-white video was poorly lit, making broadcast-quality footage impossible. With the SIT, some judges complained that in some scenes it was difficult to tell who was speaking. We felt that the SIT had demonstrated that the underlying approach was methodologically viable and theoretically interesting. As a result, we decided to use professional videographers to create a full-color, broadcast-quality next generation. The result is the IPT.

We had several goals in mind when we created the IPT and the IPT-15: to move beyond paper-and-pencil measures; to improve on the video measures available at the time (most notably the PONS and the SIT); and to provide a brief, standardized measure with known properties that could easily be included in studies of nonverbal behavior, social perception, and social sensitivity. As social psychologists, we were mainly interested in creating an instrument for investigating the process of interpersonal perception. We were interested in using the IPT to explore the relationship between confidence and accuracy, to examine how different communication channels (i.e., verbal, vocal, and nonverbal) contribute to accurate perception, and to identify which cues people rely on when making interpersonal judgments. The "T" in IPT stands for "task" instead of "test" because our interest was not primarily psychometric.

However, most studies that have used the IPT have used it as a measure of interpersonal sensitivity. Consequently, it is important to ask, "What ability is measured by the IPT or the IPT-15?" One answer might be that the IPT measures the ability to interpret accurately the expressive behavior of others. Because achieving interpersonal goals depends significantly on our ability to correctly interpret accurately the behavior of others, the IPT measures a core component of what has been called "social intelligence" or "social competence." Of course, skill in interpreting the behavior of others is only one aspect of overall social competence. Many other component skills—for example, the ability to regulate emotional displays and the ability to influence others—are crucial to achieving interpersonal goals. Still, it is difficult to imagine a highly socially competent person who does not have a well developed ability to read or decode the expressive behavior of others.

# Concrete Design Decisions in Creating the IPT: Choices and Reasons

In making the IPT, we made conscious decisions about several major design issues, and each of them, it seemed to us, was theoretically significant. In making these decisions, we were particularly conscious of the epistemological approach we wanted to follow in our exploration of the related topics of person perception, interpersonal behavior, nonverbal communication, and interpretation. Our preferences may or may not suit other researchers, other measures, or other research programs. But design decisions clearly do matter, and because they are rarely (if ever) self-explanatory, we have tried in this section to articulate both (a) our specific design choices in making the IPT and (b) much more generally, our theoretical and epistemological reasons for making the choices we did.

## Enactments Versus Naturalistic Interaction

The PONS test used acting to create samples of behavior. The encoder, Judith Hall, enacted a series of emotional situations while facing three video cameras and Dane Archer, just off-camera. Although there is no real benchmark for such things, the enactments seemed very well done. Even so, there remain interesting epistemological questions. Was her acted performance of jealous anger similar in all or most channels to how she would have shown jealous anger in real life? Was her performance of this acted emotion idiosyncratic—or did it closely resemble the way jealous anger would be performed by other Americans, by other American women, by other American women of a certain age, by American women of a certain age in the U.S. Northeast, and so forth.

When testing with the PONS film, Dane Archer was on rare occasions asked whether the judge was supposed to indicate what emotion the PONS encoder was performing or what emotion (if any) she was really feeling. The PONS researcher's intent, of course, was that judges should try to recognize the acted emotion. But as a number of judges would sometimes say, "The correct answer is that she is really feeling none of the above."

Since systematic research on nonverbal behavior began, researchers have been divided on this question. Acted emotions have been widely used, and this choice obviously maximizes experimental control over the stimuli. In doing the IPT, we decided to avoid acted emotions. Our rationale was largely theoretical in that we wanted to study sensitivity to interpersonal behavior and not sensitivity to someone's performance of what real interpersonal behavior might look like.

This preference for naturalistic behavior served as our general rule, but there was one exception. For our "lie" items, we did have encoders provide a truthful biographical account and also an untrue biographical account. The latter, of course, was acted or performed. With the exception of the lies we included, the other IPT scenes contain naturalistic rather than acted behavior.

## Subjective Versus Objective Answers

What is the right answer in a test of interpersonal sensitivity? This is known as the criterion of accuracy problem, and there are a number of different answers. Some researchers have used the encoder's intent to determine the right answer—if the encoder intended to show jealous anger, then jealous anger is the correct answer to this item. There are other approaches. For example, researchers can videotape several different versions of jealous anger, and then have raters select the most authentic performance—in this case expert opinion becomes the right answer.

In designing the IPT, we wanted to stake out what we regard—rightly or wrongly—as firmer epistemological ground. The IPT items have an objectively correct criterion of accuracy–that is, the right answers to the IPT questions are a matter of fact. On the IPT, one of the two men really did win the basketball game; one of the men really is the father of both children; one of the two women really is the boss; and one of the two accounts of the woman's childhood really is the truth.

Objectively correct questions seem to us to be theoretically preferable on an a priori basis, but they are not for all researchers or all projects. For example, this design decision had an effect on how emotion occurs in the IPT. Instead of asking, "Which one of these two fencers feels victorious?," we ask the objective version of the question: "Which one of these two fencers just won the fencing match?" Similarly, we avoid questions about "motherly love," and instead ask simply "Which woman is the mother?"

Researchers who want to study emotions that are intense but rare (rage, extreme grief, etc.) cannot easily use our method—unless they sample behaviors from news film and similar sources. We regard this as a promising tactic for future researchers hoping to have intense emotions and objectively right answers. At this point, we tend to think there is no longer much justification for using an acted emotion to determine the right answer to an interpersonal sensitivity task. As media become more and more accessible, it is becoming more and more possible to insist on questions that have objectively correct answers, and that was our design decision in making the IPT.

## A Single Encoder Versus Real Interaction

There is no nonverbal dictionary showing what constitutes typical, fairly common, fairly uncommon, or rare nonverbal behavior in a variety of interpersonal settings. This means that we have little or no systematic way to judge how realistic or (alternately) idiosyncratic a given encoding sequence is. The researcher can voice an opinion on this, but it remains an opinion.

For this reason, it seems prudent to include many different encoders in a sensitivity task rather than just one or two. With many encoders, one minimizes the risk that idiosyncratic encoding will compromise chances of generalization from sensitivity in the lab to sensitivity in the real world. The PONS project used one encoder, because there were so many other variables (e.g., 20 scenes x 11 channels) that the researchers understandably wanted to keep the encoder as a constant. In making the IPT, we preferred the opposite design choice and filmed as many different encoders as possible. Parenthetically, this seems to be beneficial for the judges—multiple encoders seem to do a much better job of sustaining viewer interest levels.

### Channel Isolation Versus Multichannel Cues

This design choice confronts most or all researchers interested in studying interpersonal sensitivity. It is possible to divide almost any videotaped interaction into constituent channels: text or printed transcript, audio track only, still visual photograph only, silent video track only, and so forth. In the PONS film, we had four different visual channels (face, body, figure, and no visual) and three audio channels (content filter, random-splice, and no audio). If one combines the four visual channels and three audio channels, there are 11 different possibilities (not counting the 12th combination: no video and no audio). In designing the IPT, we did not use this kind of factorial design but instead made a design decision to use only naturally occurring channels of communication. The result is that the IPT scenes include verbal, coverbal, and nonverbal behavior—precisely whatever communication channels were naturally present in the interactions we videotaped.

This approach serves researchers who want to study naturalistic verbal and nonverbal behavior, and it also means that one's judges are decoding in a naturalistic manner. In order to form an interpretation, the judges have to sort among hundreds of potential cues—weighing some and discarding others—to try to answer the IPT question. This is precisely the same multichannel complexity confronted in real-life interpretation, and it seems to us a good idea to include this realistic communications environment in an interpersonal sensitivity task. Finally, there may be other advantages as well—for instance, researchers can ask judges to try to identify which cues were the most influential. This could set the stage for an understanding of how interpretation actually operates.

### Recognition Versus Interpretation

This design decision lies at the heart of what we mean by interpersonal sensitivity or interpretation. For example, the PONS scenes might be thought of as requiring recognition rather than interpretation. In the first draft of the PONS, we found that if the PONS scenes were 6 s long, everyone could recognize the emotion that the encoder was performing (i.e., we had the dreaded ceiling effect). As a result, the PONS scenes were edited down to 2 s, producing variation among the judges' accuracy scores. In our view, the judges are performing a recognition task if everyone would get the right answer if shown 6 s of behavior. If the judges are asked to perform a more complex inferential task, we believe that what is being studied is interpretation rather than recognition. In designing the IPT, we wanted to study interpretation—and this is reflected in the IPT scenes.

Our preference for interpretation over recognition reflects our view that the former is closer to the complex interpersonal perception challenges we confront in everyday life. When we interact with other people, we rarely confront recognition tasks that are completely self-evident to all observers in 6 s. Instead, we need to construct an interpretation that is not obvious, and we need to weigh subtle cues from many channels in trying to understand the other person or his or her behavior. We should emphasize that studying recognition makes perfect sense for some questions—for instance, Can men and women recognize emblematic hand gestures? But for complex interpersonal perception, we prefer a focus on interpretation, and that is how we designed the IPT.

## The Context Problem: Some Major Dimensions

One of the most abused words in the vocabulary of research, "context" assumes special importance in the study of nonverbal behavior. The essential tension is between efforts to preserve the naturalistic contexts in which a nonverbal behavior occurs, on the one hand, and a commendable scientific impulse to isolate a behavior (e.g., one photograph, a video of one gesture) so that it can be studied free of encumbrances. There are several different ways in which the issue of context bears importantly on nonverbal research. The issue here is not that some designs are always superior to some other approaches. Instead, the key is for the researcher to be aware that decisions will be made, consciously or not, that affect each of the following five forms of context.

*1. Channel Inclusion.*   Researchers can isolate a single nonverbal channel or artificially mix in only the channels that are wanted. In designing the IPT, we made a decision to include all the channels naturally present in an interaction, including both verbal and nonverbal behaviors. Our theoretical stance was that the IPT judges should confront each nonverbal cue in context with cues in other channels—just as in everyday life.

*2. Situational Antecedents.*   In real interactions, almost all behaviors have situational antecedents as a context, and almost all judgment tasks truncate this history by framing behavior samples with an arbitrary beginning point. Without knowledge of the situational antecedents, judges are forced to operate in an informational vacuum—for instance, Is the "hilarity" we see in a video sample the result of a joke or the strained release at a wake? Obviously, our work with the PONS used two-second stimuli, reducing this variety of context to near-zero. In designing the IPT, we sought to provide segments long enough (i.e., 1-3 min) that some sense of sequence and context is possible.

*3. Prior Experience With the Encoder.*    Understanding of a given nonverbal behavior is presumably enhanced and more accurate as a function of one's history with the encoder. This history allows to be interpreted behavior in light of the encoder's biography, personality, and communicative idiosyncrasies. Because most judgment tasks use standardized samples of behavior, this dimension of context is simply absent from most nonverbal research—including both the PONS and the IPT.

*4. Behavior Streams.*    Nonverbal behavior in a judgment study can be presented in static slices (e.g., photographs) or in continuous streams (e.g., video) that capture the fluidity of natural behavior as well as the onset and offset of any given nonverbal behavior. This provides a sense of embeddedness or context for any specific nonverbal cue. We believed that static slices would inevitably lose potentially important meanings associated with sequences or combinations of behaviors, and so the IPT scenes contain only fluid, videotaped behavior.

*5. Real-Time Exposures.*    In real interaction, nonverbal acts occur in the context of time. In a research design, researchers can choose to make nonverbal cues available to the judges at naturalistic real-time speeds (e.g., as in video), at slower time (e.g., still photographs), or at faster time (e.g., one or two frames of film only, tachistoscope stimuli). When decoding in face-to-face interaction, of course, nonverbal behavior occurs in real-time, with hundreds (if not thousands) of potential cues flowing past an observer each minute. This means that an observer must attach significance to a cue at the instant one is perceived, and he or she will not be able to dwell at length on any single nonverbal act. For this reason, in designing the IPT we chose to use only real-time contexts for all verbal and nonverbal behaviors.

## The Importance of a Design Menu

We very much doubt that the design decisions we made in creating the IPT reflect all-purpose solutions for future research. The choices that we describe in this chapter reflect our view of what is most critical for any research program on the interpretation of nonverbal cues and interpersonal behavior.

The choices discussed here represent our priorities and preferences; other researchers will no doubt have additional or different concerns. The point of this chapter, however, is that there is in fact a "design menu" for all researchers work-ing on these questions. Whether explicitly or not, researchers will be making de-sign decisions along many or all of the dimensions charted in this chapter. We believe it is optimal for researchers to know at the outset of a research project that they are making highly consequential design choices. A far less desirable outcome is for the researcher to discover—long after a research design has been carried out—that there were unrecognized design choices that could have been made.

## Current Knowledge and Future Directions

Several scholars use the IPT, and the video has been especially popular as a classroom tool for teaching about social perception and human communica-tion. As a teaching device, the IPT helps instructors to facilitate classroom dis-cussion, sensitize students to the subtlety and complexity of verbal and nonverbal cues, and help students understand the process of interpreting these cues (see Costanzo & Archer, 1991, 1994). The IPT has been used by teachers at more than 600 colleges and universities in several countries.

A shortened and revised version of the IPT—the IPT-15—is a briefer, less difficult version of the original. The newer version also meets higher standards of reliability and validity (Costanzo & Archer, 1994). Although the IPT-15 can be administered in half the time of the original IPT, all five areas represented in the original (deception, intimacy, status, kinship, and competition) are repre-sented in the revision.

The IPT and the IPT-15 have been used in both published and unpublished studies. The first published article (Costanzo & Archer, 1989) described the de-sign of the IPT and reported the findings of several studies demonstrating its va-lidity and reliability. We found that average performance was well above what would be expected by chance, that the cues needed for correct interpretation were available in the scenes, and that scores on the IPT correlated with other standardized measures in logical ways.

Perhaps most important, we found that people with higher scores on the IPT were rated as more socially skilled by their friends. This conclusion is supported by research conducted by other investigators. For example, in a study of 53 pairs of university roommates, Hodgins and Zuckerman (1990) found that IPT scores predicted how the relationship was perceived. In pairs where both roommates scored high on the IPT, the relationship was rated significantly higher on several important types of emotional sharing—(a) self- and other-disclosure, (b) mean-ingful involvement, (c) giving and receiving support, and so forth.

Other research with the IPT has taken a psychometric approach, examining the relationships between the IPT and other measures of social competence. In several correlational studies of interpersonal perception skills, Schroeder (1995a, 1995b; Schroeder & Ketrow, 1997) found that IPT scores were posi-tively correlated with measures of sociability and public self-consciousness but negatively correlated with measures of social anxiety, communication anxiety, and shyness. Aube and Whiffen (1996) found that people who manifested a self-critical personality type (which is associated with depression) obtained lower scores on the IPT.

In a neuropsychological study, Puschel, Hernandez, and Zaidel (personal communication October 23, 1993) examined IPT performance scores by participants who were (a) healthy, (b) left-brain-damaged patients, and (c) right-brain-damaged patients. Puschel et al. found unexpectedly lower IPT scores for left-brain-damaged patients, suggesting that some nonverbal interactions also include important verbal cues (e.g., recognizing "girls' talk"). Campbell and McCord (1996) were unable to find any reliable relationship between IPT scores and the comprehension or picture arrangement subscales of the Wechsler Intelligence Scale. This suggests that the social intelligence intentionally tapped by the IPT is very different from the intelligence measured by IQ tests and other conventional measures.

Other published studies have taken a more social-psychological, process-oriented approach. Smith, Archer, and Costanzo (1991) made use of the IPT to show that although perceivers are consciously aware of when they are using cues accurately, they have great difficulty articulating the reasons for their judgments. Costanzo and Archer (1991, 1993) described several ways of using the IPT to teach students about social perception and reported data that the use of these techniques produced greater student satisfaction and a more sophisticated understanding of human communication.

Archer, Akert, and Costanzo (1993) discussed the theoretical implications of using the IPT and other measures of social perception. Costanzo (1992) used the IPT to evaluate the effectiveness of training designed to improve the ability to decode verbal and nonverbal cues. He found that an informational lecture increased confidence but not performance, that information plus practice improved both confidence and performance, and that men were more confident that they were doing well even when their accuracy was lower than women's accuracy.

An intriguing study by Bush and Marshall (1999) suggested that other forms of interpersonal training may also enhance the accuracy of nonverbal decoding. Bush and Marshall examined the IPT scores of beginning and advanced students who were in (a) theatre or (b) various other majors. They found no differences in IPT accuracy between beginning students in theatre and beginning students in other fields. This suggests that there were no selection differences—beginning theatre students were no more accurate than students in other fields.

Among advanced students, however, Bush and Marshall (1999) found large differences: Students who had received advanced theatrical training had much higher IPT scores than either beginning theatre students or advanced students in other fields. The authors attribute this finding to theatrical training that sensitizes them to the meaning of specific gestures, facial expressions, kinesics, vocal paralanguage, and so forth. Although Bush and Marshall may have the first systematic evidence that theatrical training enhances an understanding of nonverbal behavior, the idea has long been central to theories about acting:

> Observation is an integral part of normal theatrical training. Even the most elementary lessons in acting stress the preparation and repetition of activities snatched from everyday life, developing the student's memory and sharpening his or her sense of observation. The gift of observation must be cultivated in every part of your body, not just in your sight and memory. (Boleslavsky, 1933)

Ambady, Hallahan, and Rosenthal (1995) examined how unacquainted participants judged and were judged by others. They found that accurate judges scored higher on the IPT and that performance on the IPT predicted accuracy of judgment for women. Hall, Halberstadt, and O'Brien (1997) used the IPT as part of an investigation of the hypothesis that people who have been subordinated possess an enhanced ability to interpret nonverbal cues. Their findings did not support the subordination hypotheses. Patterson and Stockbridge (1998) used either full-channel or silent forms of the IPT to examine the effect of judgment strategy and cognitive load on the accuracy of social perception. They found that for the silent version of the IPT, people were more accurate under low cognitive demand conditions.

Although the IPT is very much a new arrival in the person-perception, nonverbal communication, and interpretation research communities, we are buoyed by what we see. The early investigations suggest that the IPT may be able to make important contributions across a highly diverse range of hypotheses, questions, and research applications. The intriguing results obtained so far encourage us to be optimistic about the general usefulness of the IPT and the shorter IPT-15.

In conclusion, we believe the unique design features of the IPT and the IPT-15 include (a) naturalistic interaction, (b) the simultaneous presence of both verbal and nonverbal channels, (c) multiple encoders, (d) questions that require interpretation and not mere cue recognition, (e) real-time exposure lengths, and (f) objectively correct answers. We very much hope that these features will make the IPT and the IPT-15 attractive to any researcher eager to approximate the conditions of real person perception, naturalistic nonverbal behavior, and authentic interpretation. In addition, we are extremely encouraged by research results—our own and others—that performance on the IPT strongly (and consistently) predicts important outcomes and also the qualities of real relationships outside the laboratory. As Hodgins and Zuckerman (1990) concluded from their research with the IPT:

> Interactions between roommates who both correctly interpret nonverbal behaviors are more meaningful and characterized by more mutual disclosure and support. Apparently, emotional sharing requires that interactants tune in not only to the verbal content of messages but also to the accompanying cues from face, body, and tone of voice.

# REFERENCES

Ambady, N., Hallahan, M., & Rosenthal, R. (1995). On judging and being judged accurately in zero-acquaintance situations. *Journal of Personality and Social Psychology, 69*, 518–529.

Archer, D. (1992, Spring). A world of gestures: Culture and nonverbal communication. *Harvard Graduate Society Newsletter,* PP. Spring, 4–7.

Archer, D. (1997a). Unspoken diversity: Cultural differences in gestures. *Qualitative Sociology, 20*, 79–105.

Archer, D., & Akert, R. M. (1977). Words and everything else: Verbal and nonverbal cues in social interpretation. *Journal of Personality and Social Psychology, 35*, 443–449.

Archer, D., & Akert, R. M. (1980) The encoding of meaning: A test of three theories of social interaction. *Sociological Inquiry, 50*, 393–419.

Archer, D., Akert, R., & Costanzo, M. (1993). The accurate perception of nonverbal behavior: Questions of theory and research design. In P. D. Blanck (Ed.), *Interpersonal Expectations: Theory, Research, and Application.* New York: Cambridge University Press, 242–260.

Archer, D., & Costanzo, M. (1987). *The Interpersonal Perception Task (IPT)* [Video]. (Available from University of California Extension Center for Media and Independent Learning, 2000 Center Street, 4th Floor, Berkeley, California 94704; Phone (510) 642–0460; Fax (510) 643–9271; e-mail: cmil@uclink.berkeley.edu)

Aube, J., & Whiffen, V. (1996). Depressive styles and social acuity: Further evidence for distinct interpersonal correlates of dependency and self-criticism. *Communication Research, 23*, 407–424.

Boleslavsky, R. (1933). *Acting: The first six lessons.* New York: Theatre Art Books.

Bush, J., & Marshall, P. (1999). The inter-relationship between self-monitoring, interpersonal perception, and acting training. Unpublished manuscript.

Campbell, J., & McCord, D. (1996). The WAIS-R comprehension and picture arrangement subtests as measures of social intelligence: Testing additional interpretations. *Journal of Psychoeducational Assessment, 14*, 240–249.

Costanzo, M. (1992). Training students to decode verbal and nonverbal cues: Effects on confidence and performance. *Journal of Educational Psychology, 84*, 308–313.

Costanzo, M., & Archer, D. (1989). Interpreting the expressive behavior of others: The Interpersonal Perception Task. *Journal of Nonverbal Behavior, 13*, 225–245.

Costanzo, M., & Archer, D. (1991). A method of teaching about verbal and nonverbal communication. *Teaching of Psychology, 18*, 4, 223–226.

Costanzo, M., & Archer, D. (1993). *The Interpersonal Perception Task-15 (IPT-15).* Berkeley, CA: University of California Center for Media and Independent Learning.

Costanzo, M., & Archer, D. (1994). *The Interpersonal Perception Task-15 (IPT-15): A guide for researchers and teachers.* Berkeley, CA: University of California Center for Media and Independent Learning.

Hall, J., Halberstadt, A., & O'Brien, C. (1997). "Subordination" and nonverbal sensitivity: A study and synthesis of findings based on trait measures. *Sex Roles, 37,* 295–317.

Hodgins, H., & Zuckerman, M. (1990). The effect of nonverbal sensitivity on social interaction. *Journal of Nonverbal Behavior, 24,* 155–170.

Patterson, M., & Stockbridge, E. (1998). Effects of cognitive demand and judgment strategy on person perception accuracy. *Journal of Nonverbal Behavior, 22,* 253–263.

Rosenthal, R., Hall, J. A., DiMatteo, M. R., Rogers, P. L. & Archer, D. (1979). Sensitivity to nonverbal communication: The PONS test. Baltimore: Johns Hopkins University Press.

Schroeder, J. (1995a). Interpersonal perception skills: Self-concept correlates. *Perceptual and Motor Skills, 80,* 51–56.

Schroeder, J. (1995b). Self-concept, social anxiety, and interpersonal perception skills. *Personality and Individual Differences, 19,* 955–958.

Schroeder, J., & Ketrow, S. (1997). Social anxiety and performance in an interpersonal perception task. *Psychological Reports, 81,* 991–996.

Smith, H. J., Archer, D., & Costanzo, M. (1991). "Just a hunch": Accuracy and awareness in person perception. *Journal of Nonverbal Behavior, 15,* 3–18.

# ℰ 10 ℭ

# Nonverbal Receptivity:
# The Diagnostic Analysis
# of Nonverbal Accuracy (DANVA)

Stephen Nowicki Jr.
Marshall P. Duke
*Emory University*

Interpersonal sensitivity has been defined in various ways by researchers, but whatever definition is used it must include the idea of differences in an individual's responsivity to, as well as the accurate perception and judgment of, the social environment. In this chapter, the definition of interpersonal sensitivity is perhaps more basic and more narrow than many of those submitted by other investigators. Interpersonal sensitivity is defined here as the ability to identify the basic emotions of happiness, sadness, anger, and fear at both high and low intensity levels in nonverbal behavior in general and in facial expressions and prosody in particular.

A deficit in processing nonverbal emotional information has been called a "dyssemia" (*dys* = inability; *semia* = sign) by Nowicki and Duke (1992). The tests developed by Nowicki and Duke to measure nonverbal sensitivity are collectively called The Diagnostic Analysis of Nonverbal Accuracy (DANVA; Nowicki & Duke, 1994). The basic test stimuli of the DANVA are a combination of posed and spontaneous photographs and audio recordings (of a single standard sentence). The main assumption driving the development and construction of the nonverbal test stimuli included in the DANVA is that individuals need to be proficient in identifying the emotional communications of others in order to be able to interact with them successfully (Custrini & Feldman, 1989). Such skill is seen as a necessary but insufficient condition for interacting with others successfully; social knowledge and social skill also need to be mastered in order to have the potential to be fully socially competent. Individuals without the ability to identify the basic emotions in the nonverbal behaviors used by others in everyday interpersonal transactions are assumed to be at a higher risk for social failure. The association between interpersonal sensitivity and interpersonal functioning is hypothesized to exist for several reasons.

First, nonverbal communication is seen as important to social interaction and social competence because it is a reliable source of information about how others are feeling. In order to respond appropriately to others it is first necessary to identify their emotional states. Correct identification of emotions in others is required if individuals are to act appropriately at proper times during ongoing interactions (Vosk, Forehand, & Figueroa, 1983). Rubin (1980) went so far as to suggest that most all friendship-making skills depend on knowing how others are feeling. Nonverbal behavior is assumed to be a reliable and dependable source of information about interactants' affective states (e.g., Rosenthal, Hall, DiMatteo, Rogers, & Archer, 1979) that can be used to better understand social situations (Feldman, Philippot, & Custrini, 1991).

Second, nonverbal communication is important for successful interpersonal transactions because it is used to regulate the ongoing process of social interaction (Feldman et al., 1991; Riggio, 1992). Successful social interaction depends, to a large degree, on the accurate sending and receiving of cues for "turn taking" (e.g., Duncan, 1983). Most of these cues, in the form of gaze, gestures, and voice pitch (Friend, 1997), are nonverbal in nature, and the more adept individuals are at expressing and reading them the more likely it is that their interactions will be satisfying and reinforcing to them and to those with whom they interact.

> The general point is that a perceiver's ability to infer a target person's emotional state from the target's expressive behavior should be rewarding for the target and should therefore enhance the perceiver's attractiveness to the target and facilitate the relationship between them (Manstead, 1995, p. 153).

Third, nonverbal communication is important to social outcomes because of its use in display rules that must be mastered in order for a person to be perceived as adjusted to a culture (Ekman & Friesen, 1969). Nonverbal behavior is regulated by display rules or the norms for what are appropriate displays of emotions in social situations. Should individuals fail to read display rules accurately, they may be considered by others in that culture to be deviant and are more likely to be avoided or rejected (Feldman et al., 1991).

According to Nowicki and Duke (1992), besides being important for communicating emotional states, regulating interpersonal transactions, and following display rules, nonverbal communication is important to social competence because of the ways in which it differs from verbal communication. It is these unique differences that create the special impact that nonverbal communication can have on relationship development.

First, nonverbal communication is more continuous than verbal communication. Individuals can stop talking, but they cannot stop sending communications about how they are feeling via the nonverbal visual modalities. The statement, "You cannot not communicate, nonverbally" expresses this basic difference between nonverbal and verbal communication systems (Kiesler, 1996).

In addition to being more continuous, nonverbal communication takes place more beyond awareness than does verbal communication. Friedman (1979) pointed out that although what is being communicated nonverbally can be brought into awareness by conscious effort, the awareness is difficult to maintain. Mayo and LaFrance (1980) suggested that "given that nonverbal behavior lies out of awareness most of the time, it becomes interesting also to know when and how awareness of one's own and others' nonverbal behavior arises" (p. 225). Because so much of nonverbal communication takes place out of awareness, individuals are probably relatively less aware of their strengths, or more importantly, their deficits in these skills as compared with verbal ones. Lack of awareness also tends to make self-report tests of nonverbal processing skill, especially those assessing receptive nonverbal processing skill, less appropriate in some situations (Friedman, 1979; see also Riggio & Riggio, chap. 7, this volume).

Besides level of awareness, another important difference between the two types of communication is that an error in nonverbal communication is more likely to have a negative emotional impact than an error in verbal communication. When individuals break nonverbal rules of communication, for example, by standing too close to others or by prolonged staring at them, the result is that they make others feel frightened, anxious, or otherwise uncomfortable emotionally (Friedman, 1979). In contrast, when individuals make verbal errors such as using the wrong verb or noun–verb agreement, as in the statement, "I seen it!", the result is that they may seem uneducated or perhaps not very intelligent to others, but they are certainly not viewed as emotionally unsettling. Having a negative emotional impact on others can have a more profound effect on ongoing social interactions than having negative intellectual impact.

Because nonverbal communication is more continuous, out of awareness, and emotionally impactful, difficulties in sensitivity to others' nonverbal cues can potentially have a significant negative effect on interpersonal interactions. On the basis of these differences, it is conceivable that individuals who are dyssemic may not even be aware that they have a nonverbal social processing deficit or that the deficit may be continuously producing negative emotional reactions in others. This set of circumstances puts them at high risk for failing in their attempts to relate successfully to others.

## THE DIAGNOSTIC ANALYSIS
## OF NONVERBAL ACCURACY

The study of nonverbal behavior has increased dramatically in recent years, largely through the work begun by Ekman and Friesen (1974, 1975) and Izard (1971) among others. Not only did these researchers provide a rationale for why nonverbal behavior was important, they also suggested ways of measuring both receptive (e.g., Brief Affect Recognition Test, or BART; Ekman & Friesen, 1975) and expressive (e.g., Facial Action Coding System, or FACS; Ekman & Friesen, 1978) facial expression processing skills. Much of their research effort was spent in obtaining basic knowledge about whether the ability to recognize facial expression was universal across racial and ethnic groups (Russell, 1994). The measures they developed were based on ethological principles that assumed that common muscle movements underlay the facial expression of emotion. However, the BART included only adult facial expressions, and the expressions, which were created by actors under the direction of the experimenters, were sometimes unusual and sometimes not ecologically consistent with what individuals experience in their everyday interactions (e.g., Camras & Allison, 1985). Although there are significant exceptions (e.g., Camras, 1980), the BART was not frequently used to study the association between individual differences in receptive skill and important personal and social variables, especially in children.

In contrast to the BART, the Profile of Nonverbal Sensitivity (PONS; Rosenthal et al., 1979), was developed specifically for assessing individual differences in nonverbal sensitivity—not only in facial expressions, but also in prosody, postures, and gestures. However, the PONS was originally constructed for use with older children and adults, and it has most frequently been used with adults (Rosenthal et al., 1979). Research using the full PONS or its derivations with younger children has been far less frequent (e.g., Stone & la Greca, 1984). One potential shortcoming of the PONS is that it requires participants not only to decode the valence of the affect being presented, but then to match that judgment, via a forced-choice framework, to the correct social situation. Thus, the PONS potentially confounds sensitivity to nonverbal social cues and knowledge of adult social situations. Participants conceivably could be able to accurately identify nonverbal emotional cues and still score low on the PONS because they do not apply the information correctly. Further the audio portion uses content-filtering and random-splicing procedures, which Axelrod (1982) suggested "result in sound patterns not normally found in life situations" (p. 611).

Other attempts to measure individual differences in the ability of children to process nonverbal affect information also seem to fall short in one way or another. The Social Skills Inventory (Riggio, 1986), like the PONS, is designed primarily for use with adults. Further, it is not actually a measure of nonverbal processing ability, but a self-report instrument of the individual's self-perceived nonverbal performance (see Riggio & Riggio, chap. 7, this volume). The Inter-personal Perception Task (Costanzo & Archer, 1989; see also Archer, Costanzo, & Akert, chap. 9, this volume) uses videotaped interpersonal situa-tions as test stimuli, but it is appropriate for use primarily with adults and does not allow for the measurement of the separate basic emotions. The Vocal Emo-tion Recognition Test (Guidetti, 1989) is a test of receptive prosody and was constructed via taped phrases consisting of nonsense words made up of Indo-European phonemes. However, it does not distinguish intensity levels, has infrequently been used with English-speaking participants or children, and was developed on an ethological model (Kappas, Hess, & Scherer, 1991). The Florida Affect Battery (FAB; Bowers, Blonder, & Heilman, 1991) has primarily been used to test questions of neurological sources for nonverbal processing skills but is promising in that it provides measures for facial expressions and tones of voice. The FAB does not, however, include children's stimuli, does not measure degree of intensity, and has not been used often with children.

For these reasons, work was begun a decade ago that led to the DANVA (Nowicki & Duke, 1994) and the DANVA2 (Baum & Nowicki, 1998; Nowicki & Carton, 1993; Nowicki, Glanville, & Demertzis, 1998). Both sets of tests evaluate the ability of participants to identity the four basic emotions of happi-ness, sadness, anger, and fear. Pertinent to the focus of the present volume, the original DANVA included receptive tests of facial expressions (adults and chil-dren), postures, gestures, and prosody (children). Research has continued both to improve the test stimuli and to gather data essential in evaluating their con-struct validity. The updated and revised versions of the earlier tests are referred to as the DANVA2 and are the primary focus of the rest of this chapter. Compared with the DANVA, the DANVA2 receptive tests for facial expres-sions and prosody possess a wider range of difficulty, include stimuli that differ systematically in terms of intensity, and include stimuli from members of differ-ent racial groups. All subtests of the DANVA and DANVA2 were constructed according to the following guidelines.

1. Each Subtest was Constructed Independently. This was done because there is little theoretical or empirical agreement on the underlying relationship of separate nonverbal processing skills with one another. Intuitively it makes sense that some nonverbal communication skills should cluster together, espe-cially within the receptive and expressive areas. However, empirical results sug-gest nonverbal processing skills may be somewhat independent from one another even within expressive and receptive areas (Feldman & Thayer, 1980; Hall, chap. 8, this volume). DePaulo and Rosenthal (1979) reported that send-ing and receiving accuracy produced a median correlation of .16 across 19 stud-ies they reviewed.

2. Stimuli Were Selected on the Basis of a Preset Percentage of Judges Agreeing on the Identification of a Particular Emotion. Rather than being cho-

sen on the basis of any particular theory of emotional development or on "anatomically objective" criteria such as position of facial features or specific muscle tensions (e.g., Ekman & Friesen, 1974), DANVA test items were selected primarily on empirical-normative grounds. Of the five general ways to establish a criterion of accuracy for nonverbal processing skill described by Cook (cited in Rosenthal et al., 1979, p. 19), this is the method that most closely reflects the ecological situation individuals face in their daily interactions.

3. Judgments Regarding Stimuli Were Made by Individuals of Different Ages to Ensure That the Items Were Perceived Similarly Across Age. If an item was identified by a certain percentage of participants at one age, it would be checked against the percentage of older and younger participants to be sure that there was a linear increase in accuracy with age. Though the original DANVA was constructed to be used primarily with 6- to 10-year-old children, it was used with older children and adults by comparing their scores to the norms for the 10-year-old participants. DANVA2 subtests, in contrast, have a much greater range of difficulty than the original DANVA subtests and have been used successfully with children as young as 3 (Verbeek, 1996) and adults as old as 100 (Roberts, Nowicki, & McClure, 1998).

4. A Relatively High Percentage of Interjudge Agreement was Used for Item Selection. The major goal of the DANVA tests was to present stimuli to children and adults that would be recognized by most (80%) as communicating a particular emotion. Including viable low-intensity stimuli was an important goal of test construction for the DANVA2 subtests, because an appreciable proportion of common everyday social interactions requires the accurate reading of low-intensity emotional messages. Although low-intensity stimuli may be more difficult in general than high intensity stimuli, the 80% criterion was used for both.

5. DANVA and DANVA2 Items Measured Four Basic Core Emotions: Happiness, Sadness, Anger, and Fear. These four emotions, along with surprise and disgust, are considered to be the primary emotions (Ekman & Friesen, 1975). These four emotions are more likely to be involved in everyday interactions and are likely to be learned by most children 10 years of age (Camras & Allison, 1985). Without the ability to accurately identify basic emotions being communicated nonverbally by others, knowledge of how to behave in social situations would be relatively useless and learning to process more complex emotions such as guilt and shame would be difficult if not impossible.

6. DANVA Subtest Items Primarily Rely on Posed Stimuli. Encoding of posed or spontaneous stimuli has been found to be significantly related in past studies (median $r$ over six studies = .43; Halberstadt, 1986). Participants who generated the test stimuli of the DANVA and DANVA2 subtests were given time to practice and were read stories and descriptions of events consistent with being happy, sad, angry, or fearful. In many instances, models were photographed or recorded as they practiced and many of these test stimuli made it through the judges' item selection procedures into the final form of the test.

## Construct Validity Support
## for the DANVA2 Subtests

To establish the worth of a test of nonverbal sensitivity such as the DANVA2, especially if it is going to be used with participants of different ages, one must present evidence that the test possesses certain characteristics. Primary among these characteristics is reliability; that is, to be considered a construct valid test, DANVA2 subtests must show that they are internally consistent and reliable over time. A second important characteristic involves the association between DANVA2 scores and age of participants. Because it is assumed that nonverbal sensitivity is a learned skill, DANVA2 scores should show improvement throughout childhood and into adulthood. Finally, because nonverbal sensitivity is so much a part of interpersonal interactions and relationship formation, its deficits as measured by low DANVA2 scores should be related to lower social competence and negative personality characteristics. Brief descriptions of how each DANVA2 subtest was constructed along with selected findings in support of the construct validity of each of the DANVA2 subtests are presented next.

*Adult Facial Expressions (DANVA2-AF).*   This test consists of 24 photographs of an equal number of adult facial expressions of high- and low-intensity happiness, sadness, anger, and fear (Nowicki & Carton, 1993). Photographs were taken of adult men and women and then shown to participants. Photographs in which the emotion was agreed on by 80% of the participants (ranging in age from 8 to 26; $N = 166$) were included in the final form of the test. Construct validity evidence was initially presented by Nowicki and Carton (1993). Scores have been found to be internally consistent as measured by coefficient alpha in children as young as 4 (Verbeek, 1996; $N = 34$, $\alpha = .71$) and as old as 15 (Baum, Logan, Walker, Tomlinson, & Schiffman, 1996; $N = 27$, $\alpha = .78$) and in adults as old as 100 (Roberts et al., 1998; $N = 22$, $\alpha = .74$). Lower accuracy scores have been found to be significantly correlated with lower social competence as rated by sociometric ratings (Nowicki & Mitchell, 1997; Verbeek, 1996), teachers (Collins, 1996; Maxim & Nowicki, 1997), and parents (McClanahan, 1996), as well as with higher external control expectancies (Nowicki & Halpern, 1997) and greater depression in boys and lower self-esteem in girls (Nowicki & Carton, 1997). Scores from the DANVA2-AF correlated significantly with those from the original DANVA-AF, mean age = 8, $r(42) = .58$; mean age = 19.1, $r(34) = .54$.

*Child Facial Expressions (DANVA2-CF).*   DANVA2-CF consists of 24 photographs of child facial expressions consisting of an equal number of high- and low- intensity, happy, sad, angry, and fearful faces. Children between the ages of 6 and 12 ($N = 36$) were read vignettes with happy, sad, angry, and fearful themes and asked to respond with appropriate facial expressions. The process used to select the final 24 photographs of child expressions was similar to that reported earlier for the adult facial expressions. Scores from the DANVA2-CF correlated significantly with those from the original DANVA-CF in children aged 8.5 years of age, $r(101) = .54$, $p < .01$. Internal consistency as estimated by coefficent alpha averaged .76 across 10 studies with children as young as 4 and as old as 16 (Nowicki, 1997). Results from these same 10 studies indicated that accuracy increased significantly as a function of age. Lower accuracy scores on the DANVA2-CF were significantly correlated with lower social competence as indicated by sociometric status (Nowicki & Mitchell, 1997; Verbeek, 1996), ratings by teachers (e.g., Maxim & Nowicki, 1997; Nowicki & Mitchell, 1997) and parents (McClanahan, 1996), and with greater external control expectancies (e.g., Nowicki & Halpern, 1997).

*Adult Paralanguage (DANVA2-AP).*   This subtest is new to the DANVA series (Baum & Nowicki, 1998). There was no adult paralanguage test in the original DANVA. To construct the paralanguage stimuli, two professional actors responded to vignettes designed to elicit happy, sad, angry, and fearful feelings by saying a neutral sentence—"I am going out of the room now but I'll be back later"—to reflect the appropriate emotion at different levels of intensity. The neutral sentence was used previously by Maitland (1977), who found that it was rated as "neutral" by 90% of the undergraduates and 85% of the children surveyed. Audio samples of the sentences produced by the two actors were played for college-age ($N = 147$) and fourth grade ($N = 57$) participants who listened to each trial and judged whether it was happy, sad, angry, or fearful and how intense it was on a 5-point scale. The final 24 stimuli were selected empirically from an original sample of 133 trials produced by a professional actor and actress. Trials on which at least 80% of the raters agreed on a specific emotion were retained. The final form of the test contains equal numbers of male and female trials of high- and low-intensity happy, sad, angry, and fearful voices.

Construct validity support for the DANVA2-AP was presented by Baum and Nowicki (1998). First, linear trend analysis on data from six studies using the DANVA2-AP with different age participants (Baum, Diforio, Tomlinson, & Walker, 1996; Collins, 1996; McClanahan, 1996; Nowicki, 1995; Rowe, 1996) showed that mean accuracy increased with age. Second, studies showed coefficient alphas ranging from .71 in 4-year-old participants to .78 in college students. Test–retest reliability over 6 weeks was .83 in a sample of college students ($N = 68$, $M = 19.4$ years). Third, DANVA2-AP scores were related to indices of social competence in children as young as 3 (Verbeek, 1996), as well as in preschool (Nowicki & Mitchell, 1997), elementary school (Maxim & Nowicki, 1997; McClanahan, 1996), and high school participants (Baum et al., 1996). In addition, lower accuracy on the DANVA2-AP was related to greater external control in college students (Nowicki, 1995). Fourth, DANVA2-AP scores were found not to be related to measures of IQ in preschool (Nowicki & Mitchell, 1997; Verbeek, 1996), elementary school (McClanahan, 1996), and high school children (Baum, Logan, et al., 1996). However, greater accuracy on the DANVA2-AP was related to greater achievement in preschool (Nowicki & Mitchell, 1997) and elementary school children (Collins, 1996).

*Child Paralanguage (DANVA2-CP).*   The DANVA2-CP (Demertzis & Nowicki, 1997) is the most recent test from the original DANVA to be revised for the DANVA2 scales. The original child voices test had been used successfully in numerous studies (Nowicki & Duke, 1994), but it did not include stimuli of different intensities and its range was limited and therefore so was its ability to discriminate among older participants. The DANVA2-CP stimuli were recorded by professional child actors (age 9) in a sound studio. The actors were asked to say the Maitland (1977) sentence to reflect the emotions elicited by vignettes of emotional situations that were read to them. The voice trials were heard by college students ($N = 147$) and fourth graders ($N = 152$). As with the other subtests of the DANVA2, the DANVA2-CP is composed of 24 trials (Both 16- and 32-trial forms are also available.) There are an equal number of high- and low-intensity trials of each emotion.

Construct validity evidence for the DANVA2-CP was presented by Demertzis and Nowicki (1997). First, scores from the original DANVA child voices and the DANVA2-CP were significantly related in children 7 years old, $r(48) = .48; p < .05$; 8 years old, $r(51) = .54, p < .05$; and 9 years old, $r(43) = .51, p < .05$. Second, linear trend analysis of accuracy scores from the DANVA2-CP with children ($N = 112$) from 7 to 11 years of age showed they increased with age. Third, scores from the DANVA2-CP were internally consistent as shown by coefficient alphas for 8-year-olds ($N = 32, .74$) and 10-year-olds ($N = 31, .76$). Test–retest reliability over 6 weeks was $r(22) = .88$ in 10-year-old children. Fourth, lower accuracy on the DANVA2-CP was related to lower social competence in second and third grade children as rated by teachers, $r(51) = .43, p < .05$; lower self-esteem, $r(57) = .39, p < .05$; and greater external locus of control, $r(57) = .41, p < .05$.

## Future Directions in Assessment

With the establishment of construct valid tests for adult and child faces and voices, the next test of nonverbal sensitivity to be constructed for the DANVA2 involves postures. Because of its importance as a "long distance" mode of information about others' emotional states and its importance in regulating turn taking in seated interactions, postural accuracy is assumed to be a necessary social skill. Pitterman and Nowicki (1999) constructed a preliminary form of the DANVA2 postural sensitivity test and gathered preliminary evidence of the test's construct validity. Types of standing and sitting postures were generated, with a minimal emphasis on gestures, on the basis of primate literature and work with humans. Four models portrayed a basic set of 170 postures, which was reduced to 32 stimuli via a variety of item analysis procedures. The DANVA2 postures test consists of equal numbers of standing and seated postures of men and women communicating the basic four emotions of happiness, sadness, anger, and fear. Scores were found to be internally consistent ($N$ = 143, $\alpha$ = .69) and related to loneliness, locus of control, and social anxiety. Future research should involve extending the present findings to a wider age range, especially children; different race participants; and other personality and social correlates.

The DANVA2 nonverbal sensitivity tests can be used to help establish a baseline skill level for reading emotional cues in the nonverbal communications of others. If research questions require assessment of ecological validity, then other tests need to be constructed to assess how individuals differ in their abilities to identify emotion in more complex forms of nonverbal sensitivity that are communicated through movement and time in facial expressions, postures, gestures, and personal space. The PONS was constructed to assess these abilities, and though it is the most successful test of nonverbal sensitivity yet constructed, it did not measure specific emotions and used a response format that required not only the correct identification of nonverbal cues but the social knowledge necessary to apply that information appropriately to an adult situation. Carton and Nowicki (1999) have begun work on a test of facial expression sensitivity that includes the use of videotaped facial expressions of children. Whatever tests of nonverbal sensitivity are developed, to be considered as construct valid they must show discriminative validity over measures already in use. That is, rather than just showing a significant association between nonverbal sensitivity and social competence, the association should be independent from those already established by tests.

A recent innovation—based on the DANVA2 and the popular teacher-friendly behavioral checklists currently in wide use such as Achenbach's (1991) Child Behavior Check List (CBCL)—is the Emory Dyssemia Index (EDI; Love, Nowicki, & Duke, 1994). The EDI is filled in by a teacher or parent and is composed of 42 items describing a variety of nonverbal patterns in gaze and eye contact (e.g., "fails to look at others when addressed"), space and touch (e.g., "stands too close to others when interacting with them"), facial expressions (e.g., "facial expressions do not fit emotional states"), paralanguage (e.g., "fails to alter speech volume to fit situation"), objectics (e.g., "seems unaware of fads/styles"), social rules and norms (e.g., "seems tactless in interactions") and nonverbal receptivity (e.g., "seems insensitive to others' feelings"). Each item is rated for frequency of occurrence on a scale ranging from 1 (*never*) to 4 (*often*). In addition to subscores for each of the nonverbal channels, a total EDI score is also calculated. In preliminary work, Love et al. (1994) reported test–retest reliabilities over 6 weeks ranging from .63 to .86 depending on channel. Early validity indicators were a correlation of total EDI and Children's Piers-Harris Self-Concept (Piers, 1984) scores of –.28 ($p < .05$) and a correlation of .74 ($p < .01$) with behavioral problems as assessed by the Mann–Kenowitz Behavioral Evaluation Scale (BES-2; Mann & Kenowitz, 1985). The EDI is currently undergoing revision based on its efficacy in classroom and clinical settings. It has been found to be extremely useful in screening large groups of children for indicators of dyssemia or other troubling interpersonal patterns. It may be especially useful as an adjunct to the DANVA2 in that the EDI requires less than 5 min to complete and 5 min to score and gives a quick measure of expressive as well as receptive nonverbal difficulties.

## Use of DANVA2 in Clinical and Educational Settings

One advantage of the DANVA2 tests is that they are simple to administer and score. There is a computer program for scoring each of the DANVA2 tests. Information gleaned from the DANVA2 tests can be used in a number of ways and in a variety of educational and clinical settings. DANVA2 tests yield three different types of error scores: errors by emotion, errors by intensity, and errors by misattribution. Errors by emotion refers to the number of times participants fail to accurately identify the emotion of a nonverbal stimulus. Because there are 6 items for each emotion within a DANVA2 subtest, there can be up to 6 errors. Because each stimulus varies by intensity as well as emotion, errors by intensity occur when participants inaccurately identify the emotion in either high- or low-intensity stimuli. There are 12 high- and 12 low-intensity stimuli within each DANVA2 subtest, so there can be up to 12 errors in either level of intensity. In addition, there can be Emotion × Intensity errors as well. There are three high- and three low-intensity stimuli for each emotion. For example, there can be up to 3 errors for the high intensity sad stimuli. Finally, there are misattribution errors. These errors occur when a different emotion is given instead of the correct one. For example, one type of misattribution error is the number of times an angry emotion is given for a happy, sad, or fearful stimuli. Because there are 18 stimuli in addition to the 6 that are correct, overall misattribution scores can range from 0 to 18. Although total error scores are important, more specific error scores can be more useful and associated with different personal and social outcomes. For example, children with externalizing types of problems not only make more errors than their peers without such problems, but, in addition, they are more likely to make errors that involve low-intensity stimuli in general and anger stimuli in specific (e.g., Lancelot & Nowicki, 1997; Stevens, 1998). Such errors may play a part in both the development and maintenance of the "acting out" behaviors that characterize externalizing disorders. Differential patterns of errors have been found in internalizing difficulties such as social anxiety (McClure & Nowicki, 1998) and schizoptypal personality disorders (Baum, 1997), among others.

Once the nonverbal sensitivity of an individual or group of individuals has been found to be below what it should be for their age, this information can be used to guide interventions. Interventions—be they with individuals or with groups—should be active and direct in teaching nonverbal processing skills. Although making individuals aware that they have a nonverbal processing deficit may be helpful in improving their nonverbal processing skill, it is direct learning of what associations exist between an internal emotional state and a particular pattern of nonverbal behavior that leads to more accurate processing. If a large number of children are found to be lacking in certain areas of nonverbal sensitivity, then this skill can be taught directly in the classroom as part of the school curriculum. To accomplish this task, researchers must develop school curricula to teach nonverbal receptive skills at different age levels. One example of such a project is the de Paul curriculum developed by Harlow (as described in Duke, Nowicki, & Martin, 1996). The de Paul curriculum presents classroom content and exercises for each of the six types of nonverbal communication: rhythm, facial expressions, personal space, postures, gestures, and paralanguage. The de Paul curriculum has been applied successfully in elementary and middle school settings to teach the basics of nonverbal communication.

At the more individual level, direct remediation can be applied to help individuals learn to read the nonverbal cues of emotion that they cannot. On the basis of the work of Minskoff (1980), Nowicki (1996) developed the R-DANVA tutorial remediation program that can be administered by teacher aides to individuals or small groups. In this program, individuals are taught through a number of structured exercises first to "discriminate" between nonverbal cues and then to "identify" them. Once individuals can discriminate and identify nonverbal cues, they are taught to "meaningfully express" nonverbal information and then to "apply" this knowledge to social situations. Only in this last stage, application, do the R-DANVA procedures resemble what is usually taken to be social skills training. Many social skills training programs assume that individuals can discriminate, identify, and meaningfully use nonverbal cues (Argyle, 1988). However, if individuals lack these abilities they will be less able to make adequate use of any social skills training program.

Nonverbal sensitivity can also be an important focus of psychotherapy. Interpersonal psychotherapy approaches emphasize the importance of nonverbal communication and assume that nonverbal sensitivity deficits are a significant cause of personal and social maladjustment. Interpersonal psychotherapists focus on helping the client become aware of the errors they make in reading emotion in the nonverbal cues of others. This awareness has been found to be associated with improved personal and social adjustment. Research findings support this assumption (Garfield, Raue, & Castonguay, 1998; Kiesler, 1996).

## CONCLUSION

The DANVA2 assesses the ability to identify emotion without a stated context. However, we are aware of the fact that nonverbal communication is very much affected by the context within which it takes place. To this end, the ability to identify emotions nonverbally could also be examined within various social contexts. This could be accomplished in a number of ways. For example, ecologically valid social or academic situations could be described to a child and the child be shown a photograph or hear a tonal message from the DANVA2. After seeing or hearing the stimulus, the child could be asked to decide whether the stimulus was appropriate for that situation or which of a variety of possible nonverbal stimuli would be consistent with the described situation. Such approaches would give additional information about the social knowledge possessed by children. However, it still would not assess children's social skill. Children could be accurate on the DANVA2 and know what is the socially correct response to a particular social situation and still fail interpersonally because they are not skilled enough to produce the correct set of behaviors. On the other hand, children could possess social knowledge and social skill, but if they lacked the ability to identify basic emotions nonverbally, then they still would be at risk for social failure because they would be mistakenly applying their social knowledge and skill to the wrong emotional cue. There are so many ways to fail interpersonally that it is surprising that children succeed as often as they do socially.

Nonverbal sensitivity is just beginning to be recognized as an important basic social skill necessary for forming satisfactory relationships. With this recognition comes the responsibility not only to develop adequate assessment procedures to help identify those individuals who lack this crucial interpersonal skill, but once the deficit is discovered, to construct effective interventions to deal with this difficulty. Without effective nonverbal processing abilities the goal of developing satisfactory relationships with others becomes all the more difficult.

## REFERENCES

Achenbach, T. (1991). *The Child Behavior Checklist*. Burlington, VT: University of Vermont, Department of Psychiatry.

Argyle, M. (1988). *Bodily communication*. New York: International Universities Press.

Axelrod, L. (1982). Social perception in learning disabled adolescents. *Journal of Learning Disabilities, 15*, 610–613.

Baum, K .M. (1997). *Emotion perception in adolescents with schizotypal personality disorder*. Unpublished doctoral dissertation, Emory University, Atlanta.

Baum, K. M., Diforio, D., Tomlinson, H., & Walker, E. F. (1996, March). *Emotion recognition deficits in schizotypal personality.* Paper presented at the annual meeting of the Society for Research in Psychopathology, Iowa City, IA.

Baum, K. M., Logan, M. C., Walker, E. F., Tomlinson, H., & Schiffman, J. (1996, March). *Emotion recognition in adolescents with schizotypal personality disorder.* Poster presented at the annual meeting of the Society for Research in Psychopathology, Atlanta, GA.

Baum, K., & Nowicki, S. Jr. (1996, March). *A measure of receptive prosody for adults: The Diagnostic Analysis of Nonverbal Accuracy–Adult Voices.* Paper presented at the meeting of the Society for Research in Personality, Atlanta, GA.

Baum, K., & Nowicki, S. Jr. (1998). Perception of emotion: Measuring decoding accuracy of adult prosodic cues varying in intensity. *Journal of Nonverbal Behavior, 22,* 89–108.

Bowers, D., Blonder, L. X., & Heilman, K. M. (1991). *The Florida Affect Battery.* Gainesville, FL: Center for Neuropsychological Studies, University of Florida, Department of Neurology.

Camras, L. A. (1980). Children's understanding of facial expressions used during conflict encounters. *Child Development, 51,* 879–885.

Camras, L. A., & Allison, K. (1985). Children's understanding of emotional facial expressions and verbal labels. *Journal of Nonverbal Behavior, 9,* 84–94.

Carton, J., & Nowicki, S. Jr. (1999). *Measuring emotion in video presentations of facial expressions.* Unpublished manuscript, Emory University, Atlanta, GA.

Collins, M. (1996). *Personality and achievement correlates of nonverbal processing ability in African American children.* Unpublished doctoral dissertation, Emory University, Atlanta.

Constanzo, M., & Archer, D. (1989). Interpreting the expressive behavior of others: The Interpersonal Perception Task. *Journal of Nonverbal Behavior, 13,* 225–245.

Custrini, R. J., & Feldman, R. S. (1989). Children's social competence and nonverbal encoding and decoding of emotion. *Journal of Clinical Child Psychology, 18,* 336–342.

Demertzis, A., & Nowicki, S. Jr. (1997, April). *Perception of emotion: Measuring decoding accuracy of child prosodic cues varying in emotional intensity.* Paper presented at the meeting of the Southeastern Psychological Association, Mobile, AL.

DePaulo, B. M., & Rosenthal, R. (1979). Telling lies. *Journal of Personality and Social Psychology, 37,* 1713–1722.

Duke, M. P., Nowicki, S. Jr., & Martin, E. (1996). *Teaching your child the language of social success.* Atlanta, GA: Peachtree.

Duncan, S. (1983). Speaking turns: Studies of structures and individual differences. In J. M. Wiemann & R. Harrison (Eds.), *Nonverbal interaction* (pp. 149–178). Beverly Hills, CA: Sage.

Ekman, P., & Friesen, W. V. (1969). The repertoire of nonverbal behavior: Categories, origins, usage, and coding. *Semiotica, 1,* 49–98.

Ekman, P., & Friesen, W. V. (1974). Detecting deception from the body or face. *Journal of Personality and Social Psychology, 29,* 288–298.

Ekman, P., & Friesen, W. V. (1975). *Unmasking the face.* Englewood Cliffs, NJ: Prentice-Hall.

Ekman, P., & Friesen, W. V. (1978). *Facial Action Coding System.* Palo Alto, CA: Consulting Psychologists Press.

Feldman, R. S., Philippot, P., & Custrini, R. J. (1991). Social competence and nonverbal behavior. In R. S. Feldman & B. Rimé (Eds.), *Fundamentals of nonverbal behavior* (pp. 329–350). New York: Cambridge University Press.

Feldman, M., & Thayer, S. (1980). A comparison of three measures of nonverbal decoding ability. *Journal of Social Psychology, 112,* 91–97.

Friedman, H. S. (1979). The concept of skill in nonverbal communication: Implications for understanding social interaction. In R. Rosenthal (Ed.), *Skill in nonverbal communication: Individual differences.* (pp. 1–34). Cambridge, MA: Oelgeschlager, Gunn, & Hain.

Friend, M. J. (1997). From prosodic to paralinguistic function: Implication for affective development. *Dissertation Abstracts International, 56,* 6417.

Garfield, M. R., Raue, P. J., & Castonguay, L. G. (1998). The therapeutic focus in significant sessions of master therapists: A comparison of cognitive–behavioral and psychodynamic–interpersonal interventions. *Journal of Consulting and Clinical Psychology, 66,* 803–810.

Guidetti, M. (1991). Vocal expression of emotions: A crosscultural and developmental approach. *Annee Psychologique, 91,* 383–396.

Halberstadt, A. G. (1986). Family socialization of emotional expression and nonverbal communication styles and skills. *Journal of Personality and Social Psychology, 31,* 827–836.

Izard, C. E. (1971). *The face of emotion.* New York: Appleton-Century-Crofts.

Kappas, A., Hess, U., & Scherer, K. R. (1991). Voice and emotion. In R. S. Feldman & B. Rimé (Eds.), *Fundamentals of nonverbal behavior: Studies in emotion and social interaction* (pp. 200–238). New York: Cambridge University Press.

Kiesler, D. J. (1996). *Contemporary interpersonal theory and research.* New York: Wiley.

Lancelot, C., & Nowicki, S. Jr. (1997). The association between nonverbal processing abilities and internalizing/externalizing problems in girls and boys. *Journal of Genetic Psychology, 158,* 287–296.

Love, E. B., Nowicki, S. Jr., & Duke, M. P. (1994). The Emory Dyssemia Index: A brief screening instrument for the identification of nonverbal language deficits in elementary school children. *Journal of Psychology, 128,* 703–705.

Maitland, G. E. (1977). The perception of facial and vocal expressions by emotionally disturbed and normal children (Doctoral Dissertation, University of Virginia, 1977). *Dissertation Abstracts International, 38,* 5396A.

Mann, L., & Kenowitz, L. (1985). Review of the Behavior Evaluation Scale. In J. Mitchell (Ed.), *The Ninth mental measurements yearbook* (pp. 160–161). Lincoln, NE: The Buros Institute.

Manstead, A. S. R. (1995). Children's understanding of emotion. In J. A. Russell & J. M. Fernandez-Dols, *Everyday conceptions of emotion* (pp. 146–161). Amsterdam: Kluwer Academic.

Mayo, C., & LaFrance, M. (1980). On the acquisition of nonverbal communication: A review. *Merrill-Palmer Quarterly, 24,* 213–225.

Maxim, L., & Nowicki, S. Jr. (1997, April). *Receptive nonverbal accuracy in elementary school age children.* Poster presented at the meeting of the Southeastern Psychological Association. Atlanta, GA.

McClanahan, P. (1996). *Social competence correlates of individual differences in nonverbal behavior.* Unpublished master's thesis, Emory University, Atlanta, GA.

McClure, E., & Nowicki, S. Jr. (1998). *Nonverbal processing deficits and social anxiety.* Unpublished manuscript, Department of Psychology, Emory University, Atlanta, GA.

Minskoff, E. (1980). Teaching approach for developing nonverbal communication skills in students with social perception deficits: Part I. The basic approach and body language cues. *Journal of Learning Disabilities, 13,* 118–124.

Nowicki, S. Jr. (1995). *A study of the DANVA-AV in college students.* Unpublished manuscript, Emory University, Atlanta, GA.

Nowicki, S. Jr. (1996). *The Diagnostic Analysis of Nonverbal Accuracy-2: Remediation.* Unpublished manuscript, Emory University, Atlanta, GA.

Nowicki, S. Jr. (1997). *Internal consistency of the DANVA2 child voices test.* Unpublished manuscript, Emory University, Atlanta, GA.

Nowicki, S. Jr., & Carton, E. (1997). Self-esteem, depression, and nonverbal processing difficulties in boys and girls. *Journal of Genetic Psychology, 158,* 357–364.

Nowicki, S. Jr., & Carton, J. (1993). The measurement of emotional intensity from facial expressions. *Journal of Social Psychology*, *133*, 749–750.

Nowicki, S. Jr., & Duke, M. P. (1992). *Helping the child who doesn't fit in*. Atlanta, GA. Peachtree.

Nowicki, S. Jr., & Duke, M. (1994). Individual differences in the nonverbal communication of affect: The Diagnostic Analysis of Nonverbal Accuracy Scale. *Journal of Nonverbal Behavior*, *18*, 9–35.

Nowicki, S. Jr., Glanville, D., & Demertzis, A. (1998). A test of the ability to recognize emotion in the facial expressions of African American adults. *Journal of Black Psychology*, *24*, 333–348.

Nowicki, S. Jr., & Halpern, A. (1997). *The association between mothers' ability to recognize emotional expressions and their children' recognition ability and locus of control*. Unpublished manuscript, Emory University, Atlanta, GA.

Nowicki, S. Jr., & Mitchell, J. (1997). Accuracy in identifying affect in child and adult faces and voices and social competence in preschool children. *Genetic, Social and General Psychology Monographs*, *124*, 39–59.

Nowicki, S., & Carton, E. (1997). *The relation of nonverbal processing ability in faces and voices and children's feelings of depression and competence*. Unpublished manuscript, Emory University, Atlanta, GA.

Piers, F. (1984). *Piers-Harris Children's Self-Concept Scale*. Los Angeles: Western Psychological Services.

Pitterman, H., & Nowicki, S. Jr. (1999). *A measure of the ability to read emotion in postures*. Unpublished manuscript, Emory University, Atlanta, GA.

Riggio, R. E. (1986). Assessment of social skill. *Journal of Personality and Social Psychology*, *51*, 649–660.

Riggio, R. E. (1992). Social interaction skills and nonverbal behavior. In R. S. Feldman (Ed.), *Applications of nonverbal behavioral theories and research*. Hillsdale, NJ: Lawrence Erlbaum Associates.

Roberts, V. J., Nowicki, S. Jr., & McClure, E. (1998, February). *Emotional prosody recognition and right hemisphere functioning in the elderly*. Paper presented at the 26th Annual Meeting of the International Neuropsychological Society, Honolulu, HI.

Rosenthal, R., Hall, J. A., DiMatteo, M. R., Rogers, P. L., & Archer, D. (1979). *Sensitivity to nonverbal communication: The PONS test*. Baltimore, MD: Johns Hopkins University Press.

Rowe, E. (1996). *Gender differences in elementary school age children and social adjustment*. Unpublished doctoral dissertation, Emory University, Atlanta, GA.

Rubin, A. (1980). *Children's friendships*. London: Fontana.

Russell, J. A. (1994). Is there universal recognition of emotion from facial expression? A review of the cross-cultural studies. *Psychological Bulletin*, *115*, 102–141.

Stevens, D. (1998). *Nonverbal receptive accuracy in psychopathic individuals*. Unpublished doctoral dissertation, University of London.

Stone, W. L., & la Greca, A. M. (1984). Comprehension of nonverbal communication: A reexamination of the social competencies of learning-disabled children. *Journal of Abnormal Child Psychology*, *12*, 505–518.

Verbeek, P. (1996). *Conflict instigation and conflict resolution in preschool children*. Unpublished doctoral dissertation, Emory University, Atlanta, GA.

Vosk, B. N., Forehand, R., & Figueroa, R. (1983). Perception of emotions by accepted and rejected children. *Journal of Behavioral Assessment*, *5*, 151–160.

# IV

Dyadic Interaction Approaches

# ᛓ 11 ᛏ

# Correlational Method for Assessing Interpersonal Sensitivity Within Dyadic Interaction

### Sara E. Snodgrass
*Florida Atlantic University*


Psychologists have been interested in how accurately one person perceives another for at least 6 decades (e.g., Asch, 1946; Cronbach, 1955; Dymond, 1949; Funder, 1995; Harackiewicz & DePaulo, 1982; Rosenthal, Hall, DiMatteo, Rogers, & Archer, 1979). Much past research in person perception has centered on the perception of another person's personality traits, such as leadership or extraversion (e.g., Asch, 1946; Bernieri, Zuckerman, Koestner, & Rosenthal, 1994; Funder, 1995; Kenny, 1994; Vogt & Colvin, 1998).

When research began measuring the perception of emotion rather than personality traits, participants attempted to recognize feelings from static targets depicted in photographs or films (e.g., Costanzo & Archer, 1989; Ekman, 1973; Izard, 1971; Rosenthal et al., 1979). Since the 1970s, research on the ability to recognize feelings and thoughts from isolated nonverbal behaviors has proliferated (e.g., DePaulo & Friedman, 1998; Hall, 1978; Riggio, 1992; Rosenthal et al., 1979). The vicarious experiencing of another person's emotional response (empathy), as depicted in pictures or stories, has interested some researchers (e.g., Buck, 1984; Doherty, 1997; Hamilton, 1973; Hoffman, 1977). Some sought to measure interpersonal sensitivity through self-reports with forced-choice item tests (e.g., Empathy Scale, Hogan, 1969; Affective Communication Test, Friedman, Prince, Riggio, & DiMatteo, 1980; Social Skills Inventory, Riggio, 1986, 1989; Perceived Encoding Ability and Perceived Decoding

Ability, Zuckerman, & Larrance, 1979). Until the past decade, most of the research involved ratings of stimulus persons presented in written descriptions or on videotapes (e.g., Bernieri, Gillis, Davis, & Grahe, 1996; Costanzo & Archer, 1989; Harackiewicz & DePaulo, 1982; Ickes, 1993; Rosenthal et al., 1979).

Although the majority of person perception research has focused on decoding ability, or the ability to sense what another person's personality is like, or what another person is thinking or feeling, there has also been an interest in encoding ability, or the ability to express what one is like, or what one is thinking or feeling (Buck, 1984; Costanzo & Archer, 1989; Ekman, 1973; Friedman et al., 1980; Hall, 1984; Hamilton, 1973; Izard, 1971; Snodgrass, Hecht, & Ploutz-Snyder, 1998; Zuckerman & Larrance, 1979).

To summarize, past research has focused on (a) the perception of stable personality traits, (b) nonverbal behaviors isolated from their context, (c) self-reports of ability to perceive others' traits or feelings, (d) separating perception from expression, or a combination of these. These ways of studying person perception have much greater control of extraneous variables, thus greater reliability, than the correlational method described later. Also, these methods allow the researcher to separate various facets of sensitivity such as nonverbal from verbal cues and perception from expression, therefore focusing on a cleaner and clearer dependent variable. There are many research questions that necessitate using a more focused measure, isolating it from confounds with other variables. However, we were interested in studying the effects of the social environment on interpersonal sensitivity, so we wanted a method that measured the total of interpersonal sensitivity within an ongoing interaction. The total of interpersonal sensitivity would include nonverbal and verbal cues, perception by one person as well as expression by another, the natural stereotypes and biases assumed about other people (see Kahneman, Slovic, & Tversky, 1982, for descriptions of some of these biases), and many other variables occurring within natural interpersonal interactions.

Therefore, we created a correlational measure in which a perceiver's perceptions (what A thinks B is feeling) is correlated with an expressor's expressions (what B reports feeling). Such a measure is more complex (i.e., including and therefore confounding several variables) than the more focused measures. It is also more comprehensive, in that it measures interpersonal sensitivity between two people within an ongoing interaction, including expression and perception (and their biases), verbal and nonverbal cues, and natural changes within an interaction. When two people interact, they are continually changing their perceptions and expressions as the interaction evolves. As we find a social environmental effect, it is interesting to begin to separate out the various confounds to find just what aspect of interpersonal sensitivity is most influential in this context, such as was done in Snodgrass et al. (1998, described later).

In one attempt to use correlation as a measure of sensitivity within a real interaction between two people, Ickes (1993; chap. 12, this volume) measured empathic accuracy by having two people interact while being videotaped. Later, while watching the videotaped interaction, they reported their own thoughts and feelings and their perceptions of the thoughts and feelings of the other person. Although a realistic interaction took place, the interactants watched the videotape after the interaction was over and tried to remember what they had been feeling and to interpret what the other person had been feeling. An accuracy score was created by an outside judge who interpreted the descriptions of the affects of one interactant and compared them with those of the other person. Thus the accuracy score was an outside judge's perception of the participants' perceptions of the other person's affect in a past interaction. This does not really measure interpersonal sensitivity within an ongoing interaction because it allows the participants to interpret their behavior on the videotape, perhaps to produce a positive self-presentation. Also, they may forget just what they had been feeling, and interpret their feelings in the context of what they now see the other person expressing.

Snodgrass (1985, 1992; Snodgrass, Ploutz-Snyder, & Hecht, 1999) looked at person perception within ongoing dyadic interactions. We needed a measure that would capture the natural variations of expression and perception over time and would provide the opportunity to study the social context of a real interaction. We needed to complement the more focused research with a more comprehensive and realistic (i.e., combined variables as within a real interaction between two people) measure. Such a measure combines the variables that have been carefully separated by the more focused measures but is more realistic because of this confounding. Different measures are needed to thoroughly study interpersonal sensitivity. We were interested in studying the effects of the social context on interpersonal sensitivity, so created this more comprehensive (less focused) measure. We call this a measure of interpersonal sensitivity rather than a measure of perception or empathy because this correlational measure encompasses the sensitivity between two people, one perceiving and one expressing. It includes stereotyping and guesses based on social skills, as well as nonverbal cues accompanying the verbal content, as in all natural interactions.

While two people interacted in various tasks, they filled out questionnaires on which they rated what they were thinking and feeling and also rated how they thought the other person was thinking and feeling. Accuracy at interpersonal sensitivity was measured by correlating what one person thought the other person was thinking and feeling with what the other person reported thinking and feeling. This complex (nonfocused) measure of interpersonal sensitivity includes (a) both verbal and nonverbal cues; (b) both expression by one person and perception (and the inherent biases such as stereotyping) by the other person; and (c) an interactional context, that is, the participants rated how they were feeling and thinking several times during the evolving interaction. Interpersonal sensitivity is defined by this correlational measure as sensitivity to another person's current feelings and thoughts (*states*), rather than more stable personality *traits* (see questionnaire items in the Appendix, reflecting states within this interaction rather than more general traits).

In reporting our research findings (Snodgrass, 1985, 1992; Snodgrass et al. 1999), we used interpersonal sensitivity as if it were only one person's perceptions of the other person, regardless of the other person's expressions. However, we explained in each report that interpersonal sensitivity, as measured, included both the perception of one person and the expression of the other person. Even though a perceiver might guess fairly accurately based on stereotypes and minimal nonverbal cues, she or he will not have nearly as accurate interpersonal sensitivity if the other person is not very expressive or does not express his or her feelings clearly. Also, a very inept perceiver will not have accurate interpersonal sensitivity even if the other person has exceptionally clear expression. The use of sensitivity as if it were a perceiver's skill is just for simplicity of description; we use "sensitivity" to refer to a measure that includes both perception and expression, and we use "perception" to refer to perceiving ability only. Because we measured sensitivity for each interactant in a dyad, we used "Bill's sensitivity" to mean Bill's perception and Tom's expression, and "Tom's sensitivity" to mean Tom's perception and Bill's expression. In all three studies, we were interested in the effect of the social context on interpersonal sensitivity, more specifically, the effects of gender and status role differences on sensitivity.

In the first study (Snodgrass, 1985), 96 pairs of participants were assigned randomly to the teacher or student role, and the first activity was for the teacher to teach the letters of the alphabet in sign language to the student. The teacher had a card depicting the letters of the signed alphabet that he or she used for reference. The roles were randomly assigned, and this random selection was obvious to the participants. After the 6-min lesson, the teacher tested the student and gave him or her a grade. The second activity was a competitive game of "Blockhead" in which they took turns stacking odd-shaped blocks until one person's (the loser of the game) block caused the stack to tumble (no status roles were assigned). The third activity was a cooperative game in which they played "password" in which one is given a word, then that person gives clues for the other one to guess the word (again, no assigned roles). These three interactions were videotaped.

Interpersonal sensitivity scores were constructed to represent the interactants' perceptivity and expressivity to various thoughts and feelings about the current interaction. Each participant completed a total of 12 questionnaires, a set of 3 immediately after each activity and one summary set of 3 at the end of the interaction. The participants were asked to rate on 7-point scales (1 = not at all, 7 = very much) their impressions (feelings and thoughts) concerning themselves and the other person throughout the current activity. They also rated how they thought the other person felt about the same items. The items referred to their affects (i.e., current feelings rather than more stable traits) during that particular activity (sample questionnaires can be found in the

Appendix). Across the four sets of questionnaires there was a total of 48 items (11–13 on each questionnaire). Sample items were "I liked him," "I felt confident," "I was a good teacher," and "I was the dominant one." Each of these 11–13 items was rated three ways (the sets of 3 questionnaires): for example, (a) "I was the dominant one," (b) "She was the dominant one," and (c) "She thought I was the dominant one." The items on the three questionnaires were the same; only the viewpoint changed (from "I was … " to "She was … " to "She thought I was … "; see questionnaires in the Appendix).

The measure of accuracy in interpersonal sensitivity was calculated to create two different measures: (a) sensitivity to how the other person felt about her- or himself, and (b) sensitivity to the impression one is making on the other person (or how the other person felt about her or him often referred to as "meta-perception"). Suppose the two interactants were A, a man, and B, a woman. The first type of sensitivity is A's accuracy at perceiving (and B's accuracy at expressing) how B felt about herself ("B Sees Self"); and the second type of sensitivity is A's accuracy at perceiving (and B's accuracy at expressing) how B felt about A ("B Sees Me"). The first (B Sees Self) is created by correlating A's 48 ratings of how the other person feels (e.g., "she enjoys the task" on A's Questionnaire B) with B's 48 ratings of how she feels (e.g., "I enjoy the task" on B's Questionnaire A). The second (B Sees Me) is created by correlating A's 48 ratings of how B feels about A (e.g., "she thinks that I enjoy the task" on A's Questionnaire C) with B's 48 ratings of how A feels (e.g., "he enjoys the task" on B's Questionnaire B). These measures were calculated for each participant in an interaction. These correlations represent the degree of sensitivity to a person's variation in affect over time and over different affects. One can argue that correlations of ratings such as these will naturally be influenced by one person's stereotypes of how another would feel in that situation—making the perceiver a "good guesser." If one person tends to use the higher numbers on the rating scale and their partner tends to use the lower numbers on the rating scale, they might still have a high correlation. That indicates that they may be accurate at interpreting the changes in feelings over time, or the variations in another's feelings on various states even though one favors lower ratings and one favors high ratings. Other measures would confound the tendency to use higher versus lower numbers with inaccuracy. However, these "biases" are inherent in all natural interaction and perception.

These correlations were transformed by Fisher's $z$ to create two sensitivity scores ("B Sees Me" and "B Sees Self") for each participant. These sensitivity scores served as dependent variables that were analyzed with analyses of variance (ANOVAs).

The second study (Snodgrass, 1992) was very much like the first, except that the status variable of leader–follower was established as "boss" and "employee" rather than "teacher" and "student." The first activity involved the randomly selected boss to interview the prospective employee. The boss could make up questions to ask the employee as if the employee was being interviewed for a job. The interview lasted 10 min. Then the boss was given a picture of the solution to a 4–7-piece puzzle, and the employee was given the pieces of the puzzle. The boss was to instruct while the employee put the pieces of the puzzle together. The third activity was a decision-making task in which the boss and employee were to work together discussing a problem and come up with a solution before 10 min was up. All activities were videotaped.

After each activity, the participants completed sets of three questionnaires, similar to those in Snodgrass (1985), except the items related to the particular activities performed in this study. Interpersonal sensitivity scores were calculated by correlating one participant's items with the other participant's similar items, as described earlier.

The third study (Snodgrass et al., 1999) differed from these in that there was only one activity and only one set of three questionnaires. Also, no leader–follower roles were assigned. Instead, an expectancy for one of the dyad members to have a "better aptitude" for leadership than the other was planted in one interactant. In the first two studies, the leader role was randomly assigned and the participants were fully informed that one had been chosen to be leader randomly. Also, the tasks involved one leader role and one follower role. In this third study, nothing was mentioned about a leader or a follower, and the task called for cooperation, with no one was assigned to be superior to the other.

After being tested in large groups on several personality tests, participants were randomly selected to come to the laboratory in pairs (who did not know each other). When they arrived, each was shown his or her own and the other person's "scores" on leadership potential supposedly based on the previous personality tests. Actually, the bogus scores had been assigned so that one person (randomly chosen) saw scores that reflected that one was superior to the other on leadership potential (the "expectancy" participant). The bogus scores for one half of the expectancy group indicated that their own potential for leadership was greater than that of the other person, and one half indicated that the other person had greater potential. The other person (randomly chosen by default) was shown scores reflecting that both interactants were average in leadership potential (the "control" participant).

They were then given a decision-making task (rank-ordering 10 ways to spend a generous grant given to the university) to discuss and come to an agreement within 10 min. This discussion was videotaped. After the task was completed, they were given a set of three questionnaires in which they rated items reflecting what they felt and thought during the discussion, what they thought the other person felt and thought during the discussion, and what they thought the other person thought about them during the discussion, as in the two studies discussed earlier. Sensitivity scores were calculated as described earlier.

Snodgrass (1985, 1992; Snodgrass et al., 1999) was interested in assessing how the social context (in particular, status and gender) affected interpersonal sensitivity. Stereotypes suggest that women are more sensitive than men, and research has indicated that women are better than men at decoding nonverbal cues (e.g., Hall, 1978). Are women more sensitive than men even when they are in a superior role over men?

All three studies (Snodgrass, 1985, 1992; Snodgrass et al., 1999) were analyzed by using a four-way ANOVA with two repeated measures and pairs as units of analysis. The between-groups factors were superior's gender (male or female) and subordinate's gender (male or female). The within-groups factors were status role (superior or subordinate) and type of sensitivity ("B sees me" or "B sees self").

All three studies found no significant differences in sensitivity between women and men. However, all three studies found an interaction between type of sensitivity ("B sees me" or "B sees self") and role (leader or subordinate), even when the role was not assigned or mentioned, but one participant's expectancies for leadership potential were manipulated relative to the other person. We found that subordinates were more perceptive of (and/or leaders were more expressive of) the leader's feelings about the subordinate ("B sees me"), relative to leaders who were more perceptive of (and/or subordinates more expressive of) the subordinate's feelings about him- or herself ("B sees self"), regardless of gender (see Table 11.1 for typical results).

**TABLE 11.1**

**Means Representing Typical Results: Mean Sensitivity Scores by Role and Type of Sensitivity**

| Type of Sensitivity | Leader | Role Subordinate | Total M |
|---|---|---|---|
| B Sees Me | | | |
| M | .189 | .547 | .368 |
| SD | .20 | .21 | |
| B Sees Self | | | |
| M | .470 | .257 | .364 |
| SD | .29 | .24 | |
| Total M | .330 | .402 | .366 |

Note. From "Further Effects of Role Versus Gender on Interpersonal Sensitivity," by S. E. Snodgrass, 1992, Journal of Personality and Social Psychology, 62, 156. Copyright 1992 by the American Psychological Association. Reprinted with permission. M = mean. SD = standard deviation.

What does this interaction mean? In a dyadic interaction in which there are status roles, whether teacher–student, boss–employee, or merely expectations about which participant has the greatest potential for leadership, we found a significant $2 \times 2$ interaction between status role and type of sensitivity. Examples include the following: (a) The subordinates' answers to "B sees me" questions such as "Does the leader like me?" and "Does he think I am doing a good job?" are more accurate (i.e., correlated higher with the other person's self-ratings) than the leaders' answers to "Does my subordinate like me"? (b) The leaders' answers to "B sees self" questions such as "Is she enjoying her work?" and "Does she feel confident?" are more accurate than the subordinates' answer to "Does he like being boss?" These results have face validity. As an example, using Al, the leader, and Bev, the subordinate, it is more important for Bev to attend to and care about how her leader, Al, feels about her personally and about her performance, because this will influence promotions and raises; it is less likely, however, that Al will care much about what Bev thinks about him, as long as the work is satisfactory. Also, Bev will not openly express her feelings about Al because it might be perceived as ingratiation or disrespect, and Al will express his thoughts and feelings about Bev and her work in order to have the work accomplished more satisfactorily. However, Al will be more perceptive of Bev's feelings about herself—is she pleased with her assignment? Does she understand the instructions?—whereas Bev doesn't really care how Al feels about himself. Also, Bev will be expressing her feelings about herself and her work in order to gain recognition or assistance, and Al will not express his feelings about himself to his subordinates.

Snodgrass' measure of interpersonal sensitivity has received some criticisms. For example, Hall and Halberstadt (1994) criticized the Snodgrass studies because they confound perceptivity with expressivity, and the results, therefore, do not contribute to the study of either decoding or encoding sensitivities. How does one interpret these results? Are subordinates more perceptive, or are leaders more expressive of their feelings about the subordinate? Snodgrass et al. (1998) proceeded to examine the relative contributions of perception and expression to this correlational measure of interpersonal sensitivity. Using the videotaped interactions from Snodgrass (1992) and Snodgrass et al. (1999), we did two studies in which naive judges observed the videotaped interactions and rated how they thought their target participant felt about himself or herself and the other person. The items on the judges' rating sheets were identical to those on which the participants had rated their own feelings about themselves and the other person (see sample questionnaires in the Appendix). Therefore, sensitivity scores for the judges could be calculated in the same way they were calculated for the participants. Each judge rated items for only one of the two participants in each interaction (their "target"). One would expect observers of videotaped interactions to be perceptive of the feelings of the participants on the videotape to some extent. However, the two-way Status Role × Type of Sensitivity interaction as found in the previous studies is very subtle. There is no common expectation that people will perceive another person's feelings about themselves or about their interacting partners differentially depending on their status within the interaction.

If neutral observers of the videotapes (people not involved in the interaction nor in a role of higher or lower status than the interactants) are able to sense the interactants in the same two-way interaction pattern as that found in Snodgrass (1985, 1992; Snodgrass et al., 1999), then the status of the one expressing thoughts and feelings must be a significant factor in determining the perceiver's sensitivity scores (the judges have no status within the interaction to influence them). This is referred to as the expressivity hypothesis, that interpersonal sensitivity is more an indication of the clear expression of a person's affect depending on the relative status of the expressor than of the perception of the other person.

However, if it is the status of the perceiver that really caused him or her to be more or less perceptive, then these neutral observers who are not in any status role should be relatively equally sensitive to both subordinates and superiors on both types of sensitivity. If this perceptivity hypothesis is correct, then the two-way Status Role x Type of Sensitivity interaction should become statistically insignificant, indicating that interpersonal sensitivity is more an indication of a person's accurate perception of another person's affects depending on the status role of the perceiver.

Snodgrass et al. (1998) found the same two-way interaction pattern in the sensitivity scores of the neutral judges to be statistically significant, thus supporting the expressivity hypothesis more than the perceptivity hypothesis. Those in higher power roles are relatively more expressive about what they think of the subordinate, whereas subordinates are relatively more expressive about what they think about themselves. Previous interpretations of this correlation measure still hold: This measure of interpersonal sensitivity represents both the perception of one interactant and the expression of the other. Perception has still not been completely isolated from expression in these correlated scores. The observers may have been "good guessers" by using stereotypes and other inherent biases in rating the feelings and thoughts of the target. However, this study demonstrates that expression plays the most significant role. Other researchers have found that expression plays a significant role in the various measures of person perception, as well (e.g., Hancock & Ickes, 1996; Kenny & La Voie, 1984; Nakamura, Buck, & Kenny, 1990; Sabatelli, Buck, & Dreyer, 1982; Sabatelli, Buck, & Kenny, 1986).

This correlational measure also does not separate verbal from nonverbal cues. This problem could be addressed by having outside judges observe the videotapes with no sound or listen to audio tapes with no picture. Because it has been found that the status role of the one expressing contributes to the two-way interaction pattern more than the status of the one perceiving, it can be expected that the interpersonal sensitivity scores of outside judges will fall into the same pattern, although more so when observing video with no sound or when listening to sound with no video.

The use of correlations to create interpersonal sensitivity scores has several advantages. By correlating several items, researchers avoid the biases inherent in difference scores (Cronbach, 1955, 1958). Unlike difference scores, correlations are not biased by the number of data points, the variability, or even nonnormality. Also, rather than a measure of how well one can guess another's actual rating (as in difference scores), these sensitivity scores are a measure of how well one senses and another expresses a pattern of variation in another's ratings on related items made several times throughout the interaction, that is, sensitivity to changing states in another person. (See Bronfenbrenner, Harding, & Gallwey, 1958; Funder, chap. 16, this volume; Kenny & Winquist, chap. 14, this volume, for further discussion of correlation scores.)

This correlational method of producing interpersonal sensitivity scores is most appropriately used to investigate the effects of social context on the ability for two people to communicate feelings and thoughts concerning the ongoing interaction. When studying the effects of the social context, researchers want realistic and comprehensive scores to represent sensitivity, that is, scores that include both the expression and the perception within the interaction and both the verbal and nonverbal cues to feelings and thoughts. If other measures that isolate a particular variable within sensitivity are used, then researchers will find how the social context affects only the specific isolated ingredient in sensitivity. Perhaps this correlational measure is best for studying the effects of outside influences on interpersonal sensitivity (a *macro* sensitivity), whereas those measures that isolate various factors within sensitivity are best used only for more *micro* studies whose purpose is to pull apart communication into its various factors. Other researchers have used this correlational measure to study different social factors (e.g., Bernieri, 1990, 1991; Patterson, Churchill, Faraq, & Borden, 1992).

In the Appendix are examples of questionnaires used in Snodgrass (1985) and Snodgrass et al. (1998). The items on the questionnaires determine what elements of the interaction one particularly wants to study. Of course, any items of interest could be used to create a questionnaire. One might want to focus the items more toward the motivations of each interactant or more toward the tasks involved. This measure can be used in larger groups than dyads by giving each interactant a questionnaire on which to rate his or her own feelings and thoughts and questionnaires to rate each of the other interactants' feelings and thoughts about self and other. The method is very flexible, as long as one wants to measure the comprehensive (confounded, but more natural) sensitivity. Also, the items on the questionnaires can be written to access other types of sensitivity than "B sees me" and "B sees self." For example, one could study sensitivity to "B sees task" or to B's motivations just by changing the items and the formats of the questionnaires.

This comprehensive measure of interpersonal sensitivity invites social psychologists to explore further the variables in the social context that may affect interpersonal sensitivity, variables such as the tasks involved in the interaction, the motivation of the interactants, and the size and composition of the group interacting. Interpersonal sensitivity is definitely a social phenomenon, and the exploration of the contextual variables affecting sensitivity will contribute to the improvement of all social interactions.

## REFERENCES

Asch, S. E. (1946). Forming impressions of personality. *Journal of Abnormal and Social Psychology, 41,* 258–290.

Bernieri, F. (1990, July). *Interpersonal coordination and emotion contagion.* Presented at the International Society for Research on Emotions Annual Conference, New Brunswick, NJ.

Bernieri, F. (1991). Interpersonal sensitivity in teaching interactions. *Personality and Social Psychology Bulletin, 17,* 98–103.

Bernieri, F. J., Gillis, J. S., Davis, J. M., & Grahe, J. E. (1996). Dyad rapport and the accuracy of its judgment across situations: A lens model analysis. *Journal of Personality and Social Psychology, 71,* 110–129.

Bernieri, F. J., Zuckerman, M., Koestner, R., & Rosenthal, R. (1994). Measuring person perception accuracy: Another look at self–other agreement. *Personality and Social Psychology Bulletin, 20,* 367–378.

Bronfenbrenner, U., Harding, J., & Gallwey, M. (1958). The measurement of skill in social perception. In D. C. McClelland, A. L. Baldwin, U. Bronfenbrenner, & F. L. Strodtbeck (Eds.), *Talent and society: New perspectives in the identification of talent* (pp. 29–111). Princeton, NJ: Van Nostrand.

Buck, R. (1984). *The communication of emotion.* New York: Guilford.

Costanzo, M., & Archer, D. (1989). Interpreting the expressive behavior of others: The Interpersonal Perception Task. *Journal of Nonverbal Behavior, 13,* 225–245.

Cronbach, L. J. (1955). Processes affecting scores on "understanding of others" and "assumed similarity." *Psychological Bulletin, 52,* 177–193.

Cronbach, L. J. (1958). Proposals leading to analytic treatment of social perception scores. In R. Tagiuri & L. Petrullo (Eds.), *Person perception and interpersonal behavior* (pp. 353–379). Stanford, CA: Stanford University Press.

DePaulo, B. M., & Friedman, H. S. (1998). Nonverbal communication. In D. T. Gilbert, S. T. Fiske, & G. Lindzey (Eds.), *The handbook of social psychology* (4th ed., vol. 2, pp. 3–40). Boston: McGraw-Hill.

Doherty, R. W. (1997). The Emotional Contagion Scale: A measure of individual differences. *Journal of Nonverbal Behavior, 21,* 131–154.

Dymond, R. F. (1949). A scale for the measurement of empathic ability. *Journal of Consulting Psychology, 13,* 127–133.

Ekman, P. (1973). Cross cultural studies of facial expression. In P. Ekman (Ed.), *Darwin and facial expression* (pp. 169–222). New York: Academic.

Friedman, H. S., Prince, L. M., Riggio, R. E., & DiMatteo, M. R. (1980). Understanding and assessing nonverbal expressiveness: The Affective Communication Test. *Journal of Personality and Social Psychology, 39,* 333–351.

Funder, D. C. (1995). On the accuracy of personality judgment: A realistic approach. *Psychological Review, 102,* 652–670.

Hall, J. A. (1978). Gender effects in decoding nonverbal cues. *Psychological Bulletin, 85,* 845–857.

Hall, J. A. (1984). *Nonverbal sex differences: Communication accuracy and expressive style.* Baltimore: Johns Hopkins University Press.

Hall, J. A., & Halberstadt, A. G. (1994). "Subordination" and sensitivity to nonverbal cues: A study of married, working women. *Sex Roles, 31,* 149–165.

Hamilton, M. L. (1973). Imitative behavior and expressive ability in facial expression of emotion. *Developmental Psychology, 8,* 138.

Hancock, M., & Ickes, W. (1996). Empathic accuracy: When does the perceiver–target relationship make a difference? *Journal of Social and Personal Relationships, 13,* 179–199.

Harackiewicz, J. M., & DePaulo, B. M. (1982). Accuracy of person perception: A component analysis according to Cronbach. *Personality and Social Psychology Bulletin, 8,* 247–256.

Hoffman, M. L. (1977). Sex differences in empathy and related behaviors. *Psychological Bulletin, 84,* 712–722.

Hogan, R. (1969). Development of an empathy scale. *Journal of Consulting and Clinical Psychology, 33,* 307–316.

Ickes, W. (1993). Empathic accuracy. *Journal of Personality, 61,* 587–610.

Izard, C. E. (1971). *The face of emotion.* New York: Appleton-Century-Crofts.

Kahneman, D., Slovic, P., & Tversky, A. (Eds.). (1982). *Judgment under uncertainty: Heuristics and biases.* New York: Cambridge University Press.

Kenny, D. A. (1994). *Interpersonal perception: A social relations analysis.* New York: Guilford.

Kenny, D. A., & La Voie, L. (1984). The social relations model. In L. Berkowitz (Ed.), *Advances in Experimental Social Psychology* (Vol. 18, pp. 142–182). Orlando, FL: Academic.

Nakamura, M., Buck, R., & Kenny, D. A. (1990). Relative contributions of expressive behavior and contextual information to the judgment of the emotional state of the other. *Journal of Personality and Social Psychology, 59,* 1032–1039.

Patterson, M. L., Churchill, M. E., Faraq, F., & Borden, E. (1992). Impression management, cognitive demand, and interpersonal sensitivity. *Current Psychology—Research and Reviews, 10,* 263–271.

Riggio, R. E. (1986). Assessment of basic social skills. *Journal of Personality and Social Psychology, 51,* 649–660.

Riggio, R. E. (1989). *Manual for the Social Skills Inventory.* Palo Alto, CA: Consulting Psychologists Press.

Riggio, R. E. (1992). Social interaction skills and nonverbal behavior. In R. S. Feldman (Ed.), *Applications of nonverbal behavioral theories and research* (pp. 3–30). Hillsdale, NJ: Lawrence Erlbaum Associates.

Rosenthal, R., Hall, J. A., DiMatteo, M. R., Rogers, P. L., & Archer, D. (1979). *Sensitivity to nonverbal communication: The PONS test.* Baltimore: Johns Hopkins University Press.

Sabatelli, R. M., Buck, R., & Dreyer, A. (1982). Nonverbal communication accuracy in married couples: Relationship with marital complaints. *Journal of Personality and Social Psychology, 43,* 1088–1097.

Sabatelli, R. M., Buck, R., & Kenny, D. A. (1986). A social relations analysis of nonverbal communication accuracy in married couples. *Journal of Personality, 54,* 513–527.

Snodgrass, S. E. (1985). Women's intuition: The effect of subordinate role on interpersonal sensitivity. *Journal of Personality and Social Psychology, 49,* 146–155.

Snodgrass, S. E. (1992). Further effects of role versus gender on interpersonal sensitivity. *Journal of Personality and Social Psychology, 62,* 154–158.

Snodgrass, S. E., Hecht, M. A., & Ploutz-Snyder, R. (1998). Interpersonal sensitivity: Expressivity or perceptivity? *Journal of Personality and Social Psychology, 74,* 238–249.

Snodgrass, S. E., Ploutz-Snyder, R., & Hecht, M. A. (1999). *The effect of leadership expectations on interpersonal sensitivity.* Unpublished manuscript.

Vogt, D. S., & Colvin, C. R. (1998). *The good judge of personality: Gender differences, personality correlates, and Cronbachian "artifacts."* Manuscript submitted for publication.

Zuckerman, M., & Larrance, D. T. (1979). Individual differences in perceived encoding and decoding abilities. In R. Rosenthal (Ed.), *Skill in nonverbal communication: Individual differences* (pp. 171–203). Cambridge, MA: Oelgeschlager, Gunn & Hain.

## APPENDIX

## Rating Scales .

Items on rating scales should be written for each separate interaction, pertaining to their feelings and thoughts about this interaction. Examples of rating scales used follow.

## Examples

Rating Scale 1-A:          My self-ratings of how I felt and thought.

Rating Scale 1-B:          My ratings of how the other person felt and thought.

Rating Scale 1-C:          My ratings of how the other person rated my feelings and thoughts.

Rating Scale J1-A:         Judges' ratings of how the target person felt and thought.

Rating Scale J1-B:         Judges' ratings of how the target felt about the other person.

## Creating Sensitivity Scores

Original Participants' Scores (A's sensitivity):

B SEES SELF: Correlate A's ratings of "He felt.... " (1-B) with B's ratings of "I felt.... " (1-A).

B SEES ME: Correlate A's ratings of "She thought that I felt.... " (1-C) with B's ratings of "He felt.... " (1-B)

Judges' (Observers') Scores (T = Target):

T SEES SELF: Correlate Observer's ratings of "She felt.... " (J1-A) with Target's ratings of "I felt.... " (1-A)

T SEES OTHER: Correlate Observer's ratings of "She thought he felt.... " (J1-B) with Target's ratings of "He felt.... " (1-B)

Transform correlations into $z$ scores using Fisher's $z$ before analysis.

# RATING SCALE 1-A

## The Interview

Answer each of the following questions by circling the number that best represents your thoughts or feelings during the interview in which you have just participated. Please be very honest. Your answers will never be seen by the other person, nor will your name ever appear on this questionnaire. Also, please answer quickly—usually the first response that comes to mind best reflects your true feelings (your "gut" reaction). Don't think about each question for very long. Thank you.

|  | *Not at all* |  |  |  |  |  | *Very much* |
|---|---|---|---|---|---|---|---|
| 1. I enjoyed the interview. | 1 | 2 | 3 | 4 | 5 | 6 | 7 |
| 2. I felt comfortable as the interviewer. | 1 | 2 | 3 | 4 | 5 | 6 | 7 |
| 3. I was a good interviewer. | 1 | 2 | 3 | 4 | 5 | 6 | 7 |
| 4. I felt self-confident. | 1 | 2 | 3 | 4 | 5 | 6 | 7 |
| 5. I was the dominant one. | 1 | 2 | 3 | 4 | 5 | 6 | 7 |
| 6. I learned a lot about my subordinate. | 1 | 2 | 3 | 4 | 5 | 6 | 7 |
| 7. I made my subordinate feel comfortable. | 1 | 2 | 3 | 4 | 5 | 6 | 7 |
| 8. I made a good impression on my subordinate. | 1 | 2 | 3 | 4 | 5 | 6 | 7 |
| 9. I controlled the interaction. | 1 | 2 | 3 | 4 | 5 | 6 | 7 |
| 10. I liked my subordinate. | 1 | 2 | 3 | 4 | 5 | 6 | 7 |
| 11. I was the leader. | 1 | 2 | 3 | 4 | 5 | 6 | 7 |
| 12. I took the interview seriously (really "got into it"). | 1 | 2 | 3 | 4 | 5 | 6 | 7 |
| 13. I enjoyed getting to know my subordinate. | 1 | 2 | 3 | 4 | 5 | 6 | 7 |

HAND THIS QUESTIONNAIRE TO THE EXPERIMENTER
AND GO ON TO THE NEXT ONE

# RATING SCALE 1-B

## The Interview

Answer each of the following questions by circling the number that best represents your thoughts or feelings during the interview in which you have just participated. Please be very honest. Your answers will never be seen by the other person, nor will your name ever appear on this questionnaire. Also, please answer quickly—usually the first response that comes to mind best reflects your true feelings (your "gut" reaction). Don't think about each question for very long. Thank you.

|  | Not at all |  |  |  |  |  | Very much |
|---|---|---|---|---|---|---|---|
| 1. S/He enjoyed the interview. | 1 | 2 | 3 | 4 | 5 | 6 | 7 |
| 2. S/He felt comfortable as the interviewer. | 1 | 2 | 3 | 4 | 5 | 6 | 7 |
| 3. S/He was a good interviewer. | 1 | 2 | 3 | 4 | 5 | 6 | 7 |
| 4. S/He felt self-confident. | 1 | 2 | 3 | 4 | 5 | 6 | 7 |
| 5. S/He was the dominant one. | 1 | 2 | 3 | 4 | 5 | 6 | 7 |
| 6. S/He learned a lot about me. | 1 | 2 | 3 | 4 | 5 | 6 | 7 |
| 7. S/He made me feel comfortable. | 1 | 2 | 3 | 4 | 5 | 6 | 7 |
| 8. S/He made a good impression on me. | 1 | 2 | 3 | 4 | 5 | 6 | 7 |
| 9. S/He controlled the interaction. | 1 | 2 | 3 | 4 | 5 | 6 | 7 |
| 10. S/He liked me. | 1 | 2 | 3 | 4 | 5 | 6 | 7 |
| 11. S/He was the leader. | 1 | 2 | 3 | 4 | 5 | 6 | 7 |
| 12. S/He took the interview seriously (really "got into it"). | 1 | 2 | 3 | 4 | 5 | 6 | 7 |
| 13. S/He enjoyed getting to know me. | 1 | 2 | 3 | 4 | 5 | 6 | 7 |

HAND THIS QUESTIONNAIRE TO THE EXPERIMENTER
AND GO ON TO THE NEXT ONE

# RATING SCALE 1-C

## The Interview

Now, please answer each item as you think the other person felt about *you* during the interview in which you have just participated. Try to put yourself in the other person's shoes—we want to know to what extent you can sense what the other person was thinking about you. Just guess if you feel you have to—a guess is often intuitively quite accurate.

| *He/She thought that:* | Not at all | | | | | | Very much |
|---|---|---|---|---|---|---|---|
| 1. I enjoyed the interview. | 1 | 2 | 3 | 4 | 5 | 6 | 7 |
| 2. I felt comfortable as the interviewer. | 1 | 2 | 3 | 4 | 5 | 6 | 7 |
| 3. I was a good interviewer. | 1 | 2 | 3 | 4 | 5 | 6 | 7 |
| 4. I felt self-confident. | 1 | 2 | 3 | 4 | 5 | 6 | 7 |
| 5. I was the dominant one. | 1 | 2 | 3 | 4 | 5 | 6 | 7 |
| 6. I learned a lot about my subordinate. | 1 | 2 | 3 | 4 | 5 | 6 | 7 |
| 7. I made my subordinate feel comfortable. | 1 | 2 | 3 | 4 | 5 | 6 | 7 |
| 8. I made a good impression on my subordinate. | 1 | 2 | 3 | 4 | 5 | 6 | 7 |
| 9. I controlled the interaction. | 1 | 2 | 3 | 4 | 5 | 6 | 7 |
| 10. I liked my subordinate. | 1 | 2 | 3 | 4 | 5 | 6 | 7 |
| 11. I was the leader. | 1 | 2 | 3 | 4 | 5 | 6 | 7 |
| 12. I took the interview seriously (really "got into it"). | 1 | 2 | 3 | 4 | 5 | 6 | 7 |
| 13. I enjoyed getting to know my subordinate. | 1 | 2 | 3 | 4 | 5 | 6 | 7 |

HAND THIS QUESTIONNAIRE TO THE EXPERIMENTER
AND GO ON TO THE NEXT ONE

## RATING SCALE J1-A

### The Interview

Rate how you think the person you watched felt about the following statements by circling the number that best represents how you think he or she felt or thought during the interview. Try to work quickly, going with your original "gut reaction" rather than thinking too long about each statement. Some statements will seem difficult to answer, but give it your best guess. Answer all items and circle only one number for each.

| | Not at all | | | | | | Very much |
|---|---|---|---|---|---|---|---|
| 1. S/He enjoyed the interview. | 1 | 2 | 3 | 4 | 5 | 6 | 7 |
| 2. S/He felt comfortable as the interviewer (or interviewee). | 1 | 2 | 3 | 4 | 5 | 6 | 7 |
| 3. S/He thought that s/he was a good interviewer (interviewee). | 1 | 2 | 3 | 4 | 5 | 6 | 7 |
| 4. S/He felt self-confident. | 1 | 2 | 3 | 4 | 5 | 6 | 7 |
| 5. S/He thought s/he was the dominant one. | 1 | 2 | 3 | 4 | 5 | 6 | 7 |
| 6. S/He thought s/he learned a lot about the boss (employee). | 1 | 2 | 3 | 4 | 5 | 6 | 7 |
| 7. S/He thought s/he made the boss (employee) feel comfortable. | 1 | 2 | 3 | 4 | 5 | 6 | 7 |
| 8. S/He thought s/he made a good impression on the boss (employee). | 1 | 2 | 3 | 4 | 5 | 6 | 7 |
| 9. S/He thought s/he controlled the interview. | 1 | 2 | 3 | 4 | 5 | 6 | 7 |
| 10. S/He liked the boss (employee). | 1 | 2 | 3 | 4 | 5 | 6 | 7 |
| 11. S/He thought s/he was the leader. | 1 | 2 | 3 | 4 | 5 | 6 | 7 |
| 12. S/He thought s/he took the interview seriously (really "got into it"). | 1 | 2 | 3 | 4 | 5 | 6 | 7 |
| 13. S/He enjoyed getting to know the other person. | 1 | 2 | 3 | 4 | 5 | 6 | 7 |

# RATING SCALE J1-B

## The Interview

Rate how you think the person you watched felt about the other person with whom he or she interacted by circling the number that best represents how you think he or she felt or thought during the interview. Try to work quickly, going with your original "gut reaction" rather than thinking too long about each statement. Some statements will seem difficult to answer, but give it your best guess. Answer all items, and circle only one number for each.

| She/He thought that the other person: | Not at all | | | | | | Very much |
|---|---|---|---|---|---|---|---|
| 1. Enjoyed the interview. | 1 | 2 | 3 | 4 | 5 | 6 | 7 |
| 2. Felt comfortable as the interviewer (or interviewee). | 1 | 2 | 3 | 4 | 5 | 6 | 7 |
| 3. Was a good interviewer (interviewee). | 1 | 2 | 3 | 4 | 5 | 6 | 7 |
| 4. Felt self-confident. | 1 | 2 | 3 | 4 | 5 | 6 | 7 |
| 5. Was the dominant one. | 1 | 2 | 3 | 4 | 5 | 6 | 7 |
| 6. Learned a lot about her/him. | 1 | 2 | 3 | 4 | 5 | 6 | 7 |
| 7. Made her/him feel comfortable. | 1 | 2 | 3 | 4 | 5 | 6 | 7 |
| 8. Made a good impression on her/him. | 1 | 2 | 3 | 4 | 5 | 6 | 7 |
| 9. Controlled the interview. | 1 | 2 | 3 | 4 | 5 | 6 | 7 |
| 10. Liked her/him. | 1 | 2 | 3 | 4 | 5 | 6 | 7 |
| 11. Was the leader. | 1 | 2 | 3 | 4 | 5 | 6 | 7 |
| 12. Took the interview seriously (really "got into it"). | 1 | 2 | 3 | 4 | 5 | 6 | 7 |
| 13. Enjoyed getting to know her/him. | 1 | 2 | 3 | 4 | 5 | 6 | 7 |

# ℬ 12 ℭ

# Measuring Empathic Accuracy

**William Ickes**
*University of Texas at Arlington*

Q: Can you really measure people's ability to "read" other people's minds?
A: Yes.
Q: Is it a lot of work to do that?
A: Yes.
Q: Is it worth all the effort?
A: Yes.
Q: Can you answer a question without saying "Yes"?
A: Yes.

Is the person who answered "Yes" to this series of questions being flippant? Or merely factual? Or is the answerer just responding affirmatively to whatever question he is asked? Perhaps the questioner can decide among these possibilities by drawing on information acquired in previous interaction with the answerer, on the answerer's reputation as a smart-aleck, or on the answerer's ironic smile or tone of voice. It is difficult, however, for the rest of us to decide, having to rely only on the few short lines of conversation that are available. The point of this example is that knowing the answerer's words (or, in this case, word) isn't always sufficient for us to determine what our next response should be. To make that decision, we would want to know what the answerer meant or intended by saying "Yes" to every question. In other words, we would want to "read" the answerer's mind.

Empathic inference is the "everyday mind reading" that people do whenever they attempt to infer other people's thoughts and feelings. Empathic accuracy is the extent to which such mind reading attempts are successful (Ickes, 1993, 1997). According to Goleman (1995), the ability to accurately "read" other people's thoughts and feelings is an important skill that affects people's social

219

adjustment in all phases of their life: as students in the classroom, as playmates and platonic friends, as dating and marriage partners, as parents, as members of the work force, and as members of the larger community. Indeed, this ability may be the quintessential aspect of what is commonly termed "social intelligence." All else being equal, it is this ability that distinguishes "the most tactful advisors, the most diplomatic officials, the most effective negotiators, the most electable politicians, the most productive salespersons, the most successful teachers, and the most insightful therapists" (Ickes, 1997, p. 2).

Empathic accuracy is the newest area of study within the accuracy tradition of interpersonal perception research, being the most recent of four areas to emerge. The first and longest studied area focuses on perceivers' accuracy in judging other people's personality traits (e.g., Asch, 1946; Cronbach, 1955; Estes, 1938; Funder & Colvin, 1988; McCrae, 1982; Norman & Goldberg, 1966). The second and next-longest studied area focuses on dyad members' accurate perceptions or understanding of each other's attitudes, values, and self-conceptions (e.g., Knudson, Sommers, & Golding, 1980; Laing, Phillipson, & Lee, 1966; Newmark, Woody, & Ziff, 1977; Rogers & Dymond, 1954; Sillars, 1989). The third and more recent area focuses on perceivers' affective sensitivity in inferring the emotional state(s) of one or more target persons (e.g., Costanzo & Archer, 1989; Ekman & Friesen, 1975; Hall, 1984; Kagan, 1977; Noller, 1980, 1981; Rosenthal, Hall, DiMatteo, Rogers, & Archer, 1979; see also, in this volume, Archer, Costanzo, & Akert, chap. 9; Hall, chap. 8; Noller, chap. 13; Nowicki & Duke, chap. 10). The fourth and most recent area focuses on perceivers' empathic accuracy—that is, their ability to accurately infer the specific content of another person's covert thoughts and feelings (e.g., Ickes, Stinson, Bissonnette, & Garcia, 1990; Levenson & Ruef, 1992; Marangoni, Garcia, Ickes, & Teng, 1995; Simpson, Ickes, & Blackstone, 1995; Stinson & Ickes, 1992).

Carl Rogers called attention to the importance of *accurate empathy* in the therapist–client relationship as early as 1957. His work suggested that an ideal measure of empathic accuracy would be one that (a) could be used to track the accuracy of the therapist's inferences over the course of the client–therapist interaction, and (b) would be objective in defining accuracy in terms of the degree to which the perceiver's inferences matched the client's actual reported thoughts and feelings. During the next 4 decades, many attempts to develop such a measure were made by researchers in areas such as clinical and counseling psychology, communication studies, marriage and family studies, psychiatry, and personality and social psychology.

Two of the most promising measurement approaches were introduced in the early 1990s in studies reported by Ickes, Stinson, et al. (1990) and by Levenson and Ruef (1992). The approach that my colleagues and I developed is used to assess how accurately perceivers can infer online the specific content of other people's successive thoughts and feelings. The approach that Levenson and

Ruef developed is used to assess how accurately perceivers can infer online the valence and intensity of other people's changing emotional states. In both approaches, perceivers attempt to infer aspects of a target person's reported subjective experience while viewing a videotape of the target person in conversation with either a therapist or another interaction partner. Accuracy is objectively defined in terms of the degree to which the perceiver's inference matches the target's reported subjective experience, and the accuracy scores for individual inferences can be aggregated across time or across targets to assess changes across time or to create a single, cross-target index.

The present chapter describes how empathic accuracy is measured using the approach that my colleagues and I developed. Specifically, I review the procedures we use to assess empathic accuracy, the evidence for its interrater reliability and cross-target consistency, and the growing body of data that support its construct validity. In the interest of space, I do not attempt to review Levenson and Ruef's (1992) approach, which focuses more specifically on emotional empathic accuracy and the degree of "physiological linkage" between the perceiver and the target. For excellent (indeed, definitive) descriptions of that approach, see Levenson and Ruef (1992, 1997).

## MEASURING EMPATHIC ACCURACY

With respect to the approach that my colleagues and I have developed, the measurement of empathic accuracy implicates three major issues: assessment, reliability, and validity. Each of these issues is addressed in turn in the following sections.

## Assessment

Our procedure for assessing empathic accuracy varies somewhat, depending on the type of research paradigm in which it is applied. In the studies that we have conducted in the University of Texas at Arlington (UTA) Social Interaction Lab, two such paradigms have predominated. The first is the *unstructured dyadic interaction paradigm*, in which dyad members attempt to infer each other's thoughts and feelings from a videotape of their spontaneous interaction during a brief period in which the experimenter left them alone together (Ickes & Tooke, 1988; Ickes, Bissonnette, et al., 1990; Ickes & Stinson, 1990; Stinson & Ickes, 1992). The second is the *standard stimulus paradigm*, in which individual participants each view the same standard set of videotaped interactions and attempt to infer the thoughts and feelings of the same set of target persons (Gesn & Ickes, 1999; Marangoni et al., 1995).

*The Unstructured Dyadic Interaction Paradigm.*   The dyadic interaction paradigm is used in studies of dyad members' ability to infer the specific content of each other's thoughts and feelings during a brief interaction period. In the first of these studies, we examined the factors influencing the empathic accuracy of opposite-sex strangers (Ickes, Stinson, et al., 1990). In subsequent studies, we have compared the empathic accuracy of same-sex strangers with that of same-sex friends (Graham, 1994; Stinson & Ickes, 1992). More recently, studies have explored the factors influencing the empathic accuracy of dating couples (Simpson et al., 1995) and married couples (Bissonnette, Rusbult, & Kilpatrick, 1997; Thomas, Fletcher, & Lange, 1997).

As conducted in the UTA Social Interaction Lab (depicted in Fig. 12.1), a typical dyadic interaction study begins when the participants have been recruited for a given session. If the participants are strangers, two different sign-up sheets—each carrying the name of an ostensibly different experiment—are used to help ensure that only previously unacquainted individuals will be run together in the same experimental session. If the participants are friends, dating partners, or marriage partners, more elaborate recruitment procedures (e.g., posting fliers around campus promising payment to dating couples who participate together) may be required.

Following the directions they are given on the telephone or on their respective sign-up sheets, the participants for a given session report to the appropriate waiting areas of the psychology building. (When the participants are strangers, they are asked to report to different waiting areas to ensure that their laboratory interaction will be the very first one they have.) The experimenter then collects the two participants from their waiting areas and escorts them into the observation room (see Fig. 12.1 see above, upper left). This room is furnished with a long couch in which a wireless microphone is concealed. A videocamera is concealed in a darkened storage room across the hallway from the observation room. When the doors of both rooms are left open, the dyad members' interaction can be unobtrusively videotaped with a minimal likelihood of the camera being detected.

Once they are inside the observation room, the participants are asked to place their books and belongings on the table nearest the door and to be seated on the couch. Depending on the cover story being used in a given study, the experimenter then "discovers" a reason for having to run a quick errand (either to retrieve additional consent forms or to replace a slide projector bulb that has apparently burned out). The experimenter's "unplanned" errand results in the participants being left alone together while the errand is completed. At the point at which the experimenter leaves the observation room, a research assistant in the control room activates the video equipment to begin taping the dyad members' unstructured interaction. Exactly 6 min later, at the end of the observation period, the experimenter returns to the observation room and the videotaping is terminated.

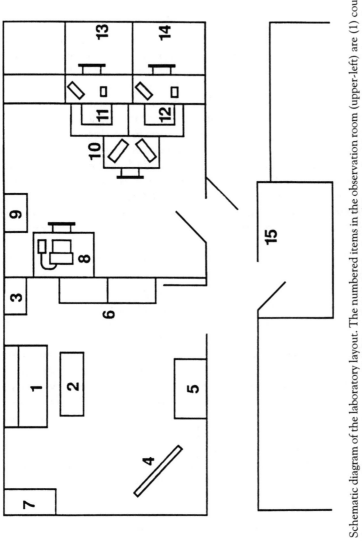

FIG. 12.1   Schematic diagram of the laboratory layout. The numbered items in the observation room (upper-left) are (1) couch, (2) coffee table, (3) slide projector, (4) projection screen, (5) table, and (6 and 7) bookcases. The numbered items in the control room (upper-right) are (8 and 9) PC and printer; (10) experimenter's workstation with identical VCRs; and (11 and 12) 27-inch color TV monitors, which face into the individual test cubicles (13 and 14). The single numbered item at the bottom (15) is the storage room in which the videocamera is concealed.

After probing for any evidence of suspicion, the experimenter conducts a partial debriefing. The participants are told that they have been videotaped for the purpose of studying their naturally occurring interaction behavior. The experimenter describes the videotaping procedure, explains the methodological importance of not telling them about the taping in advance, and informs them that their written consent is required for the tape to be used as a source of data. To assure the participants that their rights to privacy have been protected, the experimenter explains that the videotape has not yet been reviewed or studied in any way. If either participant objects to having been videotaped without permission, the tape is erased immediately. (To date, fewer than 1% of our participants have asked to have the tape of their interaction erased.)

If both participants agree to release their taped interaction as a source of data, they are asked to read and sign a consent form indicating their willingness to do so. On the same consent form, they are also asked to give their signed consent to participate in a subsequent phase of the study. In this phase, the participants are asked to view the tape of the interaction in which they have just participated and provide written records of (a) their own thoughts and feelings during the interaction and (b) their inferences about the thoughts and feelings recorded by their interaction partner. It is explained to the participants that because they are the only authorities on what their actual thoughts and feelings were during the interaction, we would like them to assist us by providing the most complete, honest, and accurate record of the content of these thoughts and feelings that they possibly can. It is further explained that they should report all of the thoughts and feelings they distinctly remember having had during the interaction, but should not report any thoughts or feelings that they experience for the first time while viewing the videotape.

If both dyad members consent to participate in the thought–feeling assessment, they are seated in separate but identical cubicles. Here they are instructed, either by means of a standard instructional videotape or by means of verbal instructions provided by the experimenter, to view a copy of the videotaped interaction in which they have just participated. The participants each view a copy of the videotape on a large color TV monitor that faces into the cubicle through a window in the control room. Each cubicle also contains a supply of thought–feeling coding forms of the type represented in Figure 12.2 and a help-button that can be used to signal the experimenter if further instruction or assistance is required.

Each participant is shown how to use a remote start–pause control to start and stop the copy of the videotape that he or she has been asked to view. The participants' task during the first pass through the tape is to view the entire interaction, but to stop the tape at each point at which they distinctly remember having had a specific thought or feeling. At each of these "tape stops," the participants use the thought–feeling coding form to record (a) the time the thought or feeling occurred (available from a time counter that is superimposed

DATE_____

NUMBER _____

M     F

| TIME | THOUGHT OR FEELING | +, 0, – | |
|------|--------------------|---------|---|
| | ☐ I was thinking:<br>☐ I was feeling: | +<br>0<br>– | |
| | ☐ I was thinking:<br>☐ I was feeling: | +<br>0<br>– | |
| | ☐ I was thinking:<br>☐ I was feeling: | +<br>0<br>– | |
| | ☐ I was thinking:<br>☐ I was feeling: | +<br>0<br>– | |
| | ☐ I was thinking:<br>☐ I was feeling: | +<br>0<br>– | |
| | ☐ I was thinking:<br>☐ I was feeling: | +<br>0<br>– | |

FIG. 12.2    Sample thought–feeling reporting form (self).

on the video image), (b) whether they were experiencing a thought or a feeling at that time, and (c) the specific content of the thought or feeling, expressed in sentence form. This procedure is repeated until both dyad members have recorded all of their actual thoughts and feelings during the videotaped interaction sequence.

The participants are then asked to view the tape a second time, this time for the purpose of inferring the specific thoughts and feelings that their interaction partner reported having had at each of his or her tape stops. The experimenter gives each participant a supply of thought–feeling inference forms to use for this purpose (see Fig. 12.3), and instructions are again provided either by an instructional videotape or by the experimenter. On this pass through the tape, the participants do not use their remote control to pause the tape. Instead, the experimenter, seated in the control room, pauses the tape at each of the times the participant's interaction partner reported having had a specific thought or feeling (i.e., each perceiver has a different set of tape stops that occur at the times when that perceiver's partner reported having had a specific thought or feeling). The participants write down their thought–feeling inferences at each of these tape stops and then use their remote controls to re-start their copy of the tape until the next tape stop occurs.

DATE_____

NUMBER_____

M     F

| TIME | THOUGHT OR FEELING | +, 0, – | |
|---|---|---|---|
| | ☐He/she was thinking:<br>☐He/she was feeling: | +<br>0<br>– | |
| | ☐He/she was thinking:<br>☐He/she was feeling: | +<br>0<br>– | |
| | ☐He/she was thinking:<br>☐He/she was feeling: | +<br>0<br>– | |
| | ☐He/she was thinking:<br>☐He/she was feeling: | +<br>0<br>– | |
| | ☐He/she was thinking:<br>☐He/she was feeling: | +<br>0<br>– | |
| | ☐He/she was thinking:<br>☐He/she was feeling: | +<br>0<br>– | |

FIG. 12.3   Sample thought–feeling inference form (other).

At each of these tape stops, the participants' task is to use the thought–feeling inference form to record (a) the time the thought or feeling occurred (as a check to ensure that all of the tape stops were accurate), (b) whether their interaction partner appeared to be experiencing a thought or a feeling at that time, and (c) their inference about the specific content of the thought or feeling, expressed in sentence form. After each thought–feeling inference has been recorded, the participant uses the remote control to re-start the videotape, which runs until the experimenter pauses it when the next tape stop occurs. This procedure is repeated until both dyad members have recorded all of their inferences about their partner's thoughts and feelings. When both participants have completed the empathic inference task and have filled out a short posttest questionnaire (the content of which varies according to the goals of the study), they are debriefed completely and then thanked and released.

As described earlier, the dyadic interaction paradigm is used to study the empathic inferences that two interactants make about each other's thoughts and feelings. Interesting variations on this paradigm can also be used, however. For examples of how the dyadic interaction paradigm can be extended to study the empathic inferences of four individuals whose role as participant versus observer can vary within the four-member groups, see Hancock and Ickes (1996) and Buysse and Ickes (1999).

*The Standard Stimulus Paradigm.*    The standard stimulus paradigm is used in studies of individual perceivers' ability to infer the specific content of the thoughts and feelings of the same set of target persons whom they view in a standard set of videotaped interactions. The prototype for these studies was Marangoni et al.'s (1995) study of empathic accuracy in a clinically relevant setting. In this study, individual participants were asked to view three videotaped interactions. Each interaction depicted a female client discussing a real-life personal problem with a male client-centered therapist.

Each client knew beforehand that her therapy session would be videotaped for use in future research, and had signed a consent form granting permission for the tape to be used for this purpose. Though simulated for research purposes, the psychotherapy sessions were videotaped live, without any rehearsal, and the genuineness and spontaneity of the sessions were evident in the clients' range of emotional expression. Immediately after their respective sessions with the therapist were completed, each client was debriefed and asked to sign a second consent form indicating her willingness to participate in an assessment of the specific thoughts and feelings she had experienced during the videotaped session. She was then escorted to the UTA Social Interaction Lab and seated in a cubicle, where she made a complete video-cued record of her thoughts and feelings during the interaction using the same thought–feeling assessment procedure described earlier.

Using these videotaped psychotherapy sessions as the standard stimulus materials, Marangoni et al. (1995) gave 80 undergraduate research participants a
chance to play amateur therapist. Each participant independently viewed all
three stimulus tapes, and in each case attempted to infer the content of the
thought or feeling the client had reported at each of 30 tape stops. Using a written log of the times at which each client's tape stops had occurred, the experimenter paused the tape at each tape stop. The participant then wrote down her
or his thought–feeling inference on the empathic inference form and re-started
the tape by means of the remote control.

It should be noted that researchers who would like to use the standard stimulus
paradigm to measure empathic accuracy need not use tapes of psychotherapy sessions as their standard stimuli. Videotapes of the unstructured interactions of
strangers, friends, dating partners, marriage partners, parent–child, teacher–student, supervisor–employee, salesperson–customer, and so on, could all be used as
the standard stimuli, depending on the goals of the particular research project in
which the tapes are presented. For an interesting application in which standard
stimulus tapes were used to study perceivers' ability to infer the thoughts and feelings of individuals who were trying to influence their partner's behavior by carrying out an assigned "hidden agenda," see Kelleher, Ickes, Dugosh (2000).

*Differences Between the Two Paradigms.*    There are four key
differences between the dyadic interaction paradigm and the standard stimulus
paradigm that have implications for the assessment of the participants' empathic accuracy. First, and most obvious, in the dyadic interaction paradigm the
dyad members are run together as paired interactants, whereas in the standard
stimulus paradigm the participants are run individually.

Second, in the dyadic interaction paradigm each of the dyad members is both
a perceiver who infers the other dyad member's thoughts and feelings and a perceptual target whose thoughts and feelings are inferred by the other dyad member. In contrast, in the standard stimulus paradigm each participant is only a
perceiver who infers the thoughts and feelings of the same set of targets to which
all other perceivers in the study are also exposed.

Third, as a corollary of the first two differences, the researcher must consider
and test the possibility that the empathic accuracy scores of the dyad members
in the first paradigm will prove to be interdependent (i.e., correlated), whereas
the researcher can generally assume that the empathic accuracy scores of the
individual participants in the second paradigm can be treated as independent
observations. Fourth, perceivers in the dyadic interaction paradigm will vary
greatly in the number of thought–feeling inferences they are asked to make, depending on the number of actual thoughts and feelings their interaction partners reported having had. In contrast, because perceivers in the standard
stimulus paradigm all see the same set of stimulus targets, they will always be
asked to make the same number of thought–feeling inferences.

Finally, there is a fifth important difference between the two paradigms that does not have implications for the assessment of the participants' empathic accuracy but does have important analytic and interpretive implications. Because each perceiver is uniquely paired with a unique target person in the dyadic interaction paradigm, perceivers are confounded with targets in a way that precludes partitioning the variance in empathic accuracy scores to obtain estimates of the respective strengths of the *perceiver effect* and the *target effect*. In other words, random-effects analysis of variance models such as the Social Relations Model (Kenny, 1994; Kenny & Albright, 1987; Malloy & Kenny, 1986) cannot be applied to dyadic interaction paradigm studies. If the goals of a given research project require that the perceiver and target effects be estimated, researchers should use either (a) a variant of the unstructured interaction paradigm in which all the members of larger groups (minimally, 4-member groups) attempt to infer all of the remaining group members' thoughts and feelings, or (b) a standard stimulus design in which many perceivers rate the same (not too small) set of target persons from videotaped stimuli. (For further discussion of this and related issues, see Ickes et al., 2000.)

*Obtaining Subjective Ratings of Empathic Accuracy.* The major problem in measuring empathic accuracy boils down to this question: How do you assess the degree to which the content of each of the perceiver's empathic inferences matches the content of the corresponding thought or feeling that the target person actually reported? Clearly, ratings of the degree of matching are required. To facilitate the collection and aggregation of such ratings, Victor Bissonnette, Stephen Trued, and I developed an interactive software program that was part of a larger DOS-based software package called *Collect Your Thoughts* (see Ickes & Trued, 1985; Ickes, Bissonnette, et al., 1990). With the aid of this program, a set of independent raters make subjective judgments about the similarity between the content of each actual thought or feeling and the corresponding inferred thought or feeling. These similarity ratings are input to the computer, where they are automatically saved into electronic data files from which the data are later retrieved, transformed, and aggregated for statistical analysis.

A similar and more powerful program, called *Read Your Mind*, was recently completed by Golden Strader. It has better data entry and data editing capabilities than its predecessor program; it is designed to run in Windows as well as in DOS; and it features a more sophisticated (and more colorful) graphics interface. Using the *Read Your Mind* program, a member of the research team can create text files that contain all of the actual thoughts and feelings reported by a given target and the corresponding inferences made by one or more perceivers. The program's graphic interface is designed to present each of the target's actual thoughts or feelings in a rectangular box at the top of the computer screen and the perceiver's corresponding inferred thought or feeling in a similar box in the middle of the screen. A "prompt box" in the lower-right corner of the screen displays the response options that independent raters should use when judging the degree of similarity in the content of each actual versus inferred thought–feeling pair. The three response options are 0 (essentially different content), 1 (similar, but not the same, content), and 2 (essentially the same content).

The raters' task is a relatively simple one. They compare the actual thought or feeling at the top of the screen with the inferred thought or feeling in the middle of the screen and input a similarity rating of 0, 1, or 2. A rating of 0 is assigned if there is no apparent similarity in the content of the actual thought–feeling versus the inferred thought–feeling; a rating of 2 is assigned if the same content is evident (though paraphrased or expressed in different words); and a score of 1 is assigned to all of the "gray area" cases in between. Table 12.1 provides examples of cases drawn from different dyads in which all of the raters displayed perfect agreement in assigning scores of 0, 1, or 2 when judging the similarity between the content of the actual versus the inferred thought–feeling.

How many raters should be assigned to this task for an empathic accuracy study? In terms of interrater reliability, the standard rule is: The more raters, the better the reliability. Without disputing this rule of thumb, I would draw on my own experience (more than 12 years of studying empathic accuracy) to suggest that a point of diminishing returns is reached in the general range of 6 to 8 raters. Below that number, interrater reliability can decline substantially; however,

TABLE 12.1

Sample Thought–Feeling Entries with Corresponding Inferences
and Mean Empathic Accuracy Ratings

| Dyad Member's Actual Thought–Feeling | Partner's inference | Average Empathic Accuracy Rating (Max = 2, Min = 0) |
|---|---|---|
| I was feeling silly because I couldn't remember my teacher's name. | She was maybe feeling sorta odd for not remembering her teacher's name. | 2 |
| I was thinking that I was not missing anything I didn't want to miss. I was thinking that I came to school to learn, not to join organizations. | He was thinking about what he was missing in school. | 1 |
| I was thinking about a previous production of the play in another city that a local radio personality was in. | She was thinking if I would ask her out. | 0 |

Note. From "Implementing and Using the Dyadic Interaction Paradigm," in C. Hendrick & M. Clark (Eds.), Review of Personality and Social Psychology: Volume 11, Research Methods in Personality and Social Psychology (p. 33), by W. Ickes, V. Bissonette, S. Garcia, & L. Stinson, 1990, Newbury Park, CA: Sage. Copyright ©1990 by Sage Publications. Reprinted with permission.

above that number, interrater reliability may not improve substantially. Whatever number of raters is used, it obviously pays to train them by conducting group training sessions that are designed to discourage the use of idiosyncratic decision rules.

More specific information about the typical levels of interrater reliability achieved in this research are provided later, in the section pertaining to the reliability of the empathic accuracy measure. Of greater immediate interest is the question of how the raters' similarity judgments are aggregated in the dyadic interaction paradigm and in the standard stimulus paradigm to create more global indices of empathic accuracy.

*Creating an Aggregated Index of Empathic Accuracy.* The procedure used to create an aggregated index of empathic accuracy is essentially the same in both the unstructured dyadic interaction paradigm and the standard stimulus paradigm. However, because of the key differences in the paradigms that I discussed earlier, some paradigm-specific variations must also be considered.

The basic assumption underlying our empathic accuracy measure is that the degree to which the perceiver "understands" the target person is a function of the degree to which the content of the perceiver's thought–feeling inferences match the content of the target's actual thoughts and feelings. From this assumption it follows that an aggregate index of empathic accuracy can be derived by measuring the perceiver's empathic accuracy for each thought–feeling inference made, and then summing or averaging the resulting empathic scores across the entire set of thought–feeling inferences. Because an aggregate index of this type can be computed for any given target person, a more global measure of empathic accuracy can be derived by summing or averaging the target-specific indices to create a single cross-target index.

In the dyadic interaction paradigm, each dyad member reports a set of actual thoughts and feelings, which the other dyad member subsequently attempts to infer. Because the number of thoughts and feelings reported is quite variable, both within and between dyads, it is necessary to control for the number of inferences made when computing an aggregated index of empathic accuracy for each dyad member. The simplest way to do this begins by treating the similarity values assigned by each rater as "accuracy points," which can vary from 0 to 2 for a single rater's judgment of a single thought–feeling inference. Assuming high interrater reliability, the accuracy points assigned by the raters can be averaged for each inference made, and these averages can then be summed across all of the inferences made by the perceiver to compute the "total accuracy points" the perceiver has achieved.

It is important to recognize, however, that the total accuracy points will be greater for perceivers who make many inferences than for those who make few inferences. The most straightforward way of correcting for this complication in dyadic interaction studies is to divide each perceiver's total accuracy points by the number of inferences made to yield an index of the proportion of accuracy points obtained relative to the total number of accuracy points possible. When this index is further divided by 2 (effectively changing our 0-to-2 similarity rating scale to a 0-to-1 scale) and then multiplied by 100 to convert the first two digits from decimals to integers, the result is a percentage-scaled empathic accuracy index that has a theoretical range of 0 to 100.

This percentage measure of empathic accuracy is conveniently scaled, easy to interpret, and corrects reasonably well for differences in the total number of inferences made. It is by no means a perfect index, however. For one thing, as with many percentage or percentage-analogue measures, its distribution can be skewed and require normalization through an appropriate transformation (e.g., arc sine). For another, it provides less stable estimates of empathic accuracy when the number of inferences made is small (e.g., 5 or less) than when the number of inferences made is large (e.g., 20 or more). To help minimize this problem, researchers should establish a predetermined criterion according to which they will delete the empathic accuracy data for dyads in which one or both members report a very small number of thoughts and feelings.

Creating an aggregated index of empathic accuracy is further complicated in the dyadic interaction paradigm by the possibility that the dyad members' empathic accuracy scores may be interdependent (i.e., correlated). If significant interdependence is evident, the appropriate unit of analysis might be the dyad-level empathic accuracy score rather than the individual-level one (Kenny & Judd, 1986). The obvious first step to take in addressing this complication is to compute the intraclass correlation of the dyad members' empathic accuracy scores (or the partial intraclass correlation for data sets in which the dyad members are distinguishable on the basis of a characteristic such as gender). This computation will enable the researcher to assess the degree of interdependence and its likelihood of occurring by chance (Gonzalez & Griffin, 1997). If substantial interdependence is evident, special statistical techniques may be required to analyze the data (see Kenny, 1988; Gonzalez & Griffin, 1997).

Fortunately, the complications of creating an aggregated index of empathic accuracy in the dyadic interaction paradigm are rarely an issue in the standard stimulus paradigm. In this second paradigm, the researcher can typically ensure that (a) the number of thought–feeling inferences made will be the same for all perceivers; (b) this number will be relatively large, rather than small; and (c) the perceivers' empathic accuracy scores can be treated as independent observations because the perceivers were tested separately, rather than in dyads or in larger groups.

## Reliability of the Empathic Accuracy Measure

How reliably can empathic accuracy be measured using the assessment procedure I just described? The short answer is: very reliably. The longer and more detailed answer requires that I start by distinguishing two types of reliability that are relevant to the empathic accuracy measure: interrater reliability and cross-target consistency. Although other aspects of reliability could also be computed (e.g., interitem reliability, cross-situational or cross-temporal reliability), the most commonly reported types are the ones I now review.

*Interrater Reliability.*    The first way to assess the reliability of the empathic accuracy measure is in terms of interrater reliability. Assuming that all raters have provided content similarity judgments for all of the thought–feeling inferences made in a given study, one can assess interrater reliability by creating a data matrix in which the columns are defined by the various raters and the rows are defined by the various thought–feeling inferences whose accuracy (i.e., content similarity) each of the raters has assessed. Cronbach's alpha can then be computed for the data in this matrix, treating raters (the column variable) as analogous to the items on a psychological scale and treating the individual thought–feeling inferences (the row variable) as analogous to the respondents who completed the scale.

Assessed in this way, interrater reliability in our empathic accuracy studies has consistently been quite high, ranging from a low of .85 in a study in which only 4 raters were used to a high of .98 in two studies in which either 7 or 8 raters were used. Across all of the studies we have conducted to date, the average cross-rater correlation has been about .55, and the average interrater alpha coefficient has been about .90. One way to maximize interrater reliability in a given study is to use the output of the Cronbach's alpha analysis to exclude the data for one or more raters whose data, if included, would substantially lower the overall alpha value. A complementary way that we have found useful is to factor analyze the same rating data (using the default, principal components solution) and then examine the output to see if any of the raters uniquely define a secondary factor, rather than loading highly on the first, common factor. If such raters exist, the odds are good that they used a uniquely different criterion in doing the content similarity rating task than the other raters did. In general, we find that they are the same raters who are identified by the output of the alpha analysis as the ones whose data should probably be excluded.

*Cross-Target Consistency.*    The second way to assess the reliability of the empathic accuracy measure is in terms of cross-target consistency. This aspect of the measure's reliability is applicable only in the standard stimulus paradigm—that is, only in designs in which individual perceivers infer the thoughts and feelings of the same set of multiple target persons. Cross-target consistency is assessed by treating the perceiver's aggregated empathic accuracy score for each of the target persons as analogous to one of the items on an $n$-item scale, and then computing Cronbach's alpha to estimate the degree to which the perceivers maintain the same rank ordering in their empathic accuracy scores across the set of "items" (i.e., target persons).

Cross-target consistency in the first standard stimulus study conducted by Marangoni et al. (1995) was .86 across the three target tapes used. In a more recent study using highly edited versions of the same three tapes, Gesn and Ickes (1999) reported an alpha of .91. These high alpha values might be partly attributable to homogeneity in the set of target persons (all three were middle-class, college-educated, Anglo-American women) and in the problems they discussed (women's relationship issues). Still, the data are compelling in their implication that our empathic accuracy measure reflects a stable and reliably measured social skill that perceivers can apply to different target persons with a striking degree of cross-target consistency (Gesn & Ickes, 1999).

## Validity of the Empathic Accuracy Measure

What evidence is there for the construct validity of our empathic accuracy measure? The short answer is: quite a bit. The longer and more detailed answer emphasizes the measure's face validity and predictive validity but essentially draws a blank with respect to the measure's convergent and discriminant validity.

*Face Validity.*    In psychometric theory, face validity refers to the extent to which the measure would appear, on the surface, to be a plausible measure of the construct it is intended to assess. The appeal here is to logic, common sense, and consensus: Would most reasonable people agree that the measure appears to address the intended construct? By this criterion, I think most reasonable people would agree that a face valid measure of empathic accuracy would be one that assessed the degree to which people can accurately infer the specific content of other people's reported thoughts and feelings.

It is important to note, however, that the face validity—and, indeed, the overall construct validity—of our empathic accuracy measure depends not only on the accuracy of the perceiver's inferences but also on the accuracy of the target person's report of his or her actual thoughts and feelings. It is for this reason that our methodology contains a number of safeguards designed to ensure the completeness and accuracy of such reports. These safeguards include a video-cued recall procedure that occurs immediately after the respondents' interaction has occurred, a "research collaborator" task set that encourages targets to report their thoughts and feelings accurately and completely, and the written assurance that perceivers will never see the targets' actual reported thoughts and feelings. In addition, there is considerable evidence for the content validity of target persons' reported thoughts and feelings, and much of this evidence is reported in Ickes, Robertson, Took, and Teng (1986). In the final analysis, however, we must take the accuracy of the target's reported thoughts and feelings largely on faith, as there is no realistic way of second-guessing the target's own judgments in this regard.

*Predictive Validity.* Face validity, though certainly important, is often less important than predictive validity in convincing the scientific community that one's measure validly assesses the intended underlying construct. For a dramatic example that is especially pertinent in the present case, consider Davis and Kraus's (1997) quantitative meta-analysis of potential individual difference predictors of various measures of interpersonal accuracy and sensitivity. This ambitious meta-analysis included 36 studies conducted since Cronbach's (1955, 1958) critiques and examined 251 effects involving 32 individual-difference variables and 30 interpersonal accuracy measures.

Highly represented in these studies were several self-report measures of empathy, social intelligence, and social sensitivity—measures that most reasonable people would readily characterize as having good face validity. Ironically, however, Davis and Kraus found essentially no evidence for the predictive validity of these measures with respect to relevant performance measures of interpersonal accuracy and sensitivity. The results of their meta-analysis revealed mean effect sizes of nearly zero for various measures of self-reported dispositional empathy (.01), femininity (.00), social intelligence (.08), and social sensitivity and thoughtfulness (.04). Clearly, the face validity of such measures was no guarantee of their predictive validity—a finding that led my colleagues and me to propose that either "individuals are so biased or so lacking in self-insight that they cannot report accurately/objectively about their own level of empathic ability, or [else] individual differences on this dimension are remarkably subtle and difficult to discern" (Ickes et al., 2000, p. 220). (See also Riggio & Riggio, chap. 7, this volume, for a discussion of the validity of self-reported interpersonal sensitivity.)

Fortunately, the evidence for the predictive validity of our performance-based measure of empathic accuracy is considerably better than that for the predictive validity of the kinds of self-report measures discussed earlier. A number of predictive validity studies were conducted early in our program of research. One of our first predictions was that if our procedure for assessing empathic accuracy was indeed valid, close friends should display higher levels of accuracy than strangers when inferring the content of each other's thoughts and feelings. This prediction was confirmed in studies by Stinson and Ickes (1992) and Graham (1994), which revealed that, on average, the empathic accuracy scores of close, same-sex friends were about 50% higher than those of same-sex strangers—a statistically significant difference in both studies.

In the clinically relevant study conducted by Marangoni et al. (1995), the predictive validity of our empathic accuracy measure was further tested with respect to the hypotheses that (a) perceivers' empathic scores should be significantly greater at the end of the psychotherapy tapes than at the beginning, reflecting their greater acquaintance with the clients and their problems, and (b) perceivers who receive immediate feedback about the clients' actual thoughts and feelings during the middle portion of each tape should subsequently achieve higher empathic accuracy scores than perceivers who do not receive such feedback. Statistically significant support for both of these hypotheses was obtained.

Simpson et al. (1995) proposed that, if our measure of empathic accuracy is predictively valid, dating partners should display particularly low empathic accuracy scores in relationship-threatening conditions in which they should be motivated to inaccurately infer each other's thoughts and feelings. They reported converging support for this prediction in their study of 82 dating couples. More recently, Gesn and Ickes (1999) predicted that empathic accuracy in the clinically relevant situation studied by Marangoni et al. (1995) should depend more on the clients' verbal cues than on their nonverbal cues. They found strong support for this hypothesis in a study that varied the information channels to which the perceivers were exposed.

Finally, Kelleher, Ickes, and Dugosh (2000) predicted that perceivers who had been given an accurate "frame" for interpreting a target person's motivation in a social situation would be more accurate in reading the target person's frame-relevant thoughts and feelings than would perceivers who had been given either an inaccurate frame or no frame at all (cf. Goffman, 1974). This prediction was also confirmed, contributing further to the growing body of evidence supporting the validity of our empathic accuracy measure.

*Convergent and Discriminant Validity.* Establishing the convergent and discriminant validity of our empathic accuracy measure has proved to be more difficult and complicated than my colleagues and I had expected. Although Hall (1998) reported many significant correlates of interpersonal sensitivity in her meta-analytic review, Davis and Kraus (1997) concluded that self-report measures of empathically relevant dispositions have conspicuously failed to predict performance on most interpersonal accuracy–sensitivity tests. Unfortunately, with regard to our measure of empathic accuracy, the results obtained over the past decade or so are consistent with Davis and Kraus's more pessimistic conclusion. As my colleagues and I noted in a recent article:

> As in the much larger set of interpersonal accuracy studies reviewed by Davis and Kraus (1997), self-reported dispositional empathy measures have consistently failed to predict perceivers' performance on empathic accuracy tasks. The two most relevant studies are replete with nonsignificant correlations between perceivers' empathic accuracy scores and a range of self-report measures that include (a) our own composite scales for assessing "everyday mind reading" ability, perspective-taking, and emotional contagion (rs = -.06, .05, and .11, respectively; Ickes, Stinson, et al., 1994); and (b) Davis's (1983) measures of perspective-taking, empathic concern, fantasy identification, and personal distress (rs = -.14, .04, -.11, and .06, respectively; Ickes, Stinson, et al., 1990). Even more disturbing from the standpoint of Taft's (1955) and Davis and Kraus's (1997) reviews, the more intellective measures of need for cognition and grade point average also failed to predict aggregated empathic accuracy scores (rs = .00 and -.05, respectively) in a study involving 128 participant-perceivers (Ickes, et al., 1994). (Ickes, Buysse, et al., 2000)

Given the problem of trying to use empathy-relevant self-report measures to establish convergent validity in this case, would we be more successful if we used another performance-based measure instead? The answer, with respect to our single attempt so far, is "no." In his master's thesis study, Mortimer (1996) attempted to relate his participants' cross-target measure of empathic accuracy (based on the Marangoni et al., 1995, tapes) to their scores on the Interpersonal Perception Task (IPT; Costanzo & Archer, 1989)—the interpersonal sensitivity measure that he felt should most resemble our empathic accuracy measure in its stimulus materials and available channels of information. The resulting correlation (.06) was not significantly different from zero.

It is tempting to attribute this null result to the likelihood that empathic accuracy scores are influenced more by verbal cues than by nonverbal cues (see Gesn & Ickes, 1999), in contrast to other measures of interpersonal sensitivity (e.g., the IPT and the PONS—the Profile of Nonverbal Sensitivity test) for which nonverbal cues are the predominant, or even exclusive, influence. The explanation cannot be this simple, however, because comparable null results have also been reported when researchers have attempted to correlate perceivers' scores on primarily "nonverbal" measures such as the IPT and the PONS (e.g., Ambady, Hallahan, & Rosenthal, 1995; Bernieri & Gillis, 1995; Gesn, Bernieri, Grahe, & Gada, 1998). The explanation for these null findings is not yet clear, although they appear to suggest that different types of interpersonal sensitivity exist and that they are not necessarily related to each other (see also Hall, chap. 8, this volume). At any rate, if performance-based measures of interpersonal sensitivity are uncorrelated and fail to demonstrate convergent validity, then establishing the discriminant validity of such measures becomes equally problematic, and other validity criteria (in particular, predictive validity) must be relied on instead.

## POINTS OF DEPARTURE

The lines of dialogue that opened this chapter can also be used to close it. In this chapter, I have attempted to provide a more complete (and less flippant?) answer to the question "Can you really measure people's ability to 'read' other people's minds?" By now it should be evident that the procedure my colleagues and I have developed for assessing empathic accuracy is not only reliable in terms of its interrater reliability and cross-target consistency, but is also valid in terms of its predictive and face validity. Although using this procedure admittedly involves a lot of work, we think that it is worth the effort when one considers the range of important research issues that are opened up for scientific exploration.

Many of the research issues that have already been addressed in empathic accuracy research are discussed at length in the book, *Empathic Accuracy* (Ickes, 1997). They include:

the evolutionary and social-developmental origins of empathic accuracy, its physiological aspects, its relation to gender and other individual difference variables, its dynamic role in the context of personal relationships, its relevance to applied domains
such as clinical and counseling psychology, and its sensitivity to the processes of mental control (p. 6).

These issues will continue to be of interest in empathic accuracy research, but
they will increasingly compete for attention with a host of new issues that interpersonal sensitivity researchers will want to explore. We hope the procedures
described in this chapter leave them better equipped for their research expedi-
tions than they might otherwise have been.

Q: So, is that it? Are you finished now?
A: What do you think? (Tell me. I'd really like to know.)

## ACKNOWLEDGMENTS

I thank Ann Buysse, Paul R. Gesn, Sara Hodges, David A. Kenny, Golden
Strader, and the editors for their comments on a previous version of this chapter.

## REFERENCES

Ambady, N., Hallahan, M., & Rosenthal, R. (1995). On judging and being judged accurately
in zero-acquaintance situations. Journal of Personality and Social Psychology, 69, 518–529.
Asch, S. E. (1946). Forming impressions of personality. Journal of Abnormal and Social Psychology, 41, 258–290.
Bernieri, F., & Gillis, J. S. (1995). Personality correlates of accuracy in a social perception
task. Perceptual and Motor Skills, 81, 168–170.
Bissonnette, V. L., Rusbult, C. E., & Kilpatrick, S. D. (1997). Empathic accuracy and marital
conflict resolution. In W. Ickes (Ed.), Empathic accuracy (pp. 251–281). New York:
Guilford.
Buysse, A., & Ickes, W. (1999). Topic-relevant cognition and empathic accuracy in labora-
tory discussions of safer sex. Psychology and Health, 14, 351–366.
Costanzo, M., & Archer, D. (1989). Interpreting the expressive behavior of others: The In-
terpersonal Perception Task. Journal of Nonverbal Behavior, 13, 225–245.
Cronbach, L. J. (1955). Processes affecting scores on "understanding of others" and "assumed
similarity." Psychological Bulletin, 52, 177–193.
Cronbach, L. J. (1958). Proposals leading to analytic treatment of social perception scores. In
R. Tagiuri & L. Petrullo (Eds.), Person perception and interpersonal behavior (pp. 353–379).
Stanford, CA: Stanford University Press.
Davis, M. H. (1983). Measuring individual differences in empathy: Evidence for a multidi-
mensional approach. Journal of Personality and Social Psychology, 51, 167–184.
Davis, M. H., & Kraus, L. A. (1997). Personality and empathic accuracy. In W. Ickes (Ed.),
Empathic accuracy (pp. 144–168). New York: Guilford.

Ekman, P., & Friesen, W. V. (1975). *Unmasking the face: A guide to recognizing emotions from facial cues.* Englewood Cliffs, NJ: Prentice-Hall.

Estes, S. G. (1938). Judging personality from expressive behavior. *Journal of Abnormal and Social Psychology, 33,* 217–236.

Funder, D. C., & Colvin, C. R. (1988). Friends and strangers: Acquaintanceship, agreement, and the accuracy of personality judgment. *Journal of Personality and Social Psychology, 55,* 149–158.

Gesn, P. R., Bernieri, F., Grahe, J. E., & Gada, N. (1998). *Performance measures of interpersonal perception accuracy do not correlate.* Unpublished manuscript, University of Toledo, OH.

Gesn, P. R., & Ickes, W. (1999). The development of meaning contexts for empathic accuracy: Channel and sequence effects. *Journal of Personality and Social Psychology, 77,* 746–761.

Goffman, E. (1974). *Frame analysis.* Boston: Northeastern University Press.

Goleman, D. (1995). *Emotional intelligence.* New York: Bantam.

Gonzalez, R., & Griffin, D. (1997). On the statistics of interdependence: Treating dyadic data with respect. In S. Duck, K. Dindia, W. Ickes, R. Milardo, R. Mills, & B. Sarason (Eds.), *Handbook of personal relationships: Theory, research, and interventions* (2nd ed., pp. 271–302). Chichester, England: Wiley.

Graham, T. (1994). *Gender, relationship, and target differences in empathic accuracy.* Unpublished masters thesis, University of Texas at Arlington.

Hall, J. A. (1984). *Nonverbal sex differences: Communication accuracy and expressive style.* Baltimore: Johns Hopkins University Press.

Hall, J. A. (1998). How big are nonverbal sex differences? The case of smiling and sensitivity to nonverbal cues. In D.J. Canary & K. Dindia (Eds.), *Sex differences and similarities in communication* (pp. 155–177). Mahwah, NJ: Lawrence Erlbaum Associates.

Hancock, M., & Ickes, W. (1996). Empathic accuracy: When does the perceiver–target relationship make a difference? *Journal of Social and Personal Relationships, 13,* 179–199.

Ickes, W. (1993). Empathic accuracy. *Journal of Personality, 61,* 587–609.

Ickes, W. (1997). Introduction. In W. Ickes (Ed.), *Empathic accuracy* (pp. 1–16). New York: Guilford Press.

Ickes, W., Bissonnette, V., Garcia, S., & Stinson, L. (1990). Implementing and using the dyadic interaction paradigm. In C. Hendrick & M. Clark (Eds.), *Review of personality and social psychology: Volume 11, Research methods in personality and social psychology* (pp. 16–44). Newbury Park, CA: Sage.

Ickes, W., Buysse, A., Pham, H., Rivers, K., Erickson, J. R., Hancock, M., Kelleher, J., & Gesn, P. R. (2000). On the difficulty of distinguishing "good" and "poor" perceivers: A social relations analysis of empathic accuracy data. *Personal relationships, 1,* 219–234.

Ickes, W., Hancock, M., Graham, T., Gesn, P. R., & Mortimer, D. C. (1994). *(Nonsignificant) individual-difference correlates of perceivers' empathic accuracy scores.* Unpublished data, University of Texas at Arlington.

Ickes, W., Robertson, E., Took, W., & Teng, G. (1986). Naturalistic social cognition: Methodology, assessment, and validation. *Journal of Personality and Social Psychology, 51,* 66–82.

Ickes, W., Stinson, L., Bissonnette, V., & Garcia, S. (1990). Naturalistic social cognition: Empathic accuracy in mixed-sex dyads. *Journal of Personality and Social Psychology, 59,* 730–742.

Ickes, W., & Tooke, W. (1988). The observational method: Studying the interactions of minds and bodies. In S. Duck, D. F. Hay, S. E. Hobfoll, W. Ickes, & B. Montgomery (Eds.), *Handbook of personal relationships: Theory, research, and interventions* (pp. 79–97). Chichester, England: Wiley.

Ickes, W., & Trued, S. (1985). A system for collecting dyadic interaction data on the Apple II. *Electronic Social Psychology. [Online serial]*, 1, Article no. 8501012.

Kagan, N. (1977). *Affective sensitivity test: Validity and reliability.* Paper presented at the convention of the American Psychological Association, San Francisco.

Kelleher, J., Ickes, W., & Dugosh, J. (2000). *Hidden and revealed agendas: Effects of frames on empathic accuracy.* Manuscript under editorial review.

Kenny, D. A. (1988). The analysis of data from two-person relationships. In S. Duck, D. Hay, S. Hobfoll, W. Ickes, & B. Montgomery (Eds.), *Handbook of personal relationships: Theory, research, and interventions* (pp. 57–77). Chichester, England: Wiley.

Kenny, D. A. (1994). *Interpersonal perception: A social relations analysis.* New York: Guilford.

Kenny, D. A., & Albright, L. (1987). Accuracy in interpersonal perception: A social relations analysis. *Psychological Bulletin, 102,* 390–402.

Kenny, D. A., & Judd, C. M. (1986). Consequences of violating the independence assumption in analysis of variance. *Psychological Bulletin, 99,* 422–431.

Knudson, R. A., Sommers, A. A., & Golding, S. L. (1980). Interpersonal perception and mode of resolution in marital conflict. *Journal of Personality and Social Psychology, 38,* 251–263.

Laing, R. D., Phillipson, H., & Lee, A. R. (1966). *Interpersonal perception: A theory and a method of research.* New York: Springer.

Levenson, R. W., & Ruef, A. M. (1992). Empathy: A physiological substrate. *Journal of Personality and Social Psychology, 63,* 234–246.

Levenson, R. W., & Ruef, A. M. (1997). Physiological aspects of emotional knowledge and rapport. In W. Ickes (Ed.), *Empathic accuracy* (pp. 44–72). New York: Guilford.

Malloy, T. E., & Kenny, D. A. (1986). The social relations model: An integrative model for personality research. *Journal of Personality, 54,* 199–225.

Marangoni, C., Garcia, S., Ickes, W., & Teng, G. (1995). Empathic accuracy in a clinically relevant setting. *Journal of Personality and Social Psychology, 68,* 854–869.

McCrae, R. R. (1982). Consensual validation of personality traits: Evidence from self-reports and ratings. *Journal of Personality and Social Psychology, 43,* 293–303.

Mortimer, D. C. (1996). *"Reading" ourselves "reading" others: Actual versus self-estimated empathic accuracy.* Unpublished master's thesis, University of Texas at Arlington.

Newmark, C. S., Woody, G., & Ziff, D. (1977). Understanding and similarity in relation to marital satisfaction. *Journal of Clinical Psychology, 33,* 83–86.

Noller, P. (1980). Misunderstandings in marital communication: A study of couples' nonverbal communication. *Journal of Personality and Social Psychology, 39,* 1135–1148.

Noller, P. (1981). Gender and marital adjustment level differences in decoding messages from spouses and strangers. *Journal of Personality and Social Psychology, 41,* 272–278.

Norman, W. T., & Goldberg, L. R. (1966). Raters, ratees, and randomness in personality. *Journal of Personality, 4,* 681–691.

Rogers, C. R. (1957). The necessary and sufficient conditions of therapeutic personality change. *Journal of Consulting Psychology, 21,* 95–103.

Rogers, C. R., & Dymond, R. F. (1954). *Psychotherapy and personality change.* Chicago: University of Chicago Press.

Rosenthal, R., Hall, J. A., DiMatteo, M. R., Rogers, P. L., & Archer, D. (1979). *Sensitivity to nonverbal communication: The PONS test.* Baltimore: Johns Hopkins University Press.

Sillars, A. L. (1989). Communication, uncertainty and understanding in marriage. In B. Dervin, L. Grossberg, B. O'Keefe, & E. Wartella (Eds.), *Rethinking communication: Vol. 2. Paradigm exemplars* (pp. 307–328). Newbury Park, CA: Sage.

Simpson, J. A., Ickes, W., & Blackstone, T. (1995). When the head protects the heart: Empathic accuracy in dating relationships. *Journal of Personality and Social Psychology, 69,* 629–641.

Stinson, L., & Ickes, W. (1992). Empathic accuracy in the interactions of male friends versus male strangers. *Journal of Personality and Social Psychology, 62,* 787–797.

Taft, R. (1955). The ability to judge people. *Psychological Bulletin, 52,* 1–23.

Thomas, G., Fletcher, G. J. O., & Lange, C. (1997). On-line empathic accuracy and projection in marital interaction. *Journal of Personality and Social Psychology, 72,* 839–850.

# ❧ 13 ❧

# Using Standard
# Content Methodology
# to Assess Nonverbal
# Sensitivity in Dyads

Patricia Noller
*University of Queensland, Australia*

When one member of a couple continually misunderstands the other, it may be important to know the answers to such questions as, Is the problem most likely to be in the encoding (or message sending) or in the decoding (or message receiving)? In other words, is the communication problem occurring because the message is not clear, or is it occurring because of the receiver's (or listener's) attitude to the message or to the person sending the message? Communication problems can occur in either mode. There are several other relevant questions. Is the problem in the words or in the nonverbal behavior accompanying those words (i.e., is the problem what he said or the way that he said it)? What is needed to answer these and other related questions is a methodology that allows the researcher to assess the effects of encoding and the effects of decoding separately. This chapter is about the development of such a methodology, using the standard content paradigm (Duckworth, 1975; Kahn, 1970; Mehrabian & Ferris, 1967). The methodology described herein is based on the work of these researchers, but it involves developments that allow a more sophisticated exploration of the kinds of questions raised.

The standard content methodology was primarily devised to test a particular type of nonverbal sensitivity: sensitivity or accuracy in decoding nonverbal messages that accompany verbal statements. If communication problems tend to be related to the way a message is sent rather than the content of the message

(Gottman, Markman, & Notarius, 1977), then a way must be found to separate the nonverbal component of the message (facial expressions, gestures, gaze, tone of voice) from the verbal component (the words that are actually said). In standard content methodology, the words are controlled by having all the participants use the same words to send messages of different emotional valence (e.g., positive, neutral, or negative). For example, participants may be asked to say "What are you doing?" with positive, neutral, and negative intentions (Duckworth, 1975). In the positive situation the words would mean "I'm pleased to see you doing that"; in the negative situation they would mean "How many times have I asked you not to do that"; and in the neutral situation they would mean "I'm just interested to know what you are doing."

It is important to note that the words used in standard content messages need to be ambiguous, so that the meaning of those words can be altered, depending on the nonverbal behaviors that accompany the words. Central to the method is the assumption that if words are held constant, then changes in the meaning of the message must be the result of changes in the nonverbal behavior accompanying that message.

Sometimes standard content can be in the form of meaningless content, such as when participants are asked to express a particular emotion or attitude (e.g., anger, sadness, happiness, inferiority) while repeating the alphabet or counting (e.g., Argyle, Salter, Nicholson, Williams, & Burgess, 1970; Davitz & Davitz, 1959). Davitz and Davitz had individuals recite the alphabet while expressing 10 different emotions in the nonverbal channels, whereas Argyle and his colleagues asked participants to count while expressing superior, inferior, or neutral status to another person. These tasks would seem to be both artificial and difficult, although the advantage of the latter task is that the messages were at least sent to other people in a relational context.

Standard content tasks involving ambiguous messages have been used by a number of researchers. Mehrabian and Ferris (1967) had participants encode the single words "really" and "maybe" while varying the affective tone of the message they were sending. Duckworth (1975) had the participants in his study ask the question "What are you doing?" in ways that expressed different feelings such as anger or surprise. (See also Nowicki & Duke, chap. 10, this volume).

## THEORETICAL ISSUES

The impetus for studying nonverbal accuracy in couple relationships comes from the contention that the marriage relationship is likely to be particularly prone to misunderstandings because of its intensity and intimacy (Bach & Wyden, 1969). These problems are particularly likely to occur when the verbal component of messages is ambiguous. Given an ambiguous message from his or her partner, a person who is feeling hurt or angry is likely to interpret that message negatively, whereas a person who is feeling happy and relaxed may be more likely to interpret the message in a positive way.

Standard content methodology is primarily used to assess the extent to which members of a dyad understand or misunderstand the nonverbal aspects of the messages they send to one another. As Gottman et al. (1976) explained, the important issue is whether the intention of the message sent by the encoder equals the impact of that message on the receiver or decoder. In such a situation, the nonverbal component of the message is likely to be crucial in determining whether the message is understood correctly (Gottman et al., 1977). Of course, misunderstandings are not necessarily due to problems in the decoder or listener. The message may not be encoded clearly for a range of reasons, including lack of communication skill, lack of expressivity, ambivalence about the issue, or affect that interferes with the sending of the message (Noller, 1984).

Gottman et al. (1976) explored misunderstandings between married couples using a technique called the talk-table that enabled participants to rate the positivity of the intention of their messages when they were the message-sender and the positivity of the impact of the partner's message on them when they were the message-receiver. These researchers were particularly interested in the issue of whether distressed and nondistressed couples differed in terms of the number of misunderstandings that occurred. Gottman and his colleagues found that distressed and nondistressed participants did not differ with regard to the intent of their messages (as reported) but that they differed with regard to the impact of the partner's messages on them, with messages sent to distressed spouses having a more negative impact.

There are several possible explanations for why the distressed couples differed in terms of impact, but not in terms of intention. It may be, as suggested earlier, that the unhappy couples had more negative perceptions of their spouses and thus interpreted their messages more negatively. It is also possible that the ratings of intent were affected by social desirability, with encoders rating the intention of their messages as more positive than their actual intention. Alternatively the negative perceptions of their marriages held by distressed couples may have affected the way their messages were sent, making those messages more negative than intended because of the negative attitude being "leaked" through the nonverbal channels (Ekman & Friesen, 1969). Whatever the explanation, the difficulty in separating encoding effects from decoding effects with the talk-table highlights the problems with this methodology.

## STANDARD CONTENT METHODOLOGY
## WITH MARRIED COUPLES

The first researcher to use standard content methodology to assess the encoding and decoding skills of married couples was Kahn (1970). Kahn designed two sets of standard content messages: eight messages to be sent by husbands to wives and eight messages to be sent by wives to husbands. Sample cards used by encoders and decoders are presented in Tables 13.1 and 13.2, and the messages are presented in full in the Appendix. Note that the message "What are you doing?" as used by Duckworth (1975) was added to each set by Noller (1980), making nine messages in each set.

I followed Kahn (1970) in using a different set of messages for husbands and wives. In order to be able to test for gender differences, it is important that the two sets of messages are of a similar level of difficulty and that the alternatives are similarly positive, neutral, and negative. This issue could be tested by having an independent group of participants rate the alternatives on a scale of positivity–negativity, and then comparing positivity ratings for positive, neutral, and negative alternatives.

### TABLE 13.1

**Example of an Encoding Card**

| Section | Content |
| --- | --- |
| Situation | You and your husband are sitting alone on a winter evening. You feel cold. |
| Intention | You feel that he is being inconsiderate in not having turned up the heat by now and you want him to turn it up right away. |
| Statement | I'm cold, aren't you? |

### TABLE 13.2

**Example of a Decoding Card**

| Situation—as provided to the encoder | You and your husband are sitting alone on a Winter evening. You feel cold. |
| --- | --- |
| Alternatives—as provided to the encoder | a. You wonder if it's only you who are cold, or he is cold, too. |
| | b. You want him to warm you with physical affection. |
| | c. You feel that he is inconsiderate in not having turned up the heat by now, and you want him to turn it up straight away. |

*Note.* These alternatives are worded in exactly the same way as on the encoder's card. An alternative would be to word the alternatives in the third person. For example, "She wonders whether she is the only one who is cold or whether I am cold, too."

In Kahn's (1970) experiment using the Marital Communication Scale, each partner was asked to send a number of messages to their partner, using words set by the experimenter (Marital Communication Scale) but encoding one of three possible meanings that those words could convey, if accompanied by the appropriate nonverbal behavior. The task of the other partner was to decide which of the three possible meanings was intended.

In his own experiment, Kahn (1970) did not attempt to differentiate the separate contributions of each member of the dyad. Instead, he added together the score (i.e., the number of items "correctly" decoded or consistent with the intention), when the wife was the encoder and the husband the decoder, and the score obtained when the husband was the encoder and the wife was the decoder. Adding the two sets of scores together in this way implies that individual differences in the contribution of each member of the dyad to the total score are irrelevant or uninteresting. This position is unlikely to be supported by the data, given that there are individual differences in both the encoding and decoding of nonverbal messages, as well as evidence for gender differences (Hall, 1978). It is interesting to note that Kahn found that happy couples had significantly higher total scores than did unhappy couples. Despite this finding, however, Kahn left many questions unanswered.

## METHODOLOGICAL ISSUES

### Separating the Contributions of Encoders and Decoders

There are several problems with the way that Kahn (1970) carried out his study of misunderstandings in married couples using standard content methodology. The most critical one is the failure to separate the contributions of the encoder and the decoder. It is possible that a couple could receive a particular score because of their skill at encoding, their skill at decoding, or some combination of the two. It is also possible that one member of the dyad could encode and decode more accurately than the other. What is needed is a way to give each partner an encoding score and a decoding score.

Noller (1980, 1984) solved this problem by videotaping the messages as they were encoded and then showing these messages to a different sample of decoders who were asked to decide whether the message had a positive, negative, or neutral intent. Each message thus received a score that was the proportion of decoders other than the spouse (external decoders) who correctly identified the intent of the message (as set by the experimenter). If two thirds or more of these external decoders correctly identified the intent of the message, then that message was considered as successfully sent and was labeled a "good communication." If fewer than two thirds of the external decoders correctly identified the intent of the message, it was considered a "bad communication," with an "encoding error" being defined as a bad communication incorrectly decoded by the spouse. "Decoding errors" were scored when a good communication was incorrectly decoded by the spouse. "Idiosyncratic communications," on the other hand, were scored when a bad communication was correctly decoded by the spouse. It is important to acknowledge that these cut-off points were arbitrary, and generally conservative. The terms "good" and "bad" are not used in any absolute sense.

In other words, whether a message was a good communication or a bad communication was determined by how well the external decoders were able to understand the message. Good communications were assumed to be sent clearly and easily decoded, whereas bad communications were assumed to be poorly sent and difficult to decode. Encoding errors were messages that both the external decoders and the spouse had difficulty decoding. Decoding errors were messages that the external decoders were able to understand accurately but that the spouse was unable to understand correctly. The situation where the spouse was able to decode a message correctly when the external decoders were wrong was classified as an idiosyncratic message and as indicative of a "private message system" in the couple (Gottman & Porterfield, 1981).

## Criterion of Accuracy

The criterion of accuracy for all messages was whether intent (as set by the experimenter) was equal to the impact reported by the decoder. Although using this strategy could have been problematic if the encoder was not very accurate at message sending, potential problems are dealt with by having all messages checked for ease of decoding as described earlier. Using this procedure provides an objective criterion of accuracy and enables the independent contributions to be assessed of both the encoder and the decoder, as well as of each member of the dyad. In contrast to the talk-table study discussed earlier, the experimenter did not have to rely on self-reports of intention, but had a relatively objective criterion by which to assess the message.

## Calculating Scores

In Noller's (1980, 1984) study, four scores were derived from the data for each participant:

1. The percentage of messages objectively rated as being adequately sent, or good communications. This score was seen as a measure of overall encoding skill, with higher scores indicating higher levels of skill (for high-adjustment women, 52% of positive messages, 42% of neutral messages, and 60% of negative messages were good communications).

2. The percentage of the spouse's good communications on which decoding errors were made. This score was a measure of decoding skill that took into ac-

count the number of opportunities a participant had to decode correctly. High scores on this measure indicated a lack of decoding skill, at least with the spouse (for high-adjustment women, 26% of positive messages, 28% of neutral messages, and 9% of negative messages were decoding errors).

3. The percentage of total errors on a participant's messages that could be accounted for by his or her encoding. This score was a measure of the extent to which a participant's encoding, rather than the spouse's decoding, accounted for errors on that participant's messages (for high-adjustment women, 70% of positive messages, 58% of neutral messages, and 51% of negative messages were encoding errors).

4. The percentage of a participant's bad communications that the spouse decoded correctly, with this score indicative of a private message system, as noted earlier.

## OTHER QUESTIONS ANSWERED
## WITH THIS METHODOLOGY

### Gender Differences

Because of the fact that this method allowed the calculation of individual scores on encoding and decoding, it was possible to look at gender differences in encoding and decoding. It was also possible to look at the interaction of gender and message type (as discussed later). Wives were found to be more accurate message senders than husbands over all groups, particularly when sending positive messages. More details about these effects can be found in Noller (1980, 1984).

Because it makes intuitive sense that in happy couples a spouse is likely to distort the partner's message in a positive direction, whereas in unhappy couples a spouse is likely to distort the partner's messages in a negative direction, I decided to examine the data to see whether spouses had a tendency to make errors in decoding in a particular direction. I devised a scoring scheme to take account of the direction in which decoding errors were made, as well as the magnitude of the error. If the spouse decoded an item incorrectly and made the error in a negative direction (i.e., decoded a neutral item as negative or a positive item as neutral or negative), he or she received a negative score (-1 for decoding a positive item as neutral or a neutral item as negative, and -2 for decoding a positive item as negative). However, if he or she decoded an item incorrectly but made the error in a positive direction (that is, neutral as positive, or negative as neutral or positive) then he or she received a positive score (+1 for decoding a neutral item as positive or a negative item as neutral and +2 for decoding a negative item as positive). What I found was an effect for gender, with wives tending to make errors in a positive direction and husbands tending to make errors in a negative direction.

## Message Type Effects

Given that the spouses in Noller's (1980, 1984) study each sent 27 messages, 9 of which were positive, 9 negative, and 9 neutral, it was possible to look at the effects of message type and to see whether some types of messages tended to be encoded or decoded more accurately than others. It was also possible to see whether husbands and wives differed in terms of the types of messages they encoded and decoded accurately and whether nondistressed and distressed couples differed in terms of their encoding and decoding accuracy for different types of messages. I found that message type interacted with gender, with wives being particularly better than husbands at sending positive messages. I also found that more negative messages were rated as good communications than was true for other types of messages and that neutral messages were more often incorrectly decoded.

## Channel Effects

Because the messages were videotaped, it was possible to have each of the spouses decode their partner from the videotape using a single channel of non-verbal communication (i.e., either the vocal channel or the visual channel). Each spouse individually watched the videotape of the partner's messages, using either the picture only with the sound turned off (visual channel) or the sound only with the picture turned off (vocal channel). I was then able to look at which types of messages (wife-to-husband or husband-to-wife) were decoded more accurately in which channel. In other words, were husbands and wives as decoders more accurate when decoding using only the visual channel, or using only the vocal channel?

In addition, using correlational analyses, I was able to look at the correlations between accuracy at decoding the visual channel, and accuracy at decoding the vocal channel, and I discovered that these two skills were unrelated. I could also look at the links between the single-channel decoding and the decoding using the complete videotaped message (i.e., visual, vocal, and verbal channels, as used in the original task). This task could be interpreted as revealing the extent to which the visual and vocal channels were relied on when decoding the original messages.

### COMPARING DECODING
### WITH SPOUSES AND STRANGERS

I was also interested in exploring the question of whether decoders were more accurate with spouses or with strangers (see Noller, 1981, 1984 for more detail about this study). This question is very important because it asks whether decoding is a stable skill or whether it is affected by the relationship between the message sender and the receiver. To look at this issue, I made a videotape of five couples (not included in the main study) who sent the same sets of messages to one another as were used in the main study. These 270 messages were then shown to groups of decoders who then decoded all of them. On the basis of these data, item–total correlations were used to identify the most discriminating version of each item (one positive, one negative, and one neutral version of each message)—that is, the version that good decoders tended to decode accurately and that poor decoders tended to get wrong. The most discriminating items were chosen to ensure that the test discriminated between those who were good decoders (i.e., those who were generally sensitive to nonverbal cues, even from strangers) and those who were poor decoders in our sample of married couples in the main study. A new tape was then made using the 54 items selected—27 sent by wives and 27 sent by husbands. All of the couples in the main study decoded these messages from the videotape during the experimental session.

This study showed that happy couples were more accurate at decoding their spouses than they were at decoding strangers, whereas unhappy couples were more accurate with strangers than they were with their partner. These results point to a performance deficit, particularly for unhappy husbands, who seemed to possess decoding skills that they were unable to use in decoding the spouse, presumably because of the negative perceptions they had of their partner. This study was similar to one carried out by Gottman and Porterfield (1981), who also had couples decode both the spouse and a stranger, although they did not use a standardized instrument for assessing decoding with strangers, and they used correlational analyses. Their results were similar to those of Noller (1981, 1984) in that they found that husbands, but not male strangers, were deficient in decoding wives' nonverbal messages.

## AWARENESS OF ENCODING
## AND CONFIDENCE IN DECODING

A further interesting issue was explored using the standard content paradigm in a new study. In this study, we explored the issue of whether, in ongoing relationships, individuals are conscious of the possibility of misunderstanding or being misunderstood (Noller & Venardos, 1986). When a husband sends a message that is unclear, is he aware that the message is unclear and may not be understood by his wife? When a wife misinterprets a message from her husband, is she totally confident that she is right, or does she leave open the possibility that she may have misinterpreted what he said?

To explore these questions, we had spouses encode and decode the same set of messages as used in the earlier study (Noller, 1980, 1984) and also make some additional ratings. When encoding, participants were asked to rate how clearly they thought they sent the message, and to predict whether the partner would accurately decode that message. When decoding, participants were asked to rate how confident they were of their interpretation of the message sent by the encoder. Although this study was limited by the fact that videotapes were not made of the encoders' messages, and therefore only a decoding score was calculated, the scores for confidence, clarity, and correct predictions could be related to this decoding score. It was also possible to compare confidence, clarity, and correct prediction scores for items correctly and incorrectly decoded. The analyses showed that wives in the low-marital-adjustment group were significantly different from other wives in terms of their encoding awareness and their decoding confidence. These wives were more confident when decoding incorrectly than were the high-adjustment wives, and they were less able than the high-adjustment wives to predict whether their husbands would decode their own messages correctly.

## MICROANALYSIS OF NONVERBAL BEHAVIORS ON THE STANDARD CONTENT MESSAGES

Noller and Gallois (1986) microcoded the messages from the original study (Noller, 1980) to see whether they could explain the gender differences in encoding and decoding found in the original study (Noller, 1980, 1984). Each message was coded for the presence of 16 different nonverbal behaviors (see Noller & Gallois, 1986, for a list of the behaviors coded and their operational definitions). The number of items on which each nonverbal behavior occurred was calculated for each message type. Analyses were conducted to look at the behaviors that discriminated between the three message types. Negative messages were characterized by frown and eyebrow furrow, and positive messages were characterized by open smile, closed smile, eyebrow raise, and forward lean. There were no behaviors that discriminated neutral messages from the other types of message, suggesting that neutral messages may be characterized by the absence of distinctive nonverbal behavior.

We found that standard content messages were highly suitable for this purpose. Because the words were standardized, we could be confident that the change in the meaning of the message could be attributed to changes in the nonverbal behavior accompanying the message. In addition, the intention of the message was set by the experimenter, and we did not need to rely on the encoder to tell us what message he or she sent. Another advantage of using the standard content methodology for this purpose was that all participants sent messages of approximately the same length, and the word lengths were the same for different types of messages.

We found that wives' nonverbal behavior differed from that of husbands in two important ways. Wives differentiated more clearly between positive and negative messages and used different behaviors for positive and negative messages (smiles on positive messages and frowns on negative messages). In addition, the behaviors that the wives used were those that clearly discriminated between the two types of messages. Husbands, on the other hand, tended to use the eyebrow raise on both types of messages. We were also able to show that husbands high in marital adjustment behaved more like the wives and that good communicators did not smile on negative messages.

## STRENGTHS OF STANDARD CONTENT METHODOLOGY

The primary advantage of the standard content methodology is that it is a way to ensure that the nonverbal channel is the focus of the participants (whether encoders or decoders), because the verbal channel is controlled so that changes in intention or interpretation (impact) can be validly attributed to changes in the nonverbal behavior. In addition, the test is easy to administer, particularly once the sets of encoding and decoding cards have been made (see details in Appendix). This method, which involves live messages, is superior to still photographs, which are often used to assess accuracy at identifying emotions (Ekman & Friesen, 1967).

It is important to keep in mind that this method assesses sensitivity to intended nonverbal communications, and it may be more clearly generalizable to situations where a person plans a message that he or she wants to get across to the partner and is clear about the intention that should be conveyed. The method does not generalize as clearly to the nonverbal expression of affective states (although that skill may be relevant for some messages) or to the expression of true motivational states. It is also important to keep in mind, however, that spouses' past experiences with each other and with each other's communication are likely to affect their decoding.

Another important point to note about this methodology is that, unlike tests of nonverbal skill such as the Profile of Nonverbal Sensitivity (PONS test; Rosenthal, Hall, Archer, DiMatteo, & Rogers, 1979; Hall, chap. 8, this volume), or the Interpersonal Perception Task (Costanzo & Archer, 1989; Archer, Costanzo, & Akert, chap. 9, this volume), it is designed to be used dyadically. In other words, accuracy can be assessed in terms of the dyadic relationship. How accurate are these two people when encoding and decoding nonverbal messages to each other? As was shown in Noller's (1981) study comparing both married couples and strangers, accuracy in a dyadic relationship can be very different from the accuracy of the same individual on an objective test, because, particularly in poor quality relationships, nonverbal accuracy in dyadic relationships is affected by relationship history and expectations of the partner. Noller and Ruzzene (1991) showed that the accuracy of husbands' decoding was affected by the negativity of the intentions they attributed to their wives.

Sillars and Scott (1983) discussed the perceptual biases (or tendency to misunderstand messages from the partner) that may be operating in intimate relationships. They conceptualized the situation in terms of a trade-off between familiarity and objectivity. The spouse may be the one who knows the partner best, but he or she is also likely to be the least partial observer. They noted that perceptual biases may become particularly strongly entrenched in intimate relationships, with familiarity increasing confidence in one's understanding of the partner, often beyond actual understanding.

## LIMITATIONS OF STANDARD CONTENT METHODOLOGY

Harper, Wiens, and Matarazzo (1978) pointed out four problems they saw as related to standard content methodology. These include the potential interaction between the speaker and the verbal content; microphone fright; the confound between voice quality and speech-related paralinguistic phenomena; and the fact that problems in the relationship, such as dominance, may not be aroused when standard content methods are used. In talking about the potential interaction between the speaker and the verbal content, these authors raised the possibility that the words that the experimenter asks the participants to use may not have the same meaning for all participants. It is also possible that a word, or even a situation, that is aversive for one couple because of their particular relationship history, will be positive for another. For this reason, it is important for experimenters, as far as possible, to avoid including words with the potential for highly emotive interpretations.

There is also the possibility of problems arising because the words used in the message designed by the experimenter are different from those that the participants would normally use in their daily conversations. Some of the participants in Noller (1980) told me that they did not rely on nonverbal cues to get messages across, because they relied on the use of words to make their messages positive or negative. These couples may have been in the minority, however, because my overall finding was that, particularly for positive messages, neutral words and positive nonverbals were the norm.

A second problem raised by Harper et al. (1978) concerns nervousness or microphone fright. From this perspective, the task is seen as one involving acting rather than just communicating a message to the partner. As noted earlier, I prefer to think of the task as equivalent to the messages sent when a spouse has thought about an issue for a while and wants to raise it with a partner. In this situation, couples are likely to plan what they are going to say and how they are going to say it. Although some nervousness might be involved, particularly if the issue is a contentious one, the task is basically about sending a message to the partner.

The third problem raised by Harper et al. (1978) concerns the possibility that "individual differences in speech-related paralinguistic phenomena" such as accent or voice quality may be confounded with the vocal cues accompanying the message. In other words, if someone has a harsh voice, the effects of that voice quality may cause the message to be interpreted more negatively than the speaker intended. Although this issue might be highly salient when strangers are decoding one another, it would not seem to be an issue when married or dating couples or friends are involved in the study.

The fourth problem raised by Harper et al. (1978) is really about the fact that the situation in which the couple perform the standard content task is an artificial one. They argue that characteristics of the relationships such as dominance may not come into play in this artificial situation where stylized messages are being used. In answering this criticism, let me give an example of how an issue that was salient for a couple at the time of the study affected the decoding of standard content messages. The situation is described in Noller's (1984) book.

In one of the situations, husbands were asked to send a message to their wives using the words, "Do you know what a trip like that costs?" The context for the message was that the wife had been talking about a trip that a friend and her husband had taken. Each time the encoding husband sent the message, the wife had to decide which of three possible meanings was intended. The three possible meanings were as follows:

1. He felt that a trip to that place was totally unappealing and would hardly be worthwhile.
2. He was pleased that she would want to go with him on such a trip and would like to make serious inquiries about it.
3. He was interested in finding out whether she knew the approximate cost of such a trip before committing himself one way or the other.

Although the husband actually attempted to send all three of the messages at different times, because the wife's perception of the husband was that he was unwilling to spend money on holidays, she interpreted each of the messages negatively. It is interesting to note that the wife reacted in this way although she knew that one of the messages should have been positive and one should have been neutral.

Another related problem is that one of the alternative intentions may be so far out of the couple's experience that the partner would not believe that the spouse could send such a message, even in a game-like situation. For example, in the "chicken item" (Message 1 in the husbands' set; see Appendix), wives may consider it so unlikely that their husband could mean the negative alternative that they might never select that alternative intention.

Nevertheless, I would not want to deny the fact that the standard content methodology involves spouses decoding one another's messages in an artificial situation, and possibly being required to use words that they would not normally use. Because of this problem, I have used a number of other methodologies to look at the issue of family members' understandings of one another.

These methodologies tend to involve family members engaging in a video-taped interaction that they can then watch and answer particular questions about, or make various types of ratings on. For example, Guthrie and Noller (1988) had couples interact about an emotional incident in their marriage. Following the interaction, they were asked to report what they were trying to do in the interaction and what they thought their spouse was trying to do in the interaction. A sample of undergraduate students was then asked to rate the similarity of the two statements of intention (e.g., the intention the husband reported, and the intention his wife attributed to him). We found that unhappy spouses were less accurate than happy spouses (i.e., their attributions of the spouse's intention tended to be quite different from those the spouse attributed to him- or herself). In addition, unhappy spouses tended to attribute more negative intentions to their partners than did happy spouses.

In another study (Noller & Ruzzene, 1991), we had couples discuss a long-standing problem and then provide information about their own and their partner's affect and intentions during the interaction. As in the previous study, similarity ratings of the spouses' reports of their own intentions and their partners' judgments of their intentions, as well as the similarity of their reported affect and their partners' judgments of their affect, were obtained. The accuracy with which they judged one another's affect depended on marital adjustment level, supporting the findings using standard content methods in the earlier studies (Noller, 1980, 1984).

## CONCLUSION

Overall, I believe that standard content methodology, despite the limitations, is useful for assessing nonverbal accuracy as an interpersonal skill. The methods described herein could be adapted for use with other groups such as parents and children (with competence in reading) or teachers and children. Different sets of messages, suitable for these different groups, could be written and appropriate contexts and alternative intentions devised. This method is very useful for separating the verbal and nonverbal components of messages and for looking at the effects of gender, message type, and channel on the encoding and decoding of nonverbal messages in dyadic interaction.

## REFERENCES

Argyle, M., Salter, V., Nicholson, H., Williams, M., & Burgess, P. (1970). The communication of inferior and superior attitudes by verbal and nonverbal signals. *British Journal of Social and Clinical Psychology, 9,* 222–231.

Bach, G. R., & Wyden, P. (1969). Marital fighting: A guide to love. In B. N. Ard & C. C. Ard (Eds.), *Handbook of marriage counseling* (pp. 313–321). Palo Alto, CA: Science and Behavior Books.

Costanzo, M., & Archer, D. (1989). Interpreting the expressive behavior of others: The Interpersonal Perception Task. *Journal of Nonverbal Behavior, 13,* 225–245.

Davitz, J. R., & Davitz, L. J. (1959). Correlates of accuracy in the communication of feelings. *Journal of Communication, 9,* 110–117.

Duckworth, D. (1975). Personality, emotional state and perceptions of nonverbal communication. *Perceptual and Motor Skills, 40,* 325–326.

Ekman, P., & Friesen, W. V. (1967). Head and body cues in the judgment of emotion: A reformulation. *Perceptual and Motor Skills, 24,* 711–724.

Ekman, P., & Friesen, W. V. (1969). Nonverbal leakage and cues to deception. *Psychiatry, 32,* 88–106.

Gottman, J. M., Markman, H., & Notarius, C. (1977). The topography of marital conflict: A sequential analysis of verbal and nonverbal behavior. *Journal of Marriage and the Family, 39,* 461–477.

Gottman, J. M., Notarius, C., Markman, H., Banks, S., Yoppi, B., & Rubin, M. E. (1976). Behavior exchange theory and marital decision-making. *Journal of Personality and Social Psychology, 34,* 461–477.

Gottman, J. M., & Porterfield, A. L. (1981). Communicative competence in the nonverbal behavior of married couples. *Journal of Marriage and the Family, 4,* 817–824.

Guthrie, D. M., & Noller, P. (1988). Spouse' perceptions of one another in emotional situations. In P. Noller & M. A. Fitzpatrick (Eds.), *Perspectives on marital interaction* (pp. 53–77). Philadelphia: Multilingual Matters.

Hall, J. A. (1978). Gender effects in decoding nonverbal cues. *Psychological Bulletin, 85,* 845–857.

Harper, R. G., Wiens, A. N., & Matarazzo, J. D. (1978). *Nonverbal communication: The state of the art.* New York: Wiley.

Kahn, M. (1970). Nonverbal communication and marital satisfaction. *Family Process, 9,* 449–456.

Mehrabian, A., & Ferris, S. R. (1967). Inference of attitudes from nonverbal communication in two channels. *Journal of Consulting Psychology, 31,* 248–252.

Noller, P. (1980). Misunderstandings in marital communication: A study of couples' nonverbal communication. *Journal of Personality and Social Psychology, 39,* 1135–1148.

Noller, P. (1981). Gender and marital adjustment level differences in decoding messages from spouses and strangers. *Journal of Personality and Social Psychology, 41,* 272–278.

Noller, P. (1984). *Nonverbal communication and marital interaction.* Oxford, England: Pergamon.

Noller, P., & Gallois, C. (1986). Sending emotional messages in marriage: Nonverbal behavior, sex and communication clarity. *British Journal of Social Psychology, 25,* 287–297.

Noller, P., & Ruzzene, M. (1991). Communication in marriage: The influence of affect and cognition. In G. O. Fletcher & F. D. Fincham (Eds.), *Cognition in close relationships* (pp. 203–233). Hillsdale, NJ: Lawrence Erlbaum Associates.

Noller, P., & Venardos, C. (1986). Communication awareness in married couples. *Journal of Social and Personal Relationships, 3,* 31–42.

Rosenthal, R., Hall, J., Dimatteo, M. R., & Rogers, P. L., & Archer, D. (1979). *Sensitivity to nonverbal communication: The PONS test.* Baltimore: The Johns Hopkins University Press.

Sillars, A. L., & Scott, M. D. (1983). Interpersonal perception between intimates: An integrative review. *Human Communication Research, 10,* 153–176.

# APPENDIX

Two sets of cards are required for using standard content methodology. The first set is the encoding set, which comprises 27 cards, each of which includes three parts:

1. description of the situation or context in which the communication takes place;
2. the intention that the message should convey;
3. the statement, or words that the encoder is to use.

Each of these cards has the number of the message being sent (i.e., 1 to 9) on the back so that it can be easily seen by the decoder and also so that it can be seen on the videotape, if the messages are being recorded. The cards are shuffled so that the messages are presented in random order, and the encoder's task is to send the message to the partner, using the words provided (see Table 13.1 for an example of an encoding card).

The second set of cards is the decoding set, which comprises nine cards (one for each statement) that include the three possible alternative meanings for that statement. Decoders are required to find the appropriate card (matching it to the number of the card that the encoder has selected). They are then asked to choose which of the three alternatives they thought their partner was trying to send, and to record it on an appropriate form, out of the sight of the encoder (see Table 13.2 for an example of a decoding card).

The nine sets of contexts, ambiguous statements, and alternative intentions used by Noller (1980, 1984) for husbands are presented in Table 13.3, and those for wives are presented in Table 13.4.

The encoder and the decoder sit opposite each other at a table large enough for the decoder to be able to spread out the nine decoding cards. This procedure is followed so that the appropriate card can easily be located once the encoder picks up the message he or she will send next and shows the number on the back (1–9). If the encoders' messages are to be video-recorded, then the camera should be positioned to record the encoder from the waist up (or above the table). The encoder's 27 cards should be shuffled so that the messages are sent in random order. Both the encoder and the decoder need to make a note of the message numbers (e.g., 5b) as they are sent, with the list being kept out of sight of the partner. Scoring involves comparing the decoder's list with the encoder's list. The encoder's list is assumed to be a correct record of messages sent. Provided that the encoder keeps the cards in the order in which they were sent, any concerns can be checked.

## TABLE 13.3

### Context, Statement, and Alternative Intentions for Husbands' Messages

| Message | Context | Statement | Alternative Intentions |
|---|---|---|---|
| 1 | You come to the dinner table as your wife begins to serve chicken, a main course you recall having had four days ago for dinner, too. | Didn't we have chicken for dinner a few nights ago? | a. You are irritated with her for preparing the same meal again and are warning her that she had better not make the same mistake in the future of a closely repeated meal.<br>b. You do not mind but are curious to see if your memory for meals is accurate.<br>c. You are elated because chicken is your one of your favorites and she doesn't usually serve it so often. |
| 2 | Your wife is modeling a new outfit for you that she just bought. She asks you how you like it. | That's really something. Where did you get the money to buy an outfit like that? | a. You are curious to know how she managed to save the money to buy such an outfit.<br>b. You think that the outfit looks good, are pleased with the purchase and are pleasantly surprised that she could afford such an expensive-looking outfit.<br>c. You think that the outfit is totally unbecoming on her and therefore not worth the money. |
| 3 | Your wife tells you about the wonderful vacation that one of her friends just took with her husband. She wishes that you and she could also take a trip to the same place. | Do you know what a trip like that costs? | a. You think that a trip to that place is unappealing and would hardly be worthwhile.<br>b. You are pleased that she would want to go with you on such a trip and would like to make serious inquiries about it.<br>c. You are interested in finding out whether she knows the approximate cost of the trip before committing yourself one way or the other. |

*(Table 3.3 continues)*

259

| Message | Context | Statement | Alternative Intentions |
|---------|---------|-----------|------------------------|
| 4 | You and your wife are discussing a life insurance policy that you recently purchased. | I'm not sure you'll need all this insurance, because if I die you'll probably remarry. | a. You hope that your wife would remarry so that her happiness and welfare would be maintained. <br> b. You want your wife to say that she would never consider remarrying, and would never love another man. <br> c. You wonder what her attitude to remarriage is, as you've not talked about it before. |
| 5 | You and your wife are both ready for bed at night. It is a night when sexual relations are a possibility. | Do you really want to have sex tonight? | a. You are not interested in having sexual relations that night. <br> b. You are interested in having sexual relations and want to let her know, but you are afraid she might be unwilling. You hope that your eagerness will convince her to agree. <br> c. You would like to make love only if she would like to, and are interested in her attitude. |
| 6 | A neighbor phones and invites you and your wife to visit him at a get-together at their home on the following Saturday evening. You and your wife had previous plans to go out alone that evening. You tell your neighbor to hold on while you confer with your wife. | Would you prefer us to go on our own as we planned? | a. You would much prefer to go out with your wife. <br> b. You are not really keen to go out with your wife and would rather go to your neighbor's house. <br> c. You have no preference at the moment and will accept whatever alternative your wife selects. |

(Table 13.3 continues)

| Message | Context | Statement | Alternative Intentions |
|---|---|---|---|
| 7 | Your wife tells you to clean up a mess you made in the apartment. | I was going to clean it up, fusspot. | a. You are annoyed and will not clean up the mess because she nagged you.<br>b. You intended to clean up the mess, and are just letting her know that.<br>c. You are quite happy to clean up the mess, but you enjoy affectionately teasing your wife about her housekeeping. |
| 8 | As you walk into the bathroom unbuttoning your shirt, you find your wife partly undressed and turning on the shower. You were on your way to have a shower yourself. | I didn't know you were thinking of a shower, I'm planning to take one myself. | a. You are glad to find her going into the shower so that you can take one together and enjoy the sex play.<br>b. You are annoyed and expect her to wait until you take your shower first.<br>c. You are just surprised at the coincidence. |
| 9 | You walk into the room and unexpectedly come across your wife. You ask her what she is doing. | What are you doing? | a. You are just curious to know what she is doing.<br>b. She is obviously doing something you have asked her not to do and you are angry.<br>c. You have caught her doing something to surprise you. |

261

**TABLE 13.4**

Contexts, Statements and Alternative Intentions for Wives' Messages

| Message | Context | Statement | Alternative Intentions |
|---|---|---|---|
| 1 | It is approximately the time when you and your husband usually go to bed together but he seems engrossed in a TV show. | Do you really want to watch the rest of that? | a. You hope that he will turn off the TV and come to bed with you so that you can make love.<br>b. You are tired and will not mind if he continues to watch his show while you fall asleep.<br>c. You are annoyed because he knows this is not the kind of show you enjoy, and you want him to turn to another channel. |
| 2 | At a social gathering, an attractive single girl wearing a dress with a plunging neckline is introduced to you and your husband. She acts very flirtatiously toward your husband and then leaves your company. | She was really something, wasn't she? | a. You think that she was vulgar and you are angry at your husband for the attention he paid her.<br>b. You just wonder what he thought of her.<br>c. You thought this woman was attractive, and you feel flattered that she has taken notice of your husband. |
| 3 | Your husband just presented you with your birthday present. You had been expecting a completely different gift. | You really surprised me this time. | a. You are quite satisfied with the gift, although you really would have preferred what you were expecting.<br>b. You are very disappointed and annoyed that he didn't get you what you expected.<br>c. You are pleasantly surprised by the unexpected gift. |

(*Table 13.4 continues*)

| Message | Context | Statement | Alternative Intentions |
|---|---|---|---|
| 4 | You and your husband are sitting alone in your living room on a winter evening. You feel cold. | I'm cold, aren't you? | a. You wonder if he is also cold, or if it is only you who are cold.<br>b. You want him to warm you with physical affection.<br>c. You're feeling that he is being inconsiderate in not having turned up the heat by now, and you want him to turn it up right away. |
| 5 | You come home to find the wash you had left in the washing machine hanging on the line. | Did you do that? | a. You are angry because some of the clothes are hung in a way that would spoil their shape and you wish it had been left for you.<br>b. You are curious about whether it was your husband or one of the children who hung it out.<br>c. You are pleased that he has done such a thing to help you. |
| 6 | It's time for you and your husband to get dressed for a special event you were planning to go to that evening. You have a headache and feel uncomfortable. | I've got a headache and I'm not sure whether to go. | a. You want to find out how much he wants to go before making up your mind.<br>b. You are angry with him about something that happened earlier and don't think you'd enjoy going out with him.<br>c. You want him to encourage you to go and enjoy the performance despite the headache, because you are keen to go out with him. |

(*Table 13.4 continues*)

263

| Message | Context | Statement | Alternative Intentions |
|---|---|---|---|
| 7 | You and your husband have begun talking about the purchase of new bedroom furniture. Assume that you currently own a set with a double bed. You point out a twin bed set in a shop window. | Look at that twin bed set. Why don't we get it? | a. You know that you both want another double bed because you cherish the closeness it fosters, but you sometimes tease about twin beds.<br>b. You are serious in bringing up the possibility of twin beds because they would give you some escape from his sexual advances that you don't enjoy. You want your husband to realize this.<br>c. You have never really talked about the issue of twin versus double beds, and you are interested in knowing his attitude. |
| 8 | You have just come out of the bathroom. It is a few days past when your menstrual period usually begins, but you have seen no sign of it starting. You tell your husband about the current situation. | You know, I'm a few days late on my period this month. | a. If you are pregnant you regard it as his fault for not taking better precautions and you will be extremely angry at him.<br>b. You are delighted that you might be pregnant and want to share the good news with him.<br>c. You just want him to know, although you don't really care one way or the other. |
| 9 | You walk into a room and unexpectedly come across your husband. You ask him what he is doing. | What are you doing? | a. You are just curious to know what he is doing.<br>b. He is obviously doing something you have asked him not to do and you are angry.<br>c. You have caught him doing something to surprise you. |

264

# ဆ $14$ ෭

# The Measurement
# of Interpersonal Sensitivity:
# Consideration of Design,
# Components, and
# Unit of Analysis

David A. Kenny
Lynn Winquist
*University of Connecticut*

Accuracy is a very general construct, and as this volume testifies, it has been studied in many different ways. Consider the following examples:

Levesque and Kenny (1993) studied whether women who, after a brief period of observation, were perceived as extraverted talked more in dyadic interaction.

Shechtman and Kenny (1994) studied whether education students in discussion groups would be able to know how the other group members viewed them.

Funder and Colvin (1988) examined the agreement between the judgments made by strangers and friends across 100 Q-sort items of personality.

Levenson and Ruef (1992) studied whether people were able to gauge the online emotional feelings of their partners over time.

Accuracy research can be divided into four basic types (Ickes, 1997; chap. 12, this volume). First, researchers have examined the accuracy of people's judgments of fairly stable characteristics of the target. For instance, if Clyde thinks Bonnie is extraverted, then is Bonnie in fact extraverted? Among these characteristics would be the target's personality, values, and dispositions. This form of accuracy has been called *target accuracy* (Kenny, 1994; Malloy & Albright, 1990). Second, researchers have studied whether perceivers know what targets are thinking and feeling about others and perceivers themselves. For instance, does Clyde know whether Bonnie likes Clyde? We have called this form of accuracy *meta-accuracy* (Kenny, 1994; Kenny & DePaulo, 1993). Third, researchers have studied the ability of perceivers to identify the emotions of targets. For instance, does Clyde know whether Bonnie is angry? This type of accuracy is often referred to as *nonverbal sensitivity* (Rosenthal, Hall, DiMatteo, Rogers, & Archer, 1979). Fourth, researchers have studied the ability of perceivers to read the minds of targets. For instance, does Clyde know that Bonnie is bored right now and wishes that she were at the beach? This type of accuracy is commonly called *empathic accuracy* (Ickes, 1997).

Accuracy is usually defined as the correspondence between a judgment made by a perceiver of a target person and some criterion measure (Kruglanski, 1989). For instance, Bonnie's belief that Clyde is angry would be the judgment, and Clyde's emotional state would be the criterion. There are very difficult issues concerning defining and measuring the criterion, issues that we largely skirt in this chapter. Instead, we concentrate on the measurement of accuracy, assuming that the judgment and criterion are validly measured.

There are two important features that often characterize both the judgment and criterion measures in accuracy. First, they are *dyadic* in that they refer to two persons, a perceiver and a target. (There is the important exception where the perceiver and the target are the very same person, as in self-perception.) Second, the measurements are typically *multivariate* in that a perceiver makes multiple judgments of the target. The analysis of accuracy in this chapter emphasizes both the dyadic and multivariate features of most accuracy research.

## THE COMPONENTIAL APPROACH

Accuracy as an area of research is complex, in part, by the necessity of measuring many types of accuracy. In essence, Cronbach (1955) suggested a partitioning of the judgment and the criterion into four components: constant, trait, target, and uniqueness. This componential decomposition is a two-way analysis of the variance of target by trait data structure. In this section, we refer to the multiple judgments of a target as *traits* because that is the term usually used when discussing a Cronbach partitioning. In the rest of the chapter we use the term *measures* in that they are not always measurements of traits.

Considering the judgment, the constant component represents the judge's general response style. It reflects the judge's tendency to rate all targets on all of the traits at the same level. The trait component reflects the judge's tendency to rate all targets the same way for a particular trait, and the target component represents the extent to which a target is generally viewed as favorable or unfavorable across all traits by a judge. The uniqueness or target by trait interaction component reflects the degree to which a target is viewed high or low on a specific trait, controlling for the effects of the constant, trait, and target components.

Considering the criterion, the constant component represents the average standing of all the targets on all the traits. The trait component reflects how the targets on average differ on the criterion measure. The target component represents the extent to which a target scores high or low on the criterion measure across all traits. The uniqueness component reflects the degree to which a target scores high or low on a specific trait on the criterion, controlling for the effects of the constant, trait, and target components.

As illustrated in Fig. 14.1, accuracy is determined by the correspondence between the components in the judgment and the components in the criterion measure (Kenny & Albright, 1987). Cronbach (1955) developed four types of accuracy, which are defined for each perceiver as follows:

*Elevation accuracy:* The degree of correspondence between the constant of the judgment and the constant of the criterion. It reflects the discrepancy between the perceiver's mean judgment across targets and traits and the overall mean across targets and traits on the criterion.

*Differential elevation accuracy:* The degree of correlation between the target effects of the judgment and the target effects of the criterion. This form of accuracy reflects the correspondence between the mean of a perceiver's judgments of each target and the overall mean level for the target on the criterion.

*Stereotype accuracy:* The extent to which there is a correlation between the trait effects of the judgment and the trait effects of the criterion. This type of accuracy concerns the degree of correspondence between the mean of a perceiver's judgments of each trait across targets and the overall mean level for the trait on the criterion.

*Differential accuracy:* The degree of correlation between the uniqueness component of the judgment and the uniqueness component of the criterion. This form of accuracy reflects the degree of correspondence between the perceiver's judgment of each trait for each target and the criterion scores of each trait for each target.

So if Mary judges Matthew, Mark, Luke, and John on the traits of intelligence, friendliness, and conscientiousness and her average rating across targets and traits agreed with the average of the 12 criterion scores, then there is elevation accuracy. There would be differential elevation accuracy if her average judgment for each of the four targets corresponded to the average of each of the four on the criterion scores. There would be stereotype accuracy if her rank ordering of

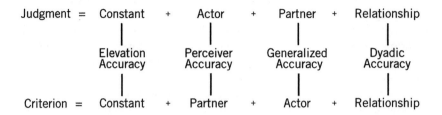

FIG. 14.1. Cronbach's (1955) four components of accuracy. From "Accuracy in Interpersonal Perception? A Social Relations Analysis," by D. A. Kenny & L. Albright, 1987, *Psychological Bulletin, 102*, p. 391. Copyright 1987 by the American Psychologi-

the three traits corresponded to the rank ordering for the traits on the criterion. Finally, there would be differential accuracy if—after the overall mean, the target averages, and the trait averages were removed—her judgments for the four targets on each trait corresponded to the criterion scores for each target on each trait.

A Cronbach partitioning of ratings is done on the target by trait data for each perceiver. However, the partitioning can be done in different ways. For instance, Kenny and Albright (1987) partitioned the perceiver by target data for each trait into actor, partner, and relationship (to be discussed later in this chapter). Such a partitioning is the social relations model (SRM; Kenny, 1994). In this chapter, we repeatedly partition both the judgment and criterion into components and define the different types of accuracy as the correlation between these components.

## THE UNIT OF ANALYSIS OF ACCURACY RESEARCH: IDIOGRAPHIC VERSUS NOMOTHETIC

A key decision in accuracy research is whether the focus of the research is idiographic or nomothetic. The term *idiographic* (Allport, 1937) originally referred to research aimed at developing a comprehensive understanding of the individual. The primary concern is describing unique patterns of characteristics within persons, rather than drawing conclusions across persons. However, over time the term idiographic has evolved to mean the following (Jaccard & Dittus, 1990; Lamiell, 1981): Analyses are conducted for each individual, and the results from those analyses are explored (e.g., a mean across persons is computed). So our use of the term idiographic is consistent with modern usage of the term, and not Allport's.

An idiographic focus requires measuring individual differences in levels of accuracy. That focus is typically on "who" is more accurate, sometimes the focus is on "whom" or what type of target is easier to judge, and even less frequently the focus is on "which" relationships show greater levels of accuracy. Within the idiographic tradition, there is often a set of external variables or moderator variables that are correlated with the idiographic measure of accuracy for each person or relationship. For instance, the researcher might specify that women are more accurate than men.

Researchers usually measure idiographic accuracy by profile similarity (e.g., Bernieri, Zuckerman, Koestner, & Rosenthal, 1994; Pelham, 1993) or the correspondence between two sets of measures. Although profile similarity measures of accuracy have been in use for over 50 years (e.g., Dymond, 1950), their modern revival is due to Snodgrass (1985). Interestingly, part of the impetus of focusing on such measures was an attempt to remove elevation and differential elevation from the measurement of accuracy. In profile similarity, the set of judgments is mapped onto the set of criterion measurements. In computing the association between two sets of scores, the unit of analysis is the measure, not the person. Very often the correlation coefficient is used to tap the degree of similarity between the judgment and the criterion, but other statistics are possible (e.g., regression coefficient with the criterion as the predictor, and discrepancy scores). Snodgrass (chap. 11, this volume) and Bernieri and Gillis (chap. 4, this volume) discuss the use of correlations to measure accuracy.

Given that the judgment and criterion measures can be conceptualized as being the sum of a series of components (Cronbach, 1955; Kenny & Albright, 1987), it is reasonable to remove one or more of these components before computing the profile similarity between two sets of scores. In this chapter, idiographic accuracy involves the subtraction of components of variance that are deemed as not the core of what is usually meant by accuracy.

In nomothetic research, the focus is on the level of accuracy across persons and what situational factors lead to increases in accuracy. Correlations are computed for each measure between the judgment and the criterion across perceivers, targets, and relationships, and so the unit in the statistical analysis is the perceiver, the target, or the relationship. Very often these nomothetic accuracy correlations are compared across conditions, measures, and times. For instance, are people more accurate in judging extraversion than neuroticism? As in idiographic accuracy, it is usually necessary to subtract the sources of variance that are deemed irrelevant.

Historically, the early focus of accuracy research was idiographic. Recall that Cronbach (1955) criticized work on individual differences in accuracy by Dymond (1950) and others. Swann (1984) and Kenny and Albright (1987) urged a refocusing of interest on nomothetic accuracy. More recently, Pelham (1993) took the position that idiographic research is much more informative than nomothetic research: "An idiographic assessment of the relation between our self-appraisals and the appraisals we receive from others should reveal levels of congruence that could easily elude nomothetic analyses" (p. 669). A major goal of this chapter is to reorient the thinking about this fundamental dichotomy in accuracy research. We argue that it is as much an empirical issue as a theoretical issue whether accuracy should be studied in a nomothetic or idiographic fashion. Moreover, we show that at least in some circumstances, these two very different foci lead to essentially the same answer. Thus, the two approaches may not be as different as might appear.

## THE DESIGN OF ACCURACY RESEARCH

Another key issue in accuracy research is that of design or the arrangement of perceivers and targets. We adopt the following notation: Designs can either be 1P or MP in that there can be just one perceiver per target (1P) or multiple perceivers per target (MP). For example, if Clyde is the target and is rated only by Bonnie, we have a 1P design; but if both Bonnie and Bill rate Clyde, we have an MP design. Designs can either be 1T or MT in that there can be just one target per perceiver (1T) or multiple targets per perceiver (MT). For example, if Clyde is the perceiver and rates only Bonnie, we have a 1T design; but if Clyde rates Bonnie and Bill, we have an MT design. Finally, designs can also be reciprocal in the sense that for each perceiver–target pair, both people serve as a perceiver and a target. If the design were reciprocal, we would add an "-R" to it. Table 14.1 presents the set of possible designs using the new design notation.

Quite often in research each target is evaluated by a single perceiver who judges only that one target, a 1P1T design. An example of this design is the study conducted by Bernieri et al. (1994) in which each student rated his or her roommate's personality. The dyadic unstructured interaction studies used by Ickes (chap. 12, this volume) to study empathic accuracy are usually 1P1T-R designs.

Sometimes each target is judged by multiple perceivers, but each perceiver judges only a single target. John and Robins (1993) used such a design, designated here as MP1T. The design is used often by Funder (chap. 16, this volume). Less commonly, each person judges multiple targets, but only one perceiver judges each target. For instance, if a teacher were to judge the social skills of his or her students, the design would be a 1PMT design. It is interesting that making a 1PMT design reciprocal requires a MP1T design and vice versa. So making either a 1PMT or an MP1T design reciprocal results in the same design.

In the most complicated design, each judge evaluates multiple targets, and multiple judges evaluate each target. We refer to this design as the MPMT design. One important type of this design is the classic (Kenny & Albright, 1987) or half-block (Kenny, 1994) design in which judges and targets are different people and so the design is not reciprocal. The standard stimulus studies of Ickes (chap. 12, this volume) and the rapport judgment accuracy work of Bernieri and

**TABLE 14.1**

**Design Typology**

| Design | Not Reciprocal | Reciprocal |
|--------|----------------|------------|

**1P1T**

Not Reciprocal:

|   | A | B | C | D | E | F |
|---|---|---|---|---|---|---|
| A |   | X |   |   |   |   |
| B |   |   |   |   |   |   |
| C |   |   |   | X |   |   |
| D |   |   |   |   |   |   |
| E |   |   |   |   |   | X |
| F |   |   |   |   |   |   |

Reciprocal:

|   | A | B | C | D | E | F |
|---|---|---|---|---|---|---|
| A |   | X |   |   |   |   |
| B | X |   |   |   |   |   |
| C |   |   |   | X |   |   |
| D |   |   | X |   |   |   |
| E |   |   |   |   |   | X |
| F |   |   |   |   | X |   |

**MP1T**

Not Reciprocal:

|   | A | B | C | D | E | F | G | H | I |
|---|---|---|---|---|---|---|---|---|---|
| A |   | X | X |   |   |   |   |   |   |
| B |   |   |   |   |   |   |   |   |   |
| C |   |   |   |   |   |   |   |   |   |
| D |   |   |   | X | X |   |   |   |   |
| E |   |   |   |   |   |   |   |   |   |
| F |   |   |   |   |   |   |   |   |   |
| G |   |   |   |   |   |   | X | X |   |
| H |   |   |   |   |   |   |   |   |   |
| I |   |   |   |   |   |   |   |   |   |

Reciprocal:

|   | A | B | C | D | E | F | G | H | I |
|---|---|---|---|---|---|---|---|---|---|
| A |   | X | X |   |   |   |   |   |   |
| B | X |   |   |   |   |   |   |   |   |
| C | X |   |   |   |   |   |   |   |   |
| D |   |   |   |   | X | X |   |   |   |
| E |   |   |   | X |   |   |   |   |   |
| F |   |   |   | X |   |   |   |   |   |
| G |   |   |   |   |   |   |   | X | X |
| H |   |   |   |   |   |   | X |   |   |
| I |   |   |   |   |   |   | X |   |   |

**1PMT**

Not Reciprocal:

|   | A | B | C | D | E | F | G | H | I |
|---|---|---|---|---|---|---|---|---|---|
| A |   |   |   |   |   |   |   |   |   |
| B | X |   |   |   |   |   |   |   |   |
| C | X |   |   |   |   |   |   |   |   |
| D |   |   |   |   |   |   |   |   |   |
| E |   |   | X |   |   |   |   |   |   |
| F |   |   | X |   |   |   |   |   |   |
| G |   |   |   |   |   |   |   |   |   |
| H |   |   |   |   | X |   |   |   |   |
| I |   |   |   |   | X |   |   |   |   |

*(Table 14.1 continues)*

| Design | | Not Reciprocal | | | | | | | | Reciprocal | | | | |
|---|---|---|---|---|---|---|---|---|---|---|---|---|---|---|
| | | A | B | C | D | E | F | G | H | | A | B | C | D |
| | A | | | | | X | X | X | X | A | | X | X | X |
| | B | | | | | X | X | X | X | B | X | | X | X |
| | C | | | | | X | X | X | X | C | X | X | | X |
| MPMT | D | | | | | X | X | X | X | D | X | X | X | |
| | E | | | | | | | | | | A | B | C | D |
| | F | | | | | | | | | A | | | X | X |
| | G | | | | | | | | | B | | | X | X |
| | H | | | | | | | | | C | X | X | | |
| | | | | | | | | | | D | X | X | | |

Note. Rows represent perceivers (P), and columns represent targets (T), each of which is designated by a bold capital letter.

Gillis (chap. 4, this volume) have this structure. Also studies that use test materials such as Costanzo and Archer's (1989; Archer, Costanzo, & Akert, chap. 9, this volume) Interpersonal Perception Task (IPT) have this structure. Two fairly common MPMT-R designs are the round-robin design in which the perceivers and targets judge each other and the block design in which a subset of people judge the remaining subset. Most of SRM accuracy research uses one of these two MPMT-R designs.

So far we have concentrated on the design of the judgment measure, but there is also a design of the measurement of the criterion. These two designs might well be different, so that if multiple perceivers judge a target, there might be different criterion scores for each perceiver or there might be only one. If perceivers judge how extraverted in general each target would be, there would be a single score for each target. If, however, the perceiver were to judge how extraverted the target would be when interacting with the perceiver, there would be multiple scores for each target. Kenny and Albright (1987), responding to the concerns of Swann (1984), argued that there should be a different criterion measure for each target whenever possible.

A second feature of the designs in this chapter concerns the multiple measures for each perceiver–target combination. Recall that measurements in accuracy research are typically multivariate. For many of the analyses, the units of measurements should be the same. For example, the measures are all on seven-point scales. Additionally, the measures also need to be oriented in the same way. Usually, that orientation is in terms of positivity, and so larger numbers refer to more of something good. Sometimes the measures cannot be oriented in terms of a positivity continuum because the opposite pole of a measure may not necessarily imply something negative (e.g., masculine–feminine). Measures can be oriented in other ways; for example, larger scores mean more stereotypically masculine. For an illustration of how results can change when some of the measures are reoriented, consult Richards and Cline (1963).

Besides the orientation of the measures, there should be a sufficient number of measures to compute a correlation coefficient of some measure of profile similarity. However, the usual guidelines for sample sizes used in nomothetic research are inappropriate for idiographic research. As shown later in this chapter, meaningful results for idiographic accuracy are obtained with as few as four measurements.

In some situations, the measures have very different units. For instance, the perceiver might judge the target's intelligence in IQ points, weight in kilograms, and age in years. In such a case, the units might be made "equivalent" through standardization or $Z$ scoring. However, it can at times be difficult to decide exactly how to perform the standardization.[1] For instance, in MTMP designs, is the standardization done across targets within a perceiver, across perceivers within targets, or across relationships?

A final feature concerns not so much the design, but the analysis. We have emphasized that accuracy research very often involves multiple perceivers, targets, and measures. Each of these factors can be treated as either fixed or random. If the factor were fixed, the conclusions of the study would refer to only those units that were sampled. For instance, if the classic design were used and targets were treated as fixed, then the conclusions would refer to only those targets sampled. However, treating a factor as random greatly complicates the analysis. Ideally in accuracy research, perceivers, targets, and measures should be treated as random factors. We note that research using tests (e.g., the IPT) conventionally treats target or item as fixed, but modern psychometric methods do allow for treating these factors as random.

A design factor not considered much in this chapter is that of roles (Kenny, 1996). For instance, in some groups people are designated as mothers, fathers, and children. In this chapter, we generally treat persons, both perceivers and targets, as if they were interchangeable and so presume that there are no roles.

## THIS CHAPTER'S FOCUS

In this chapter, we concentrate on the measurement of accuracy for the 1P1T and MPMT designs, although we give some consideration to the MP1T and

---

[1] Standardization is just one form of linear transformation. Alternatively, it is possible to choose the coefficients for transformations empirically. That is, for the measure $Y$, the coefficients $a$ and $b$ that form $a + bY$ would be empirically derived.

1PMT designs. Additionally, for each, we consider both a nomothetic and an idiographic analysis. For each of these analyses, we provide a partitioning of variance of both the judgment and the criterion measures into components. We illustrate the methods by the analysis of data. The details of the computation are presented in the Appendix for smaller data sets.

We develop four types of accuracy for the 1P1T design, two for nomothetic analysis and two for idiographic analysis. An important concern is the degree of homogeneity in the accuracy correlations. The homogeneity question in the idiographic analysis is whether persons vary in their accuracy. Homogeneity in the nomothetic analysis concerns whether accuracy is the same for the different measures. For the MPMT design, we develop eight measures of accuracy for the nomothetic analysis and four for the idiographic analysis.

The approach that we develop in this chapter can be applied to many questions in dyadic research besides accuracy. If the research problem is bivariate and dyadic, this new approach can be used. For instance, self–other agreement can be studied by the methods developed in this chapter, and in fact one of our example data sets concerns self–other agreement. Also, the criterion variable need not be the "truth," but it might be a "bias" that the perceiver uses to approximate the truth. For instance, the criterion score might be how similar the perceiver feels he or she is to the target. Thus, the bias of assumed similarity can be studied by the same method as accuracy. Ideally, accuracy and bias can be studied in a combined analysis (Kenny & Acitelli, in press) in which both the truth and bias compete to explain variance in the judgments. For example, to what extent is the judgment determined by the truth and assumed similarity?

## THE 1P1T DESIGN

In this design, each perceiver judges a single target on a set of measures, and for each of these measurements there is a criterion score. This is probably the most common design in accuracy research. Sometimes the design is reciprocal, as when husbands judge wives and vice versa.

The example data set is taken from Winquist (1999). Forty students judged their own personality and were judged by a parent on 10 measures, 2 for each of the Big Five factors. The following were measures of each factor: *extraversion*—sociable, outgoing; *agreeableness*—good-natured, courteous; *conscientiousness*—responsible, serious; *emotional stability*—calm, sedate; and *culture*—intelligent, scholarly. We treat the parent rating as the judgment and the self-rating as the criterion.[2]

---

[2]Kenny (1994) did not treat self–other agreement as accuracy, but most other treatments of accuracy do (Funder, 1995).

## Idiographic Analysis

We begin by computing the correlation between the judgment and the criterion for each perceiver–target pair using the 10 measures as the units of analysis. These correlations are sometimes called $q$ correlations. When we did so for the Winquist data set, we obtained an average correlation (transformed into Fisher's $z$, averaged, and this average transformed back to $r$) of .498. We present this value and others to follow in Table 14.2. We can test the statistical significance of this correlation by multiplying the average Fisher $z$ value by the square root of the product of $k - 3 \times N$, where $k$ is the number of measures (10 for the example) and $N$ the number of perceiver–target dyads (40 for the example). The resulting value is a standard normal or $Z$ variable. We can then test the null hypothesis that the average correlation is zero. For the example, we have .547(7 $\times$ 40)$^{1/2}$ yielding a $Z = 9.16$ ($p < .001$).

Such idiographic correlations contain stereotype accuracy (Cronbach, 1955). That is, the judgment and the criterion might be correlated because their mean profiles are correlated. A parent might be just as accurate at predicting some other child's self-rating as his or her own child. To determine the extent to which there is stereotype accuracy, we compute, for each measure, the mean rating of the judgments made by the 40 parents; we also compute for each measure the mean rating of the criterion (i.e., self-ratings made by the 40 students), and then correlate the two. For the Winquist data set, there is very

TABLE 14.2

Accuracy Results in the 1P1T Design From Winquist's (1999) Data

| Measure | Correlation |
| --- | --- |
| Idiographic | |
| Undifferentiated | .498, $p < .001$ |
| Differentiated | |
| Stereotype accuracy | .932, $p < .001$ |
| Adjusted | .311, $p < .001$ |
| Test of homogeneity | $\chi^2(38) = 39.14, p = .418$ |
| Nomothetic | |
| Undifferentiated | .325, $p < .001$ |
| Differentiated | |
| Differential elevation accuracy | .352, $p = .026$ |
| Adjusted | .300, $p < .001$ |
| Test of homogeneity | $\chi^2(8) = 11.26, p = .187$ |

strong stereotype accuracy, the correlation being .932, a statistically significant correlation despite the small number of measures. Thus, the mean ratings of parents and students are virtually identical.

One simple way to remove the effects of stereotype accuracy, used by many investigators (e.g., Bernieri et al., 1994), is to subtract the mean across persons for each measure before computing the correlations. To be clear, we compute the means across perceivers in the judgments for each measure and subtract that mean from the judgments of that measure. We also compute the mean for each criterion measure across targets and subtract that mean from each corresponding criterion measurement. We then correlate the sets of adjusted scores for each perceiver–target pair. When we do so for the Winquist data set, we find that the average value (transformed into Fisher's $z$, averaged, and transformed back to $r$) is .311. Thus, removing stereotype accuracy lowers the correlation by about 40%. To test this correlation, we use the test $Z = z[(N - 1)(k - 3)]^{1/2}$, where $z$ is the Fisher's $z$ of the average correlation and $N$ and $k$ are defined as earlier. The test of the .311 correlation yields a $Z = 5.32, p < .001$.

An alternative strategy is to allow for the possibility that perceivers differentially endorse the stereotype. In essence, the judgments are regressed on the stereotype (the mean judgment). The details of this approach are described in Kenny and Acitelli (1994). We have generally found that the simple subtraction of the means is as effective as the more complicated method developed by Kenny and Acitelli (1994).

We next test whether the correlations vary, or the degree of heterogeneity in the correlations. That is, is the correlation the same for all perceiver–target pairs? Can we explain the variation in correlations by sampling error? The usual expectation in an idiographic analysis is that correlations do in fact vary by persons. The test of homogeneity statistically evaluates the hypothesis that the correlations do not vary by person. Statistically, this test can be accomplished by computing $(k - 3)\Sigma(z-\bar{z})^2$, where $k$ is the number of measures, $z$ is the Fisher's $r$-to-$z$ transformation of the idiographic correlations, and the summation is across persons. If the correlations are homogeneous, then the above quantity is distributed as chi = square with $N - 2$ degrees of freedom, where $N$ is the number of perceiver–target pairs.[3] When we applied this test to the Winquist data set, we obtained $\chi^2(38) = 39.14, p = .418$. Thus, in this data set there is no evidence of individual differences in accuracy. Therefore, we believe that it would be inappropriate to correlate the idiographic correlations, whether $z$ transformed or not, with individual difference variables because the data suggest that the correlations do not vary by persons.

We should note that others differ with our approach. They advocate a search for moderators even if there is not statistically significant variation in the corre-

---

[3] The degrees of freedom are $N - 2$ not $N - 1$, because of the removal of the effects due to stereotype accuracy.

lations. However, we do not see the utility of taking a variable that has essentially zero reliability and correlating it with other variables. Of course, we should not confuse a statistically nonsignificant test statistic with the absence of variance. Work is needed on the power of these tests of homogeneity.

## Nomothetic Analysis

Traditionally the nomothetic correlational analysis involves computing the simple correlations of judgments across targets for each measure. Accuracy is the correlation between judgment and criterion (i.e., parent and student) for each of the 10 measures. When we do this for the Winquist data set, we obtain the correlations of .519, .219, .403, .200, .207, .558, .316, .116, .193, and .215. To pool these correlations we use structural equation modeling. For statistical reasons,[4] we use unrestricted least squares, not the more conventional maximum likelihood estimation. Each measure becomes a latent variable (the loading matrix is an identity matrix, and there is no error variance), and the correlations are set equal to each other. Using this method, the average of the 10 correlations is .325, which is reported in Table 14.2.

In the idiographic analysis, there is the potential confounding due to stereotype accuracy, whereas in the nomothetic analysis, there is the potential confounding due to differential elevation accuracy. How the perceiver generally evaluates the target across the measures may be correlated with the average of the target's scores on the criterion. Although differential elevation accuracy can be considered to be a form of a true accuracy (Cronbach, 1955), it is valuable to understand, if there is accuracy, how that accuracy is obtained. Thus, it seems sensible to partition the nomothetic accuracy correlation into differential elevation accuracy and differential accuracy.

To measure differential elevation accuracy, we compute for each perceiver–target pair the mean perceiver's judgments across measures and correlate it with mean of criterion scores across measures. For the Winquist data set, the correlation is .352 ($p = .026$). Thus, this result suggests that parents' average rating (i.e., favorability) of their child modestly correlates with the average self-rating of the child (i.e., favorability).

To remove the effects of differential elevation accuracy, we subtract the mean of the measures for each perceiver from the judgments and the mean of the criterion scores from each target and then correlate the adjusted ratings for each measure. For the 10 measures of the Winquist study, we find that the correlations are .510, −.110, .058, .263, .404, .551, .147, .246, .318, and .353. To pool these correlations, we again use structural equation modeling, again using unre-

---

[4]The reason that this method of statistical estimation should be used is that we remove differential elevation components, and when this is done, the correlation matrix becomes singular and maximum likelihood estimation is impossible.

stricted least squares, and their average is .300. The standard chi-square test is a test of homogeneity. For the example $\chi^2(8) = 11.26$, $p = .187$. (Note the degrees of freedom are 8, not 9, because 1 degree of freedom is lost for the controlling for differential elevation.) Thus, we conclude that the correlations do not vary as a function of measure.

## Summary

There are strong parallels between the idiographic and nomothetic analyses. A naive researcher ignores the Cronbach components: The standard idiographic analysis ignores the trait component resulting in stereotype accuracy, and the standard nomothetic analysis ignores the target component resulting in differential elevation accuracy. In a complete analysis, these components are removed before the correlations are computed. Moreover, we can also determine whether these correlations are equal, homogeneous across persons in the idiographic analysis, and homogeneous across measures in the nomothetic analysis. The search for moderation (of persons for the idiographic analysis and measures for the nomothetic analysis) begins only after significant variation is found.

The careful reader may have noticed that the average adjusted correlations from the nomothetic and idiographic analyses are essentially the same (.311 for idiographic and .300 for nomothetic). We obtain essentially the same value from what are apparently two different forms of analysis. Because the very same data are being analyzed by different methods, the results must be parallel. However, past researchers (e.g., Pelham, 1993) have not been familiar with this essential similarity, obscured by the varying influences of components. These researchers have reported results demonstrating that for a given data set, an idiographic analysis produces higher levels of congruence than a nomothetic analysis between self-ratings and personality appraisals received from others. A reanalysis using our componential approach will yield analogous interpersonal agreement estimates.[5]

## THE MPMT DESIGN

In this design, each perceiver judges multiple targets, and each target is judged by multiple perceivers. The prototypical design is one in which the perceivers and targets are different people and each perceiver judges each target. Another common MPMT design is the round-robin design. In this design, the perceivers and the targets are the same persons and they all judge one another. Some MPMT designs, such as the round-robin design, are reciprocal in the sense that

---

[5]With large samples and perfect homogeneity of variance and covariance, the idiographic and the nomothetic analyses would be exactly identical. However, with finite samples and some heterogeneity, there would be some discrepancy between the two analyses.

if Clyde judges Bonnie, Bonnie also judges Clyde. However, we are not focusing on reciprocity in this chapter.

The example data set was gathered by DePaulo, Kenny, Hoover, Webb, and Oliver (1987) and is a study of metaperception: Do perceivers know how others view them? The study is a symmetric block design in which six persons are divided into two sets of three, and a member of each set interacts with all members of the other set. The people interacted and rated their partner on how competent they viewed the partner (the sum of dominant, intelligent, and confident), and they guessed how their partner rated them. Meta-accuracy is the degree of correspondence between how one thinks another sees him or her and how that other actually sees them. The measurements took place at four different times. Therefore, in this case, time is treated as a multiple measurement.

## Nomothetic Analysis: The Traditional Analysis

The analysis of accuracy in this case begins with a traditional SRM analysis. As described in Kenny and Albright (1987) and Kenny (1994), we partition the judgment and criterion measures into mean, actor, partner, and relationship. Consider that we have judgments of competence by a set of perceivers on a set of targets. The meanings of the four SRM components of the judgment data are as follows:

Grand Mean: The average of the competence judgments across perceivers and targets.
Actor: How much competence a given perceiver sees in others.
Partner: How competent a given target is generally seen by others.
Relationship: How competent a given perceiver sees a given target after actor and partner effects are removed.

To keep the discussion general, we use the terms *actor* and *partner*, and not *perceiver* and *target*. Assuming that there is a criterion measurement for each actor–partner combination, a parallel SRM decomposition of the criterion measure can be undertaken. For metaperception, an actor guesses how a partner views that actor. The SRM decomposition of metaperception is:

Grand Mean: The average of the metaperceptions across actors and partners.
Actor: How competent an actor thinks others view him or her.
Partner: How competent a partner is thought by others to generally view others.
Relationship: How competent an actor thinks that a partner views that actor after actor and partner effects are removed.

For those not familiar with SRM decomposition, actor, partner, and relationship are treated as random variables. The focus in an SRM analysis is the variance associated with each component. Computations of SRM variances are rather complex (see Appendix C of Kenny, 1994, for details). Programs for computing SRM variances and correlations can be downloaded at http://nw3.nai.net/~dakenny/srm.htm. Moreover, the appendix of this chapter details the computations.

Following Kenny and Albright (1987), the links between the SRM components define four different types of accuracy, which are illustrated in Fig. 14.2:

Elevation: Degree of correspondence between the judgment mean and the criterion mean.

Perceiver: Degree of correlation between the actor effect in the judgments and the partner effect in the criterion measure.

Generalized: Degree of correlation between the partner effect in the judgments and the actor effect in the criterion measure.

Dyadic: Degree of correlation between the relationship effect in the judgments and the relationship effect in the criterion measure.

Elevation accuracy can be measured only if the units of measurement of the judgment and the criterion are the same. As Kenny and Albright (1987) pointed out, these four types of accuracy—given that only one feature (competence in this case) is being judged—parallel the classic Cronbach types of accuracy (cf. Figs. 14.2 and 14.1).

Several studies have used Kenny and Albright's system to study meta-accuracy (Does Bonnie know that Clyde likes her?), as opposed to target accuracy (Does Bonnie know what Clyde is really like?). For meta-accuracy, generalized accuracy refers to the correlation between the actor effect in the judgment and the partner effect in the criterion. Perceiver accuracy is also "flipped" in a parallel fashion. The evidence from previous studies (Kenny & DePaulo, 1993) is consistent in showing little or no evidence of dyadic accuracy for both target accuracy and meta-accuracy. The finding of no dyadic target ac-

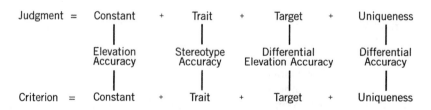

FIG. 14.2. Kenny and Albright (1987) four types of accuracy.

curacy is contrary to the theorizing of Swann (1984) and others. There is, however, some evidence for dyadic meta-accuracy of liking. People know who particularly likes and dislikes them. When there is partner variance in the judgments, there is typically evidence for generalized accuracy for both target accuracy as well as meta-accuracy. There is virtually no evidence for perceiver accuracy for either target or meta-accuracy.

## Nomothetic Analysis:
## A New Analysis

Kenny and Albright's (1987) analysis of accuracy is limited in that it considers only the accuracy for a single variable. Having multiple variables allows for a more detailed analysis of accuracy. In this section we show how to extend Kenny and Albright's (1987) analysis to multiple variables.

The variance of each of the four SRM components can be considered to be stable and unstable across the multiple measures. That is, the variance of the SRM component would be stable if it correlated across measures and unstable if it did not. Table 14.3 presents this SRM partitioning for the judgment variables. *Stable* refers to a theoretical average of the SRM component averaged over the population of measures, and so it is a latent or random variable. *Unstable* refers to the measure minus the stable component—that is, variance that changes across measures.

If the measures were treated as fixed, then the stable component would be estimated by the simple average of the measures. A fixed analysis would require two SRM analyses: one on the average of the set of measures and the other on the deviations from this average. A random effects analysis, described by Kenny (1994), is used here.

As seen in Table 14.4, there are eight types of nomothetic accuracy. Each of the four SRM types of accuracy developed by Kenny and Albright (1987) can be examined in terms of stable and unstable sources of variance. For the stable components, we use the same terms as those of Kenny and Albright. The new terms are for the unstable components. For the means, we use the term *nomothetic stereotype accuracy* because it refers to the correspondence in the means across perceivers and targets. To be clear, stereotype accuracy in the Cronbach system refers to accuracy in knowing the stereotype (the mean profile) for each perceiver (i.e., accuracy in predicting the generalized other), whereas here we mean it to refer to accuracy across perceivers and targets.

For the remaining three components we use the term *differential* in the unstable case. There is differential perceiver, generalized, and dyadic accuracy. For each, we compute the mean across measures of the SRM component and subtract that mean from each measure. Using these residual effects, accuracy correlations are computed for each measure and then averaged. *Differential perceiver accuracy* refers to the correspondence of the residual actor effect in the

TABLE 14.3

Social Relations Model (SRM) Partitioning of the Judgment
With Multiple Measures

Mean

- Stable: How perceivers generally see all of the targets across the set of measures.
- Unstable: How perceivers generally see all of the targets differentially for each measure.

Actor

- Stable: How perceivers differ on how they see all the targets across all the measures.
- Unstable: How perceivers differ on how they see all the targets differentially for each measure.

Partner

- Stable: How targets differ on how they are seen by all the perceivers across all the measures.
- Unstable: How targets differ on how they are seen by all the perceivers differentially for each measure.

Relationship

- Stable: How a perceiver uniquely views a target across all the measures.
- Unstable: How a perceiver uniquely views a target differentially for each measure.

judgments with the residual partner effect in the criterion measure. *Differential generalized accuracy* refers to the correspondence of the residual partner effect in the judgments to the residual actor effect in the criterion measure. *Differential dyadic accuracy* refers to the correspondence of the residual relationship effect in the judgments to the residual relationship effect in the criterion measure. (Differential generalized accuracy parallels differential accuracy in the nomothetic analysis for the 1P1T design; additionally, generalized accuracy is similar to nomothetic differential elevation accuracy for the 1P1T design.)

Recall that for 1P1T designs, we examined whether the accuracy varied across measures. The analysis that we have described assumes such homogeneity without ever testing for it. One complication in testing for homogeneity in MPMT designs is that there are three different ways in which homogeneity might be violated: actor, partner, and relationship. If the homogeneity of the correlations of the measures is a key question, then effect estimates of the relevant component might be estimated (see Appendix B in Kenny, 1994), and the data structure would become a 1P1T design, and so the analysis method for that design would be used.

## TABLE 14.4

Nomothetic Target Accuracy for Social Relations Model (SRM) Designs

| Judgment | Criterion | Name | Description[a] |
|---|---|---|---|
| Mean | Mean | | |
| Stable | Stable | Elevation | Discrepancy in overall means |
| Unstable | Unstable | Nomothetic stereotype accuracy | Correlation of the measure means |
| Actor | Partner | | |
| Stable | Stable | Perceiver accuracy | Correlation of the average actor effect with the average partner effect |
| Unstable | Unstable | Differential perceiver accuracy | Correlation of the residual partner effect with the residual actor effect |
| Partner | Actor | | |
| Stable | Stable | Generalized accuracy | Correlation of the average partner effect with the average actor effect |
| Unstable | Unstable | Differential generalized accuracy | Correlation of the residual partner effect with the residual actor effect |
| Relationship | Relationship | | |
| Stable | Stable | Dyadic accuracy | Correlation of the average relationship effect with the average relationship effect |
| Unstable | Unstable | Differential dyadic accuracy | Correlation of the residual relationship effect with the residual relationship effect |

Note. [a]The "average" is across measures, and the "residual" is the deviation of the measure from the average.

We have assumed that the criterion has the same design as that for the judgments, and this may not be the case (see Kenny & Albright, 1987). For instance, it is possible that the criterion score may be the same for every perceiver. For instance, students might judge the personality of teachers that they have in common, and the criterion is the self-rating of those teachers.[6] In such a situation, the criterion would have no partner or relationship variance, and so only elevation, nomothetic stereotype, generalized, and differential generalized accuracy can be measured.

---

[6]We might ask the teachers to rate their teaching style for each of the different students, but this measurement strategy is not commonly done.

Table 14.5 presents the nomothetic results from our reanalysis of DePaulo et al.'s (1987) study of meta-accuracy. We first consider the sources of variances in the measures. For judgments (metaperceptions), the bulk of the variance (49%) is stable actor variance. People think that they make the same impression on every measure for every partner, but people vary on what this impression might be. The next largest source of variance is relationship unstable: The person thinks that different people see him or her differently on the different measures. Very often this source of variance is treated as error.

For the criterion measure (impressions), the largest source of variance is actor stable: Some people generally see others as competent and others do not. The next largest source of variance is relationship unstable.

We computed accuracy correlations between terms that explained at least 5% of the total variance. All of the correlations are positive. The correlation between the unstable means reflects the fact that changes in the means of the metaperceptions paralleled changes in the means of impressions. The correlation between the stable actor effect of metaperceptions with stable partner in impressions means that people who think that they generally make a good or a bad impression are right. The correlation between the relationship stable components means that if a person thinks that overall he or she made a good or bad

TABLE 14.5

Nomothetic Results From DePaulo et al.'s (1987) Data

| Judgment | % Variance | Criterion | % Variance | Accuracy r |
|---|---|---|---|---|
| Mean | | Mean | | |
| Stable | 44.66[a] | Stable | 45.15[a] | .49[b] |
| Unstable | 0.10 | Unstable | 0.07 | 1.00 |
| Actor | | Partner | | |
| Stable | 0.49 | Stable | 0.06 | .37 |
| Unstable | 0.02 | Unstable | 0.00 | |
| Partner | | Actor | | |
| Stable | 0.03 | Stable | 0.35 | |
| Unstable | 0.00 | Unstable | 0.04 | |
| Relationship | | Relationship | | |
| Stable | 0.08 | Stable | 0.17 | .47 |
| Unstable | 0.29 | Unstable | 0.31 | .30 |

Note. Empty cells indicate that there was insufficient variance to compute the correlation.
[a]The value is a mean not a variance.
[b]The value is the absolute difference between means and not a correlation.

impression on a particular other person, the person was right. Finally, the correlation between the relationship unstable component implies that if Clyde sees Bonnie as especially competent at one particular time, then Bonnie believes that Clyde sees her as especially competent at that time.

Because of the complexity of the concepts, a second example might help even if it is only hypothetical. Consider strangers who interact with each other and rate their partner on each of the Big Five factors. Observers code each person's behavior in these interactions, and so these behavioral measures are aggregated to create a behavioral Big Five measurement. We describe the meaning of eight types of accuracy.

It is likely that the units of measurement of the stranger ratings and the observer codings, which serve as the criterion, would not be comparable. If they were, however, elevation accuracy would answer the question, Are the interactions perceived to be as positive by the interactants as by the observers? Nomothetic stereotype accuracy would concern the relative prevalence of the Big Five characteristics. For instance, if extraversion were the most prevalent Big Five factor as rated by interactants, would it be seen as most prevalent by observers?

Perceiver accuracy would imply that perceivers who generally see their partners positively have partners who behave positively. Differential perceiver accuracy would imply that perceivers who generally see their partners positively for one Big Five factor and negatively on a second had partners who behave positively on the one factor and negatively on the other. Perceiver accuracy and differential perceiver accuracy imply that perceivers have some insight into how others in general uniquely behave with them.

Generalized accuracy would imply that a person who is generally seen positively by others actually behaves positively with others. Differential generalized accuracy would imply that a person who is seen positively on one Big Five factor and negatively on a second actually behaves that way with others. *Generalized accuracy* and *differential generalized accuracy* imply that perceivers' consensual judgments of others correspond to the judgments of the observers.

Finally, *dyadic accuracy* would imply that a person who is seen positively by one perceiver and is not seen so positively by other perceivers behaves positively with that one perceiver. Differential dyadic accuracy would imply that a person who is seen as particularly positive on one Big Five factor by another person and not so positively on another factor behaves that way with that person. Dyadic accuracy and differential dyadic accuracy would imply that how a person uniquely sees his or her interaction partner corresponds with how the observers uniquely view that partner with that person.

## Idiographic Analysis

As in the 1P1T design, we can relate the set of judgments to the set of criterion measures. The basic plan for the MPMT design is to compute a measure of judgment–criterion association for each relationship and submit the set of measures to a social relations analysis to decompose the variance of idiographic accuracy into SRM components (e.g., Sabatelli, Buck, & Kenny, 1986).

When we considered the 1P1T design, the measure of profile similarity was the correlation coefficient. We correlated the judgment and the criterion variable. However, other measures of association, besides the correlation coefficient, can be computed. Although not often realized, virtually all measures of nonverbal sensitivity and empathic accuracy measures can be viewed as profile similarity measures. Measures of the number correct, the typical measure in these studies, can be viewed as a reverse discrepancy score, and so is a measure of the correspondence between a judgment and a criterion.

Imagine that we have judgment and criterion data, and the correlation across measures between the two is the measure of accuracy. There are many different ways to compute such a correlation. One reasonable plan is to use the relationship unstable component, rather than correlating the raw scores. Thus, the mean, actor, partner, and relationship components are removed before computing the correlations. In the example, we use these values to compute the correlations that are akin to the Cronbach differential accuracy computed for each perceiver–target combination.

As we discussed earlier, even if the judgment has a MPMT structure, the criterion may not vary as a function of the interaction partner. Consider the question of self–other agreement; self-ratings serve as the criterion measure. If the self-measurements are taken only once, the criterion has a two-way data structure: Person × measure. Before computing the idiographic correlations, we would remove the person and measure components and use the residuals to compute the correlations.

The resulting set of profile similarity measures has a MPMT structure, which can be submitted to an SRM analysis (e.g., Ickes et al., in press). Table 14.6 presents the four types of accuracy that result from the SRM analysis of idiographic accuracy. Consider first *average idiographic accuracy*, which reflects the mean accuracy coefficient computed across all perceivers and all targets. Average idiographic accuracy corresponds to differential dyadic accuracy in the

TABLE 14.6

Idiographic Accuracy for MPMT Designs

| Component | Type of Accuracy |
| --- | --- |
| Mean | Average idiographic accuracy |
| Actor | Perceiver idiographic accuracy |
| Partner | Target idiographic accuracy |
| Relationship | Relational idiographic accuracy |

nomothetic analysis. As in the 1P1T analysis, there are parallels between the nomothetic and the idiographic analysis.

The next two types of accuracy concern individual differences in nomothetic accuracy. One type measures the "good judge" (see Colvin & Bundick, chap. 3, this volume) and is denoted as *perceiver idiographic accuracy*. This measure estimates the extent to which some judges are consistently more accurate than others. The other measures the "good target" (Colvin, 1993; Funder, 1995) and is denoted as *target idiographic accuracy*. This measure shows the extent to which some targets are consistently judged more accurately than other targets. It is possible to correlate these accuracy measures with individual difference variables.

The final measure of accuracy is *relational idiographic accuracy*, which represents the extent to which relationships differ in accuracy. Because this measure is confounded with error, to separate error from relationship, one would need two or more replications of idiographic accuracy. For instance, the measures would be divided into two sets, and the idiographic correlations would be computed within each set. Even without replications, one way to establish its meaningfulness is by correlations. For instance, if there were dyadic reciprocity (Bonnie is good at reading Clyde, and Clyde is good at reading Bonnie), that would begin to establish the reliability of relational idiographic accuracy.

It is helpful to think of the meaning of the four types of accuracy where the measure is of nonverbal sensitivity. Actors take on the role of decoders or receivers, and partners take on the role of encoders or senders.[7] Imagine that the measure is the percentage of correct judgments. Average idiographic accuracy would refer to the grand mean. If chance accuracy could be determined, we could judge whether the encoders and decoders were performing above chance. Perceiver idiographic accuracy refers to decoding differences. Target idiographic accuracy refers to encoding differences. Finally, relational idiographic accuracy refers to whether some encoders are especially able to send to specific decoders.

For the idiographic analysis of DePaulo et al.'s (1987) data set, we computed regression slopes using the criterion to predict the metaperception. First, the level of average idiographic accuracy equals .36, which, when expressed as a correlation,[8] equals .30 (the same value as differential dyadic accuracy of .30 in Table 14.5). The average idiographic accuracy is statistically significantly greater than zero. People are aware of how competent or incompetent other people think they are in their interactions.

---

[7]Some readers may be familiar with the paper by Zuckerman, Lipets, Koivumaki, and Rosenthal (1975), in which they measured both encoding and decoding skill in the same sample. Our approach is similar to theirs, but we prefer to measure a skill score for each encoder–decoder dyad. Thus, from the one set of skill scores, both decoding and encoding accuracy can be measured.

[8]To convert a regression coefficient into a correlation coefficient, one computes $b(s^x/s^y)$, where $b$ is the regression coefficient, $s^x$ the standard deviation of the predictor, and $s^y$ the standard deviation of the criterion.

We have evidence for perceiver idiographic accuracy (18% of the total variance, $p < .05$), indicating that some perceivers were more accurate than others. We do not find any evidence for target idiographic accuracy (0% of the total variance). The largest source of variance is relational idiographic accuracy (82% of the total variance), but this is confounded with error. To determine how much of the variance is error, we would need multiple measures of idiographic accuracy.

Given that there is evidence for perceiver accuracy but not target accuracy, we can examine the extent to which individual differences correlate with perceiver accuracy, but not target accuracy. The two statistically significant correlates that we found with perceiver idiographic accuracy are that perceivers higher in social anxiety ($r = .79$, $p < .05$) and those lower on the extraversion subscale of self-monitoring ($r = -.91$, $p < .05$) were more accurate. The two variables correlate with a value of $-.71$. Thus, introverts were more accurate than extraverts.

We examined whether idiographic accuracy is reciprocal. At the individual level, we did not test whether more accurate perceivers were also targets who were more accurately perceived because there was no idiographic target variance. There was virtually no evidence for reciprocity at the dyadic level ($r = -.04$, ns). Thus, if Clyde is an especially good reader of Bonnie, Bonnie is not necessarily a good reader of Clyde.

## Conclusion

As with the 1P1T design, we find a parallel in the nomothetic and idiographic analyses in the MPMT designs. However, it is much more difficult to see. We find that the differential dyadic accuracy in the nomothetic analysis is about equal to the average idiographic accuracy.

MPMT designs allow for much more detail than do other designs. This detail might well intimidate some. We have identified 12 types of accuracy, 8 for the nomothetic analysis and 4 for the idiographic analysis.[9] We need to realize that although the full model is potentially very complex, rarely will the data from studies exhibit this full complexity. We return to issues of complexity in computation and interpretation in the final section of this chapter.

### MP1T AND 1PMT DESIGNS

In the MP1T design, multiple perceivers judge each target, whereas in the 1PMT design, each perceiver judges multiple targets. These designs are mixtures of both the 1P1T and MPMT designs, and their analysis is also a mixture of the methods used to analyze those designs.

---

[9]It would be possible to have eight types of idiographic measures, as there are for nomothetic accuracy, if there were multiple measure or replications of the idiographic measure.

The analysis of an MP1T design would begin by showing that the perceivers agree in their judgments of the targets.[10] One way of doing so would be to compute the intraclass correlation for each variable (Funder & Colvin, 1988). This analysis is essentially a one-way analysis of variance (ANOVA) in which the target is the independent variable and the perceivers are the "subjects." In some MP1T designs, the perceivers can be distinguished by roles (e.g., male and female; parent and friend; friend and stranger). For such a case, the data can be treated as a series of 1P1T designs. Consider, for example, Kenrick and Stringfield's (1980) classic study in which a parent and a friend rated the same target. We could treat this as a 1P1T design by making one set of judgments the criterion and so determine the extent to which the parent's or friend's judgments correlate.

If perceivers are indistinguishable and the perceivers agree, we could average or aggregate the ratings of the perceivers for each target and measure. The resulting data structure would have a 1P1T structure, and the data could be analyzed by those methods for that design. Alternatively, we could undertake a variance decomposition approach as we did in the analysis of the MPMT designs. In terms of the SRM, actor and relationship effects are confounded for the MP1T design, whereas partner and relationship are confounded for the 1PMT design. Because the central focus in accuracy research is very often the target or partner, MP1T are much more common than 1PMT designs. Henss (1997) empirically compared MP1T and MPMT designs. He was interested in the degree of consensus (i.e., the degree of agreement about targets or partner variance). He found that the estimates were essentially the same in the two designs.

Particularly in accuracy research, 1PMT designs are uncommon. In principle, when a 1PMT and a MP1T are combined in a reciprocal design, actor, partner, and relationship effects can be separated. We return to the questions of design and components in the next section.

## CONCLUSION

One major theme of this chapter is the importance of research design to illuminate the components in the measurement of accuracy. We can learn much more about accuracy from MPMT designs than from 1P1T designs. Table 14.7 presents what sources of variance can be studied in the different designs. In 1P1T designs, actor, partner, and relationship effects are all confounded. Relationship effects are confounded with actor in the MP1T designs, and relationship effects are confounded with partner in 1PMT designs. Only in the MPMT designs can the three sources of variances be separated.

---

[10]It is possible for two perceivers to disagree, yet both be partially accurate. Strictly speaking, then, agreement is not a prerequisite of accuracy. However, when perceivers have access to the same reality, it would seem that agreement is necessary for accuracy.

TABLE 14.7

Sources of Social Relations Model (SRM) Variance for the Different Designs

| 1P1T |
|---|
| Score = (Actor + Partner + Relationship) |
| MP1T |
| Score = (Actor + Relationship) + Partner |
| 1PMT |
| Score = Actor + (Partner + Relationship) |
| MPMT |
| Score = Actor + Partner + Relationship |

*Note.* Terms in parentheses are confounded (effects cannot be independently estimated).

It might be argued that for simplification, the initial studies in an area should be 1P1T studies. Assuming that some degree of accuracy is found, then an MPMT study can be conducted, and the results would suggest what sort of future studies should be done. Alternatively, it might be argued that an MPMT study should be the first study in an area. Because this design separates the sources of variance, it would serve as a guide for the design of future studies. Hopefully, this chapter has communicated that the 1P1T is not a deficient research design. We have detailed the vast amount of information that can be gleaned from this design. We suspect that it would remain the most prevalent design for the analysis of accuracy.

One very surprising (even to the authors) but recurrent theme of this new approach is that idiographic and nomothetic are more alike than different. Some (e.g., Pelham, 1993) have argued that the two types of analyses are fundamentally different, and our intuition would seem to reinforce that view. However, we have illustrated their essential similarity. We believe that the decision as to whether variation is idiographic or nomothetic is more empirical than theoretical; that is, the data may reveal the necessity for an idiographic versus a nomothetic approach. For instance, if the correlations vary by person, then an idiographic analysis is necessary; but if the correlations vary by measure, then a nomothetic analysis is indicated. We strongly endorse the strategy, perhaps first introduced by Bernieri et al. (1994), to examine simultaneously the data by both the idiographic and nomothetic methods. Note that if there is no person or measure variation, the two approaches result in essentially the same result.[11]

---

[11]Factor analysts have already learned this lesson. They have shown that conventional factor analysis and *q* factor analysis yield the same information.

Certainly the analyses that we have proposed are very complicated. We have created 4 new types of accuracy for the 1P1T design and 12 new types for the MPMT design. Complications are further enhanced by the difficulty of computation and the fact that all of the analyses cannot be accomplished by one mouse click. Some of the computations must be done by hand, and others require software that is not readily available. We need to emphasize that the analyses, although difficult, are not impossible. Although the SRM is complicated, the method has been used in many articles, chapters, and dissertations.[12]

Our approach to the 1P1T design can be viewed as a form of moderator analysis. The idiographic analysis focuses on person moderators, whereas the nomothetic analysis focuses on measure moderators. Ideally, the search for person and measure moderators might be combined in a single analysis, perhaps by some form of multilevel analysis (Snijders & Kenny, in press). However, to our knowledge such an analysis cannot be accomplished now. We expect in the near future that the analyses we sketch in this chapter will become simple to accomplish. We also note that there is not an exact parallelism between the analyses of the 1P1T and MPMT designs. We believe that a single unified analysis strategy will eventually emerge.

Moreover, these complicated analyses permit a much more detailed probing into the data and will likely lead to greater theoretical refinements. We think that the problems posed by accuracy literature require the best possible design and analysis that is currently available. Accuracy research is something that is talked about a lot, but not really done very much. We hope that this volume signals an end of just talk and that researchers start doing it.

Very often the oldest paper cited by most contemporary accuracy researchers is Cronbach (1955). This chapter clearly continues the Cronbach tradition. However, there was accuracy research before Cronbach; after all he had to criticize something. Contemporary accuracy researchers owe a debt of gratitude to Rosalind Dymond and others who were the real pioneers in accuracy research. They did not have the high-speed computers, the elaborate statistical models, and the intricate statistical software to assist them in their analyses. Let us hope that this generation of accuracy researchers exploits this marvelous opportunity.

## ACKNOWLEDGMENTS

This chapter was supported in part by National Institute of Mental Health Grant R01-MH51964. We also thank the volume editors, who made many useful suggestions.

---

[12]Those interested can consult the Web site at http://nw3.nai.net/~dakenny/srmbib.htm for a compendium of papers using the SRM.

# REFERENCES

Allport, G. W. (1937). *Personality: A psychological interpretation.* New York: Holt.
Bernieri, F. J., Zuckerman, M., Koestner, R., & Rosenthal, R. (1994). Measuring person per-
ception accuracy: Another look at self–other agreement. *Personality and Social Psychology
Bulletin, 20,* 367–378.
Colvin, C. R. (1993). "Judgable" people: Personality, behavior, and competing explanations.
*Journal of Personality and Social Psychology, 64,* 861–873.
Costanzo, M., & Archer, D. (1989). Interpreting the expressive behavior of others: The In-
terpersonal Perception Task. *Journal of Nonverbal Behavior, 13,* 225–245.
Cronbach, L. J. (1955). Processes affecting scores on "understanding of others" and "assumed
similarity." *Psychological Bulletin, 52,* 177–193.
DePaulo, B., Kenny, D. A., Hoover, C., Webb, W., & Oliver, P. V. (1987). Accuracy of person
perception: Do people know what kinds of impressions they convey? *Journal of Personality
and Social Psychology, 52,* 303–315.
Dymond, R. F. (1950). Personality and empathy. *Journal of Consulting Psychology, 14,*
343–350.
Funder, D. C. (1995). On the accuracy of personality judgment: A realistic approach. *Psychological Review, 102,* 652–670.
Funder, D. C., & Colvin, C. R. (1988). Friends and strangers: Acquaintanceship, agreement,
and the accuracy of personality judgment. *Journal of Personality and Social Psychology, 55,*
149–158.
Henss, R. (1997, October). Face and personality impressions: Consensus at zero acquain-
tance. Poster presented at the 4th Arbeitstagung Differentielle Psychologie,
Persönlichkeitspsychologie und Psychologische Diagnostik, Bamberg, Germany.
Ickes, W. (1997). Introduction. In Ickes, W. (Ed.), *Empathic accuracy* (pp. 1–16). New York:
Guilford.
Ickes, W., Buysse, A., Pham, H., Rivers, K., Erickson, J. R., Hancock, M., Kelleher, J., & Gesn,
P. R. (2000). On the difficulty of distinguishing "good" and "poor" perceivers: A social re-
lations analysis of empathic accuracy data. *Personal Relationships, 1,* 219–234.
Jaccard, J., & Dittus, P. (1990). Idiographic and nomothetic perspectives on research meth-
ods and data analysis. In C. Hendrick & M. S. Clark (Eds.), *Review of personality and social
psychology: Vol. 11. Research methods in personality and social psychology* (pp. 312–351).
Thousand Oaks, CA: Sage.
John, O. P., & Robins, R. W. (1993). Determinants of interjudge agreement on personality
traits: The big five domains, observability, evaluativeness, and the unique perspective of
the self. *Journal of Personality, 61,* 521–551.
Kenny, D. A. (1994). *Interpersonal perception: A social relations analysis.* New York: Guilford.
Kenny, D. A. (1996). The design and analysis of social-interaction research. *Annual Review of
Psychology, 47,* 59–86.
Kenny, D. A., & Acitelli, L. K. (1994). Measuring similarity in couples. *Journal of Family Psy-
chology, 8,* 417–431.
Kenny, D. A., & Acitelli, L. K. (in press). Accuracy and bias in the perception of the partner a
in close relationships. *Journal of Personality and Social Psychology,* in press.
Kenny, D. A., & Albright, L. (1987). Accuracy in interpersonal perception: A social relations
analysis. *Psychological Bulletin, 102,* 390–402.
Kenny, D. A., & DePaulo, B. M. (1993). Do people know how others view them?: An empirical and theoretical account. *Psychological Bulletin, 114,* 145–161.

Kenrick, D. T., & Stringfield, D. O. (1980). Personality traits and the eye of the beholder: Crossing some traditional philosophical boundaries in the search for consistency in all of the people. *Psychological Review, 87,* 88–104.

Kruglanski, A. W. (1989). The psychology of being "right": The problem of accuracy in social perception and cognition. *Psychological Bulletin, 106,* 395–409.

Lamiell, J. T. (1981). Toward an idiothetic psychology of personality. *American Psychologist, 36,* 276–289.

Levenson, R. E., & Ruef, A. M. (1992). Empathy: A physiological substrate. *Journal of Personality and Social Psychology, 63,* 234–246.

Levesque, M. J., & Kenny, D. A. (1993). Accuracy of behavioral predictions at zero acquaintance: A social relations analysis. *Journal of Personality and Social Psychology, 65,* 1178–1187.

Malloy, T. E., & Albright, L. (1990). Interpersonal perception in a social context. *Journal of Personality and Social Psychology, 58,* 419–428.

Pelham, B. W. (1993). The idiographic nature of human personality: Examples of the idiographic self-concept. *Journal of Personality and Social Psychology, 64,* 665–677.

Richards, J. M., Jr., & Cline, V. B. (1963). Accuracy components in person perception scores and the scoring system as an artifact in investigations of the generality of judging ability. *Psychological Reports, 12,* 363–373.

Rosenthal, R., Hall, J. A., DiMatteo, M. R., Rogers, P. L., & Archer, D. (1979). *Sensitivity to nonverbal communication: The PONS test.* Baltimore: Johns Hopkins University Press.

Sabatelli, R. M., Buck, R., & Kenny, D. A. (1986). A social relations analysis of nonverbal communication accuracy in married couples. *Journal of Personality, 53,* 513–527.

Shechtman, Z., & Kenny, D. A. (1994). Meta-perception accuracy: An Israeli study. *Journal of Basic and Applied Social Psychology, 15,* 451–465.

Snijders, T. A. B., & Kenny, D. A. (1999). The social relations model for family data: A multilevel approach. *Personal Relationships, 6,* 471–486.

Snodgrass, S. E. (1985). Women's intuition: The effect of subordinate role on interpersonal sensitivity. *Journal of Personality and Social Psychology, 49,* 146–155.

Swann, W. B., Jr. (1984). Quest for accuracy in person perception: A matter of pragmatics. *Psychological Review, 91,* 457–477.

Winquist, L. A. (1999). *Componential accuracy model (CAM): Implications for the idiographic–nomothetic debate.* Unpublished masters thesis, University of Connecticut.

Zuckerman, M., Lipets, M. S., Koivumaki, H. J., & Rosenthal, R. (1975). Encoding and decoding nonverbal cues of emotion. *Journal of Personality and Social Psychology, 32,* 1068–1076.

## APPENDIX

Computational details of the analyses methods for the 1P1T and MPMT designs are presented using small data sets to enhance comprehension of the strategies outlined in this chapter. We consider both the idiographic and nomothetic analysis. For each of these analyses, we demonstrate the partitioning of both the judgment and criterion measures into components. The interested researcher can reproduce our results by following the sets of computational steps outlined in the following pages using the raw data that is provided.

### 1P1T Design

There are 10 judges each rating a different target on 10 measures. Table 14.1A presents the 10 × 10 matrix of judgments. Self-ratings made by the target on the 10 measures serve as the criterion. Table 14.2A presents these self-ratings. The raw data are extracted from a larger data set (Winquist, 1999). Ratings were all made on a nine-point scale.

*Nomothetic Analysis.*    The unit of analysis is dyad, and the correlation is computed between the judgment and the criterion for each measure. When we do this, we obtain correlations of −.156, −.336, .213, −.094, −.472, −.073, .299, .133, −.368, and .231. To pool these correlations, we use structural equa-

TABLE 14.1A

Raw Judgment Data for 1P1T Design

| Judge | Variable | | | | | | | | | | M |
|-------|-----|-----|-----|-----|-----|-----|-----|-----|-----|-----|------|
|       | 1 | 2 | 3 | 4 | 5 | 6 | 7 | 8 | 9 | 10 | |
| 1  | 7.0 | 6.0 | 4.0 | 4.0 | 8.0 | 8.0 | 6.0 | 3.0 | 3.0 | 8.0 | 5.7 |
| 2  | 8.0 | 5.0 | 7.0 | 3.0 | 7.0 | 6.0 | 6.0 | 4.0 | 4.0 | 7.0 | 5.7 |
| 3  | 6.0 | 6.0 | 6.0 | 6.0 | 6.0 | 7.0 | 6.0 | 4.0 | 4.0 | 5.0 | 5.6 |
| 4  | 8.0 | 8.0 | 9.0 | 6.0 | 8.0 | 7.0 | 8.0 | 8.0 | 5.0 | 7.0 | 7.4 |
| 5  | 7.0 | 6.0 | 7.0 | 6.0 | 7.0 | 6.0 | 4.0 | 6.0 | 4.0 | 6.0 | 5.9 |
| 6  | 7.0 | 7.0 | 8.0 | 6.0 | 8.0 | 9.0 | 7.0 | 6.0 | 5.0 | 9.0 | 7.2 |
| 7  | 7.0 | 5.0 | 8.0 | 8.0 | 8.0 | 9.0 | 8.0 | 8.0 | 4.0 | 6.0 | 7.1 |
| 8  | 8.0 | 7.0 | 7.0 | 6.0 | 8.0 | 7.0 | 8.0 | 7.0 | 6.0 | 8.0 | 7.2 |
| 9  | 7.0 | 2.0 | 6.0 | 1.0 | 8.0 | 4.0 | 4.0 | 2.0 | 1.0 | 8.0 | 4.3 |
| 10 | 7.0 | 8.0 | 6.0 | 6.0 | 8.0 | 5.0 | 8.0 | 6.0 | 6.0 | 5.0 | 6.5 |
| M  | 7.2 | 6.0 | 6.8 | 5.2 | 7.6 | 6.8 | 6.5 | 5.4 | 4.2 | 6.9 | 6.26 |

TABLE 14.2A

Raw Criterion for the 1P1T Design

| Target | 1 | 2 | 3 | 4 | 5 | 6 | 7 | 8 | 9 | 10 | M |
|--------|---|---|---|---|---|---|---|---|---|----|---|
| | | | | | *Variable* | | | | | | |
| 1 | 8.0 | 6.0 | 6.0 | 5.0 | 8.0 | 8.0 | 7.0 | 5.0 | 5.0 | 7.0 | 6.5 |
| 2 | 8.0 | 6.0 | 4.0 | 3.0 | 8.0 | 5.0 | 7.0 | 5.0 | 5.0 | 7.0 | 5.8 |
| 3 | 8.0 | 8.0 | 6.0 | 6.0 | 8.0 | 9.0 | 7.0 | 6.0 | 9.0 | 7.0 | 7.4 |
| 4 | 7.0 | 7.0 | 5.0 | 7.0 | 6.0 | 7.0 | 8.0 | 5.0 | 6.0 | 5.0 | 6.3 |
| 5 | 6.0 | 5.0 | 8.0 | 5.0 | 7.0 | 6.0 | 6.0 | 8.0 | 5.0 | 7.0 | 6.3 |
| 6 | 7.0 | 3.0 | 7.0 | 2.0 | 6.0 | 7.0 | 4.0 | 6.0 | 2.0 | 6.0 | 5.0 |
| 7 | 7.0 | 7.0 | 8.0 | 6.0 | 8.0 | 6.0 | 7.0 | 6.0 | 6.0 | 7.0 | 6.8 |
| 8 | 7.0 | 3.0 | 7.0 | 4.0 | 7.0 | 4.0 | 8.0 | 7.0 | 6.0 | 8.0 | 6.1 |
| 9 | 8.0 | 7.0 | 4.0 | 7.0 | 7.0 | 8.0 | 6.0 | 6.0 | 7.0 | 5.0 | 6.5 |
| 10 | 7.0 | 6.0 | 5.0 | 4.0 | 6.0 | 7.0 | 6.0 | 4.0 | 4.0 | 3.0 | 5.2 |
| M | 7.3 | 5.8 | 6.0 | 4.9 | 7.1 | 6.7 | 6.6 | 5.8 | 5.5 | 6.2 | 6.19 |

tion modeling using unrestricted least squares. Each measure is treated as a latent variable. The loading matrix is an identity matrix and there is no error variance. The correlations of the latent variables are set equal to each other. When we do so for this data, we find that the average of the 10 correlations is $.164, p = .113$. This and other summary values are presented in Table 14.3A.

To estimate differential elevation accuracy, for each perceiver–target pair the mean perceiver's judgments across measures (row means in Table 14.1A) are computed and correlated with the mean of criterion scores across measures (row means in Table 14.2A). For this data set, the differential elevation accuracy correlation is $-.345$ ($p = .329$). To remove the effects of elevation and differential elevation components, we subtract the mean of the measures for each perceiver from the judgments and the mean of the criterion scores for each target.

Next we compute the correlation between the judgment and criterion adjusted scores for each measure. When we do so, we obtain the following adjusted correlations: .308, $-.009$, $-.191$, $-.061$, .102, .110, .519, .261, $-.002$, and .261. To pool these correlations, we again use structural equation modeling with unrestricted least squares. When we do so, we find that the average of the ten correlations is $.226, p = .055$. The chi-square test from the structural equation modeling program is a test of homogeneity of the correlations. For this data, we obtain $\chi^2(8) = 6.31, p = .737$. The degrees of freedom for the result from the program are 9, but we lose 1 degree of freedom when we remove the differential elevation components. So, the degrees of freedom are 8, and the $p$ value needs to be adjusted accordingly.

TABLE 14.3A

Summary of the 1P1T Results

| Measure | Correlation |
|---------|-------------|
| Nomothetic | |
| Undifferentiated | $.164, p = .113$ |
| Differentiated | |
| Differential elevation accuracy | $-.345, p = .329$ |
| Adjusted | $.226, p = .055$ |
| Test of homogeneity | $\chi^2(8) = 6.31, p = .737$ |
| Idiographic | |
| Undifferentiated | $.457, p < .001$ |
| Differentiated | |
| Stereotype accuracy | $.822, p = .004$ |
| Adjusted | $.265, p = .031$ |
| Test of homogeneity | $\chi^2(8) = 13.27, p = .102$ |

*Idiographic Analysis.* We compute the correlation between the judgment and the criterion for each perceiver–target pair using measure as the unit of analysis. When we do so, we obtain correlations of .915, .701, .157, –.107, .461, .698, .106, .613, –.235, and .472 for each perceiver–target pair. The resulting average correlation is .457 (transforming the $r$s to $z$s, averaging, and then transforming back to $r$). To test the statistical significance of this correlation, we multiply the average Fisher $z$ value by the square root of the product of $k - 3 \times N$, where $k$ is the number of measures and $N$ is the number of perceiver–target dyads. The resulting value is a standard normal or $Z$ variable that can be used to test the null hypothesis that the average correlation is 0. For this example, $.4931(7 \times 10) = 4.13, p < .001$.

Next, we compute the estimate of stereotype accuracy for the data. For each variable, we compute the mean ratings of the judgment and the criterion (column means in Tables 14.1A and 14.2A). The correlation between the two sets of means is .822, $p = .004$.

To remove the effects of stereotype accuracy, we compute the mean of each trait for the judgment and criterion score, the column means in Tables 14.1A and 14.2A. We then subtract the measure mean across persons for each measure. We compute the correlation between the adjusted judgment and criterion using measure as the unit of analysis. When we do so, we obtain .838, .434, .500, .033, .394, .291, –.168, .430, –.672, and .253 for each perceiver–target pair respectively. The resulting adjusted average correlation is .265 (transformed into Fisher's $z$'s, averaged, and transformed back to $r$). We then test this correlation we use the equation $Z = z[(N-1)(k-3)]^{1/2}$. For the example, we obtain $.2717(9 \times 7)^{1/2}$ that equals 2.16, $p = .031$.

Next we calculate the homogeneity of these adjusted correlations. Statistically, this is accomplished by computing $(k-3)\Sigma(z-\bar{z})^2$, where $k$ is the number of measures, $z$ is the Fisher's $z$ transformation of the idiographic correlation, and the summation is across persons. If the correlations are homogeneous, then the quantity is distributed as a chi square with $N-2$ degrees of freedom, where $N$ is the number of perceiver–target pairs. For this data set, we obtained $\chi^2(8) = 13.27$, $p = .102$.

## MPMT

The data that we consider in Table 14.4A are a small part of DePaulo et al.'s (1987) study. In this mini data set, there are three people (A, B, and C) who attempt to determine how competent three other people (D, E, and F) view them at four different times. We have metaperceptions (the upper table) and impressions (the lower table). Note that the design is not reciprocal, in that we have not included D, E, and F's views of A, B, and C. The analysis of this data set is

TABLE 14.4A

Raw Data for the Four Time Points

| Metaperception (Judgment) | | | | | | | | | | | |
|---|---|---|---|---|---|---|---|---|---|---|---|
| Partner | | | | | | | | | | | |
| D | | | | E | | | | F | | | |
| Actor | 1 | 2 | 3 | 4 | 1 | 2 | 3 | 4 | 1 | 2 | 3 | 4 |
| A | 40 | 44 | 47 | 49 | 34 | 51 | 52 | 53 | 45 | 49 | 53 | 50 |
| B | 33 | 43 | 43 | 45 | 39 | 36 | 32 | 41 | 33 | 41 | 35 | 44 |
| C | 54 | 54 | 54 | 53 | 49 | 51 | 50 | 53 | 38 | 40 | 39 | 47 |

| Impressions (Criterion) | | | | | | | | | | | |
|---|---|---|---|---|---|---|---|---|---|---|---|
| Partner | | | | | | | | | | | |
| A | | | | B | | | | C | | | |
| Actor | 1 | 2 | 3 | 4 | 1 | 2 | 3 | 4 | 1 | 2 | 3 | 4 |
| D | 43 | 46 | 46 | 51 | 51 | 55 | 57 | 59 | 53 | 43 | 51 | 48 |
| E | 41 | 39 | 44 | 45 | 42 | 52 | 51 | 51 | 46 | 52 | 54 | 53 |
| F | 43 | 46 | 46 | 44 | 56 | 54 | 58 | 56 | 44 | 43 | 60 | 55 |

Note. T1–T4 = Times 1–4.

considerably simpler than other designs, such as round-robin (everyone rates everyone).

*Nomothetic Analysis.*    We begin by performing an SRM analysis on the four variables separately. We compute the means of each measure across the nine scores, and they are presented in Table 14.5A. Next we compute the actor and partner effect estimates. For the actor effect, we compute a mean for each row and then subtract the mean for that measure. For the partner effect, we compute a mean for each column and then subtract the mean for that measure. The relationship effect is the score minus the actor effect, the partner effect, and the mean. So for example, the relationship effect of A's metaperception of D is as follows:

$$40 - (-0.89) - 1.78 - 40.56 = -2.11$$

The entire set of relationship effects is contained in Table 16.6A.

**TABLE 14.5A**

**Nomothetic Effect Estimates**

|    | *Metaperceptions* | | | | *Impressions* | | | |
|----|----|----|----|----|----|----|----|----|
|    | *T1* | *T2* | *T3* | *T4* | *T1* | *T2* | *T3* | *T4* |
| Ms | 40.56 | 45.44 | 45.00 | 48.33 | 46.56 | 47.78 | 51.89 | 51.33 |

*Actor and partner effect estimates*

|   | *Metaperceptions—actor* | | | | *Impressions—partner* | | | |
|---|----|----|----|----|----|----|----|----|
|   | *T1* | *T2* | *T3* | *T4* | *T1* | *T2* | *T3* | *T4* |
| A | −0.89 | 2.56 | 5.67 | 2.33 | 2.44 | 0.22 | −0.56 | 1.33 |
| B | −5.56 | −5.44 | −8.33 | −5.00 | −3.56 | −0.11 | −2.22 | −1.67 |
| C | 6.44 | 2.89 | 2.67 | 2.67 | 1.11 | −0.11 | 2.78 | 0.33 |

|   | *Metaperceptions—partner* | | | | *Impressions—actor* | | | |
|---|----|----|----|----|----|----|----|----|
|   | *T1* | *T2* | *T3* | *T4* | *T1* | *T2* | *T3* | *T4* |
| D | 1.78 | 1.56 | 3.00 | 0.67 | −4.22 | −4.11 | −6.56 | −4.67 |
| E | 0.11 | 0.56 | −0.33 | 0.67 | 3.11 | 5.89 | 3.44 | 4.00 |
| F | 1.89 | −2.11 | −2.67 | −1.33 | 1.11 | −1.78 | 3.11 | 0.67 |

*Note.*   T1–T4 = Times 1–4.

# TABLE 14.6A

## Relationship Effects

### Metaperception

| Actor | Partner D | | | | Partner E | | | | Partner F | | | |
|---|---|---|---|---|---|---|---|---|---|---|---|---|
| | T1 | T2 | T3 | T4 | T1 | T2 | T3 | T4 | T1 | T2 | T3 | T4 |
| Metaperception | | | | | | | | | | | | |
| A | -1.44 | -5.56 | -6.67 | -2.33 | -5.78 | 2.44 | 1.67 | 2.33 | -7.22 | 3.11 | 5.00 | 0.67 |
| B | -3.78 | 1.44 | 3.33 | 1.00 | 3.89 | -4.56 | -4.33 | -2.67 | -0.11 | 3.11 | 1.00 | 2.00 |
| C | 5.22 | 4.11 | 3.33 | 1.33 | 1.89 | 2.11 | 2.67 | 0.33 | -7.11 | -6.22 | -6.00 | -2.67 |

### Partner

| Actor | Partner A | | | | Partner B | | | | Partner C | | | |
|---|---|---|---|---|---|---|---|---|---|---|---|---|
| | T1 | T2 | T3 | T4 | T1 | T2 | T3 | T4 | T1 | T2 | T3 | T4 |
| Impression | | | | | | | | | | | | |
| D | -1.78 | 2.11 | 1.22 | 3.00 | -1.11 | 1.11 | 2.22 | 2.33 | 2.89 | -3.22 | -3.44 | -5.33 |
| E | 2.22 | -4.56 | 0.89 | 0.00 | -4.11 | -1.56 | -2.11 | -2.67 | 1.89 | 6.11 | 1.22 | 2.67 |
| F | -0.44 | 2.44 | 2.11 | -3.00 | 5.22 | 0.44 | -0.11 | 0.33 | -4.78 | -2.89 | 2.22 | 2.67 |

*Note.* T1–T4 = Times 1–4.

The relationship variances are defined as the sum of each effect squared divided by the product of the number of actors minus 1 multiplied times the number of partners minus 1, or 4 for the example. The covariance between two sets of relationship effects (e.g., the Time 1 relationship in metaperceptions and Time 2) is the sum of the product of the two effects divided by the product of the number of actors minus 1 multiplied times the number of partners minus 1, or 4 for the example. For example, the relationship variance of the Time 1 metaperceptions is 49.61 and the covariance between Times 1 and 2 is 15.64.

The estimates of variances and covariances for actor and partner effects are more complicated than those for relationship effects. Consider the actor variance. We first compute the usual variance of actor effect estimates. Because we treat actor as a random variable, we subtract the relationship variance divided by the number of partners. For the partner variance, we also subtract the relationship and divide by the number of actors. The estimated actor variance at Time one for metaperceptions is 20.06, and the actor covariance between Times 1 and 2 for metaperceptions is 18.08.

We can summarize the set of variances and covariances in a covariance matrix. Each covariance matrix has 16, elements or $4^2$. For metaperceptions and impressions, there is an actor, partner, and relationship matrix whose diagonal consists of variances. There are three covariance matrices that summarize the association between the two variables. They are the actor effect in metaperceptions with the partner effect in impressions (generalized accuracy), the partner effect in metaperceptions with the actor effect in impressions (perceiver accuracy), and the covariance in the two sets of relationship effects (dyadic accuracy). We present the actor covariance matrix for metaperceptions and relationship covariance between metaperceptions and impressions in Table 14.7A.

Stable variance is estimated by the average of the off-diagonal values. For the actor matrix in Table 14.7A, this average of off-diagonal values is 20.76. Unstable variance is the average of the diagonal values minus the average of the off-diagonal values, and so for the actor matrix, the unstable actor variance is 1.23.

The unstable mean variance is given by the variance in the means minus the following terms: (a) unstable actor variance divided by the number of partners, (b) unstable partner variance divided by the number of actors, and (c) unstable relationship variance divided by the number of observations.

Subtracted from the covariance of means are the unstable covariances, actor-partner, partner-actor, and relationship. The entire set of estimates of stable and unstable variances and covariances for this data set is contained in Table 14.8A.

*Idiographic Analysis.*    The basic plan is to take a measure of judgment-criterion association for each actor and partner and submit that measure to a social relations analysis to decompose the variance of idiographic accuracy into components. To compute the measure of association, we use the relationship effect

## TABLE 14.7A

### Covariance Matrices (Time as Variable)

| Time | T1 | T2 | T3 | T4 |
|------|------|------|------|------|
| Actor by actor for metaperceptions | | | | |
| 1 | 20.056 | 18.083 | 23.250 | 20.500 |
| 2 | 18.083 | 10.667 | 22.028 | 15.000 |
| 3 | 23.250 | 22.028 | 41.222 | 25.667 |
| 4 | 20.500 | 15.000 | 25.667 | 16.000 |
| Relationship in metaperceptions (row) with relationship in impressions (column) | | | | |
| 1 | 6.694 | 11.472 | −17.556 | −21.750 |
| 2 | 23.222 | 3.111 | −6.028 | −10.583 |
| 3 | 19.000 | 6.083 | −5.583 | −10.500 |
| 4 | 12.083 | 1.833 | −0.833 | −2.167 |

Note. T1–T4 - Times 1–4.

## TABLE 14.8A

### Stable and Unstable Variance and Covariance Partitioning Table

| Judgment | Variance | Criterion | Variance | Covariance |
|------|------|------|------|------|
| Mean | | Mean | | |
| Stable | 44.833[a] | Stable | 49.389[a] | 4.556[b] |
| Unstable | 6.235 | Unstable | 9.946 | 6.529 |
| Actor | | Partner | | |
| Stable | 20.755 | Stable | 18.861 | −16.963 |
| Unstable | 1.232 | Unstable | −1.569 | −0.801 |
| Partner | | Actor | | |
| Stable | −2.394 | Stable | 1.028 | −0.583 |
| Unstable | −4.509 | Unstable | −2.319 | −0.417 |
| Relationship | | Relationship | | |
| Stable | 17.329 | Stable | 2.954 | 0.537 |
| Unstable | 15.685 | Unstable | 15.005 | −0.023 |

Note. [a]The value is a mean not a variance.
[b]The value is the absolute difference between means and not a covariance.

estimates in Table 14.6A. The regression coefficient is defined as the sum of cross-products of the two variables divided by the sum of squares of the criterion variable, in this case impressions. Consider the A–D dyad or the ability of A to know how D perceives A. The sum of cross-products is –6.086, and the sum of squares for the impression variable is 12.923. The resulting slope is –. 471. Table 14.9A contains the slopes for the other eight possible combinations. The table also presents estimates of the row (actor), the column (partner), and grand means.

As in the nomothetic SRM analysis, we compute actor, partner, relationship, and mean effects, which are presented in Table 14.10A (see the earlier nomothetic section for how these are computed). Using these estimates, we can conduct an SRM analysis, the results being presented in Table 14.10A. The variance for partner is negative. When this occurs, the usual practice is to treat it as if the variance were zero.

### TABLE 14.9A

#### The Measures of Idiographic Accuracy for Actor–Partner Combinations

| Actor | Partner | | | |
| --- | --- | --- | --- | --- |
| | D | E | F | M |
| A | –0.471 | 2.183 | 0.692 | 0.801 |
| B | –0.435 | –3.495 | 0.531 | –1.133 |
| C | 0.440 | –0.044 | 0.393 | 0.263 |
| M | –0.155 | –0.452 | 0.539 | –0.023 |

### TABLE 14.10A

#### Effect Estimates and Social Relations Model (SRM) Variance for the Idiographic Analysis

| Effect estimates | D | E | F | Effect |
| --- | --- | --- | --- | --- |
| A | –1.140 | 1.811 | –0.671 | 0.824 |
| . B | 0.830 | –1.933 | 1.102 | –1.110 |
| C | 0.309 | 0.122 | –0.432 | 0.286 |
| Effect | –0.132 | –0.429 | 0.562 | –0.023 |

#### SRM variances

| Term | Estimate |
| --- | --- |
| Actor | 0.083 |
| Partner | –0.655 |
| Relationship | 2.741 |

# V

## Where Can We Go From Here?

# ❧ 15 ❧

# Interpersonal
# Sensitivity Research
# and Organizational Psychology:
# Theoretical and Methodological
# Applications

**Ronald E. Riggio**
*Claremont McKenna College*

Although there has been relatively little research directly examining the role of interpersonal sensitivity in organizational settings, the construct has important implications for the effective functioning of work groups and organizations. For example, being an effective workplace manager or leader requires sensitivity to followers and to others in the organization. Recruiting, screening, selection, and placement of employees also involve accurate perceptions of others' skills, abilities, experiences, career interests and aptitudes, and work-related personality dimensions if human resources professionals are to create a highly productive workforce. Interpersonal sensitivity is critical to the development of highly functioning work teams. In addition, successful salespersons and service industry personnel need to be responsive to customer needs and establish good relationships with them. Interpersonal sensitivity, like interpersonal communication in general, plays a key role in work organizations.

Even a cursory review of some of the hot topics in industrial–organizational (I/O) psychology and organizational behavior can provide insight into the role that interpersonal sensitivity plays in the workplace. For example, the explosion of interest in the construct of emotional intelligence has spread to the workplace, as evidenced by the popularity of recent books such as Goleman's (1998)

*Putting Emotional Intelligence to Work* and Weisinger's (1998) *Emotional Intelligence at Work*. Interpersonal sensitivity, broadly defined, is considered a core component of emotional intelligence. Standardized measures of emotional intelligence, such as Mayer and Salovey's Multifactor Emotional Intelligence Scale (MEIS; Mayer & Salovey, 1997; Mayer, Salovey, & Caruso, 1997), include measures of emotional decoding ability (nonverbal sensitivity) and sensitivity to emotional content of stories or scenarios as core components of emotional intelligence. Goleman's applications of emotional intelligence to the workplace draw on much of the interpersonal sensitivity research discussed in this volume. Most of these applications of interpersonal sensitivity to work settings view interpersonal sensitivity as a broad and general set of trait-like skills. Given the importance organizations place on recruiting and selecting highly skilled individuals, and the emphasis on continuous training and "upgrading" the skills of the existing workforce, it is not surprising that work organizations are most interested in the potential of interpersonal sensitivity as an identifiable individual difference, and one that can be learned and developed.

More recently, however, organizations have become aware of the need for managers to be "perceptually sensitive" to those they supervise—particularly sensitive to the presence of strong negative emotions in the workplace (see Hall & Halberstadt, 1997). Research on negative or dysfunctional emotions in the workplace has emerged in the past few years, fueled by the increased attention given to instances of workplace violence (see VandenBos & Bulatao, 1996). Literature on recognizing and managing negative or dysfunctional emotions in the workplace is appearing, with workplace managers being explicitly instructed to be more sensitive and attuned to employees' negative emotions as well as being provided with guidelines for dealing with them (Fineman, 1993; Ostell, 1996).

Another topic that has garnered a great deal of attention concerns issues of employee loyalty and "prosocial" behaviors on the part of employees—what has been collectively termed *organizational citizenship behavior* (OCBs) include extrarole behaviors—behaviors that are not part of a worker's formal job requirements—such as employees helping one another, workers sharing positive attitudes about their fellow employees and about the work organization, and workers showing increased concern for others in the workplace (Organ, 1988; Organ & Ryan, 1995; Podsakoff & MacKenzie, 1997). Recent research by Penner, Midili, and Kegelmeyer (1997) suggested that OCB is linked to personality dimensions, such as other-oriented empathy and helpfulness as well as to notions of volunteerism. Commensurate with this increased interest in employee loyalty and OCB is an increasing emphasis on developing interdependent work teams. There is no doubt that interpersonal sensitivity and sensitivity to the social environment of the workplace contribute in these areas. However, interpersonal sensitivity in these areas of organizational functioning more likely refers to workers' abilities to accurately infer other team members' attitudes, desires, and moods. It likely involves online processing of cues that are specific to these organizational team members.

In a related vein, the increasing diversity of the workforce also highlights the importance of this type of interpersonal sensitivity in the workplace. For example, a recent investigation of diversity and work group cohesiveness suggests that work group members need to be sensitive to their colleagues' "attitudes, beliefs, and values. Information about these factors is communicated through verbal and nonverbal behavior patterns and is only learned through extended, individualized interaction and information gathering" (Harrison, Price, & Bell, 1998, p. 98). However, most workplace diversity training programs involve simply increasing perceptual sensitivity—emphasizing employees' awareness of employees' racial, ethnic, gender, and cultural differences (Hofstede, 1980; Nahavandi & Malekzadeh, 1999; Thayer, 1997).

I now turn to an in-depth look at some traditional topics of research in I/O psychology, and how the construct of interpersonal sensitivity relates to these topic areas. I also explore research possibilities that involve the merging of interpersonal sensitivity research and traditional research topics in I/O psychology.

## INTERPERSONAL SENSITIVITY
## AND LEADERSHIP

Notions of interpersonal sensitivity figure prominently in many leadership theories. For the most part, leadership theorists view interpersonal sensitivity as a trait-like skill or characteristic. Early research that attempted to identify the key traits and characteristics associated with effective leadership were as likely to mention social and interpersonal skills as they were to mention technical and administrative skills as core leadership components (Bass, 1990). In his classic work on leadership–managerial skills, Mintzberg (1973) listed eight critical leadership skills. Half of these are interpersonal skills: the ability to establish and maintain social networks with peers, the ability to deal with subordinates, skills in conflict resolution, and the ability to understand and empathize with top-level leaders. Leadership research has also specifically explored the role of social insight and empathy in leadership. As Bass (1960) noted, "The leader must be able to know what followers want, when they want it, and what prevents them from getting what they want" (p. 167). Kenny and Zaccaro (1983), in an analysis of leader emergence, concluded that a sensitivity-related "leadership trait" was a major component of leadership, accounting for more than 50% of the variance in leadership. They defined this trait as "the ability to perceive the needs and goals of a constituency and to adjust one's personal approach to group action accordingly" (Kenny & Zaccaro, 1983, p. 678).

In the 1950s, the behavioral theories of leadership dichotomized effective leader behavior into two categories: "initiating structure," also known as "task-orientation," and "consideration," which is sometimes referred to as "employee-" or "relationship-orientation" (Halpin & Winer, 1957; Likert, 1961). Consideration behaviors are related to interpersonal sensitivity and include such things as showing concern for the feelings, attitudes, and needs of followers; helping them; doing favors for followers, being friendly and available, and showing them respect and trust (Hollander, 1985; Riggio, 1996). Research has consistently shown that leaders who demonstrate consideration behaviors (leaders who are presumably more interpersonally sensitive) lead work groups who are more cohesive, more satisfied, and more productive (see Bass, 1990).

Several of the more modern leadership theories emphasize the importance of the leader's sensitivity to followers' needs. For example, charismatic and transformational leadership theories both mention that exceptionally charismatic leaders, and those who have the ability to "transform" followers into committed and dedicated followers, are particularly sensitive to followers' needs, and according to Conger and Kanungo (1998) are sensitive to changes in the social environment. Although much of charismatic leadership involves the ability to arouse and inspire followers and articulate a shared vision, sensitivity to both the social and emotional needs of followers is critical for the success of charismatic and transformational leaders (Bass, 1998; Conger & Kanungo, 1998; Riggio, 1987). This sort of interpersonal and "social" sensitivity likely requires general ability to decode emotions and attitudes as well as sensitivity to particular followers or groups of followers that may develop over time.

Another popular leadership theory, known as the *leader–member exchange* (LMX) theory, emphasizes that effective leadership is determined by the quality of the interaction between a leader and a particular work group member (Dansereau, Graen, & Haga, 1975; Graen, 1976; Graen & Uhl-Bien, 1995). According to LMX theory, leader effectiveness is determined by the quality of the relationship with each work group supervisee, with a high-quality relationship characterized by the leader providing support and encouragement to the member (including emotional support), and by having a relationship featuring mutual respect and trust (Dienesch & Liden, 1986). The sort of interpersonal sensitivity suggested by LMX theory most likely involves target-specific ability to accurately decode feelings and attitudes. This sensitivity becomes a major contributor to a leader's ability to establish high-quality relationships with some followers, while relationships with other followers are deficient. In fact, it may be that followers contribute to whether relationships with leaders are high- or low-quality because they are easy or difficult to read.

Effective leadership also requires skills in negotiation and conflict resolution. Awareness and understanding of others' positions and viewpoints is critical for the effective negotiator or conflict manager. Accurate listening skills (including both verbal and nonverbal decoding), leading to a true understanding of another's perspective and attitudes, are often mentioned as the most important set of skills for conflict negotiators (Hughes, Ginnett, & Curphy, 1999; Johnson & Johnson, 1997). Again, in most leadership research, sensitivity is viewed as a trait-like skill, and emphasis is often placed on the development of sensitivity (e.g., listening) skills.

In summary, research on leadership has historically noted the contributions of sensitivity-related constructs to successful and effective leaders. Modern leadership theories seem to be putting even more emphasis on interpersonal skills, consistent with the trend toward more relationship-based theories of leadership, such as charismatic leadership, transformational leadership, and LMX theory. This should be a fertile area of research as measures of interpersonal sensitivity are refined and as leadership researchers become more aware of developments in interpersonal sensitivity research. Although much of this research is likely to focus on leaders' sensitivity skills (e.g., general decoding skill), there may be opportunities to study the online dynamics of leader–follower relationships under the auspices of leadership theories such as LMX and charismatic leadership, where the relationship between leader and follower is key. To date, it is clear that little research has been focused on followers, with even less research studying the dynamics of specific leader–follower relationships (Hughes et al., 1999).

## INTERPERSONAL SENSITIVITY
## AND PERSONNEL FUNCTIONS

Although interpersonal sensitivity doubtless contributes to leadership–management effectiveness, interpersonal sensitivity also plays an important role in the success of many personnel (human resources) processes. I focus on two core personnel activities—employee hiring and employee performance appraisal.

The hiring interview is perhaps the workplace event where interpersonal sensitivity figures most prominently. Nearly every employee undergoes some form of interview in order to get a job (Riggio, 1996). In the hiring interview, the goal of the interviewee is successful impression management—emphasizing strengths, hiding shortcomings, while simultaneously trying to discern what the interviewer is looking for in a prospective employee so that the interviewee can appear to "fit the bill" (Fletcher, 1989). The interviewer has a more formidable task—trying to determine the truth by accurately assessing which applicant has the requisite knowledge, skills, abilities, and other characteristics to best perform the job. Another interviewer goal is to decide whether the applicant has the right personality, attitudes, interests, and loyalties to be a proper match to the existing work group and the organizational culture. In essence, the successful interviewer must be accurate at decoding subtle verbal communication (e.g., determining from the applicant's use of jargon and technical language how much relevant work experience the applicant possesses), must be a good nonverbal decoder (e.g., able to pick up on cues that the interviewee is being evasive, or that he or she has a "bad attitude"), as well as being able to judge relevant personality traits such as conscientiousness, and, if appropriate for the position, ascertaining whether the individual has leadership potential.

In many ways, the hiring interview is similar to a deception scenario. Decoding skills are important on both sides. The interviewee is trying to decode interview questions that may or may not be loaded. Sophisticated interviewers will pose questions that ask how the prospective employee might handle a difficult work situation. The interviewee needs to ascertain what the correct, or desirable, answer is if he or she is to be successful. Similar to the deception scenario, the interviewee uses both verbal and nonverbal decoding skills to look for subtle feedback cues that indicate whether the interview is going well or poorly.

On the other side, the interviewer's sensitivity and decoding skills are called into play to try to understand whether a prospective employee does indeed have the requisite knowledge or skills for the job, and whether the individual has the right temperament, attitudes, and personality to be a good colleague. There is some limited evidence that certain interviewers are better able to select successful job applicants than others (e.g., Graves, 1993; Heneman, Schwab, Huett, & Ford, 1975; Zedeck, Tziner, & Middlestadt, 1983). Additionally, there is some evidence that suggests interviewers can be trained to increase their accuracy (e.g., Pulakos, Schmitt, Whitney, & Smith, 1996). However, the role of interviewer sensitivity in contributing to greater selection accuracy has not been studied directly. Interestingly, research on improving the validity of interviewer ratings has focused primarily on overcoming systematic interviewer biases and errors (Arvey & Campion, 1982; Campion, Pursell, & Brown, 1988; Schmitt, 1976) rather than on efforts to heighten interviewer sensitivity and accuracy.

In short, given its ubiquity and the importance of interviewing for organizational entry, the hiring interview presents an ideal opportunity for applied research in interpersonal sensitivity. Researchers could use the interview scenario to examine the accuracy of judgments of interviewees' personalities or attitudes. A useful line of research that has implications for human resource professionals would be to explore the role of individual differences in interviewers' sensitivity and decoding skills in the validity of judgments made from hiring interviews. Hiring interviews might also serve as a framework for deception studies or for applied research on the predictive value of "thin slices" of behavior (Ambady, LaPlante, & Johnson, chap. 5, this volume).

A more in-depth evaluation of prospective employees occurs in the assessment center. Typically used for selecting managers, the assessment center usually consists of a full day's (or multiple days') evaluation of prospective candidates via work simulations, interviews, group interactions, and the like (Bray & Grant, 1966; Riggio & Mayes, 1997; Thornton, 1992). The obvious advantage of an assessment center over a traditional hiring interview is that it affords more opportunity to evaluate applicants in a wider variety of behavioral settings. Jones (1997) argued that assessment centers provide an opportunity to study person perception accuracy in an applied setting, and he compared and contrasted judgment accuracy in assessment centers with accuracy research conducted in laboratories.

Another·critical personnel function where interpersonal sensitivity plays a major part is the performance appraisal. Interpersonal sensitivity is actually involved in two aspects of the performance appraisal process. First, sensitivity is called into play when the appraiser (typically the employee's supervisor) is asked to make a judgment of an employee's overall work performance. Although primarily intended to focus on work task performance, typical performance appraisals also include some evaluation of an employee's interpersonal skills and attitudes about the job, work team, and organization. Therefore, the appraiser's task may involve attempts to judge attitudes and certain personality dimensions.

A second critical element of the performance appraisal process, and one that also involves interpersonal sensitivity, is providing performance feedback. Performance feedback sessions are often likened to a counseling session. They typically occur in a face-to-face session where the supervisor provides a detailed analysis of the worker's performance and gives constructive criticism and suggestions for improvement, if necessary (Bernardin & Beatty, 1984; Riggio, 1996). Employees often have strong emotional reactions to performance appraisals, so it is important that supervisors have good emotional decoding skills in order to be sensitive to employees' reactions if the supervisor is to deal with them effectively.

A relatively recent development in the area of performance appraisal is the increasing use of 360-degree feedback, where performance ratings are obtained from supervisors, subordinates, peers, and customers (London & Beatty, 1993; Waldman, Atwater, & Antonioni, 1998). In essence, 360-degree feedback involves multiple judges evaluating the same individual's performance. This offers a natural opportunity to explore cross-rater consistency in person perception.

In summary, personnel functions such as selecting appropriate candidates for jobs and evaluating elements of effective job performance require interpersonal sensitivity and accuracy in person perception. Effective interviewers and workplace supervisors need to be accurate judges of performance-related attitudes and personality characteristics if they are to successfully perform their jobs. Supervisors must also be able to decode subordinates' emotions and feelings in order to counsel and coach them effectively. The hiring interview, assessment centers, and the performance appraisal process all offer opportunities for conducting interpersonal sensitivity research in organizational settings.

## INTERPERSONAL SENSITIVITY AND THE DEVELOPMENT AND FUNCTIONING OF WORK TEAMS

Next to relationships with spouses and other family members, relations with people at work represent perhaps the most significant interpersonal relationships for most individuals. As discussed in chapter 10 (Nowicki & Duke, this volume), interpersonal sensitivity is critical to the development of interpersonal relationships, and the same is true for relationships at work. More and more, organizations are moving away from traditional status-oriented hierarchies and making greater use of collaborative work teams (Brannick, Salas, & Prince, 1997). Effective work teams are characterized as having a strong sense of identification with other team members, shared goals, and task interdependence (Hughes et al., 1999). To share common goals and work interdependently, team members must be interpersonally sensitive in order to coordinate activities and keep the team focused and on track. A surgical team is a good example. Members must read and anticipate other members' needs and intentions if the surgery is to be quick, efficient, and successful. Surgical nurses and assistants must be particularly sensitive to cues from the surgeon about what is needed. Members read nonverbal cues that may indicate whether something is amiss. Another team member may pick up on an air of potentially disruptive tension and make a joke to change the group's mood.

The increasing use of teams in work organizations offers greater opportunity to study the role that interpersonal sensitivity plays in the effective functioning of work units. For example, previous research has examined the role of team member individual differences in team performance in important work teams such as nuclear power plant crews (Toquam, Macaulay, Westra, Fujita, & Murphy, 1997). Intact work teams could be assessed for members' levels of interpersonal sensitivity, and associations with both individual and team performance measures could be explored. It might be possible, as part of a team-building training exercise, to conduct some online assessment of accuracy judgments made by team members. Feedback could later be given to team members concerning the accuracy of their judgments as a way of improving team members' levels of sensitivity and the communication process.

## INTERPERSONAL SENSITIVITY AND CUSTOMER SERVICE

In order to remain competitive, U.S. businesses are putting greater emphasis on customer service and service quality (Schmit & Allscheid, 1995; Zeithaml, Parasuraman, & Berry, 1990). Traditionally, business sales and service providers have realized the importance of expression of positive affect in providing sales or services to consumers (i.e., "service with a smile"; see Hochschild, 1983; Rafaeli, 1989; Rafaeli & Sutton, 1987). More recently, however, businesses are emphasizing that sales and service representatives, and the organizations themselves, need to be sensitive to consumer needs, demands, and tastes. Although marketing experts have always solicited consumer feedback about product preferences and customer service, it is only relatively recently that marketing researchers are beginning to mention the importance of empathy and responsiveness to customers' needs, preferences, and feelings for salespersons and service providers (Adelman, Ahuvia, & Goodwin, 1994; Parasuraman, Zeithaml, & Berry, 1988; Schneider & Bowen, 1995). From the personnel perspective, Hogan and Hogan (1985) developed employee screening tests of dimensions such as "service orientation," ostensibly designed to help select salespersons and service providers who possess the sensitivity-related skills that will make them effective in their jobs.

It appears that there is tremendous opportunity to merge research on interpersonal sensitivity with customer-oriented marketing research (Cottle, 1990). In addition, measures of interpersonal sensitivity may play an important future role in the screening, selection, and development of salespersons, service providers, and other positions that require sensitive interactions with clients, customers, or other organizational members (e.g., workplace leaders and managers, public relations personnel).

## SUMMARY AND CONCLUSIONS

Although research on interpersonal sensitivity has not moved far from laboratory investigations concerned primarily with understanding and measuring the phenomenon as it is broadly conceived, there is a great deal of opportunity to extend interpersonal sensitivity research to the workplace. However, as is the case with any applied research in field settings, there are limitations to how intrusive a researcher can be and limitations to the amount of control the researcher has over the participants and the situation. In addition, in work organizations, time is money, so there are even more severe limitations on participants' time than might be the case in other applied settings. As a result, most research on interpersonal sensitivity in the workplace is likely to focus on sensitivity as a trait-like skill. Moreover, measurement methods used to assess interpersonal sensitivity of incumbent employees in the workplace may often be limited primarily to self-report methods (see Riggio & Riggio, chap. 7, this volume), peer ratings, or to relatively brief "standardized" performance measures such as the Profile of Nonverbal Sensitivity or the Interpersonal Perception Task (see Archer, Costanzo, & Akert, chap. 9, this volume; Hall, chap. 8, this volume).

Employers may be willing to allow more detailed assessments of interpersonal sensitivity of job applicants and new employee trainees if researchers can convince employers that interpersonal sensitivity is a relevant, performance-related variable that can be used in screening and selecting prospective employees or candidates for managerial and leadership positions. Thus, it may be possible to conduct both self-report and performance-based assessments of general decoding accuracy for prospective employees. Similarly, self-report assessments of interpersonal sensitivity can be included in employment test batteries and used for screening and selecting employees for positions where interpersonal sensitivity is predictive of effective job performance. For example, we have had considerable success using both self-report measures of interpersonal skill such as the Social Skills Inventory (Riggio, 1989), and self-report measures of empathy such as Davis's (1980, 1994) Interpersonal Reactivity Index, in predicting the performance of high-level managers and hospice workers (Riggio & Cole, 1989; Riggio & Taylor, 1999). Assessment centers for the selection and development of managers and managerial training programs may offer other opportunities for researchers to study the role of interpersonal sensitivity in both personnel selection and leadership. Again, employers are more likely to allow researchers access to workers if it does not detract from work time and if researchers can demonstrate potential benefits for the organization.

In short, the construct of interpersonal sensitivity is important to many facets of work organizations, ranging from leadership to employee selection and development to improving the functioning of work teams and the quality of customer service. It is only a matter of time before the more basic research on defining, refining, and measuring interpersonal sensitivity meets up with and converges with organizational theorists and practitioners who are beginning to recognize the importance of interpersonal sensitivity in the world of work.

## REFERENCES

Adelman, M. B., Ahuvia, A., & Goodwin, C. (1994). Beyond smiling: Social support and service quality. In R. T. Rust & R. L. Oliver (Eds.), *Service quality: New directions in theory and practice* (pp. 139–171). Thousand Oaks, CA: Sage.

Arvey, R. D., & Campion, J. E. (1982). The employment interview: A summary and review of recent research. *Personnel Psychology, 35,* 281–322.

Bass, B. M. (1960). *Leadership, psychology, and organizational behavior.* New York: Harper.

Bass, B. M. (1990). *Bass & Stogdill's handbook of leadership: Theory, research, & managerial applications* (3rd ed.). New York: Free Press.

Bass, B. M. (1998). *Transformational leadership: Industry, military, and educational impact.* Mahwah, NJ: Lawrence Erlbaum Associates.

Bernardin, H. J., & Beatty, R. W. (1984). *Performance appraisal: Assessing human behavior at work.* Boston: Kent.

Brannick, M. T., Salas, E., & Prince, C. (Eds.). (1997). *Team performance assessment and measurement: Theory, methods, and applications.* Mahwah, NJ: Lawrence Erlbaum Associates.

Bray, D. W., & Grant, D. L. (1966). The assessment center in the measurement of potential for business management. *Psychological Monographs, 80* (Whole No. 625), 1–27.

Campion, M. A., Pursell, E. D., & Brown, B. K. (1988). Structured interviewing: Raising the psychometric properties of the employment interview. *Personnel Psychology, 41,* 25–42.

Conger, J. A., & Kanungo, R. N. (1998). *Charismatic leadership in organizations.* Thousand Oaks, CA: Sage.

Cottle, D. W. (1990). *Client-centered service: How to keep them coming back for more.* New York: Wiley.

Dansereau, F., Graen, G., & Haga, B. (1975). A vertical dyad linkage approach to leadership within formal organizations: A longitudinal investigation of the role making process. *Organizational Behavior and Human Performance, 13,* 46–78.

Davis, M. H. (1980). A multidimensional approach to individual differences in empathy. *JSAS Catalog of Selected Documents in Psychology, 10,* 85.

Davis, M. H. (1994). *Empathy: A social psychological approach.* Madison, WI: Brown & Benchmark.

Dienesch, R. M., & Liden, R. C. (1986). Leader–member exchange model of leadership: A critique and further development. *Academy of Management Review, 11,* 618–634.

Fineman, S. (Ed.). (1993). *Emotion in organizations.* London: Sage.

Fletcher, C. (1989). Impression management in the selection interview. In R. A. Giacalone & P. Rosenfeld (Eds.), *Impression management in the organization* (pp. 269–281). Hillsdale, NJ: Lawrence Erlbaum Associates.

Goleman, D. (1998). *Working with emotional intelligence.* New York: Bantam.

Graen, G. (1976). Role making processes within complex organizations. In M. D. Dunnette (Ed.), *Handbook of industrial and organizational psychology* (pp. 1201–1245). Chicago: Rand McNally.

Graen, G. B., & Uhl-Bien, M. (1995). Relationship-based approach to leadership: Development of leader–member exchange (LMX) theory of leadership over 25 years. *Leadership Quarterly, 6,* 219–247.

Graves, L. M. (1993). Sources of individual differences in interviewer effectiveness: A model and implications for future research. *Journal of Organizational Behavior, 14,* 349–370.

Hall, J. A., & Halberstadt, A. G. (1997). Subordination and nonverbal sensitivity: A hypothesis in search of support. In M. R. Walsh (Ed.), *Women, men & gender: Ongoing debates* (pp. 120–133). New Haven, CT: Yale University Press.

Halpin, A. W., & Winer, B. J. (1957). A factorial study of the leader behavior descriptions. In R. M. Stogdill & A. E. Coons (Eds.), *Leader behavior: Its description and measurement* (pp. 39–51). Columbus, OH: Ohio State University Bureau of Business Research.

Harrison, D. A., Price, K. H., & Bell, M. P. (1998). Beyond relational demography: Time and the effects of surface- and deep-level diversity on work group cohesion. *Academy of Management Journal, 41,* 96–107.

Heneman, H. G., Schwab, D. P., Huett, D. L., & Ford, J. J. (1975). Interviewer validity as a function of interview structure, biographical data, and interviewee order. *Journal of Applied Psychology, 60,* 748–753.

Hochschild, A. R. (1983). *The managed heart.* Berkeley, CA: University of California Press.

Hofstede, G. (1980). *Culture's consequences: International differences in work-related values.* Beverly Hills, CA: Sage.

Hogan, R., & Hogan, J. (1985). *Hogan personnel selection series.* Minneapolis, MN: National Computer Systems.

Hollander, E. P. (1985). Leadership and power. In G. Lindzey & E. Aronson (Eds.), *The handbook of social psychology* (3rd ed., pp. 485–538). New York: Random House.

Hughes, R. L., Ginnett, R. C., & Curphy, G. J. (1999). *Leadership: Enhancing the lessons of experience.* Boston: Irwin McGraw-Hill.

Johnson, D. W., & Johnson, F. P. (1997). *Joining together: Group theory and group skills* (6th ed.). Boston: Allyn & Bacon.

Jones, R. G. (1997). A person perception explanation for validation evidence from assessment centers. *Journal of Social Behavior and Personality, 12,* 169–178.

Kenny, D. A., & Zaccaro, S. J. (1983). An estimate of variance due to traits in leadership. *Journal of Applied Psychology, 68,* 678–685.

Likert, R. (1961). *New patterns of management.* New York: McGraw-Hill.

London, M., & Beatty, R. W. (1993). 360-degree feedback as a competitive advantage. *Human Resource Management, 32,* 353–372.

Mayer, J. D., & Salovey, P. (1997). What is emotional intelligence? In P. Salovey & D. Sluyter (Eds.), *Emotional development and emotional intelligence: Implications for educators* (pp. 3–31). New York: Basic Books.

Mayer, J. D., Salovey, P., & Caruso, D. R. (1997), *Emotional intelligence test* [CD-ROM]. Needham, MA: Virtual Knowledge.

Mintzberg, H. (1973). *The nature of managerial work*. New York: Harper & Row.

Nahavandi, A., & Malekzadeh, A. R. (1999). *Organizational behavior: The person–environment fit*. Upper Saddle River, NJ: Prentice-Hall.

Organ, D. W. (1988). *Organizational citizenship behavior: The good soldier syndrome*. Lexington, MA: Lexington.

Organ, D. W., & Ryan, K. (1995). A meta-analytic review of attitudinal and dispositional predictors of organizational citizenship behavior. *Personnel Psychology, 48*, 775–802.

Ostell, A. (1996). Managing dysfunctional emotions in organizations. *Journal of Management Studies, 33*, 525–557.

Parasuraman, A., Zeithaml, V. A., & Berry, L. L. (1988). SERVQUAL: A multiple-item scale for measuring customer perceptions of service quality. *Journal of Retailing, 64*, 12–40.

Penner, L. A., Midili, A. R., & Kegelmeyer, J. (1997). Beyond job attitudes: A personality and social psychology perspective on the causes of organizational citizenship behavior. *Human Performance, 10*, 111–131.

Podsakoff, P. M., & MacKenzie, S. B. (1997). Impact of organizational citizenship behavior on organizational performance: A review and suggestions for future research. *Human Performance, 10*, 133–151.

Pulakos, E. D., Schmitt, N., Whitney, D., & Smith, M. (1996). Individual differences in interviewer ratings: The impact of standardization, consensus discussion, and sampling error on the validity of a structured interview. *Personnel Psychology 49*, 85–102.

Rafaeli, A. (1989). When clerks meet customers: A test of variables related to emotional expressions on the job. *Journal of Applied Psychology, 74*, 385–393.

Rafaeli, A., & Sutton, R. I. (1987). The expression of emotion as part of the work role. *Academy of Management Review, 12*, 23–37.

Riggio, R. E. (1987). *The charisma quotient*. New York: Dodd Mead.

Riggio, R. E. (1989). *Manual for the Social Skills Inventory*. Palo Alto, CA: Consulting Psychologists Press.

Riggio, R. E. (1996). *Introduction to industrial/organizational psychology* (2nd ed.). New York: HarperCollins.

Riggio, R. E., & Cole, E. J. (1989, August). *Leadership and communication skills of firefighter supervisors*. Paper presented at the 97th Annual Convention of the American Psychological Association, New Orleans, LA.

Riggio, R. E., & Mayes, B. T. (Eds.). (1997). Assessment centers: Research and applications. *Journal of Social Behavior and Personality, 12* (Whole No. 5), 1–338.

Riggio, R. E., & Taylor, S. J. (2000). Personality and communication skills as predictors of hospice nurse performance. *Journal of Business and Psychology, 15*, 351–359.

Schmit, M. J., & Allscheid, S. P. (1995). Employee attitudes and customer satisfaction: Making theoretical and empirical connections. *Personnel Psychology, 48*, 521–536.

Schmitt, N. (1976). Social and situational determinants of interview decisions: Implications for the employment interview. *Personnel Psychology, 29*, 79–101.

Schneider, B., & Bowen, D. E. (1995). *Winning the service game*. Boston: Harvard Business School Press.

Thayer, P. W. (1997). A rapidly changing world: Some implications for training systems in the year 2001 and beyond. In M. A. Quinones & A. Ehrenstein (Eds.), *Training for a rapidly changing workplace: Applications of psychological research* (pp. 15–30). Washington, DC: American Psychological Association.

Thornton, G. C. III (1992). *Assessment centers in human resource management.* Reading, MA: Addison-Wesley.

Toquam, J. L., Macaulay, J. L., Westra, C. D., Fujita, Y., & Murphy, S. E. (1997). Assessment of nuclear power plant crew performance variability. In M. T. Brannick, E. Salas & C. Prince (Eds.), *Team performance assessment and measurement: Theory, methods, and applications* (pp. 253–287). Mahwah, NJ: Lawrence Erlbaum Associates.

VandenBos, G. R., & Bulatao, E. Q. (Eds.). (1996). *Violence on the job: Identifying risks and developing solutions.* Washington, DC: American Psychological Association.

Waldman, D. A., Atwater, L. E., & Antonioni, D. (1998). Has 360-degree feedback gone amok? *Academy of Management Executive, 12,* 86–94.

Weisinger, H. (1998). *Emotional intelligence at work.* San Francisco: Jossey-Bass.

Zedeck, S., Tziner, A., & Middlestadt, S. (1983). Interview validity and reliability: An individual analysis approach. *Personnel Psychology, 36,* 355–370.

Zeithaml, V. A., Parasuraman, A., & Berry, L. L. (1990). *Delivering service quality.* New York: Free Press.

# 16

## Three Trends in Current Research on Person Perception: Positivity, Realism, and Sophistication

David C. Funder
*University of California, Riverside*

Research on person perception has changed a good deal, and for the better, since the late 1980s. This evolution of the broader field is clearly reflected in the contents of the present volume on interpersonal sensitivity. I submit that three trends are particularly important and can be seen both in the person perception literature and within the pages of this volume.

### POSITIVITY

The first trend is positivity. For too many years, research on person perception had an awfully negative tone. The literature on "error" that dominated the 1970s and early 1980s was particularly depressing and sometimes even insulting, wherein researchers described their fellow humans as characteristically naïve, overconfident, oblivious, insensitive, and just plain wrong (Funder, 1992). Of course, the whole point of the error literature was to point out where judgment goes awry, so this emphasis was not surprising. However, research on topics such as interviewer ratings, as Riggio points out (chap. 15, this volume), more often focused on how to correct biases and errors than on how to actually make a correct judgment.

Several factors led this emphasis to change. One is simply that the "everything you know is wrong" approach, and its associated rhetoric, became old.

Some of us will never forget how at the high-water moment of the error paradigm one researcher exclaimed in the pages of *American Psychologist* that "mistakes are fun!" (Crandall, 1984, p. 1499). Not long after that enthusiastic comment was uttered, more and more readers of the literature began to feel that mistakes were becoming tiresome. The insight that people are not perfect eventually lost its novelty. In addition, the implicit pose of every error researcher—that psychologists, especially error researchers, are smarter than ordinary humans—became less plausible as close analyses began to poke an increasing number of holes in the normative models used to evaluate errors (e.g., Funder, 1987, 1999; Gigerenzer, 1991; Jussim, 1993; Lopes & Oden, 1991).

The most important factor leading to the gradual change of emphasis, however, was that as demonstrations of error continued to accumulate, it became increasingly apparent how uninformative they were about some of the issues that really matter. Once one accepts the premise that human social judgment is imperfect—and do we really need extensive research programs to prove that?—relatively little is gained by continuing to add exhibits to the Museum of Incompetence. The reason is simple. The best and surest way to avoid error is to make no judgment at all.[1]

To say that continued demonstrations of error gain us relatively little is not to say they gain us nothing at all. Demonstrations of overgeneralization, overconfidence, and oversimplification, to name a few, can all stand as warnings of pitfalls to avoid when thinking about fellow humans. But they fundamentally cannot get us started toward a correct judgment. For this, a different approach is necessary.

This different approach can be characterized as the "accuracy approach" (Funder, 1995, 1999). The approach can be defined in various ways, but one definition is particularly simple and serves to characterize all (or nearly all) of the research in this volume. If the dependent variable of a study reflects participants' departures from a (hypothetical) standard of perfection, it is an error study. If, however, the dependent variable reflects participants' level of achievement, it is an accuracy study.[2]

By this definition, the wide range of research described in this volume is nearly all accuracy research. Dependent variables as diverse as consensus (Kenny & Winquist, chap. 14, this volume), affective empathy (Losoya & Eisenberg, chap. 2, this volume), empathic accuracy (Ickes, chap. 12, this volume), deception detection (Malone & DePaulo, chap. 6, this volume), and scores on the Profile of Nonverbal Sensitivity (PONS; Hall, chap. 8, this volume) and the IPT (Archer, Costanzo, & Akert, chap. 9, this volume) all reflect

---

[1]Indeed, researchers who consider any personality judgment to manifest a fundamental attribution error appear to advocate just that.

[2]Some accuracy tests count number of items missed rather than number of items correct, but it is a simple matter to reflect the score to index achievement. In error research, by contrast, no index of achievement can be derived.

the degree to which participants manage to make judgments that are congruent with a reasonable criterion for accuracy.

The emphasis of this book reflects a sea change that is simultaneously occurring in the wider literature. The change is important not only because the tone of the research is more optimistic and less arrogant than what came before. Once researchers begin to estimate the degree to which people can detect lies, guess what others are thinking, or come to consensus in their opinions about others, the question naturally arises as to how people manage to do any of these things at all. And this question leads in turn to a new and exciting way to conceptualize and do research on person perception.

## REALISM

A second important trend in current research is realism. By this, I mean that researchers are more often willing to assume that person perceivers are attempting to judge something that is really there.

For many years, research on person perception was dominated by studies in which participants had to guess the attitudes or personalities of "stimulus persons" who did not actually exist (see Funder, 1987). Their judgments were evaluated in terms of whether they followed the prescriptions of a putatively normative model rather than the degree to which they matched the actual attributes of the stimulus (the hypothetical stimulus had no actual attributes at all).[3] This approach worried Gordon Allport (one of the founders of research on nonverbal behavior) from the very beginning. Concerning one of the first meetings where this kind of research on hypothetical person perception was presented, he wrote the following:

> Recently I attended a conference of psychologists working on the problem of the "perception of persons" (see Tagiuri & Petrullo, 1958). At this conference one heard much about perception but little about persons, the object of perception. The reason, I think, is that the participants ... much preferred to ... evade the question of what the person is really like. (Allport, 1958, p. 243)

> In many investigations of "person perception," to try to discover the traits residing within a personality is regarded as either naïve or impossible. Studies, therefore, concentrate only on the process of perceiving or judging, and reject the problem of validating the perception and judgment (Allport, 1966, p. 2).

With these observations, Allport was prescient as he so often was (Funder, 1991). The very research approach about which he expressed such concern went on to dominate the literature on person perception for the next 3 decades.

---

[3]See Hammond (1996) for a useful comparison of "coherence" criteria (in terms of normative models) versus "correspondence" criteria (in terms of actual attributes of stimuli).

A few hardy souls, mostly in industrial–organizational psychology and in the study of nonverbal behavior (particularly including the study of the detection of deception) managed to go a separate route that was largely ignored by the mainstream literature. For the most part however, social psychologists became content to restrict themselves to studying how participants make judgments of hypothetical stimulus persons about which nothing accurate (or inaccurate, for that matter) really can be said.

Since the 1990s, a change back towards real stimuli has become apparent in the research literature, and is even more apparent in this book. Across the various chapters we can see participants judging what other people are really thinking (Ickes, chap. 12, this volume), really doing (Archer et al., chap. 9, this volume), what they are really like (Ambady, LaPlante, & Johnson, chap. 5, this volume, Colvin & Bundick, chap. 3, this volume, among others), and whether they are really lying (Malone & DePaulo, chap. 6, this volume). Realistic criteria like these raise their own philosophical complications and methodological difficulties, to be sure (see Funder, 1999, chap. 4). It is heartening though to see so many researchers—and more all the time—willing to tackle these complications and difficulties head-on rather than continuing to try to side-step them.

## SOPHISTICATION

The study of person perception has a complex history that includes some unusual twists. Perhaps the most unusual of these twists is the way the whole study of accuracy in personality judgment was nearly shut down, almost half a century ago, by a single methodological critique. A thriving and active literature on the accuracy of interpersonal judgment was closely analyzed and effectively demolished in a series of papers by Lee Cronbach (e.g., 1955; Cronbach & Gleser, 1953; Gage & Cronbach, 1955). In a nutshell, Cronbach showed how the usual method of studying accuracy—which was to evaluate a personality judgment by comparing it with the target's own self-judgment—was more complicated than had been widely appreciated. The agreement score obtained by correlating (or otherwise comparing) a set of self-judgments with a set of others' judgments is the result of several different components, each of which has a different psychological interpretation. None of them—certainly not the overall agreement score—is a simple and direct reflection of the judge's "accuracy." As a result of this critique, research on the accuracy of personality judgments simply disappeared from the mainstream literature for the next several decades.[4]

---

[4]Research on the accuracy of personality judgment was maintained within the industrial–organizational literature, however (see Funder, 1987, 1999). Also, research on the accuracy of the detection of emotion using nonverbal cues continued unabated.

## New Methods for Accuracy Analysis

When in the early 1980s a few researchers tried to renew research on accuracy and submit their papers for publication, it was not uncommon to receive back reviews that said, in effect, "Cronbach proved years ago that accuracy research is impossible." Of course, Cronbach neither proved nor even argued anything of the sort. In fact, Cronbach's critique bypassed the most difficult issue in accuracy research: the criterion problem. He did not question the most widely used criterion for accuracy, which was (and still is) self–other agreement. Rather, his critique focused exclusively on the way self–other agreement (and, with lesser emphasis, interjudge agreement) was calculated.

That critique was limited even further in that it addressed only the calculation of interjudge agreement concerning profiles (in which agreement between target–rater pairs is assessed within-target across a set of traits rated by both), rather than items (in which the agreement between targets and raters is assessed across targets on a single item).[5] Indeed, many if not quite all of the "Cronbachian" problems in data analysis are bypassed if analyses are conducted on one item at a time (Funder, 1980).

Accuracy research began to revive when investigators simultaneously became less intimidated by Cronbach's critique and began to apply the lessons he had taught. New methods began to be used that responded to Cronbachian issues in three different ways. One approach was to focus analyses on single personality items. For example, a group of targets might all rate themselves on extraversion, while an acquaintance of each target makes the same rating. The simple correlation between self and others, across targets, on this one item, is unaffected by elevation, stereotype accuracy, and most of the various other components with which Cronbach was concerned (Funder, 1980).[6] A second approach is to try to directly apply the various (and difficult) analytical techniques that Cronbach advocated (e.g., Harackiewicz & DePaulo, 1982). A third approach is Kenny's social relations model (1994, also Kenny & Winquist, chap. 14, this volume), which is not literally Cronbachian, but in the spirit of Cronbach's analysis it seeks to separate out and independently estimate each of the components that can affect measurements of agreement between judges and targets, and among judges.

All three of these developments were salutary and made the renewal of accuracy research possible. In the current literature—and certainly in this book—there is little if any indication of the kind of methodological naïveté that

---

[5]Cronbach's analyses concentrated on the use of difference scores to index agreement between profiles. When correlation coefficients are used instead, some of the major components of agreement he discussed (e.g., elevation) no longer affect these scores. The discussion that follows concerns the Cronbachian components that affect correlations used as an index of profile agreement.

[6]As always, when the talk turns to these issues, there are subtleties nested within subtleties that this sentence does not fully communicate. For a fuller discussion, see Funder (1980, 1999, chap. 4).

undermined accuracy research in the 1950s, nor are there many claims that accuracy research is impossible. This increase in sophistication is, therefore, the third positive trend I wish to suggest characterizes the current literature.

## The Perils of Analytic Sophistication

However, this development should not lead us to conclude that all analytical issues are fully understood by everyone or even all solved by anyone. One issue in particular generated lively discussion at the authors' workshop that launched the present volume and continues to serve as a possible source of confusion. The issue is "stereotype accuracy."

People new to this field of research often find this term particularly confusing. Cronbach's use of the term *stereotype* in this context is potentially misleading, because it does not refer to the racist, sexist, and other kinds of stereotypes that have long been of concern in psychological research. Nor does it refer to the recently developed topic of stereotype accuracy, the possibility that at least some aspects of some social stereotypes might be accurate (e.g., Lee, Jussim, & McCauley, 1995). Rather, stereotype accuracy refers to the component of ratings that is consistent across targets, raters, or both, and it might better have been labeled "average," "baseline," "constant," or any number of other less pejorative terms. But it seems too late to change the terminology now.

Stereotype accuracy arises as a concern because out of the many different personality traits that exist some are generally rated higher than others, regardless of who is being described or who is doing the describing. For example, imagine a two-item rating profile in which the items are "honest" and "murderous." Nearly all targets will rate the first trait higher than the second, and nearly all raters will do so as well. In fact, it might be a reasonable rating strategy to always rate honesty higher than murderousness, regardless of who the rating target is, because such a differential rating will (fortunately) almost always be correct.

The problem enters in when researchers are trying to estimate the accuracy of a particular judge or judgment. Let's say you rate a new target as more honest than murderous, and the target does the same in his or her self-rating. You have achieved perfect accuracy (the self–other correlation is 1.0), but what was its source? One possibility is that you have observed the target always to return borrowed money and never to kill anybody, and made your judgments accordingly. Another possibility, though, is that you simply used the strategy described earlier—you always rate everybody as more honest than murderous—and since that is usually correct, you are usually accurate. Does this latter route to self–other agreement deserve to be called accuracy?

Unfortunately, there is no simple answer to this question. On one level, it seems that this kind of accuracy is real. After all, when you're right, you're right, and if I predict no rain in Palm Springs tomorrow, and it doesn't rain, then I gave an accurate prediction even though it hardly ever rains in Palm Springs. Indeed, perhaps I should get a bit of credit for my meteorological perspicacity because I know this fact about the desert. In the same way, the knowledge that some traits are more frequently present or usually stronger than others—most people are more honest than murderous—is nontrivial and extremely useful psychological knowledge to possess.

On another level, this kind of definition of accuracy also seems potentially misleading. If I can make an accurate judgment of your personality, we ought to be interested in the degree to which this accuracy stemmed from something I actually saw you do, our actual acquaintance, as opposed to my knowledge of people in general. For this reason, Cronbach advocated the use of self–other agreement scores that were corrected for stereotype accuracy, because it is such differential accuracy—accuracy about a specific target over and above one's accuracy about targets in general—that is often the focus of psychological interest.[7]

In recent research, it has become a fairly typical practice, following Cronbach, to attempt to subtract-out stereotype accuracy as being "not the core of what is usually meant by accuracy" (Kenny & Winquist, chap. 14, this volume). The calculation can be simple—it is effective either to subtract the average of each item across targets from the each item rating by each judge or to calculate a partial correlation that removes the average profile across targets from each judge–target correlation (see Bernieri, Zuckerman, Koestner, & Rosenthal, 1994; Funder, 1999, chap. 4). The influence of stereotype accuracy and other components can be accounted for in other ways as well (see Kenny, 1994; Kenny & Winquist, chap. 14, this volume).

This kind of adjustment in self–other agreement scores is often a good idea and raises few problems if the researcher understands exactly what he or she is doing and why. However, it is possible to be reminded in this context of a lesson from developmental psychology. As one becomes more sophisticated, one begins without awareness of a rule, then one learns a rule, and finally one learns the exceptions to the rule.[8] In the pre-1950s days of the accuracy research that was demolished by Cronbach, researchers were unaware of the influence of stereotype accuracy and did not know to correct for it. Today, researchers know about stereotype accuracy and correct for it routinely. The stage that may yet need to be attained, however, is understanding when not to adjust for stereotype accuracy.

---

[7]The present discussion focuses on self–other agreement used as an index of accuracy, but the same issues are also relevant to analyses of interjudge agreement (consensus). In the latter case, the issue of stereotype accuracy raises questions concerning the degree to which judges agree on the basis of shared stereotypes as opposed to actual observation of their target.

[8]From the field of language acquisition, the classic example is the young child who says "I went to the park," the slightly older child who says "I goed to the park" (because she has now acquired understanding of the past tense), and the still older child who again says "I went to the park" (because she now understands that this is an irregular verb).

Indeed, it seems worrisome to me that virtuous language is so often used in the context of the adjustment—beginning with the common use of the word "correction" to describe what one has done. The word "correction" implies that what one has afterwards is "correct," and in this context that is not always the case. There are three reasons why the routine removal of stereotype accuracy is potentially problematic (see also Colvin & Bundick, chap. 3, this volume).

The first reason is that corrected accuracy or consensus scores are less reliable than uncorrected ones. The average profile itself has a less than perfect reliability (always), and so using it to adjust an accuracy or consensus score as a "correction" inevitably introduces a source of noise. When it is possible to use uncorrected scores, therefore, they may sometimes be more sensitive indicators of the underlying psychological phenomena of interest (e.g., Blackman & Funder, 1998).

A second, more substantive consideration, is that as mentioned earlier, it is no trivial feat to understand what people in general are like. If a judge of personality attains some of his or her accuracy through a profound understanding of general human nature, should this be held against him or her? It seems reasonable to expect that an understanding of human nature is part of judging particular humans, and that if one is interested in the difference between judges who are more and less accurate, then one would want to include, not "correct for," this understanding (Jackson, 1982). Indeed, in the absence of specific knowledge, the most reasonable strategy is to guess the baseline or average. Colvin and Bundick (chap. 3, this volume) describe research in which judges use their knowledge of people in general (including themselves) to fill in the gaps in their knowledge early in the acquaintance process. This is not an artifact—it is part of being a good judge.

Still, one could argue that for many research purposes it is useful to remove this component of accuracy if the researcher is interested only in the specific acquaintance and judgment processes that occur between a specific judge and a specific target. It is under these circumstances that most methodologists will argue that it is unambiguously a good thing to correct for stereotype accuracy. Unfortunately, even here the situation is not so simple.

Imagine a judge who always ignores what he knows about people in general, and bases his judgments solely on what he has seen a particular person do. Now he meets someone who is truly "Jill average." That is, her real placement just happens to be very near the average on any trait you could name. The judge gets to know her, then provides accurate ratings of her on every trait—ratings that are, of course, very near the average calculated across targets. Jill describes herself accurately, too. We psychologists calculate the self–other agreement score and get a correlation near 1.0. But we are (2nd stage) sophisticated methodologists, and "know" to correct for stereotype accuracy. So now we subtract the mean self-profile from Jill's self-ratings, or partial it out from the correlation, and then recalculate. Now the self–other correlation has dropped to near 0, and we conclude the judge has achieved no accuracy at all.

What happened? The problem is that a profile agreement score corrected for stereotype accuracy only gives credit to the degree a judge makes an unusual judgment of an unusual person. Usual judgments of usual persons are precisely what gets subtracted out. The result is that if your target is deviant from the norm on one or more traits, you have a chance to earn a high accuracy score if you can identify the deviations. But if your target is really, truly average, you will not earn a (corrected) high accuracy score no matter what you do.

This is not just some esoteric example. It is, I fear, a common pitfall. It is in the very nature of averages that most people tend to be near them. To the extent that our corrected or adjusted accuracy scores identify as accurate only unusual judgments of unusual targets, and identify as inaccurate usual judgments of usual targets, then these analytic strategies are distorting what, on a psychological level, accuracy should mean.[9]

So what is the right way to compute self–other (or inter-judge) agreement? At the workshop that spawned this book, the question was raised many times. No one had a simple answer because there is not one. Personally, I often try to avoid the problem by calculating item rather than profile correlations, but there are some issues that item correlations cannot address well (Funder, 1999, chap. 4). To the degree that researchers need to use profile correlations, the field seems to be on the horns of a real dilemma. The best advice anyone can seem to offer is this: Do not make corrections or adjustments to accuracy scores (or fail to make such adjustments) blindly or reflexively, and do not think a score is better or more informative just because you have corrected it. Instead, a researcher needs to know exactly what he or she is doing, and why, on a psychological and not just a statistical level. Then the researcher needs to be very careful in reporting the results of his or her research, so that the words really communicate the psychological phenomena that the numbers actually reflect.

The situation is not completely hopeless. With some research designs, it can be possible to control influences of stereotype accuracy (and other such influences) on one's hypotheses experimentally rather than statistically. For example, in one study of changes in agreement with increases in information, judges were randomly assigned to conditions, and so any possible effects of stereotype accuracy (and other artifacts, such as projection) on the effect of information were experimentally controlled. No adjustments needed to be used at all; the simple agreement score was sufficient (Blackman & Funder, 1998). When experimental control is possible—and it sometimes is—the complications of statistical control can be avoided.

---

[9]A parallel analysis applies to corrections for the Cronbachian artifact of projection—describing other people as similar to yourself. A truly average judge who describes his or her truly average target accurately runs the danger of having his or her perspicacity "corrected" down to nothing. As an empirical phenomenon, projection is weak to nonexistent in any event (see Funder, Kolar, & Blackman, 1995). Stereotype accuracy, in contrast, is usually an empirically strong effect, whatever its interpretation.

## The Realistic Solution

Another route also leads away from this dilemma. Everything said so far concerns using self–other (or interjudge) agreement as the criterion for accuracy, and indeed to this day most research only uses comparisons among ratings as accuracy criteria. The solution is to expand the range of criteria for accuracy. Remember that personality is real, and act accordingly. This recognition means that in addition to comparing self and others' judgments of personality, one can also compare both of those judgments with other and independent criteria, behavioral predictions (e.g., Kolar, Funder, & Colvin, 1996). It is this realistic move that can break researchers out of the dilemmas that arise when data include only mutual ratings.

## THE REALISTIC ACCURACY MODEL

My own approach to person perception, the Realistic Accuracy Model (RAM; Funder, 1995, 1999), is based on the presumption that personality is real. This presumption leads to a research program that uses many different criteria for accuracy—not all at the same time of course, but over time (and across publications) we have used several. These criteria include predictions of behavior in the lab and in real life. Because we assume personality is real—not just something people construct and can therefore agree about—we assume that its accurate judgment should yield valid predictions of future behavior. The fulfillment of this assumption not only demonstrates that personality is real, but also allows us to break out of the conundrums, described earlier, that inevitably arise when you are limited to comparing self-judgments with others' judgments, and others' judgments with each other.

RAM is actually based on three assumptions. The first, as already addressed, is that personality is real. People really do have traits, in some real amount. The second assumption is that people make judgments of traits in the people they know (including themselves).[10] Third, these judgments are sometimes correct. One does not need to assume they are always correct, or even usually correct. It is necessary only to assume that someone, just once, made a judgment of a trait in another person that happened to match what it really was. If this assumption is granted, then an important question immediately arises: How is this possible?

The answer, I argue, is that four things must happen (see Fig. 16.1). For an accurate judgment of a trait to be obtained, the target of judgment must first do something that is relevant to that trait. A friendly person must smile, or use open gestures, or do something that really is a manifestation of his or her friendliness. The work by Ambady et al. (chap. 5, this volume) and others suggests

---

[10]It is sometimes argued that people judge "affordances" rather than traits, but the difference between judging someone as "friendly" and as "affording friendly interaction" has never been clear to me.

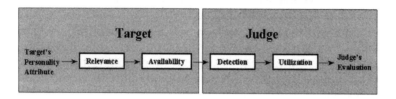

FIG. 16.1 The realistic accuracy model (RAM) describes accurate personality judgment as produced by the relevance, availability, detection and utilization of behavioral information (from Funder, 1995).

that relevant information can be emitted within surprisingly short segments of time (for a review, see Ambady, Bernieri, & Richeson, 2000).

Second, the information given off by the target must be available to the judge. Ordinarily, this just means the judge must be present. You will not know about your best friend's trait-relevant behavior at work if you never see your friend at work, but you might know all about his or her trait-relevant behavior as manifested at the bowling alley. To the extent that some life contexts are more informative than others or differentially informative about different traits, the accuracy of judges who are acquainted with their targets in these contexts will vary accordingly.

Third, the judge must detect the relevant, available information. Ordinarily, this means the judge must be attentive, not repressing information, not distracted, and so forth. Sometimes, judges are motivated not to perceive behaviors that they would find unsettling (Simpson, Ickes, & Blackstone, 1995).

Fourth and finally, the judge must correctly use the relevant, available, detected information. The entire research field of social cognition is about this final stage. It includes the way people use memory and judgmental processes as well as their implicit knowledge about people, to convert their behavioral observations into a judgment about what someone is like.

This is just a bare sketch of the RAM; much more can be said about the model as a whole and about each step (see Funder, 1995, 1999). Possible misunderstandings can also be addressed at length. For example, this is an interpersonal model of personality judgment, not a cognitive model of the sort researchers in social cognition are accustomed to seeing. The topic of social cognition, as already mentioned, is contained within the fourth step (the other three lie outside that field of research). Also, it is perhaps important to underline that this is not a model of just any judgment of personality, but of an accurate one. It does not necessarily describe how people always or even typically judge personality. Instead, it describes how accurate personality judgment happens, if and when it ever does.

Even this outline of the RAM is perhaps sufficient to point out three implications. First, accuracy is difficult. Unless the stages of relevance, availability, detection, and utilization are all traversed successfully, no accuracy will be attained at all. Moreover, imperfections at each step will combine multiplicatively (Funder, 1995, 1999). Second, the four stages of RAM identify four places where judgment can go wrong. Relevance, availability, detection, and utilization can all be and often are short-circuited for all sorts of reasons. Given these two considerations, it is really rather amazing that people manage to attain the considerable degree of accuracy that is often demonstrated. Third, the four stages of the RAM identify four places where judgment can be improved.

This final implication is perhaps the most important one. Traditionally, research to improve judgment has focused almost exclusively on the judge and his or her thinking processes. "Eliminate biases, acquire knowledge, think clearly, and don't be so defensive," judges are urged, among other suggestions. Notice, however, that in the context of the RAM these suggestions—worthy as they are—apply only to the last stage of personality judgment: utilization. There are three other places to improve accuracy as well.

For example, one might improve relevance by creating or promoting contexts in which people feel free to be themselves, to act as they really are. One might improve availability by observing one's target of judgment in a wide variety of situations, or in particularly informative ones. One might improve detection by eliminating distractions in the social environment. The point is that there are many ways to improve accuracy, only some of which involve "thinking better." These possibilities open whole new areas both for research and application. The renewed exploration of these areas will be the ultimate payoff of the field of social perception's newly attained positivity, realism, and sophistication.

## ACKNOWLEDGMENT

This research was supported in part by NIMH grant R01-MH42427.

## REFERENCES

Allport, G. W. (1958). What units shall we employ? In G. Lindzey (Ed.), *Assessment of human motives* (pp. 239–260). New York: Rinehart.

Allport, G. W. (1966). Traits revisited. *American Psychologist, 21,* 1–10.

Ambady, N., Bernieri, F. J., & Richeson, J. A. (2000). Towards a histology of social behavior: Judgmental accuracy from thin slices in the behavioral stream. *Advances in Experimental Social Psychology, 32,* 201–271.

Bernieri, F. J., Zuckerman, M., Koestner, R., & Rosenthal, R. (1994). Measuring person perception accuracy: Another look at self–other agreement. *Personality and Social Psychology Bulletin, 20,* 367–378.

Blackman, M. C., & Funder, D. C. (1998). The effect of information on consensus and accuracy in personality judgment. *Journal of Experimental Social Psychology, 34*, 164–181.

Crandall, C. S. (1984). The overcitation of examples of poor performance: Fad, fashion or fun [Comment]? *American Psychologist, 39*, 1499–1500.

Cronbach, L. J. (1955). Processes affecting scores on "understanding of others" and "assumed similarity." *Psychological Bulletin, 52*, 177–193.

Cronbach, L. J., & Gleser, G. C. (1953). Assessing similarity between profiles. *Psychological Bulletin, 50*, 456–473.

Funder, D. C. (1980). On seeing ourselves as others see us: Self–other agreement and discrepancy in personality ratings. *Journal of Personality, 48*, 473–493.

Funder, D. C. (1987). Errors and mistakes: Evaluating the accuracy of social judgment. *Psychological Bulletin, 101*, 75–90.

Funder, D. C. (1991). Global traits: A neo-Allportian approach to personality. *Psychological Science, 2*, 31–39.

Funder, D. C. (1992). Everything you know is wrong. *Contemporary Psychology, 37*, 319–320.

Funder, D. C. (1995). On the accuracy of personality judgment: A realistic approach. *Psychological Review, 102*, 652–670.

Funder, D. C. (1999). *Personality judgment: A realistic approach to person perception*. San Diego, CA: Academic.

Funder, D. C., Kolar, D., Colvin, C. R. (1995). Agreement among judges of personality: Interpersonal relations, similarity, and aquaintanceship. *Journal of Personality and Social Psychology, 69*, 656–672.

Gage, N. L., & Cronbach, L. J. (1955). Conceptual and methodological problems in interpersonal perception. *Psychological Review, 62*, 411–422.

Gigerenzer, G. (1991). How to make cognitive illusions disappear: Beyond "heuristics and biases". *European Review of Social Psychology, 2*, 83–115.

Hammond, K. R. (1996). *Human judgment and social policy*. New York: Oxford University Press.

Harackiewicz, J. M., & DePaulo, B. M. (1982). Accuracy of person perception: A component analysis according to Cronbach. *Personality and Social Psychology Bulletin, 8*, 247–256.

Jackson, D. N. (1982). Some preconditions for valid person perception. In M. P. Zanna, E. T. Higgins & C. P. Herman (Eds.), *Consistency in social behavior: The Ontario symposium* (Vol. 2, pp. 251–279). Hillsdale, NJ: Lawrence Erlbaum Associates.

Jussim, L. (1993). Accuracy in interpersonal expectations: A reflection–construction analysis of current and classic research. *Journal of Personality, 61*, 637–668.

Kenny, D. A. (1994). *Interpersonal perception: A social relations analysis*. New York: Guilford.

Kolar, D. W., Funder, D. C., & Colvin, C. R. (1996). Comparing the accuracy of personality judgments by the self and knowledgeable others. *Journal of Personality, 64*, 311–337.

Lee, Y -T., Jussim, L., & McCauley, C. (Eds.). (1995). *Stereotype accuracy: Toward appreciating group differences*. Washington, DC: American Psychological Association.

Lopes, L. L., & Oden, G. C. (1991). The rationality of intelligence. In E. Eells & T. Marusqewski (Eds.), *Probability and rationality: Studies on L. Jonathan Cohen's philosophy of science* (pp. 199–223). Amsterdam: Rodopi.

Simpson, J., Ickes, W., & Blackstone, J. (1995). When the head protects the heart: Empathic accuracy in dating relationships. *Journal of Personality and Social Psychology, 69*, 629–641.

Tagiuri, R. & Petrullo, L. (Eds.). (1958). *Person perception and interpersonal behavior*. Stanford, CA: Stanford University Press.

# ✂ 17 ✂

# Groping for the Elephant
# of Interpersonal Sensitivity

### Leslie A. Zebrowitz
*Brandeis University*

> *It was six men of Indostan*
> *To learning much inclined*
> *Who went to see the elephant*
> *(Though all of them were blind) …*
> *That each by observation*
> *Might satisfy his mind.*
>
> *And so these men of Indostan*
> *Disputed loud and long,*
> *Each in his own opinion*
> *Exceeding stiff and strong,*
> *Though each was partly in the right,*
> *And all were in the wrong!*
>
> —*John Godfrey Saxe (1816–1887).*

Reading this book may tempt one to compare psychologists who discuss interpersonal sensitivity to the six blind men, each of whom described an elephant while examining different parts of the animal's anatomy.[1] One, feeling the tusk, likened the elephant to a spear. Another, holding the trunk, said the elephant

---

[1] This heterogeneity in definitions is not unique to interpersonal sensitivity. For example, an edited book *What is Intelligence?* (Sternberg & Detterman, 1986) gathered two dozen views on its nature and definition, one of which likened conceptualizations of intelligence to the blind men's conceptualizations of the elephant.

was like a snake. Still another, seizing the tail, was sure the elephant was like a rope, and so on. Like the blind men, each psychologist who studies interpersonal sensitivity tends to explore only one of the many possible aspects of this elephant. In the chapters of this book, interpersonal sensitivity is variously conceptualized as accurately inferring others' thoughts and feelings, feeling another person's emotions, reading emotions, judging personality traits, predicting people's social outcomes, identifying social contexts and social relationships, perceiving what another feels about him or herself and you, and detecting deception. Like the views of the blind men, each of these views is surely "partly in the right." But none of them captures the entire beast of interpersonal sensitivity. And like the blind men, who lacked an overarching theory of elephantness and could not find it through local observations, psychologists lack an overarching theory of interpersonal sensitivity and will not find it through their local observations.

Just as the blind men would never grasp elephantness even if they used more refined instruments than their hands to probe separate parts of the beast's anatomy, the best measuring devices psychologists can muster will never provide a satisfactory understanding of interpersonal sensitivity so long as they continue to probe its separate components without an overarching theory to guide them. As such, the field would be better served by some serious conceptual thinking than by a proliferation of more measuring devices. Although I do not have a formal theory to propose, I will offer some suggestions about what a comprehensive theory of interpersonal sensitivity should include. These suggestions are by no means unique, and many parallel elements can be found in existing theories. However, the theory I envision is both more general and more specific than those currently found in the literature. It is more general in that it includes multiple domains of interpersonal sensitivity, and is more specific in that it provides a more fine-grained analysis of the factors that contribute to the achievement of interpersonal sensitivity.

A theory of interpersonal sensitivity should begin with a clear definition of this multifaceted construct. It should specify the target stimulus information; the contextual factors; and the affective, cognitive, and behavioral mechanisms that enable people to achieve interpersonal sensitivity in various domains. It should also explain the development and the consequences of interpersonal sensitivity in its various manifestations. With these parameters in place, one should be able to derive predictions about individual differences in interpersonal sensitivity, which is a central aim of many assessment strategies described in this book. Of course, it is possible that there is no elephantness to interpersonal sensitivity. Rather than a general faculty, it may be domain specific. Even if this is so, psychologists' understanding of the individual domains and any lack of generalizability across domains will be furthered by a careful analysis of the similarities and differences among those domains.

## WHAT IS INTERPERSONAL SENSITIVITY?

As indicated earlier, interpersonal sensitivity has been conceptualized in many ways. The chapters in this book identify at least six domains of interpersonal sensitivity—that is, to what attributes of another person perceivers are sensitive: (a) personality traits; (b) thoughts; (c) emotions, affective states, feelings; (d) social relationships and contexts; (e) social outcomes; and (f) truthfulness and deception. To this list I add one other—(g) social affordances—the opportunities for acting, interacting, or being acted on that others provide (McArthur & Baron, 1983; Zebrowitz & Collins, 1997). For example, a perceiver may accurately detect whether someone will submit to him or her, an affordance, without necessarily detecting how submissive that person is in general, a personality trait. Indeed, I have argued elsewhere that sensitivity to social affordances may be higher than sensitivity to other attributes insofar as the correct identification of affordances often has stronger implications for adaptive behavior (McArthur & Baron, 1983; Zebrowitz & Collins, 1997).[2]

However, even the foregoing seven domains oversimplify the categories of interpersonal sensitivity. For one thing, sensitivity varies within each domain (e.g., Funder & Dobroth, 1987; Wagner, MacDonald, & Manstead, 1986), which suggests that it may be appropriate to subdivide these seven domains. Moreover, there are numerous attributes to which perceivers may be sensitive that do not fit into any of these domains, including a target person's goals and motives, health, age, ethnicity, intelligence, and sexual orientation, to name a few (e.g., Ambady, Hallahan, & Conner, 1999; Borkenau & Liebler, 1993; Henss, 1991; Kalick, Zebrowitz, Langlois, & Johnson, 1998). An adequate understanding of the attributes to which perceivers may be sensitive will be better served by creating a meaningful organizational structure for these attributes than by generating an exhaustive list (cf. Zebrowitz, 1990).

Central to determining what is interpersonal sensitivity is the question of how it should be assessed. There are at least three facets to this question. One is the question of what standard should be used to assess the degree of sensitivity shown by the perceiver. Should the correct criterion response be determined by the target's self-report, by the consensus of a panel of judges who may or may not know the target, by some objective measure of the attribute in question? As discussed in many of the chapters in this book, no standard for assessing interpersonal sensitivity is perfect. The use of multiple standards is desirable, and the best one may depend on the domain. For example, the target's self-report may be inferior to the consensus of friends when assessing a perceiver's sensitivity to

---

[2]It should be noted that each of the domains of interpersonal sensitivity has a counterpart in *intrapersonal sensitivity*. People may vary in sensitivity to their own personality traits, thoughts, affective states, social roles, social outcomes, truthfulness, and social affordances.

the target's personality traits, whereas self-report may be superior when assessing a perceiver's sensitivity to the target's emotional state. A theory of interpersonal sensitivity should specify which standards for assessing sensitivity are best for which domains.

Related to the choice of a standard for assessing interpersonal sensitivity are biases that may produce a correct response. For example, perceivers may apply stereotypes that happen to be "correct" or they may project onto a target their own attributes, which happen to match the target's (Cronbach, 1955). Assessing the contribution of such biases to measures of interpersonal sensitivity requires research designs that can assess multiple components of perceivers' judgments about a target person (cf. Kenny & Winquist, chap. 14, this volume). Although stereotypical judgments and projection are biased judgments, one could nevertheless view them as showing interpersonal sensitivity insofar as the perceiver does end up knowing the target's personality, emotions, and so forth (cf. Colvin & Bundick, chap. 3, this volume; Lee, Jussim, & McCauley, 1995). Some conceptualizations seem to rule out this view. For example, Funder (1995, chap. 16, this volume) assumed that accuracy requires that the target do something relevant in the presence of a judge that is noticed and used appropriately. On the other hand, many current conceptualizations and measurements of interpersonal sensitivity do not rule out the contribution of stereotype accuracy and projection, sometimes intentionally and sometimes inadvertently. A theory of interpersonal sensitivity should take a clear stand on this issue.

A third facet of the assessment question has received less attention, but it is equally important for a theory of nonverbal sensitivity. This is the question of how interpersonal sensitivity is manifested by the perceiver. Is it shown in the perceiver's verbal report about the target attribute in question, in behavioral responses to the target, in physiological responses, in nonverbal responses, or in predictions of the target's behavior or outcomes? To determine whether the perceiver has been sensitive to a target, most researchers have assessed the perceiver's verbal reports about a target's emotions, personality, thoughts, feelings, and so forth. However, sensitivity may occur without being available to direct verbal report. For example, Malone and DePaulo (chap. 6, this volume) report that perceivers show recognition of deception in certain responses although they do not show it when directly asked to rate the deceptiveness of a communication. It is possible that interpersonal sensitivity in other domains is also underestimated by the criterion of correct verbal labels, and it may be more reliably shown in physiological, nonverbal, or affective responses. Whether one wants to call such responses "interpersonal sensitivity" is another question. One might wish to define the construct such that it requires conscious knowledge of another person's emotions, personality, and so on. The important point is that a theory of interpersonal sensitivity needs to be clear about how it can be shown by a perceiver.

## WHAT TARGET STIMULUS INFORMATION
## IS REQUIRED FOR INTERPERSONAL SENSITIVITY?

A theory of interpersonal sensitivity must specify how it is achieved. One essential question that must be answered is What stimulus information provided by a target person enables perceivers to detect that person's attributes? The central role of stimulus information is reflected in existing work on interpersonal sensitivity. For example, Funder (1995, chap. 16, this volume) argues that the accurate detection of personality traits depends on the availability of trait-relevant behavioral cues, and many assessment tools designed to measure interpersonal sensitivity explicitly vary the nature of the stimulus information provided to perceivers. The Profile of Nonverbal Sensitivity (PONS) assesses sensitivity to different channels of stimulus information reflecting 11 combinations of various visual and audio stimuli (Hall, chap. 8, this volume). The Diagnostic Analysis of Nonverbal Accuracy (DANVA) assesses sensitivity to facial expressions, gestures, and prosody (Nowicki & Duke, chap. 10, this volume). The "thin slices" methodology and the "standard content methodology" have each been used independently to assess sensitivity to visual cues and verbalizations (Ambady, LaPlante, & Johnson, chap. 5, this volume; Noller, chap. 13, this volume). Various self-report assessment tools, such as the Perceived Decoding Ability scale (Zuckerman & Larrance, 1979), also assess sensitivity to visual and vocal cues. Despite the attention to different types of target stimulus information, there is no adequate theoretical specification of the information that is needed for interpersonal sensitivity in various domains.

Psychologists have made some strides in identifying the stimulus information necessary for interpersonal sensitivity to emotions, deception, and personality traits (e.g., Ekman, 1982; Zuckerman, DePaulo, & Rosenthal, 1981; Funder & Sneed, 1993). However, our knowledge of these and other domains is incomplete. Moreover, as I have argued previously, considerable research has taken a shotgun empirical approach that yields a chaotic array of correlations. There will be greater success in identifying target stimuli that inform perceivers about others' attributes if researchers have a theoretical basis for selecting particular qualities to assess and if they assess configural qualities, which are patterns of stimulus information theoretically related to the judged attribute, as opposed to individual stimulus cues (Zebrowitz, 1997; Zebrowitz & Collins, 1997).

Developing predictions about stimulus information is not a trivial pursuit. It requires some minimal theoretical understanding of the multiple content domains to which perceivers may be sensitive. For example, in the case of interpersonal sensitivity to emotions, predictions about stimulus information require a theory of emotional expression—How are emotions manifested in behavior? In the case of interpersonal sensitivity to deception, predictions about stimulus information require some theory of how deception is manifested in behavior. In the case of interpersonal sensitivity to personality, predictions about stimulus information require a theory of how personality is manifested in behavior. In the case of interpersonal sensitivity to social relations, predictions about stimulus information require a theory of how dominance and affiliative and kinship relations are manifested in behavior. In each of these domains, perceivers may use target stimulus information from one or more modalities including verbalizations, actions, paralinguistic cues, body language, facial expression, and morphology.

## WHAT CONTEXTUAL FACTORS INFLUENCE INTERPERSONAL SENSITIVITY?

There are two general contextual influences on interpersonal sensitivity. One is the effect of the social setting on the availability of diagnostic stimulus information—whether the attributes to be detected are in fact displayed by the target. As is true for the study of target stimulus information that fosters interpersonal sensitivity, a theoretical basis is required for identifying social settings that inform perceivers about others' attributes. Thus, in the case of interpersonal sensitivity to emotions, predictions about effects of the social setting require a theory of emotional expression that specifies what settings are associated with the display of what emotions. Similarly, predictions regarding interpersonal sensitivity to personality, deception, or social relationships require theories specifying the social settings that are associated with observable indicators of each of these attributes. Inasmuch there is still no well-accepted taxonomy for describing social settings, it will be difficult to specify the ones that make diagnostic stimulus information more or less available to perceivers. Such a taxonomy not only should specify which settings are conducive to detecting particular attributes, but also what stimulus information is likely to convey those attributes in each setting.

A second contextual influence on interpersonal sensitivity is the relationship between the perceiver and the target. Although one can independently specify the stimulus information encoded by the target and the psychological and behavioral decoding mechanisms in the perceiver, the fact is that interpersonal sensitivity is an emergent property. It reflects both the stimulus properties of the target in a particular context and the context-relevant decoding abilities of the perceiver—the attunement of the perceiver to the diagnostic stimulus information that a particular target provides. Perceivers may be more motivated to read certain targets or they may be more able to do so by virtue of greater familiarity with those targets, or greater sensitivity to the particular stimulus information they provide. The significance of the unique relationship between perceiver and target is particularly apparent when one considers interpersonal sensitivity to social affordances. Some perceivers may perceive an affordance in some targets that other perceivers will not perceive because the affordance does not exist for them. For example, heterosexual female perceivers in their teens or

20s may perceive a 20-year-old man to afford a romantic relationship, while this affordance will not be perceived by 8 year olds or octogenarians.

To the extent that interpersonal sensitivity is influenced by the relationship between perceiver and target, one would expect perceivers to show considerable variation in sensitivity across targets. Consistent with this suggestion, a substantial proportion of the variance in people's impressions of others' personality traits is accounted for by the unique impression that perceivers form of particular targets (e.g., Levesque, 1997). On the other hand, perceivers' unique impressions of how targets would behave toward them were no more accurate than impressions of how those targets would generally behave (Levesque & Kenny, 1993). However, it should be noted that the latter study examined impressions of a person's likely nonverbal behaviors (e.g., voice animation, smiling, gesturing), which is very different from impressions of the adaptively relevant behavioral opportunities that a target affords the perceiver. Perceivers' impressions of attributes such as helpfulness or agreeableness may in fact show more accuracy when impressions concern how targets will behave toward them than when they concern how targets will generally behave, and this may be particularly true when perceivers and targets are acquainted.

To the extent that interpersonal sensitivity is influenced by the relationship between perceiver and target, one might also expect perceivers to show more sensitivity when judging known targets rather than strangers. Consistent with this suggestion, research has shown higher levels of empathic accuracy with increasing levels of acquaintanceship and when judging friends rather than strangers (Ickes, Marangoni, & Garcia, 1997; Stinson & Ickes, 1992) as well as higher levels of accuracy in judging the personality traits of friends than strangers (Funder & Colvin, 1988; Funder, Kolar, & Blackman, 1995). Although researchers have paid heed to the effects of the perceiver–target relationship by differentiating interpersonal sensitivity to strangers versus friends or spouses as well as by differentiating the interpersonal sensitivity of subordinates versus superiors and happily versus unhappily married couples (cf. Noller, chap. 13, this volume; Snodgrass, chap. 11, this volume), more theoretical development is needed to provide a taxonomy of those perceiver–target relations that are likely to influence interpersonal sensitivity in one or more of the various domains.

## WHAT BEHAVIORAL MECHANISMS ARE REQUIRED FOR INTERPERSONAL SENSITIVITY?

To understand interpersonal sensitivity requires not only understanding the stimulus information that is provided by targets and the social context in which sensitivity is assessed, but also the nature of the interaction between perceiver and target. Interpersonal sensitivity may be greater for active perceivers who elicit diagnostic information from targets than for those who are passive recipients of whatever stimulus information the experimenter or target provides. If so, then research paradigms that constrain the active information search of the perceiver may underestimate interpersonal sensitivity just as such paradigms underestimate the accuracy of perception of the inanimate environment (cf. Gibson, 1979). Whether this is true may depend on the domain of interpersonal sensitivity being assessed. For example, Malone and DePaulo (chap. 6, this volume) report that liars rarely experience challenges or interrogations, which suggests that constraining the active information search of lie detectors will not underestimate the interpersonal sensitivity they show in everyday life. On the other hand, constraining the information search of personality detectors may underestimate the interpersonal sensitivity shown in everyday life.

Little research has assessed whether active perceivers show greater interpersonal sensitivity, and the outcome may well depend on a variety of factors. For example, passive perceivers appear to focus more on the content of a target person's verbalizations, whereas interacting perceivers focus more on nonverbal stimulus information (e.g., Gilbert & Krull, 1988, Study 3). Therefore, whether active perceivers will show more interpersonal sensitivity will depend on which information is more diagnostic (e.g., Bernieri & Gillis, chap. 4, this volume). The effect of the perceivers' behavior is likely to depend not only on what target information is most diagnostic, but also on the nature of the perceiver's behavior and its effectiveness in evoking relevant stimulus information, the quality of the information that the target spontaneously displays, and the domain of sensitivity being assessed.[3]

## WHAT COGNITIVE AND AFFECTIVE MECHANISMS ARE REQUIRED FOR INTERPERSONAL SENSITIVITY?

For a theory of interpersonal sensitivity to specify how it is achieved, it must not only identify the diagnostic target stimulus information and the social contexts and perceiver behaviors that make this information most available; it must also specify what psychological mechanisms are required to accurately process this information. Several mechanisms are mentioned in various chapters in this book. *Attention* to diagnostic stimulus information is essential for interpersonal sensitivity unless the sensitivity derives from projection or stereotype accuracy. *Correct inferences* from that stimulus information is another psychological mechanism that may be crucial for interpersonal sensitivity. However, *emotional* or *affective reactions* to diagnostic stimulus information may yield interpersonal sensitivity in the absence of any inferences. This is particularly true when using

---

[3]Blackman and Funder (1995) found that personality judgments of perceivers who interacted with a stranger showed no more agreement with the stranger's self-ratings than did the personality judgments of perceivers who passively watched a videotape of the interaction. The lack of advantage to the active perceiver may reflect the fact that the passive observer was exposed to the same stimulus information, and that judgments pertained to the stranger's general traits rather than to the stranger's affordances for a particular perceiver.

accuracy criteria such as a perceiver's emotional matching to assess sensitivity to a target's emotions (cf. Losoya & Eisenberg, chap. 2, this volume) or a perceiver's confidence or suspiciousness to assess sensitivity to a target's deception (cf. Malone & DePaulo, chap. 6, this volume). Moreover, affective reactions may also account for interpersonal sensitivity that is assessed by direct verbal reports about a target's attributes.

Indirect evidence that inferential processes are not essential for interpersonal sensitivity is provided by data indicating that accuracy is not improved by explicitly teaching the correct cues, although it is improved by feedback that can provide implicit knowledge of cue–attribute correlations (Gillis, Bernieri, & Wooten, 1995; Ickes et al., 1997). Also suggestive is evidence that interpersonal accuracy can occur with very limited stimulus information. For example, Ambady and Rosenthal (1992) found that judgment accuracy is as high given only 30 s of stimulus information as given 4 or 5 min. However, it should be noted that although studies have controlled the time of stimulus exposure, they have not directly controlled the amount of time perceivers had to think about the stimulus. Other methods, such as response latency and priming paradigms, are needed to more definitively determine when interpersonal sensitivity is a tacit, automatic intuitive judgment, rather than an analytic inference. Such research should consider the possibility that the nature of the psychological mechanisms required for interpersonal sensitivity will vary across domains. For example, analytic inferences may be required for sensitivity to another person's personality traits or specific thoughts, while automatic affective reactions may be sufficient for sensitivity to another's emotions or deception.

## HOW DOES INTERPERSONAL
## SENSITIVITY DEVELOP?

A theory of interpersonal sensitivity should consider how it develops. It has typically been assumed that interpersonal sensitivity improves with maturation, and considerable research does show age-related improvements (cf. Hall, chap. 8, this volume; Losoya & Eisenberg, chap. 2, this volume; Nowicki & Duke, chap. 10, this volume). Almost no attention has been given to the question of whether interpersonal sensitivity continues to improve throughout adulthood or whether there are age-related declines. This is an important issue to investigate, particularly because there is some evidence that older perceivers may show less sensitivity to facial expressions of emotion and that perceivers are more sensitive to the emotions of targets who are similar in age (Malatesta, Izard, Culver, & Nicolich, 1987).

Although there is some research examining age-related changes in interpersonal sensitivity, there has been little theoretical discussion of why such changes should occur and no consideration of whether development differs across the various domains of interpersonal sensitivity. Is it the development of attention, inferential skills, emotion, or motivation that yields improved interpersonal sensitivity? The role of such processes in sensitivity to others' emotions has been demonstrated by interventions that teach children to discriminate between nonverbal cues, identify them, express them, and apply this knowledge to social situations (Nowicki & Duke, chap. 10, this volume). Although such interventions have been effective with children who show very low interpersonal sensitivity, they may not mimic the processes that contribute to the normal development of interpersonal sensitivity. In particular, some research with adults suggests that learning explicit rules is not the crucial factor, at least in sensitivity to rapport (Gillis et al., 1995).

Rather than being grounded in explicit socialization practices, interpersonal sensitivity may develop through increasing interpersonal experience that provides feedback that contributes to implicit knowledge of correlations between certain stimulus information and certain target person attributes (e.g., Hill, Lewicki, Czyzewska, & Schuller, 1990). Alternatively, it is possible that age-related improvements in interpersonal sensitivity largely reflect the development of verbal skills such that other criteria would show smaller age effects. Indeed, affective empathy has been documented in children as young as 15 months when facial and gestural measures are used as the criteria (cf. Losoya & Eisenberg, chap. 2, this volume).

## WHAT ARE THE CONSEQUENCES
## OF INTERPERSONAL SENSITIVITY?

One reason for studying interpersonal sensitivity is that it is thought to predict more effective social functioning, and various measures of individual differences in this faculty have been related to social outcome variables. Affective empathy has been used to predict a variety of prosocial behaviors (Losoya & Eisenberg, chap. 2, this volume). The inability to identify emotions as assessed by the DANVA predicts particular social problems in clinical populations (Nowicki & Duke, chap. 10, this volume). Self-report measures of interpersonal sensitivity predict job performance (Riggio & Riggio, chap. 7, this volume). Performance on the PONS test predicts job performance as clinicians and teachers, ratings of interpersonal sensitivity by peers and supervisors, and the satisfaction of physician's patients (Hall, chap. 8, this volume). Additionally, spouses' accuracy in decoding nonverbal messages of their partners predicts marital quality (Noller, chap. 13, this volume).

While the foregoing findings show that the interpersonal sensitivity construct has promising utility, there is need for a more well-articulated set of theoretical predictions regarding its social consequences. These predictions should make clear whether the consequences will vary as a function of the domain in which interpersonal sensitivity is displayed. They should also specify the factors mediating a link between interpersonal sensitivity and effective social functioning. Is interpersonal sensitivity a sufficient condition for higher functioning or only a contributing condition? If the latter, then what other factors moderate the effects of interpersonal sensitivity on social functioning? Another question is whether interpersonal sensitivity is likely to be linearly related to adaptive social functioning or whether one can be too sensitive. Such issues have rarely been considered, although there are some exceptions (e.g., Ickes & Simpson, 1997; Losoya & Eisenberg, chap. 2, this volume; Simpson, Ickes, & Grich, 1999).

## WHAT ARE THE INDIVIDUAL DIFFERENCES IN INTERPERSONAL SENSITIVITY?

### Generating Predictions

A theory of interpersonal sensitivity must be able to specify why there should be individual differences in order to know what differences to look for. Predictions about individual differences may be derived from a consideration of the target stimulus information, the contextual factors, the psychological and behavioral mechanisms, and the developmental progressions that influence interpersonal sensitivity.

Knowing what stimuli are informative may yield predictions regarding which perceivers will show the most interpersonal sensitivity. For example, some people use more visual imagery in their thinking than others, who think verbally (Paivio & Harshman, 1983). To the extent that the use of visual cues fosters interpersonal sensitivity, those who think visually may show superior performance. Knowing what target stimuli are informative will also allow predictions regarding the domains in which particular perceivers will excel. For example, those who think visually may show superior performance when reading emotions, but inferior performance when detecting deception, which can be impaired by attention to visual cues (e.g., Malone & DePaulo, chap. 6, this volume; Zuckerman, DeFrank, Hall, Larrance, & Rosenthal, 1979). Finally, knowing what target stimuli are informative will allow predictions regarding whether interpersonal sensitivity will generalize across domains. For example, to the extent that facial cues are informative about emotions, deception, and personality traits, performance may be highly correlated across these domains. However, to the extent that facial cues are informative about emotions, vocal cues informative about deception, and verbalizations informative about personality traits, interpersonal sensitivity across these domains may be relatively independent.

Knowing what social settings are informative may also yield predictions regarding which perceivers will show the most interpersonal sensitivity. For example, because cooperative contexts provide more diagnostic stimulus information for judging rapport (Bernieri, Gillis, Davis, & Grahe, 1996; Bernieri & Gillis, chap. 4, this volume), managers who establish cooperative work groups may show higher levels of sensitivity to variations in this attribute among their subordinates than managers who create a more competitive work environment. Similarly, if unstructured settings elicit behavioral information that is most informative about personality traits (Funder, 1995), then perceivers who spend considerable time in such settings may show higher levels of interpersonal sensitivity to the traits of their friends and acquaintances. Knowing the affordances of targets for particular perceivers may also yield predictions about individual differences in interpersonal sensitivity. For example, dependent perceivers are particularly sensitive to the personality trait of agreeableness in other people, whereas dominant individuals are more sensitive to the trait of assertiveness (Battistich & Aronoff, 1985).

Knowing what behavioral mechanisms foster interpersonal sensitivity may also yield predictions regarding individual differences. Insofar as some people are more interpersonally sensitive because they do more to evoke diagnostic information, various personality traits and motivational variables may predict performance. For example, an active search for diagnostic stimulus information may be more typical of extraverts than introverts. If so, then the finding that more sociable individuals are less sensitive to others' personality traits in a social situation that prohibits verbal interaction may be due to the fact that sociable people have learned to rely on explicit information that they ask for directly (e.g., Ambady, Hallahan, & Rosenthal, 1995).[4]

Individual differences in affective and cognitive mechanisms may also contribute to individual differences in interpersonal sensitivity, because these mechanisms may be more well-developed in some individuals than in others. For example, given that affective empathy requires vicariously experiencing another person's emotional state, theories of emotion were used to predict that individual differences in this domain would result from differences in emotional reactivity (Losoya & Eisenberg, chap. 2, this volume). Similarly, theories of attention may be useful in predicting individual differences insofar as some people are more interpersonally sensitive because they attend more to the stimulus information that can inform them about others' attributes. Information-processing theories and theories of cognitive abilities may also predict individual differences, insofar as some people are more interpersonally sensitive because they are better able to make the correct inferences from the available stimulus information. Indeed, intellectual functioning and cognitive style do predict interpersonal sensitivity (Davis & Kraus, 1997). However, it is not known whether this predictive power is limited to particular domains of sensitivity that require inferential processes, or for that matter what those domains may be.

---

[4]Alternatively, the expressive nonverbal behavior of sociable individuals in the presence of other people may distract them from others' personality traits, whereas they may be more interpersonally sensitive when judging people who are presented on videotape (e.g., Akert & Panter, 1988). In either event, past experimental demonstrations of greater or lesser interpersonal sensitivity among unsociable people may not generalize to real-life situations where information-seeking behavior is less constrained. ·

Knowing how interpersonal sensitivity develops may yield predictions regarding individual differences in addition to the obvious predictions of age differences. For example, if age-related improvements in interpersonal sensitivity largely reflect the development of verbal skills, then perhaps adults with higher verbal skills will show higher interpersonal sensitivity. Alternatively, age-related improvements in interpersonal sensitivity may reflect age-related increases in interpersonal experiences that reveal subtle correlations between certain stimulus information and certain target person attributes. If so, then adults who have less need or opportunity to learn these correlations may show lower interpersonal sensitivity. For example, adults who grew up in families in which emotions were frequently expressed in salient verbalizations and nonverbal behaviors were less skilled at decoding emotional expressions displayed in brief (6 s) audio and videotapes than adults who grew up in relatively unexpressive families (Halberstadt, 1986). Presumably, those growing up in unexpressive families developed more sensitivity to the subtle correlations between nonverbal cues and emotions that could be extracted from a brief slice of behavior.

The individual differences that affect the level of interpersonal sensitivity could conceivably generalize across all content domains, yielding a general trait. However, it is much more likely that they are in some way domain specific. For example, the person who attends more than others to facial cues may not necessarily attend more than others to vocal cues or verbalizations. To the extent that facial cues are diagnostic of different attributes than vocal cues or verbalizations are, this individual may show high interpersonal sensitivity in one domain but not in others. Consistent with the suggestion that interpersonal sensitivity is domain specific, various measures of individual differences in interpersonal sensitivity do not correlate (cf. Hall, chap. 8, this volume; Riggio & Riggio, chap. 7, this volume).

## Creating an Assessment Tool

Given the multifaceted nature of interpersonal sensitivity, the goal of developing a measure to assess this faculty will be difficult to achieve. One way it might be accomplished would be to develop a long self-report questionnaire that taps multiple domains, stimulus information, and contexts. If such a questionnaire could be constructed, it would provide a manageable method for determining the domains of interpersonal sensitivity that are correlated and for determining whether it is reasonable to view interpersonal sensitivity as a general faculty. However, it is difficult to develop a valid self-report questionnaire, and one of this breadth would be particularly challenging.

Another alternative would be to develop a multimethod assessment tool with separate components designed to assess sensitivity to emotions, sensitivity to social roles, sensitivity to personality traits, and so forth. Each of these components would be designed to examine a range of target stimulus information theoretically relevant to interpersonal sensitivity, as well as a range of social contexts. Each would also assess the role of theoretically relevant cognitive, affective, and behavioral mechanisms. Additionally, each would use the same set of responses to assess interpersonal sensitivity, be it verbal labels for the attribute in question, behavioral predictions, more tacit knowledge, or a combination of these. Such assessment tools would enable researchers to understand why individual differences in interpersonal sensitivity do or do not generalize across domains. For example, is generalizability shown only when the same target stimulus information is provided or only when the same behavioral mechanisms are operating? The breadth of the interpersonal sensitivity construct makes it unreasonable to expect any single researcher to develop such a multimethod assessment tool. However, if researchers subscribed to the same theoretical framework, then different components could be developed by different investigators, allowing informative comparisons across domains.

## Some Caveats

Individual differences in interpersonal sensitivity may be trivial in some domains. Indeed, some research suggests that the stimulus information provided by targets may account for more of the variance in interpersonal sensitivity than does the discernment of perceivers. For example, among perceivers and targets who were acquainted, targets accounted for more variance in judgments about four of the Big Five personality traits than perceivers did (Levesque, 1997). Even when the perceivers and targets were unacquainted, targets still accounted for more variance in judgments about extraversion than perceivers did (e.g., Albright, Kenny, & Malloy, 1988). Similarly, interpersonal sensitivity to what people think about themselves and each other was more influenced by status-related variations in the encoding of expressive cues than by status-related variations in perceivers' decoding ability (Snodgrass, Hecht, & Ploutz-Snyder, 1998).

An important question to consider is which domains are likely to show notable individual differences in interpersonal sensitivity. Although judgments of the personality traits of known others show less variance due to the perceivers making the judgments than to the targets being judged, individual differences in sensitivity to other people's thoughts about oneself reveal much more variance due to perceivers than to the targets holding those thoughts (Levesque, 1997). The likelihood of individual differences depends not only on the domain, but also on the context in which sensitivity is assessed. Judgments about strangers' personality traits show more variance due to perceivers than do judgments about acquaintances' personality traits (Albright et al., 1988; Levesque, 1997).

In those domains where attributes of the target drive social judgments, individual differences in interpersonal sensitivity may be confined to extreme groups rather than being a normally distributed faculty. There certainly are other human faculties that show such a pattern. Human beings are all sensitive to the same light spectrum, and measures of sensitivity to wavelengths are likely to pick up individual differences only in the extreme cases of colorblindness. Consistent with the suggestion that there may be a skewed distribution of individual differences in interpersonal sensitivity, one of the most useful measures, the DANVA, sets the bar very low, picking up differences between normals and those who are very insensitive.[5]

## CONCLUSIONS

To predict and assess individual differences in interpersonal sensitivity requires a theory of interpersonal sensitivity. Such a theory must begin by identifying the domains in which sensitivity may be manifested. What has been said about the construct of intelligence holds equally true for interpersonal sensitivity.

> The elephant of [interpersonal sensitivity] may be so complex that we can and should decide to add a modifier to the term [interpersonal sensitivity] for each of the several ways in which the elephant can be described.... If we could agree on appropriate modifiers, it would be easier to communicate with each other, with scientists in other disciplines, and with the general public. (adapted from Humphreys, 1996, p. 98)

A theory of interpersonal sensitivity requires not only an adequate demarcation of its domains, but it must also specify how interpersonal sensitivity is influenced by target stimulus information, contextual factors, and psychological and behavioral mechanisms in the perceiver, as well as how it develops. Given that much of the interest in assessing individual differences in interpersonal sensitivity derives from the potential practical applications of such assessments, a theory of interpersonal sensitivity should ultimately specify its consequences.

The theory of interpersonal sensitivity that I envision will allow researchers to develop measures of the separate domains of interpersonal sensitivity that permit more meaningful comparisons of individual differences across domains. Such comparisons not only will reveal whether individual differences are general or domain specific, but also why they generalize across domains or fail to do so. Researchers may find that it is reasonable to speak of a general faculty called *interpersonal sensitivity*. However, it is also possible that they will conclude that interpersonal sensitivity is made from distinct sensitivities, that have different determinants and predict different social outcomes. Even if researchers find that there is no "elephant" connecting the various domains of interpersonal sensitivity, a more unified approach to understanding each of the separate domains will yield a better understanding of these important phenomena.

---

[5]Individual differences will be found if verbal labels are used as the criterion, which illustrates the limitations of such a criterion for assessing perceptual sensitivity.

## ACKNOWLEDGMENTS

I thank Joann Montepare and Carrie Andreoletti for helpful comments on earlier drafts of this chapter.

## REFERENCES

Akert, R. M., & Panter, A. T. (1988). Extraversion and the ability to decode nonverbal communication. *Personality and Individual Differences, 9,* 965–972.

Albright, L., Kenny, D., & Malloy, T. (1988). Consensus in personality judgments at zero acquaintance. *Journal of Personality and Social Psychology, 55,* 387–395.

Ambady, N., Hallahan, M., & Conner, B. (1999). Accuracy of judgments of sexual orientation from thin slices of behavior. *Journal of Personality and Social Psychology, 77,* 538–547.

Ambady, N., Hallahan, M., & Rosenthal, R. (1995). On judging and being judged accurately in zero acquaintance situations. *Journal of Personality and Social Psychology, 69,* 518–529.

Ambady, N., & Rosenthal, R. (1992). Thin slices of expressive behavior as predictors of interpersonal consequences: A meta-analysis. *Psychological Bulletin, 111,* 256–274.

Battistich, V. A., & Aronoff, J. (1985). Perceiver, target, and situational influences on social cognition: An interactional analysis. *Journal of Personality and Social Psychology, 49,* 788–798.

Bernieri, F. J., Gillis, J. S., Davis, J. S., & Grahe, J. E. (1996). Dyad rapport and the accuracy of its judgment across situations: A lens model analysis. *Journal of Personality and Social Psychology, 71,* 110–129.

Blackman, M. C., & Funder, D. C. (1995, April). *The effect of participation vs. observation on self/stranger agreement.* Paper presented at the meeting of the Western Psychological Association, Los Angeles, CA.

Borkenau, P., & Liebler, A. (1993). Convergence of stranger ratings of personality and intelligence with self-ratings, partner ratings, and measured intelligence. *Journal of Personality and Social Psychology, 65,* 546–553.

Cronbach, L. J. (1955). Processes affecting scores on "understanding of others" and "assumed similarity." *Psychological Bulletin, 52,* 177–193.

Davis, M. H., & Kraus, L. A. (1997). Personality and empathic accuracy. In W. Ickes (Ed.), *Empathic accuracy* (pp. 144–168). New York: Guilford.

Ekman, P. (Ed.). (1982). *Emotion in the human face* (2nd ed.). Cambridge, England: Cambridge University Press.

Funder, D. C. (1995). On the accuracy of personality judgment: A realistic approach. *Psychological Review, 102,* 652–670.

Funder, D. C., & Colvin, C. R. (1988) Friends and strangers: Acquaintanceship, agreement, and the accuracy of personality judgment. *Journal of Personality and Social Psychology, 55,* 149–158.

Funder, D. C., & Dobroth, K. (1987). Differences between traits: Properties associated with interjudge agreement. *Journal of Personality and Social Psychology, 52,* 409–418.

Funder, D. C., Kolar, D. C., & Blackman, M. C. (1995). Agreement among judges of personality: Interpersonal relations, similarity, and acquaintanceship. *Journal of Personality and Social Psychology, 69,* 656–672.

Funder, D. C., & Sneed, C. (1993). Behavioral manifestations of personality: An ecological approach to judgmental accuracy. *Journal of Personality and Social Psychology, 64,* 479–490.

Gibson, J. J. (1979). *The ecological approach to visual perception.* Boston: Houghton Mifflin.

Gilbert, D. T., & Krull, D. S. (1988). Seeing less and knowing more: The benefits of perceptual ignorance. *Journal of Personality and Social Psychology, 54,* 193–202.

Gillis, J. S., Bernieri, F. J., & Wooten, E. (1995). The effects of stimulus medium and feedback on the judgment of rapport. *Organizational Behavior and Human Decision Processes, 63,* 33–45.

Halberstadt, A. G. (1986). Family socialization of emotional expression and nonverbal communication styles and skills. *Journal of Personality and Social Psychology, 51,* 827–836.

Henss, R. (1991). Perceiving age and attractiveness in facial photographs. *Journal of Applied Social Psychology, 21,* 933–946.

Hill, T., Lewicki, P., Czyzewska, M., & Schuller, G. (1990). The role of learned inferential encoding rules in the perception of faces: Effects of non-conscious self-perpetuation of a bias. *Journal of Experimental Social Psychology, 26,* 350–371.

Humphreys, L. G. (1986). Describing the elephant. In R. J. Sternberg & D. K. Detterman (Eds.), *What is intelligence? Contemporary viewpoints on its nature and definition* (pp. 97–100). Norwood, NJ: Ablex.

Ickes, W., Marangoni, C., & Garcia, S. (1997). Studying empathic accuracy in a clinically relevant context. In W. Ickes (Ed.), *Empathic accuracy* (pp. 282–310). New York: Guilford.

Ickes, W., & Simpson, J. (1997). Managing empathic accuracy in close relationships. In W. Ickes (Ed.), *Empathic accuracy* (pp. 218–250). New York: Guilford.

Kalick, S. M., Zebrowitz, L. A., Langlois, J. H., & Johnson, R. M. (1998). Does human facial attractiveness honestly advertise health? Longitudinal data on an evolutionary question. *Psychological Science, 9,* 8–13.

Lee, Y. T., Jussim, L. J., & McCauley, C. R. (1995). *Stereotype accuracy: Toward appreciating group differences.* Washington, DC: American Psychological Association.

Levesque, M. J. (1997). Meta-accuracy among acquainted individuals: A social relations analysis of interpersonal perception and metaperception. *Journal of Personality and Social Psychology, 72,* 66–74.

Levesque, M. J., & Kenny, D. A. (1993). Accuracy of behavioral predictions at zero acquaintance: A social relations analysis. *Journal of Personality and Social Psychology, 65,* 1178–1187.

Malatesta, C. Z., Izard, C. E., Culver, C., & Nicolich, M. (1987). Emotion communication skills in young, middle-aged, and older women. *Psychology and Aging, 2,* 193–203.

McArthur, L. Z., & Baron, R. M. (1983). Toward an ecological theory of social perception. *Psychological Review, 90,* 215–238.

Paivio, A., & Harshman, R.A. (1983). Factor analysis of a questionnaire on imagery and verbal habits and skills. *Canadian Journal of Psychology, 37,* 461–483.

Simpson, J. A., Ickes, W., & Grich, J. (1999). When accuracy hurts: Reactions of anxious–ambivalent dating partners to a relationship-threatening situation. *Journal of Personality and Social Psychology, 76,* 754–769.

Snodgrass, S. E., Hecht, M. A., & Ploutz-Snyder, R. (1998). Interpersonal sensitivity: Expressivity or perceptivity? *Journal of Personality and Social Psychology, 74,* 238–249.

Stinson, L., & Ickes, W. (1992). Empathic accuracy in the interactions of male friends versus male strangers. *Journal of Personality and Social Psychology, 62,* 787–797.

Wagner, M. L., MacDonald, J., & Manstead, A. S. R. (1986). Communication of individual emotions by spontaneous facial expressions. *Journal of Personality and Social Psychology, 50,* 737–743.

Zebrowitz, L. A. (1990). *Social perception.* Buckingham, England: Open University Press.

Zebrowitz, L. A. (1997). *Reading faces: Window to the soul?* Boulder, CO: Westview.

Zebrowitz, L. A., & Collins, M. A. (1997). Accurate social perception at zero acquaintance: The affordances of a Gibsonian approach. *Personality and Social Psychology Review, 1,* 204–223.

Zuckerman, M., DePaulo, B. M., & Rosenthal, R. (1981). Verbal and nonverbal communication of deception. In L. Berkowitz (Ed.), *Advances in experimental social psychology,* Vol. 14 (pp. 1–59). New York: Academic.

Zuckerman, M., DeFrank, R. S., Hall, J. A., Larrance, D. T., & Rosenthal, R. (1979). Facial and vocal cues of deception and honesty. *Journal of Experimental Social Psychology, 15,* 378–396.

Zuckerman, M., & Larrance, D. T. (1979). Individual differences in perceived encoding and decoding abilities. In R. Rosenthal (Ed.), *Skill in nonverbal communication: Individual differences* (pp. 171–203). Cambridge, MA: Oelgeschlager, Gunn & Hain.

# ❧ **18** ❧

# Paradoxes of Nonverbal Detection, Expression, and Responding: Points to PONDER

Howard S. Friedman
*University of California, Riverside*

Ponder a number of puzzling paradoxes of interpersonal sensitivity. In various situations, it appears that a tremendous amount of important interpersonal knowledge is being rapidly communicated, mostly nonverbally. Yet it is usually not understood how this occurs. On the other hand, there is a great deal of misinformation and misunderstanding in face-to-face human relations. Here, too, it's often difficult to decipher precisely what is going wrong.

Many people can describe an experience in which one look (actually, probably a minute or two of interaction) can involve an exchange that is life-changing. It could be the example of rapture and transport, in which something in the way she moves, or something in the way he grooves provides sufficient romantic information to lead to a successful marriage. Is this simply a chance association, in which almost any partner would have been suitable? If not, then important, valid information is rapidly expressed and detected. Yet this intense, deep communication is attributed only to some vague cliché like "love at first sight."

Or consider a situation in which old friends meet at a reunion after being apart for 20 years. Could one glance communicate to one's former best friend that one had married the wrong person or chosen the wrong career? Could old feelings of love be immediately rekindled, or passions of jealousy be quickly rearoused? Could these exchanges involve deep understanding as well as simple emotion? That is, can one achieve that moment of epiphany, just like Hollywood likes to show? What are the elements of such remarkable interpersonal sensitivity?

Popular books advise that the first few minutes of an encounter are key to success. Many people follow this advice, trying to make a great first impression or trying to scrutinize new acquaintances. Do individuals size up, psych out, and touch souls with each fresh companion? Alternatively, to what extent do individuals see only a self-presented image that has little ability to predict subsequent actions and outcomes? That is, is empathy often merely an illusion?

## PERSONALITY AND CHARISMA

In making a hiring decision, the crucial final step is usually the personal interview. Even in the case of a candidate who has a long track record of performance and many evaluations from expert referees, the selection committee wants to meet the candidate and see for themselves. "Sure he has won these awards and his work repeatedly has passed peer review, but I want to see him for myself."

More than 20 years ago, a "Dr. Fox" began giving lectures to unsuspecting audiences. Doctor Fox varied both the expressiveness or "seductiveness" of the lectures as well as the content. The general finding of these and related studies was that an enthusiastic, expressive lecturer is more highly rated (Marsh & Ware, 1982; Williams & Ware, 1977). Even when the speaker speaks double-talk, a fine presentation style can elicit plaudits, even from educated audiences.

Thus it has long been documented that an enthusiastic instructor tends to create positive impressions in students. This is hardly exciting news to the acting community, where that enthusiastic spark is often proclaimed as the essence of good acting. The more interesting questions for education involve the amount of learning that occurs. Certain teachers are well-liked, but do they teach better? There are no simple answers. Although an audience can be fooled by a speaker who talks double-talk in a highly engaging manner, sometimes an inspiring speaker can induce higher levels of learning, either for a single lecture or over the course of a term.

The findings often depend on the component processes. Most simply, the more attention perceivers give to important information, the more likely they are to learn it (McGuire, 1970), and the perceptual salience is related to nonverbal expressiveness (Sullins, 1989). Further, expressive presentations may be emotionally arousing, and such emotional information may be more easily remembered (McGaugh, Weinberger, & Lynch, 1995). Thus, expressive teachers indeed may be more effective. In a more complex manner, certain students with certain nonverbal sensitivities may be more highly motivated to study more when instructed by teachers with certain positive, expressive nonverbal styles. They therefore learn more and admire those teachers. (Much of this work can be found in the voluminous educational literature on how to evaluate teaching; e.g. Marsh, 1984; McKeachie, 1986.)

There are also interactional and feedback effects, both between teacher and student and involving the rest of the class. Students have some favorite teachers but they do not all have the *same* favorite teachers. There are both emotional and behavioral interactions as teachers and students transmit their expectations to each other (Harris & Rosenthal, 1986). Research has still not explained fully what makes a good teacher.

If you were a very bright physics student in 1920, you might have rated Albert Einstein quite highly as a teacher, although you might not elect him as Mr. Personality. And an Einstein class certainly would have helped your career in physics. Clearly the content of the class and the knowledge of the professor sometimes matter. Yet by definition, students are not in the best position to evaluate the knowledge of the professor.

Nevertheless, some teachers consistently win teaching awards and some teachers are universally panned. So it is not surprising that short segments or samples of teaching can capture at least some of the variance in teacher evaluations. But most teachers (or lecturers or performers or news broadcasters) are liked by some people and heartily disliked by others. Explanations are weak here as well, and suggested remedies for less-than-optimal teaching are complex (Babad, 1993). These are some of the most challenging questions for future work on interpersonal sensitivity.

So-called thin slices of behavior can be quite revealing, as the interesting studies of Ambady and colleagues have shown (Ambady & Rosenthal, 1992; Ambady, LaPlante, & Johnson, chap. 5, this volume). For example, brief (under a minute) segments of nonverbal expressive cues can be used to predict end-of-semester evaluations of professors. Yet, as noted, there is also ample documentation that other factors contribute to students' learning and to students' evaluations. Furthermore, the same teacher will often get different ratings from teaching different classes of students on the same topic. In other words, on the one hand it seems that some important information can be garnered in a matter of seconds; but on the other hand, the value of these kernels can be thrown into question. Would you feel confident hiring a teacher or a therapist based on 30 seconds of observation? Would you ever be better in making a hiring decision without any observation at all?

This line of thinking is reminiscent of the large body of work on vocal cues and the accuracy of inferences about demographic and personality characteristics, which goes back more than 50 years. In a few minutes of telephone conversation, a reasonably astute perceiver can usually gather some fairly valid information about the gender, age, and social or regional class of the speaker (Knapp & Hall, 1997). Some more subtle information is often also obtainable, such as the motivational state of the speaker and certain aspects of personality, such as extraversion. However, much research suggests that the perceiver often is also likely to be inferring vocal stereotypes. Breathy-sounding women are not necessarily sexy, shallow, and effervescent; and nasal, flat-sounding men are not necessarily cold, introverted, and distasteful. Further, women who want to sound sexy may have taken lessons in breathy speaking.

Even controlling for geographic and culturally based influences on inferential distortions, personality is notoriously difficult to judge validly from vocal cues. This is due in part to transient emotional and motivational (affective) distortions such as whether the speaker happens to be tired, hungry, ill, angry, aroused, and so on. More basically, it is difficult to know how to define the accurate judgment of personality (Colvin & Bundick, chap. 3, this volume; Funder, 1995, chap. 16, this volume). Going even further, it is problematic to define personality in terms of traits, when behavior is known to vary considerably from situation to situation and certain people commonly seek out certain preferred situations above others. Additionally, as DePaulo (e.g., 1992) has made clear, self-presentation and deception are tremendously common and involve various sorts of interpersonal skills.

Several decades of research indicate that extraversion is the aspect of personality most often shown to be able to be judged from a speaker's expressive style (Buck, 1984; Cunningham, 1977). Research with the Affective Communication Test (ACT; Friedman, Prince, Riggio, & DiMatteo, 1980) shows extraversion to be related to nonverbal emotional expressiveness. The combination of the desire to be showy (exhibition), extraversion, and clear expression of emotions constitutes the bubbly personality construct often known as "personal charisma" (Friedman, Riggio, & Casella, 1988). After gender, this charisma may be the most noticed characteristic in social interaction, but it would be a mistake to assume that this indicates that other aspects of personality are similarly so evident. Further, ongoing work in our laboratory shows that charisma can be trained or even faked, raising questions about its permanence.

In short, the key paradox here is that first impressions, especially emotional expressiveness, appear to transmit a wealth of valuable information, but researchers do not understand much about when, why, or how. In fact, it is possible that researchers are vastly underestimating *or* vastly overestimating the amount of valid information available.

Gordon Allport (1961) distinguished expressive behavior such as gait and expansiveness of gestures from emotional expressions. Others have generally followed this distinction. Twenty years ago, I suggested that this separation may have been a mistake. That is, personality may be mostly revealed through emotional expression (Friedman, DiMatteo, & Taranta, 1980; Friedman, Riggio, & Segall, 1980). The tie between emotional expression and nonverbal style (of personality) may be closer than previously thought. The implication is that interpersonal perception should be studied in emotionally arousing situations. Neither I nor others have attempted this to a significant extent as yet.

## HEALTH

The clinical examination is the cornerstone of medical practice. Indeed a physician who prescribed treatment based on a patient's e-mailed description of symptoms might face malpractice and other legal sanctions. Much valuable information results from the gestalt of the medical examination process, although clinicians would be hard put to document or explicate the processes (Roter & Hall, 1992).

On the other side of the interpersonal sensitivity dyad, there is the patient's perspective. It is increasingly well documented that the psychosocial nature of health-relevant situations is tied to the physiological processes underlying health and behavior. A simple example is white coat hypertension, in which mere presence in the doctor's exam room is often enough to elevate one's blood pressure (Pickering & Friedman, 1991). Especially interesting in this regard are the effects of perceived blessings, curses, healings, or disruptions on health-relevant physiology. Understanding that one is expected to get well (or conversely that one is expected to die) can set in motion a series of interacting behavioral and psychophysiological patterns that can become self-fulfilling (Friedman, 1991, 1993). Most of these processes involve stress, a disruption of homeostasis.

This disruption, in turn, may be visible to others. Although the communicative effects of physiological changes have not been studied very much, the potential is high. For example, consider the hypothalamic system, the part of the brain that is central to metabolism and hormonal regulation, overseeing most endocrine activity. It influences bodily functions including temperature control, the metabolism of fats and sugar, and the sex glands. Importantly, it also helps control pituitary gland function. The pituitary gland, in turn, secretes hormones that directly influence other key endocrine organs, such as gonadotrophins, which stimulate the testes or ovaries, which in turn secrete estrogen and testosterone.

When so instructed by the hypothalamus, the pituitary releases adrenocorticotropic hormone (ACTH), which stimulates the adrenal cortex. When activated by ACTH, the adrenal cortex secretes steroid hormones (such as cortisol, which acts opposite to insulin in that it increases the concentration of glucose in the blood, thus providing energy for action). These corticosteroids also fight inflammation and have other effects, some beneficial, some not. For example, while suppressing inflammation, antibody production may also be suppressed, thus reducing resistance to infection.

The sympathetic nervous system also directly affects the hormonal system. It causes the adrenal medulla (the other core part of the gland on the kidney) to secrete epinephrine and norepinephrine, which enter the blood, travel throughout the body, and increase general arousal. Thus, during stress, there is both immediate sympathetic nervous system arousal and slower endocrine arousal. The neurotransmitters and hormones such as epinephrine, norepinephrine, dopamine, and serotonin play key roles in the regulation of mood, sleep, pain, activity, and eating. In other words, they regulate the kinds of things a perceiver sees when evaluating another—whether a target person looks aroused, tired, hungry, romantic, fearful, relaxed, distressed, turned on, nervous, sleepy, enthusiastic, and so on. So it makes physiological sense that a physician (or any astute observer) can literally see if someone is mentally or physically "unbalanced," even if this is only a minor, temporary condition.

It is still not clear, however, how many of these psychophysiological processes an observer will notice. Work with a brief exposure version of the Profile of Nonverbal Sensitivity (PONS; Rosenthal, Hall, DiMatteo, Rogers, & Archer, 1979) as well as work on subliminal perception documents that individuals can perceive (at some level) nonverbal stimuli lasting a fraction of a second, even if they are unable to report what they have seen. In this sense, our sensitivity may be much better than we know. The research on subliminal suggestion points to the likelihood that sometimes very subtle information can be processed outside of awareness, but that these processes are not incompatible with normal models of cognition (Reder & Gordon, 1997). Awareness is affected by where individuals direct their attention. For example, one study used a dichotic listening task in which people wore earphones and were asked to repeat (i.e., attend to) the words presented in one ear (Mathews & MacLeod, 1986). In the other, unattended ear, the researchers presented threat words. It was found that people with anxiety disorders (but not control participants) had problems with the prescribed ongoing task when the threat words were presented, even though they did not report hearing the threat words. The (threatening) stimuli are out of conscious awareness because one's attention has been directed elsewhere, but the threatening stimuli are not inaccessible to consciousness. That is, if they tried to switch attention to the other ear, the participants would clearly hear the threatening words. Such phenomena may characterize many aspects of nonverbal sensitivity, as well as help explain some individual differences.

Further, many lines of research in nonverbal communication suggest that, overall, general molar judgments of another are somehow more valid than specific codings of nonverbal cues. How can the whole impression be greater than the sum of its components? This remains another unanswered paradox. It might be the case that the ways that a perceiver cognitively combines the observed cues holds the answer. The cognitive processing is presumably nonlinear. Or it may be that the cues that scientists observe and code are not the most relevant cues. Or it may be that there are contextual or other moderating variables that have not yet been investigated. Or it may be the case that some perceiving processes remain undiscovered. These are all unanswered issues in interpersonal sensitivity.

Finally, it is important to note that researchers of interpersonal sensitivity tend to use self-report measures. Most commonly, the perceiver is asked to make a judgment about another (target) person. Although the precise methods may vary (from Likert-type bipolar scales to Q sorts), a conscious, inferential judgment is usually required. Other processes may be overlooked.

In short, the paradox here is that interpersonal sensitivity is likely complex, sophisticated, and biologically based, but yet researchers study it by fragmenting and simplifying it and by using mostly self-report judgment tasks.

## RELATIONSHIPS

It seems almost a truism that people who are well-acquainted or even intimate should be much better at reading each others' nonverbal cues than should strangers or new acquaintances. The stereotype suggests that as marriage progresses, the couple can complete each others' sentences and read each others' minds. Studies of the associations between relationship intimacy or quality and the accuracy of nonverbal communication, however, have produced a mixed bag of results (Feeney, Noller, & Ward, 1993; Noller, 1984, chap.13, this volume). There is some evidence of increasing knowledge but many scattered failures to find such effects.

Just as one's physical perceptions can be impaired by getting too close to the object of attention, so it seems that social perception can be impaired by intimacy. One might not notice right away if a friend shaves his beard or alters her hair color. So too, one might not detect unhappiness or infidelity in a partner, as many shocked people discover.

Here also there are motivational processes as well as perceptual processes at work. Perhaps sometimes individuals do not want to know too much. This idea was first laid out and researched in detail by Rosenthal and DePaulo (1979), who focused on sex differences in accommodation to a partner. Pieces of the concept had previously shown up in work indicating the nonverbal styles of women may accommodate to the personality of their male partners (Weitz, 1976) and in evidence that even children would disregard a smiling woman as unlikely to provide valid information (because they so often see women with a constant smile; Bugental, Kaswan, & Love, 1970; Bugental, Love, & Gianetto, 1971; see also Ekman & Friesen, 1969). This means that simple judgment studies of interpersonal sensitivity are necessarily quite limited in what they can understand.

Relatedly, it seems as if one knows more after a break-up or after losing one's job than before. "I should have seen it coming; all the cues were there." It would be interesting to investigate in a comprehensive manner whether indeed all the cues were there, and if so, the sources of the failures in perception.

Such paradoxes can be more clearly addressed and understood when an elaborated version of a comprehensive lens model of perception is applied. As many scientists (going back to Brunswik, 1956) have pointed out, the communication process may be conceptualized in a model with three main components. First, there is the communicator or sender, with input factors that affect his or her behavior. Second, there is the perceiver or detector, with another set of changing inputs. Mediating the two sides of the model are the behavioral nonverbal cues (e.g., Bernieri & Gillis, chap. 4, this volume; Bernieri, Gillis, Davis, & Grahe, 1996; Friedman & Tucker, 1990).

The communicator varies on dimensions including skill, motivation, situation, and emotional state. The perceiver varies in personality, attention, motivation, and cognitive decoding processes. There are also variations in the content of the exchange and past history of such exchanges. Finally, there are the interactional components such as self-monitoring and dynamic feedback. For example, there are many differences between a divorcing couple meeting in the lawyer's office and the newly infatuated couple partying in the saloon. Looking solely at a single aspect of nonverbal sensitivity would be severely limiting.

In short, the paradox here is that processes and changes that should lead to increased interpersonal sensitivity may sometimes produce the opposite as a result of ancillary factors embedded in the primary processes.

From a motivational standpoint, consider the case in which members of a couple might not want to understand (or admit to themselves) the threats to their relationship (Simpson, Ickes, & Blackstone, 1995). This study looked at conditions in which dating people might be motivated to be inaccurate about each others' feelings. It found that dating partners who were close, insecure about their relationship, and required to evaluate highly attractive opposite-sex persons in each other's presence displayed relatively little empathic accuracy when they tried to infer each other's thoughts and feelings.

Other, nonmotivational forces from the lens model could also produce similar results in certain circumstances. For example, nonverbal sensitivity could be dulled by alcohol, impaired by poor light, or distorted by anxiety. In a case of an expressive communicator and a skilled perceiver, the perceiver could constantly modify his or her response communications, thus leading to a poor (inaccurate) reading of the partner by the communicator, even if the communicator is nonverbally sensitive. For example, a nonverbally sensitive wife might be unable to read her husband as the their relationship progresses, if the wife is also expressive and her husband is a skilled perceiver and high self-monitor.

Following on the pioneering work of Ekman and Friesen (1969), research has confirmed that information about deception is better shown through body channels than through facial expressions (Riggio & Friedman, 1983). This means that a clinician would do well to observe body movements for signs that something is being held back. It also suggests that there may be other, seemingly helpful cues that are sometimes actually invalid and misleading. Many of these remain to be discovered.

## DISCUSSION AND CONCLUSION

The 20th century got off to a promising start concerning understanding interpersonal sensitivity. Fresh on the heels of Darwin's (1872) monumental work on the expression of the emotions in man and animals, a series of experimental studies took hold. Laboratories of the 1920s intensively studied emotions, human facial expressions, and voice tones. Comparative study (of nonhuman animals) then unraveled many of the likely functions of nonverbal cues and sensitivities. For example, comparative laboratories defined the channels different animals use (e.g., the fact that nocturnal or forest animals rely mainly on nonvisual cues to communicate). Even the psychoanalysts, likewise influenced by Darwin, began to study nonverbal cues as glimpses into the unconscious. In social psychology, issues of sympathy and empathy (variously defined) dominated the social interactionist theorizing of Cooley (1912) and others.

Unfortunately, these processes never reached their full potential for study in social and personality psychology. The rise of behaviorism discouraged research about emotion and motivation in experimental labs. Perhaps more importantly, the Lewinian influences on social psychology drove attention toward social cognitive issues and not emotional communication in social psychological research. Today, the few traces of this early work appear in two places in mainstream social psychology —in some approaches to close relationships and in attempts to understand altruism (Eisenberg, Fabes, & Losoya, 1997; Eisenberg & Losoya, chap. 2, this volume; Ickes, 1997, chap. 12, this volume; Wispé, 1991).

Ironically, many social psychological studies relied implicitly on notions of interpersonal sensitivity and nonverbal communication but rarely studied it explicitly (Friedman, 1979). For example, Schachter's (1959) studies of affiliation evinced the need for emotional social comparison. Latané and Darley's (1970) studies of bystander intervention leaned heavily on explanations involving participant phenomenology, dependent on interpreting the reactions of others. Even Milgram's (1974) studies of obedience showed the powerful constraints of being face to face with a demanding "experimenter" in authority, but did not explore directly the perceptions, nonverbal cues, and feedback processes of this powerful pressure situation.

The psychology of the early part of the 20th century was also willing to study crowds, mobs, lynchings, panics, and the like. Yet there is little or no mention of such topics in most current-day social psychology texts. Researchers, as well as lay commentators, have no problem referring to ideas such as "feeling the tension" of a confrontational debate, or "sensing the electricity" of the audience during an inspiring performance, or "tasting the fear" in a group facing impending doom. Such matters undoubtedly involve the sounds, gestures, touches, odors, and faces of spreading emotion. They are fertile grounds for the future study of nonverbal sensitivity in particular, and interpersonal sensitivity in general. Much work remains to be done.

First, researchers still do not know much about which channels or which cues people use in various situations, nor about their relative validity. Second, we still do not have enough good measures that go beyond the self-report, a special failure because so much communication is not actively contemplated by the perceiver. Third, although it is known that some information can be rapidly communicated, researchers of nonverbal communication still do not know much about the necessary or optimal time frames for various sorts of information. Fourth, little is known about how the perceiver integrates the vast amount of available information. Finally, researchers do not know much about the ongoing interaction process, as individuals adjust to feedback.

Perhaps the 21st century will be more productive in addressing the many paradoxes of interpersonal sensitivity. The study of emotion is resuming its rightful place in social psychology. The methods of cognitive psychology are again addressing basic notions of vocal and facial perception. The study of nonverbal communication is making its way into the mainstream (DePaulo & Friedman, 1998). There may be a greater willingness to step outside the boundaries of classic laboratory self-report judgment studies.

Perhaps not. As computers increasingly dominate many areas of communication, the nonverbal cues are minimized or made artificial. Furthermore, normal feedback processes are interrupted. A certain unease often seems to result, as we view e-mail accompanied by emoticons, or listen to a computer-synthesized voice responding to our push-button (or voice-recognition) telephone choices. Will a world of virtual communication derail our efforts to understand interpersonal sensitivity? Or will it perhaps provide the means to digitalize and quantify the cues that have been exchanged for millennia, studied for a century, and yet still elude capture?

## REFERENCES

Allport, G. W. (1961). *Pattern and growth in personality*. New York: Holt, Rinehart & Winston.

Ambady, N., & Rosenthal, R. (1992). Thin slices of expressive behavior as predictors of interpersonal consequences: A meta-analysis. *Psychological Bulletin, 111*, 256–274.

Babad, E. (1993). Pygmalion: 25 years after interpersonal expectations in the classroom. In P. D. Blanck (Ed.), *Interpersonal expectations: Theory, research, and applications* (pp. 125–153). New York: Cambridge University Press.

Bernieri, F. J., Gillis, J. S., Davis, J. M., & Grahe, J. E. (1996). Dyad rapport and the accuracy of its judgment across situations: A lens model analysis. *Journal of Personality and Social Psychology, 71*, 110–129.

Brunswik, E. (1956). *Perception and the representative design of psychological experiments*, 2nd ed. Berkeley: University of California Press.

Buck, R. (1984). *The communication of emotion*. New York: Guilford.

Bugental, D. E., Kaswan, J. W., & Love, L. R. (1970). Perception of contradictory meanings conveyed by verbal and nonverbal channels. *Journal of Personality and Social Psychology, 16*, 647–655.

Bugental, D. E., Love, L. R., & Gianetto, R. M. (1971). Perfidious feminine faces. *Journal of Personality and Social Psychology, 17*, 314–318.

Cooley, C. H. (1912). *Social organization*. New York: Scribners'.

Cunningham, M. R. (1977). Personality and the structure of the nonverbal communication of emotion. *Journal of Personality, 45*, 564–584.

Darwin, C. (1872). *The expression of the emotions in man and animals*. London: J. Murray.

DePaulo, B. M. (1992). Nonverbal behavior and self-presentation. *Psychological Bulletin, 111,* 203–243.

DePaulo, B. M., & Friedman, H. S. (1998). Nonverbal communication. In D. Gilbert, S. Fiske & G. Lindzey (Eds.), *Handbook of social psychology* (4th ed., Vol. 2, pp. 3–40). Boston: McGraw-Hill.

Eisenberg, N., Fabes, R. A., & Losoya, S. (1997) Emotional responding: Regulation, social correlates, and socialization. In P. Salovey & D. J. Sluyter (Eds.), *Emotional development and emotional intelligence: Educational implications* (pp. 129–167). New York: Basic.

Ekman, P., & Friesen, W. V. (1969). Nonverbal leakage and clues to deception. *Psychiatry, 32,* 88–106.

Feeney, J. A., Noller, P., & Ward, C. (1993). Marital satisfaction and spousal interaction. In R. J. Sternberg & M. Hojjat (Eds.), *Satisfaction in close relationships. (pp. 160–189). New York:* Guilford.

Friedman, H. S. (1979). The concept of skill in nonverbal communication: Implications for understanding social interaction. In R. Rosenthal (Ed.), *Skill in nonverbal communication: Individual differences* (pp. 2–27). Cambridge, MA: Oelgeschlager, Gunn & Hain.

Friedman, H. S. (1991). *Self–healing personality: Why some people achieve health and others succumb to illness.* New York: Henry Holt.

Friedman, H. S. (1993). Interpersonal expectations and the maintenance of health. In P. Blanck (Ed.), *Interpersonal expectations: Theory, research, and applications* (pp. 179–93). Cambridge, UK: Cambridge University Press.

Friedman, H. S., DiMatteo, M. R., & Taranta, A. (1980). A study of the relationship between individual differences in nonverbal expressiveness and factors of personality and social interaction. *Journal of Research in Personality, 14,* 351–364.

Friedman, H. S., Prince, L. M., Riggio, R. E., & DiMatteo, M. R. (1980). Understanding and assessing nonverbal expressiveness: The Affective Communication Test. *Journal of Personality and Social Psychology, 39,* 333–351.

Friedman, H. S., Riggio, R. E., & Casella, D. (1988). Nonverbal skill, personal charisma, and initial attraction. *Personality and Social Psychology Bulletin, 14,* 203–211.

Friedman, H. S., Riggio, R. E., & Segall, D. (1980). Personality and the enactment of emotion. *Journal of Nonverbal Behavior, 5,* 35–48.

Friedman, H. S., & Tucker, J. (1990). Language and deception. In H. Giles & W. P. Robinson (Eds.), *Handbook of language and social psychology* (pp. 257–270). Chichester, England: Wiley.

Funder, D. C. (1995). On the accuracy of personality judgment: A realistic approach. *Psychological Review, 102,* 652–670.

Harris, M. J., & Rosenthal, R. (1986). Four factors in the mediation of teacher expectancy effects. In R. S. Feldman (Ed.), *The social psychology of education: Current research and theory* (pp. 91–114). New York: Cambridge University Press.

Ickes, W. J. (Ed.) (1997). *Empathic accuracy.* New York: Guilford.

Knapp, M. L., & Hall, J. A. (1997). *Nonverbal communication in human interaction,* 4th ed. Fort Worth: Harcourt Brace Jovanovich.

Latane, B., & Darley, J. M. (1970). *The unresponsive bystander: Why doesn't he help?* Englewood Cliffs, NJ: Prentice-Hall.

Marsh, H. W. (1984). Students' evaluations of university teaching: Dimensionality, reliability, validity, potential biases, and utility. *Journal of Educational Psychology, 76,* 707–754.

Marsh, H. W., & Ware, J. E. (1982). Effects of expressiveness, content coverage, and incentive on multidimensional student rating scales: New interpretations of the Dr. Fox effect. *Journal of Educational Psychology, 74,* 126–134.

Mathews, A., & MacLeod, C. (1986). Discrimination of threat cues without awareness in anxiety states. *Journal of Abnormal Behavior, 95,* 131–138.

McGaugh, J. L., Weinberger, N. M., & Lynch, G. (Eds.). (1995). *Brain and memory: Modulation and mediation of neuroplasticity.* New York: Oxford University Press.

McGuire, W. J. (1970). Attitudes and attitude change. In G. Lindzey & E. Aronson (Eds.), *Handbook of social psychology,* 2nd ed., (Vol. 3, pp. 136–314). Reading, MA: Addison-Wesley.

McKeachie, W. J. (1986). *Teaching tips: A guidebook for the beginning college teacher,* 8th ed. Lexington, MA: D.C. Heath.

Milgram, S. (1974). *Obedience to authority: An experimental view.* New York: Harper & Row.

Noller, P. (1984). *Nonverbal communication and marital interaction.* Oxford, England: Pergamon.

Pickering, T. G., & Friedman, R. (1991). The white coat effect: A neglected role for behavioral factors in hypertension. In P. M. McCabe & N. Schneiderman (Eds.), *Stress, coping, and disease* (pp. 35–49). Hillsdale, NJ: Lawrence Erlbaum Associates.

Reder, L. M., & Gordon, J. S. (1997). Subliminal perception: Nothing special, cognitively speaking. In J. D. Cohen & J. W. Schooler (Eds.), *Scientific approaches to consciousness* (pp. 125–134). Mahwah, NJ: Lawrence Erlbaum Associates.

Riggio, R. E., & Friedman, H. S. (1983). Individual differences and cues to deception. *Journal of Personality and Social Psychology, 45,* 899–915.

Rosenthal, R., & DePaulo, B. M. (1979). Sex differences in eavesdropping on nonverbal cues. *Journal of Personality and Social Psychology, 37,* 273–285.

Rosenthal, R., Hall, J. A, DiMatteo, M., Rogers, P. L., & Archer, D. (1979). *Sensitivity to nonverbal communication: The PONS test.* Baltimore: The Johns Hopkins University Press.

Roter, D., & Hall, J. A. (1992). *Doctors talking with patients/Patients talking with doctors: Improving communication in medical visits.* Westport, CT: Auburn House.

Schachter, S. (1959). *The psychology of affiliation: Experimental studies of the sources of gregariousness.* Stanford: Stanford University Press.

Simpson, J. A., Ickes, W., & Blackstone, T. (1995). When the head protects the heart: Empathic accuracy in dating relationships. *Journal of Personality and Social Psychology, 69,* 629–641.

Sullins, E. S. (1989). Perceptual salience as a function of nonverbal expressiveness. *Personality and Social Psychology Bulletin, 15,* 584–595.

Weitz, S. (1976). Sex differences in nonverbal communication. *Sex Roles, 2,* 175–184.

Williams, R. G., & Ware, J. E. (1977). An extended visit with Dr. Fox: Validity of student satisfaction with instruction ratings after repeated exposures to a lecturer. *American Educational Research Journal, 14,* 449–457.

Wispe, L. (1991). *The psychology of sympathy.* New York: Plenum.

# Author Index

# Subject Index

## A

Acquaintanceship, effects of on interpersonal sensitivity, 57-59, 109, 177, 235, 250-251, 253-254, 338-339, 346, 357

Affective Communication Test (ACT), 201, 354

Affordances, 328, 335, 338-339

Age in relation to interpersonal sensitivity, 24-25, 27-28, 32, 36, 151, 188, 190-191, 341-342, 345

Agency and communion, 60-61

Aggression, 21, 25, 28

Anxiety, 24, 32-33, 35, 91, 93, 137, 178-179, 185, 192, 194, 254, 288

Attention, *see* Interpersonal sensitivity as attention/perception

## B

Behavioral Q-sort, 55, 61-62

Big Five factors of personality, 52, 285, 346

Brief Affect Recognition Test (BART), 145, 186

Brief Exposure PONS, 130-131

## C

California Adult Q-sort, 54-55, 57, 61-62, 356

CARAT, 145-146, 155

Charisma, 308-309, 352-354

Child and Adolescent Social Perception Measure (CASP), 146-147, 153

Child Behavior Check List (CBCL), 192

Confidence in judgments, 82, 252, 341

Content-masking of speech, methods of, 91, 148-149, 186, 243-244, *see also* Standard content methodology

Correlational method for scoring judgment accuracy, 47-65, 75-76, 78, 145, 201-218, 269, 273, 286, 322-323, 327

Correlations among interpersonal sensitivity measures, *see* Interpersonal sensitivity measures, correlations among

Criterion for scoring judgment accuracy, choice of, 10-12, 50-51, 55, 71-72, 74, 76, 78-79, 84, 91, 143-145, 170, 174, 187-188, 248, 266-267, 320-321, 323, 328, 335-336

Culture, in relation to interpersonal sensitivity, 95-96, 151, 168-169

Customer service, 312-313

## D

Deception, detection of, 4, 103-124, 146, 153, 162, 309-310, 320-322, 336-337, 340-341, 343, 354, 358
and confidence, 82, 341

Demand characteristics, 27-30, 32-33, 35-36

Depression in relation to interpersonal sensitivity, 95, 189

Diagnostic Analysis of Nonverbal Accuracy (DANVA), 144, 146, 153, 156, 183-198, 224, 337, 347

Differential accuracy, 51, 106, 267, 277, 280

Differential elevation, 50, 55, 106, 267, 269, 277, 278, 280, 282, 295

Display rules, 32

Dominance, *see* Status/dominance

Dyadic sensitivity, 157-158, 201-218, 219-241, 243-264, 265-302

Dyssemia, 183, 185, 192-193